THE EMIL AND KATHLEEN SICK LECTURE-BOOK SERIES
IN WESTERN HISTORY AND BIOGRAPHY

The Great Columbia Plain: A Historical Geography, 1805–1910 by Donald W. Meinig

Mills and Markets: A History of the Pacific Coast Lumber Industry to 1900 by Thomas R. Cox

Radical Heritage: Labor, Socialism, and Reform in Washington and British Columbia, 1885–1917 by Carlos A. Schwantes

The Battle for Butte: Mining and Politics on the Northern Frontier, 1864–1906 by Michael P. Malone

The Forging of a Black Community: Seattle's Central District from 1870 through the Civil Rights Era by Quintard Taylor

Warren G. Magnuson and the Shaping of Twentieth-Century America by Shelby Scates

The Atomic West, edited by Bruce Hevly and John M. Findlay

Power and Place in the North American West, edited by Richard White and John M. Findlay

Henry M. Jackson: A Life in Politics by Robert G. Kaufman

Parallel Destinies: Canadian-American Relations West of the Rockies edited by John M. Findlay and Ken S. Coates

Nikkei in the Pacific Northwest: Japanese Americans and Japanese Canadians in the Twentieth Century, edited by Louis Fiset and Gail M. Nomura

Bringing Indians to the Book by Albert Furtwangler

Death of Celilo Falls by Katrine Barber

The Power of Promises: Rethinking Indian Treaties in the Pacific Northwest, edited by Alexandra Harmon

THE POWER OF PROMISES

RETHINKING INDIAN TREATIES

in the PACIFIC NORTHWEST

EDITED BY ALEXANDRA HARMON

CENTER FOR THE STUDY OF THE PACIFIC NORTHWEST

IN ASSOCIATION WITH

UNIVERSITY OF WASHINGTON PRESS SEATTLE AND LONDON

© 2008 by the University of Washington Press
Printed in the United States of America
Design by Pamela Canell
12 11 10 09 08   5 4 3 2 1

Center for the Study of the Pacific Northwest   University of Washington Press
P.O. Box 353587, Seattle, WA 98195   P.O. Box 50096, Seattle, WA 98145
www.cspn.washington.edu   www.washington.edu/uwpress

Library of Congress Cataloging-in-Publication Data
The power of promises : rethinking Indian treaties in the Pacific Northwest /
edited by Alexandra Harmon.
p. cm. — (The Emil and Kathleen Sick lecture-book series in western history
and biography)
Includes index.
ISBN 978-0-295-98838-2 (hardback : alk. paper)
ISBN 978-0-295-98839-9 (pbk. : alk. paper)
1. Indians of North America—Northwest, Pacific—Treaties. 2. Indians of North
America—Northwest, Pacific—Government relations. 3. Indians of North America—
Northwest, Pacific—Foreign relations. I. Harmon, Alexandra, 1945– II. Center for
the Study of the Pacific Northwest.
E78.N77P68 2008   323.11970795—dc22   2008029868

The paper used in this publication is acid-free and 90 percent recycled from at least
50 percent waste. It meets the minimum requirements of American National Standard
for Information Sciences—Permanence of Paper for Printed Library Materials, ANSI
Z39.48-1984. ♾ ♺

Contents

Foreword

John Borrows

In December of 2003, Sasha Harmon contacted me to discuss a proposed conference commemorating the sesquicentennial of the Washington Territory Indian treaties. I listened carefully to her ideas because her work has been influential in increasing our understanding of Native American identity and the definition of tribes around Puget Sound.[1] Her attentiveness to indigenous people's innovation and resilience in constructing their own identities, despite others' imposed labels, has generated insightful work.

I was enthusiastic about Professor Harmon's idea to focus on treaties from a multidisciplinary perspective. I also saw the relevance of the conference for Canada. Treaties on Vancouver Island were formalized around the same time as those in Washington Territory. Harmon hoped to engage scholars in a project to analyze broadly the repercussions and changing meanings of treaties that purportedly defined indigenous/non-indigenous relations in the Pacific Northwest. I believe she has been successful in this objective. The conference, entitled Pacific Northwest Indian Treaties in National and International Historical Perspective, took place May 13 and 14, 2004. The essays in this book present many of the issues discussed at that gathering and represent some of the finest work on treaties currently available in the literature.

Harmon's training as a lawyer and a historian has been evident throughout my association with her. This makes her both an excellent conference convener and an able editor, as is evident in these collected essays. She has a keen eye for detail yet is acutely aware of broader perspectives. Both those scholars invited to the conference and those who have contributed to *The Power of Promises* share this trait. The contributors draw on anthropology, ethnography, law, history, Native American studies, and political science, among other disciplines, in the pursuit of their research. They follow a variety of research methodologies in making their arguments and establishing their points. They are also united by their attention to the specific contexts and wider views of treaties in the Pacific Northwest. In this foreword I would like to say a few words about the conference theme, the various authors, and the essays included here, as an orientation to what follows.

There are many reasons to look at treaties in the Pacific Northwest from a wider angle, particularly across the Canadian–United States border. The two countries share common historical roots, languages, and political heritage. Furthermore, the border introduced to the territory by the Treaty of Oregon in 1846 cut across extended kinship, trade, and political relationships of indigenous people. It established distinct constitutional and legal authorities that influenced the development and judgment of treaties in different ways. However, although borders divide, they can never completely disassociate the people they ostensibly separate. This has been true for both indigenous and nonindigenous peoples of the Pacific Northwest.

Living on Vancouver Island, one is keenly aware of the connections Salish people share across the Strait of Georgia and the Strait of Juan de Fuca.[2] Though regrettably constrained by the United States–Canadian border, indigenous relationships around those and neighboring saltwater inlets (known to some as the Salish Sea) continue through such activities as marriages, trade, travel, education, feasting, and other ceremonial connections. In fact, the conference from which these essays were drawn demonstrated the saliency of these contacts. Not only did particular presentations draw on the continued relevancy of continuing cross-border Salish relationships, but also a good number of Salish students and leaders were in attendance at the conference. Their questions and informal presence added immeasurably to the spirit of the conference and helped us all appreciate the living context of the treaties under discussion. I believe many of the contributions in this book were enriched through this important exchange.

Just as cross-border contacts among indigenous people are an important source of inspiration for studies of Pacific Northwest Indian treaties, so too can profound insights be generated through international nonindigenous collaboration around this same subject. For example, during the conference I met my colleague Robert Anderson, who teaches subjects at the University of Washington Law School similar to those that I teach at the University of Victoria. Because we are not indigenous to the Pacific Northwest, I place our relationship in the nonindigenous category for the purposes of this book, but Professor Anderson and I share indigenous ancestry and citizenship in the Anishinabek Nation of central Canada and the United States. It is always good to meet a fellow citizen of the same First Nation. Though separated by international borders and living away from our homelands, we have a mutual interest in the implications of treaties our ancestors signed with the colonial governments in another region of the country.

Anderson's essay in this volume on the Alaska Native Claims Settlement Act reminded me of processes currently animating the negotiation of new treaties in British Columbia. That modern treaties might have an impact on historical treaties was mentioned at the conference and is considered in greater detail in this book. Professor Ravi de Costa from York University, closer to my own indigenous home territory in Ontario, also takes readers down that road. He discusses important concerns regarding the narrow approach he finds in contemporary British Columbia treaty negotiations. Readers will find his essay rich with insight.

Examples of nonindigenous connections across borders are also found in the work of Russel Lawrence Barsh, whose essay in this volume helps explain how tribes have been internally affected by treaty litigation in the United States. I have worked with Russel in the past in matters of international indigenous development. Through our mutual association with First Peoples Worldwide, I knew Russel had the ability to connect local concerns with issues of international importance. He does not disappoint here. His discussion of ethnonationalism among Indian tribes could easily be connected to changes taking place in the larger world, as nation-states and even indigenous nations often co-opt individual identities to serve wider collective goals.

Professor Paige Raibmon takes up a similar theme as she explores the construction of identity in relation to landownership and individual acts of dispossession directed at Indians through nonindigenous settlement and intermarriage. Although she does not refer to the processes of ethnonationalism that preface Russel's essay, Paige's work again reminds us that individuals can be used by the state to accomplish purposes that those individuals might not explicitly identify or approve if they were conscious of how their cultural propensities were being deployed. I first met Paige when she was working with the British Columbia Treaty Commission in the mid-1990s, while she was still a graduate student at Duke University. It is clear those experiences have added much to her work as a history professor at the University of British Columbia. They have enabled her to bring together the practical and academic implications of land-use policies and practices in the Pacific Northwest.

It was also a pleasure to associate with three other law professors and a lawyer at this conference. Their strong contributions are evident. Professor Kent McNeil is one of Canada's leading legal scholars in the field of Aboriginal and treaty rights. He also happens to be my former doctoral supervisor, a fact for which I am extremely grateful because of his kindness and academic guidance. The Supreme Court of Canada frequently cites McNeil, and his articles are reproduced in texts and casebooks throughout Canada. His work has also been influential in Australia and New Zealand. McNeil's essay in this volume discusses the carving up of indigenous territory through international treaties like those that dealt with the Oregon boundary. Drawing on the early Indian law decisions of United States Supreme Court Chief Justice John Marshall, McNeil's thesis is that international treaties should not be regarded as nullifying the sovereignty of First Nations that did not participate in such agreements.

Like McNeil, Canadian law professor Douglas C. Harris picks up references to U.S. law, in his case to consider how principles for interpreting rights to fish under the Washington Territory treaties bear on aboriginal fishing rights in Canada. Doug was a student in the first class I ever taught as a professor at the University of Toronto Law School. I remember his term paper very well. It drew on historian Richard White's *The Middle Ground* and argued that law could be a tool for reconciliation in contemporary Canada.[3] Doug was subsequently an outstanding graduate student at the University of British Columbia, where we again crossed paths when I taught there. He is now in the Faculty of Law at the University of British Columbia, and his work continues to examine dislocation and the possibilities for reconciliation across many "middle grounds." Doug carries this theme forward in his essay and demonstrates what Canada might learn from the fisheries disputes before the courts in Washington State.

Finally, my colleague Hamar Foster in the Faculty of Law at the University of Victoria writes with another former student of mine, Alan Grove. During law school Alan was always keen to pull Indian history away from its eastern bias. Having done graduate work in history before law school, he was convinced that courts and scholars had overlooked important interactions among government officials in Oregon, Washington, British Columbia, and Alaska. Alan later joined with Professor Foster, one of Canada's most respected legal historians, to take up this inquiry. The result of their collaboration is an insightful essay that explores the connections between colonial leaders in the Pacific Northwest in the early years of non-native settlement and traces their potential mutual influence in treaty processes. It is interesting to note modern parallels in these connections. Our interest in Pacific Northwest treaties causes us to reach across the border to learn more about treaty issues in the broader region, just as the mutual interests and shared experiences of prior generations did in their time.

The essays of Chris Friday, Andrew H. Fisher, Bruce Rigsby, and Arthur J. Ray also demonstrate how looking back across time can provide important perspectives on Pacific Northwest treaties and their subsequent interpretations. Friday, professor of history at Western Washington University, looks at performance and illustrates how treaties might be understood outside of their textual constraints and seen as living agreements that have been reenacted and applied at many points after their signing. Fisher, professor of history at the College of William and Mary, reminds us that the audience receiving performances can make a real difference in how treaty reenactments develop through time. His point—that non-native courts and officials have changed the way tribes related to one another and their resources—demonstrates the importance of viewing treaties as multicultural relationships. Fisher's work shows that native/non-native relationships are not static but rather are inflected with power, making tribes potentially more pliable and vulnerable to the state as time passes. Rigsby, emeritus professor of anthropology at the University of Queensland, demonstrates this vulnerability in his contribution by describing how tribes lack control over the burials of ancient people found within their traditional territories, contrary to their likely understandings when the treaties were signed.

Ray, professor of history at the University of British Columbia, describes another vulnerability, vividly showing how non-native people often have the last word on the treaty interpretations when these issues are taken to courts. He explains the difficulty he encounters as a historian trying to educate judges about the treaties' possible meanings. These difficulties are often compounded because of the unevenness in the experts' teaching and research qualifications. At least in the Canadian context, courts have been more heavily relying on nonacademic, professional historians, who do not have work or reputation outside their employment by the federal or provincial litigation departments. For decades Ray has been one of the most prolific and respected scholars studying Aboriginal/non-Aboriginal commercial relationships in western Canada. His personal reflections on the difficulties historians and Aboriginal claimants encounter in the courtroom are clearly presented in a wonderfully concise yet thoughtful essay.

As you read the essays throughout this volume, you will find a rich source of information that will deepen your knowledge of a dynamic field of discourse. Treaties in the Pacific Northwest are relevant today because they continue to define our relationship to one another and to the land and its resources. For example, in 2006 the Supreme Court of Canada handed down its decision in *R. v. Morris*, which examined the right of Indians on southern Vancouver Island "to hunt over the unoccupied lands . . . as formerly" under the North Saanich Treaty of 1852.[4] The Court held that First Nations treaty rights are a valid defense to charges under provincial law aimed at prohibiting night hunting. It said that Saanich people possess unextinguished rights to night hunting (where this practice does not endanger others) because their ancestors practiced that right at the time treaties were signed, and Governor James Douglas guaranteed these practices could continue without change.

The fact that First Nations treaties are constitutionally secure against provincial challenge in such controversial circumstances surely requires explanation, given the somewhat vague language by which such rights were protected. In providing such explanations the Court wrote: "The language of the Treaty stating 'we are at liberty to hunt over the unoccupied lands' exemplifies the lean and often vague vocabulary of historic treaty promises. McLachlin J., dissenting on other grounds, stated in *R. v. Marshall*, [1999] 3 *Supreme Court Reports.* 456 (*Marshall No. 1*), at para. 78, that '[t]he goal of treaty interpretation is to choose from among the various possible interpretations of common intention the one which best reconciles the interests of both parties at the time the treaty was signed.' This means that the promises in the treaty must be placed in their historical, political, and cultural contexts to clarify the common intentions of the parties and the interests they intended to reconcile at the time."

The Power of Promises places Pacific Northwest treaty promises and their interpretation within this broader context. As such, it is an important contribution to our developing understanding about how better to reconcile the varied historical, political, and cultural perspectives on these important legal agreements in both Canada and the United States today. As you read, I am sure you will learn more about the power of Indian treaty promises to have such a lasting impact. Those treaties tell us how we can live together with "good feelings" if we abide by their spirit and intent.

NOTES

1. Alexandra Harmon, *Indians in the Making: Ethnic Relations and Indian Identities Around Puget Sound* (Berkeley: University of California Press, 1998).

2. "Salish"—a term that anthropologists adopted several decades ago for a family of languages spoken by aboriginal inhabitants of several large areas in the Pacific Northwest—is now a common ethnic designation for First Nations in southwestern British Columbia and Indian tribes in western Washington.

3. Richard White, *The Middle Ground: Indians, Empires, and Republics in the Great Lakes Region, 1650–1815* (Cambridge: Cambridge University Press, 1991).

4. *R. v. Morris*, 2006 Supreme Court of Canada (SCC) 59 at paragraph 2.

THE POWER OF PROMISES

Introduction

Alexandra Harmon

The year 1855 was just under way when hundreds of travelers converged at a popular camping place on the eastern shore of Puget Sound—a low-lying point known as Mukilteo.[1] Flotillas of cedar canoes brought men, women, and children from communities in all directions. As each group arrived, the people already there lined up for a ceremonious greeting, their standard protocol at big gatherings for special occasions. This gathering, however, promised to be unusual. It was taking place at the behest of men called Bostons—newcomers in the region who referred to themselves as Americans or whites and the native inhabitants as Indians or *siwash*.[2] The Bostons had indicated that they planned some novel proceedings.

In the two weeks after the first campfires were kindled, the crowd at Mukilteo grew to more than twenty-three hundred. Finally, on January 22 of the American calendar, the Bostons convened a general assembly. With prestigious men seated in front, the native people waited to hear what their hosts would say. The man who spoke first was small in stature and had not been in the country long, but his importance among the Bostons was apparent. In English, which an interpreter converted to the regional trade jargon for succeeding interpreters who then rendered the message in local dialects, Isaac Stevens declared:

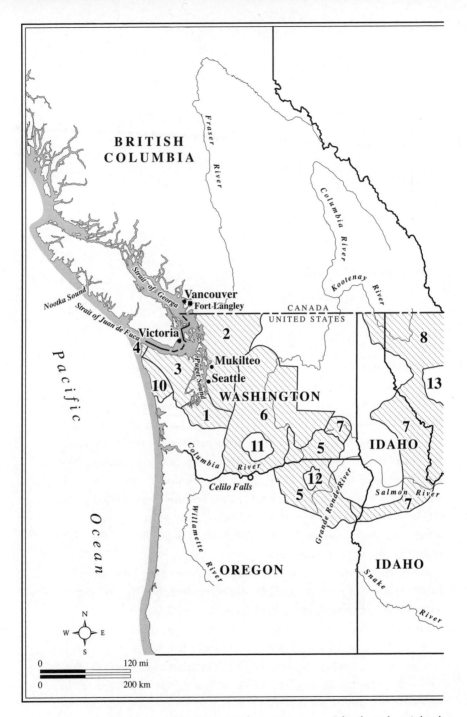

BRITISH
COLUMBIA

Fraser River

Columbia River

Nootka Sound

Strait of Georgia

Strait of Juan de Fuca

Kootenay River

Vancouver
Fort Langley

CANADA
UNITED STATES

Victoria

2

8

4

3

Puget Sound

Mukilteo

Seattle

13

10

WASHINGTON

1

6

7

7

Pacific

11

5

IDAHO

Columbia River

12

Celilo Falls

5

Grande Ronde River

Salmon River

7

O c e a n

Willamette River

OREGON

IDAHO

Snake River

N
W · E
S

0   120 mi
0   200 km

MAP I.I Washington Territory, southern Vancouver Island, and mainland
British Columbia, 1853–55

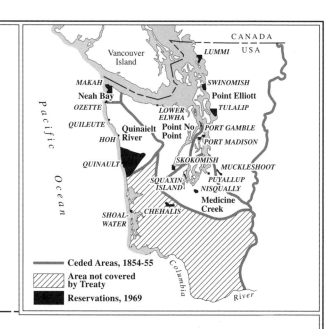

Ceded Areas, 1854-55
Area not covered by Treaty
Reservations, 1969

IDAHO

Areas Ceded in Treaties Negotiated by Isaac Stevens

1 Treaty with the Nisquallys, etc. (Treaty of Medicine Creek), December 26, 1854
2 Treaty with the Dwamish, Suquamish, etc. (Treaty of Point Elliott), January 22, 1855
3 Treaty with the S'Klallam, etc. (Treaty of Point No Point), January 26, 1855
4 Treaty with the Makah (Treaty of Neah Bay), January 31, 1855
5 Treaty with the Wallawalla, Cayuse, etc, June 9, 1855
6 Treaty with the Yakama, June 9, 1855
7 Treaty with the Nez Perces, June 11, 1855
8 Treaty with the Flatheads, etc. (Treaty of Hell Gate), July 16, 1855
9 Treaty with the Blackfeet, October 17, 1855 ("Ceded" area is a hunting reserve that the Blackfeet agreed to share with other tribes.)
10 Treaty with the Quinaielt, etc. (Treaty of Olympia), January 25, 1856

Large Areas Reserved to Indians by Stevens Treaties

11 Yakima Reservation (for fourteen tribes or bands of the mid-Columbia Plateau region)
12 Umatilla Reservation (for the Walla Walla, Cayuse, and Umatilla tribes)
13 Flathead Reservation (for the Salish, Kootenai, and Pend Oreille tribes)

My Children! You are not my children because you are the fruit of my loins but because you are children for whom I have the same feeling as if you were the fruit of my loins. You are my children for whom I will strenuously labor all the days of my life until I shall be taken hence. What will a man do for his own children? He will see that they are well cared for, that they have clothes to protect them against the cold and rain, that they have food to guard them against hunger, and as for thirst you have your own glorious streams in which to quench it. I want you as my children to be fed and clothed, and made comfortable and happy. . . . We want to place you in houses where you can cultivate the soil, raising potatoes and other articles of food, and where you may be able to pass in canoes over the waters of the sound and catch fish, and back to the mountains to get roots and berries.[3]

Stevens introduced "elder brother" Michael Simmons, whose decade-long residence in the area made him more familiar to and with Stevens's native "children." Speaking a language the minute-taker identified as "Indian" but recorded as the French- and English-sprinkled Chinook trade jargon, Simmons talked of Indians victimized by whites who stole from them, beat them, and sold them trouble-triggering rum. Implying that the Americans had a plan to solve those problems, he said, "*Konaway mesike tenass chahko kahkwa Boston tenass.* . . . All your children will be like American children." Then Stevens rose again and told the assembly that his assignment was to send a "paper" showing their "desires & wishes" to the "Great Father" in Washington, who wanted his Indian children to be virtuous, industrious, happy, and prosperous.

"The lands are yours," Stevens concluded, "and we mean to pay you for them. Thank you that you have been so kind to all the white children of the Great Father, who come to build mills, till land, build and sail ships. We will put our hearts down on paper. . . . If the Great Father says the paper is good it will stand forever." The Bostons had already put their "hearts" in written English words that they reportedly proceeded to translate in full for the Indians. When Stevens asked whether any "chiefs" objected, Seattle responded first and, according to the minutes, said: "I look upon you as my father. I and the rest regard you as such. All of the Indians have the same good feeling towards you and will send it on paper to the Great Father. All of them, men, old men, women & children rejoice that he has sent you to take care of them. My mind is like yours. I don't want to say more. My heart is very good towards Dr. Maynard [a physician who was present]. I want always to get medicine from him."

Stevens interjected a promise that the Indians would have a doctor for their bodies and a doctor for their souls, then he listened as other chiefs briefly expressed satisfaction much as Seattle had. After Stevens and eighty-two native men had marked the paper, the Bostons distributed gifts. Finally Seattle, presenting a white flag, made a public pledge: "Now by this we make friends and put away all bad feelings if we ever had any. We are the friends of the Americans. . . . We look upon you as our Father. We will never change our minds but since you have been to see us will be always the same."

The heading of the document endorsed that day in 1855 identifies it as a treaty between the United States and twenty-two listed "tribes and bands of Indians" (plus unnamed "allied and subordinate" groups). In fifteen numbered articles the text attests to what the American and tribal representatives ostensibly agreed. Among other things, the tribes conveyed to the United States all interest in the lands they occupied (a description of which the treaty drafters supplied); the parties reserved four small specified tracts of land for the Indians' exclusive use and an additional tract where the government would build a school for Indian children; the Indians promised to move to the reserved areas within a year after Americans furnished them the means; Indians retained their right to fish at traditional places and get other subsistence resources on unclaimed land; the United States pledged payments totaling $150,000 over twenty years, either in cash or in expenditures for Indians' benefit; and the American president claimed the prerogative of relocating the reservations, consolidating the Indians at fewer places, and dividing reserved lands into lots for individuals and families.[4]

According to U.S. law, that compact, now usually identified as the Treaty of Point Elliott, is an essential first link on all chains of title to land in a significant portion of Washington State. The real estate that changed hands includes the site of the city named for Chief Seattle, and within the city is a University of Washington campus. At the university, 150 years after the parley at Mukilteo, more than one hundred people convened for a conference entitled "Pacific Northwest Indian Treaties in National and International Historical Perspective." This book is an outgrowth of that commemorative event, which was an opportunity for scholars from several disciplines and countries to report on research and discuss thoughts about treaties endorsed by indigenous peoples in Washington State and elsewhere. The essays collected here present and elaborate on ideas considered at the conference.

ONE OF TEN TREATIES AND TEN OF MANY INDIAN TREATIES

It was not the anniversary of the Point Elliott treaty alone that inspired a scholarly symposium with a broad scope of inquiry. The Point Elliott treaty is representative of a distinctive historical phenomenon whose widespread political, economic, and social consequences have carried into the present day. In North America, where treaties have been employed hundreds of times to define relations between indigenous and colonial societies, many such pacts have continuing legal force, and many have been the focus of recent, high-stakes legal contests. In 2005, for example, the governments of Canada and British Columbia were even negotiating new treaties with Aboriginal groups. As the basis for current circumstances of great import to millions of people, Indian treaties are the subject of much public discourse. Thus, whenever there is occasion to ponder the significance of an individual treaty, there is also reason to consider the larger history of such treaties and the issues they have raised or sought to resolve.[5]

Furthermore, the Point Elliott council was not the only event of its kind in 1855; rather, it was one act in an epic regional drama. The document inked at Mukilteo was the second in a matched set of ten treaties, all concluded at Isaac Stevens's instigation within a thirteen-month period. As a group those agreements restructured landownership and intercultural relations in an area extending far beyond the northern Puget Sound. With his appointment as the first governor and ex-officio superintendent of Indian Affairs for Washington Territory, Stevens assumed responsibility for negotiating the terms of Americans' coexistence with indigenous peoples throughout his new jurisdiction, which encompassed present-day Idaho and western Montana as well as Washington State. Between Christmas Eve of 1854 and mid-January of 1856 he and a small crew of advisers met with Indians in nine councils at locations stretching from the tip of the Olympic Peninsula to the Rocky Mountains. Couriers subsequently carried ten "papers" bearing Indian signatures or X marks to Washington, D.C., for the "Great Father's" review.[6]

It is understandable that many people refer to the results of this diplomatic tour de force as "the Stevens treaties." The label may be a nod to the commanding persona for which Stevens is known, but it is mostly a convenient alternative to naming the several separate agreements or their many Indian parties. Either way, linking Stevens's name to the treaties reflects a bias common in public representations of history: a tendency to privilege the perspectives of the people who prevailed in struggles for hegemony. In the Pacific Northwest, Euro-Americans eventually dominated not only political institutions and economic development, but also public forums and the media for presenting stories about the region's past. And in the stories told by non-Indians, prominent Americans such as Stevens have usually been important protagonists.

But there is a better reason to speak of the Washington Territory Indian treaties as a unit, and that reason is also inseparable from Isaac Stevens's central role in their formulation. The texts of the ten documents—drafted in advance by the governor and his associates—are nearly identical. With minor exceptions they vary only in their descriptions of the lands that Indians ceded and reserved.[7] When a court has had to settle a dispute about the meaning of language in one of the treaties, its ruling has often determined how corresponding provisions of the other nine treaties will be construed.[8] As a consequence, many descendants of the indigenous people who met with Stevens in 1854, 1855, and 1856 now identify each other not only as fellow Indians but also as fellow beneficiaries of treaties so closely related that a single, shorthand name for them makes sense.[9]

Although the Stevens treaties dealt with concerns of the specific parties and accommodated local circumstances of the time, they also owed their existence and much of their content to events in a larger arena and actions taken years earlier. Subsequently, in turn, the Stevens treaties have influenced far-flung people and events, even outside the Northwest. It is with these facts in mind that organizers of the sesquicentennial conference set their sights on bringing together scholars who would consider such treaties from a wide range of chronological and geographical perspectives. The reward, they hoped, would be fresh and diverse commentaries on the evolving significance of the treaties made in Washington Territory.

To understand Isaac Stevens's actions, for example, it helps to have in mind that the history of treaties with Indians in North America reached back more than two centuries before Stevens met a *siwash* chief. By the time he requested and received congressional authorization to negotiate a purchase of lands from the Indians of his bailiwick, treaties had become a time-honored way for his country to legitimize its colonization of territory already occupied by indigenous peoples.[10] For several decades after the United States won their independence, the federal government generated revenue primarily by acquiring Indian land, then subdividing and selling it.

In proceeding by treaty, leaders of the fledgling republic emulated their colonial predecessors, who had found it necessary to work out and solemnize trading partnerships, military alliances, boundary agreements, and other terms of relations with self-governing indigenous neighbors. Architects of the United States also had a specific, recent colonial model for managing relations with Indians—a Royal Proclamation of 1763. With that decree the British Crown tried (unsuccessfully) to ensure the orderly, peaceful acquisition of Indian lands by assuming exclusive authority for negotiating purchases. The U.S. Constitution and early acts of Congress conferred the same prerogative on the new national government, although the government often invoked this power only after its constituents had swarmed into Indian country illegally, forcing its hand. By the 1850s Americans had gained considerable advantage over Indians in the contest for territory, and the purposes and terms of their treaties with Indians had changed accordingly; however, federal officials still took it for granted that treaties were necessary to smooth the way for American settlement in the Pacific Northwest.[11]

Looking forward in time from 1855 is also an essential part of assessing the Stevens treaties' significance. That year was a long, eventful decade and a half before 1871, when a majority of federal lawmakers, telling themselves that their country's power over Indians made treaties obsolete, ordered a stop to them. Moreover, the move in Congress proved premature, and for several decades after 1871 the government was obliged or chose to negotiate formal compacts with some tribal groups; it simply dubbed the results agreements instead of treaties and submitted them to both legislative houses for approval. Although Indians' near-impotence and federal policies did finally appear to render treaties and similar agreements irrelevant in the early twentieth century, old treaties remained "the law of the land" unless clearly annulled. The U.S. Supreme Court said as much in a string of decisions that included a 1959 case from the Navajo Reservation and litigation from the Pacific Northwest during the 1960s and 1970s.[12]

There is at least one more argument for locating and viewing the Stevens treaties on a timeline of Indian/non-Indian relations that extends to the present day: doing so serves as a reminder that the treaty parties did not have the benefit of our vantage point. Their words and actions are not likely to make sense unless we are mindful of what they did not know and could not foresee as well as what they knew or believed.

THE NEED TO LOOK ACROSS POLITICAL AND DISCIPLINARY BOUNDARIES

When scanning the historical background and subsequent fates of particular Indian treaties, a wide-angle geographical lens is also useful. Certainly, if treaties made in the northern United States are in the foreground, Canada should be within the range of vision. Not only are the practices of early English colonists and the Royal Proclamation of 1763 part of Canadian history as well as U.S. history, but also and more important, Indian policies in British-ruled Canada continued to affect American actions and Indians in the path of American expansion even after the United States won independence in 1783. Well into the nineteenth century, Britons carried on with colonial activities in places that would ultimately belong to the United States, including Washington Territory. Consequently, some contemporary American and Canadian tribes or indigenous nations include people whose ancestors dealt with more than one colonial government.[13] Pertinent background for the Stevens treaties is the fact that the Pacific Northwest was the subject of a joint occupation agreement between the United States and Britain from 1818 until 1846. And when the two nation-states finally agreed to divide that region roughly in equal parts at the forty-ninth parallel, the boundary they drew did not follow the boundaries of indigenous peoples' territories and movements. For these reasons and others the continuing presence and proximity of Britons was very much part of the context for the treaties that Stevens arranged.

Conference planners therefore resolved not to let present national borders and political jurisdictions determine the parameters of discussion at the University of Washington, even though the original stimulus for the meeting was the anniversary of Washington Territory Indian treaties.

Recent scholarship on related topics reinforced this determination. Histories illuminating the nature and origins of such things as ethnic groups, technologies of power, and subaltern responses to colonialism testify to the value of looking across modern international borders. David Thelen, for one, has urged his fellow historians to think "transnationally." It is important, he writes, to understand how people, "moving through time and space according to rhythms and relationships of their own, drew from, ignored, constructed, transformed, and defied claims of the nation-state."[14] Because the history of Indian treaties in North America is the history of empire builders and indigenous peoples variously asserting, negotiating, manipulating, and resisting "claims of the nation-state," students of those treaties would be wise to accept Thelen's challenge.

Organizers of the conference at the University of Washington thus had ample cause to expect that scholars who concern themselves with Canada and those who focus on the United States could learn from each other's work regarding treaties with indigenous peoples. Numerous questions are worth addressing jointly, and some lend themselves to potentially fruitful comparative studies. Why did colonial authorities make formal treaties with some indigenous peoples but not with others, for instance? How have indigenous peoples with treaties fared in comparison with indigenous peoples who did not make treaties with colonial authorities? Which colonial policies and practices regarding indigenous peoples have transcended the boundaries of colonial territories? Why and how has that occurred? What factors have affected the continuing viability and the meanings of treaties? And what have been the challenges and consequences of resolving disputes about treaties, or the lack of treaties, in colonial forums?

A keynote address underscored for conference participants the value of comparisons across time and national boundaries. The historian John Wunder, who has recently supplemented his extensive study of American Indians' legal history with investigations of other indigenous peoples' experiences, gave brief accounts of treaties involving or affecting indigenous people in four disparate places and times: medieval Scandinavia, early colonial Australia, nineteenth-century Canada, and the northern Great Plains of the United States. Although the treaties were diverse in nature, Wunder noted, their histories have an important commonality: indigenous people have ensured the treaties' evolving and present-day significance by remembering them and telling their own stories about them despite colonial authorities' efforts to suppress or discredit those indigenous representations.[15]

The quest for fresh perspectives on the Stevens treaties must also entail looking across the boundaries of academic disciplines. After all, treaties with indigenous peoples get attention in several intellectual specialties. Analyzing the language of the documents and judicial interpretations of that language has largely been the province of people trained in the law. But understanding treaties also involves knowing the circumstances in which they were made—a task that obliges lawyers and judges to seek help from people with other kinds of specialized knowledge. As Canadian scholar J. R. Miller has observed about the history of his homeland, colonists' treaties with aboriginal groups have been of several different types, each of which reflects the "character of Native-newcomer relations at the time."[16] Determining the character and context of particular relations is a challenge that historians such as Miller are disposed and equipped to tackle. But seeing those relations from the standpoints of all parties also requires information on tribal societies that anthropologists and indigenous history-keepers are practiced at collecting and interpreting. Thus it can take the combined work of analysts with three or more kinds of expertise to determine what treaties have meant to the people affected.

The essays in this volume confirm the wisdom of seizing on the 150th anniversary of the Stevens treaties as an opportunity to consider them and their broad historical context from diverse and wide-ranging scholarly perspectives. On the symposium program were historians, anthropologists, lawyers, and interdisciplinary scholars from the United States, Canada, and Australia. Joining the discussion were members of an audience that included First Nations leaders and modern treaty negotiators as well as other scholars and educators. Ten of the fifteen people chosen to speak—taking into account the presentations, conference discussions, and subsequent correspondence with each other—have since produced essays for this volume. The collection also includes a previously published article by two researchers who recounted their findings at the conference. For the people in attendance, the exchange of ideas among researchers from several fields of study and several countries did prove valuable; and now, with the publication of this anthology, it should prove valuable for anyone interested in knowing more and thinking further about the history and legacies of treaties with indigenous peoples.

Regrettably, a volume of eleven essays cannot explore every note-worthy aspect of the Stevens treaties, let alone the many other treaties with indigenous peoples. Readers seeking basic data on Indian treaties in the Pacific Northwest—a compendium of the treaties, their parties, and their terms; details of negotiations; accounts of subsequent implementation, violations, and controversies—must consult other sources.[17] This book samples but certainly does not exhaust the questions that the treaties continue to pose for scholars as well as members of the general public. The subjects of presentations proposed for the sesquicentennial symposium did not include, for example, recent campaigns in opposition to "special rights" for Indians, the contemporary importance of treaties to Indians who assert a right of political self-determination, or the current international law status of Indian treaties. Two of the conference participants who spoke on the important topic of native oral traditions had hoped to contribute essays but subsequently faced circumstances that dashed those hopes. Even so, the works included, separately and as a whole, make notable contributions to our knowledge of a historical phenomenon that has had long-lasting, complex repercussions in the Northwest and for many populations around the world.

Before highlighting some of those contributions, I should address a feature of the book that readers may find puzzling: terminology. Specifically, the authors use a variety of terms for indigenous people and the descendants who identify with them. Popular usage gives writers a choice of terms for such people in the United States, none of them uncontroversial. The most common general names—"Indians" and "Native Americans"—come in for criticism from a variety of directions. But because there is no consensus on a more appropriate designation, and because the people in question often identify themselves by one or both of those terms, our authors use either or both terms, except where a specific tribal name or indigenous language term is more fitting.

In Canada, by contrast, indigenous people have spearheaded a largely successful effort to make the term "First Nations" more common than "Indians" or "Natives." Although our Canadian contributors adopt that usage in most cases, they also use the term "Aboriginal" frequently. The latter word would likely strike Americans as quaint or pedantic but would seem familiar to Australians, whose term of choice for that continent's first inhabitants is "Aborigines." Some Canadians today may flinch on hearing Americans say "Indian," and Americans may wonder how many Canadians truly believe in the sovereignty implied by "First Nations," but speakers and audience members at the 2005 conference easily understood each other's terminology, and the differences did not prevent respectful communication. Similarly, it did not seem necessary to standardize the vocabulary throughout this book.[18]

LOOKING PAST THE U.S.–CANADA BORDER

Several essays in the collection demonstrate the particular value of linking treaty history in the northwest corner of the United States with treaty history in what is now British Columbia. They provide support for an argument that conference-goers heard from John Borrows, Professor and Law Foundation Chair of Aboriginal Justice and Governance in the University of Victoria Faculty of Law.[19] Borrows cited numerous reasons to consider Canadian and U.S. treaty making in tandem—reasons beyond the fact that the two nations share some historical roots, a language, and an English legal heritage. Treaties with indigenous peoples served the same general purposes in both countries, enabling non-natives to colonize and develop large areas in peace while assuring native peoples of home sites and access to subsistence resources. In addition, Borrows deemed it significant that the two countries share a long border. That border has simultaneously divided and connected, he said; it has created relationships even as it has marked a formal separation.

At the border's western end specifically, information and relations that crossed it were part of the context and the motivations for treaties involving native peoples on both sides. The first governor of the colonies that became British Columbia negotiated fourteen recorded treaties with Aboriginal inhabitants beginning in 1850 and ending in December 1854, the same month that Isaac Stevens called his first treaty council. Like Stevens, Governor James Douglas was dealing with people from whom his compatriots and fur-trader colleagues in the area obtained food, labor, and other vital services. Because the international boundary bisected indigenous homelands and extensive kinship networks, the two men even treated with some of the same tribal groups and individuals. Both governors—aware of each other's plans for Indians—also responded to local circumstances by proposing treaties that would reserve small parcels for Indian communities while making expanses of Aboriginal territory available for non-native settlers.

Legal historians Hamar Foster and Alan Grove offer additional, compelling reasons to meld the history of Indian treaties in Washington Territory and the history of treaty making in British Columbia. When trying to solve a puzzle of colonial B.C. history, they uncovered facts that suggest causal connections between the Indian policies of certain officials there and similar developments south of the border. Foster's and Grove's essay in this book methodically lays out evidence that Douglas was familiar with and likely to absorb ideas from U.S. law and jurisprudence regarding Indians, as was the land commissioner who subsequently declined to acknowledge native title by seeking treaties. Men charged with managing Indian affairs, note Foster and Grove, also continued to associate with each other well after taking up residence and offices on opposite sides of the international boundary. This meticulous detective work gives specificity to Borrows's observation that the line between Canada and the United States has not been a barrier to relationships or information. The border did not prevent colonial authorities from influencing each other's approach to relations with indigenous peoples.

Legal scholar Douglas Harris reports in his contribution that American interpretations of treaties have also influenced developments in Canada during recent years, thanks to Canadian courts' willingness to consider principles articulated by judges in the United States. When ruling on disputes about the fishing rights of Aboriginal people, a few Canadian justices have cited opinions or adopted language of U.S. courts construing a promise in the Stevens treaties that Indians could continue fishing at their accustomed places. Although American jurists have not returned the compliment—that is, they have not looked to Canadian court decisions for guidance—Harris's account makes it hard to understand such indifference. Every time Canadians consider and react to American conclusions regarding treaty obligations to native peoples, the reasons mount for Americans to take note.

As Harris indicates, Governors Douglas and Stevens "negotiated with peoples who shared a cultural heritage and economic base," including fish stocks that could not be neatly divided by colonial boundary lines. However, the international boundary does demarcate areas with distinct political and legal histories. Treaty making and its ramifications have taken different directions in U.S. and Canadian jurisdictions since 1854. Ironically, if Foster's and Grove's speculation is correct, one key difference—B.C. officials' apparent conclusion in 1854 that they could dispense with treaties as a means of acquiring native territory—may be traceable to a legal development in the United States. In any case differences are as instructive as similarities. One important difference—noted in Harris's essay and articulated by Borrows—"is that there is greater recognition of [Indians'] reserved rights in the United States, but greater constraint of federal sovereign power in Canada."

American courts have ruled that Congress may unilaterally abrogate treaties with Indians or terminate tribes' right to govern themselves, yet the courts have also said self-government is an inherent right that the tribes retain in the absence of an explicit cession or abrogation. By contrast, Borrows asserted at the conference, "First Nations in Canada do not currently enjoy a recognized right to self-government," but they do enjoy a measure of protection for any acknowledged rights because Canadian law requires the government to justify interference with such rights by stating a legislative objective consistent with the Crown's honor.

TREATIES AND POWER RELATIONS

In comparing U.S. and Canadian government powers to curtail native rights, Borrows alludes to another theme that runs through this volume: understanding treaties (or the lack of treaties) with indigenous populations entails analyzing power relations, and power relations have been more complex, negotiable, and variable than many broad-brush histories of Indian affairs indicate. Histories tracing the development of nation-states such as Canada and the United States understandably focus on factors that enabled them to overpower native societies. Francis Paul Prucha, author of a magisterial history of U.S. Indian policy, stresses the inequality of power reflected in most of the treaties with Indians. A typical treaty, he notes, paired ostensible recognition of the tribes' sovereignty with Indians' acknowledgment of their subservience to the United States.[20]

The essays in this book do not deny the ultimate subjugation and marginalization of indigenous peoples—indeed, the contribution by legal scholar Robert Anderson echoes Prucha's emphasis—but several of them tell stories that complicate the usual outcome-oriented perspective on power relations. They do so primarily by considering events from the historical actors' time- and culture-specific points of view. That approach carries an important lesson: a retrospective assessment of the treaty parties' relative powers will not explain the parties' words and actions; instead, it is necessary to examine what the parties knew, did not know, valued, and expected at the time they spoke and acted.

In Washington Territory, for instance, all parties came to the treaty councils with reasons for apprehension or insecurity as well as reasons for confidence. When the Indians on Stevens's circuit heard his proposals, the American presence was limited to a few thousand people around Puget Sound, most of them reliant to some extent on natives' services and goodwill. However, newcomers were rapidly swelling and emboldening the Boston population while smallpox and other plagues were taking a demoralizing toll on Indian communities. Representatives of the United States faced a need to make treaties at a time when their nation's ultimate domination of all Indians seemed assured but neither imminent nor cheap to achieve. Federal Indian policy was in disarray. During the 1840s Americans had moved into the trans-Mississippi West ahead of their government. Even after they organized U.S. territories there, the emigrants could not be sure of rapid, effective backup from the national government if their efforts to appease displaced Indians failed.

The new American communities on the Pacific coast also called into question the previous federal practice of pushing Indians westward, beyond the states of the Union, and politicians were slow to agree on another plan. Isaac Stevens took his instructions from a commissioner of Indian affairs who opined that Indians could be suffered to remain within the states, confined to small reserved tracts of land where they would have to learn the habits of "civilized" life. However, Commissioner George Manypenny and Governor Stevens were both aware that treaties embodying this proposal had no guarantee of ratification, since lawmakers and many of their constituents still favored Indians' removal from the states.[21]

In other words the balance of Indian and American power was harder to discern in the mid-1850s than it is now. Certainly, Indians did not have access to some information that would have helped them assess the looming non-Indian threat to their autonomy and prosperity. Moreover, Indians were calculating the cost-benefit ratio of a treaty by factoring in considerations that historians have overlooked or regarded as unimportant. Historian Chris Friday takes a close look in his essay at beliefs and events that would have informed the calculations of a leading Lummi man named Chowitsut. Friday concludes that Chowitsut had reason to be sanguine when he signed the Treaty of Point Elliott. Drawing on information about the nature of power and status in Lummi society, Friday infers that Chowitsut did not conceive of his signature on the treaty as submission to Americans' will; instead, the ambitious chief likely believed that he enhanced his personal power by securing an advantageous American promise.[22]

Historian Paige Raibmon offers a different kind of caveat to the general rule that nineteenth-century treaties with indigenous peoples reflected and secured the colonial states' superior power. Her essay implies that the treaties are imperfect symbols of such power because they often embodied policies the non-Indian parties could not or did not enforce. Pacific Northwest treaties, both in Washington Territory and on Vancouver Island, were efforts to stem conflict resulting or expected from settlers' demands for land and deference, and they represented a colonial policy of acquiring title to real estate without military action or moral stain where possible. Yet numerous settlers (including officials and even judges) risked the wrath of Aboriginal people by taking their land without treaties and often in defiance (or ignorance) of applicable law.[23] Since practice has never conformed entirely to policy, Raibmon argues, present circumstances (and, by implication, treaty history) cannot be understood without a history of all the practices that dispossessed natives. Their dispossession has included loss of access to fish and other resources as well as land. Detailing the process of deprivation can help non-Indians comprehend native people's complaints of injustice and their rising demands for decolonization. It makes the regional significance of Indian treaties more apparent than studies that focus solely on blackletter law.

Raibmon further complicates the issue of power by mentioning that indigenous people and immigrants have created family ties to each other, through marriage and otherwise. It will not do to tell a simple story of Aboriginals or Indians oppressed by colonists of European descent, for instance, when some people in the former category have staked their future on intimate relations with members of the latter group, including individuals who have participated in the expropriation of indigenous property. Such intergroup ties also strike Ravi de Costa as a complicating factor in the contemporary effort to redefine the balance of power between Aboriginal and other British Columbians. De Costa, an interdisciplinary scholar of colonialism's legacies among various indigenous peoples, contributes an essay on the B.C. treaty process that began during the 1970s. He observes that the nature of the native parties and their relationships to other parties is far from clear due in part to the ramifications of past and present relationships across perceived racial and cultural boundaries.

The complexity and paradoxes of power relations are also evident when indigenous people ascribe high value to treaties that have functioned as instruments of colonial domination. The essays of Friday and historian Andrew Fisher, for instance, describe dogged Indian struggles to win respect for treaties by which they had surrendered vast acreage and much of their autonomy without exacting commensurate concessions from the colonial governments. De Costa recounts the present-day efforts of First Nations in British Columbia to make treaties for the first time with governments that have ultimate power to change the ground rules entirely.

In 1994 historian Frederick Hoxie offered a succinct explanation for Indians' partiality to a way of defining relations that facilitated non-Indian rule. Indians regard their treaties as "symbols of community allegiance," Hoxie observed, and they construe recognition of the treaties as respect for their right "to affiliate as they have for centuries." Thus agreements originally meant as "a badge of sovereignty" for "weak and outnumbered Europeans" who were seeking a foothold in other people's homelands "have become badges of Native American sovereignty." Today the treaties are instruments "wielded by weak and outnumbered Native Americans to manage their passage through the legal culture" of superimposed nation-states.[24]

TREATIES AS INDIANS HAVE UNDERSTOOD THEM

Whether power relations or other aspects of treaty making are at issue, we cannot understand what happened at treaty councils and afterward without determining and accounting for what indigenous people knew, believed, wanted, and customarily did in comparable situations. And for most of the contributors to this volume, that is evidently a top-priority task. In their essays the focus is on indigenous perceptions of events and on the meanings that native people have assigned to agreements with colonial governments. The results—achieved in many cases through inspired historical detective work and methods of analysis pioneered by anthropologists—are invariably fascinating.

For example, supplementing the abundant available information on non-native treaty makers with evidence of native views means recognizing that indigenous peoples have had their own, distinctive legal cultures. Contributors Kent McNeil, Andrew Fisher, Russel Barsh, and Bruce Rigsby mention differences between Aboriginal and European or Euro-American assumptions about such legal questions as the bases of national sovereignty, the character of property rights, and the criteria of tribal landownership. Many post-treaty misunderstandings have stemmed from colonial authorities' failure or refusal to acknowledge and accommodate those differences.

Law professor McNeil carefully exposes the ethnocentricity of the legal thinking that underlay European claims of sovereignty in North America. Apologists of colonization invoked the supposedly universal law of nations—the forerunner of today's international law. However, those principles evolved in Europe and did not take Aboriginal law ways or legal capacity into account. Nor did the imperial powers involve indigenous inhabitants in plans to allocate territory for colonization. Because of this ethnocentric oversight, McNeil's essay argues, indigenous peoples of the Pacific Northwest can rightfully assert that the Canadian or American government's jurisdiction over them must rest on something other than the 1846 boundary agreement between Britain and the United States.

Non-Indians' disregard or ignorance of Indian legal culture also interests Fisher, Barsh, and Rigsby. These three authors refute a common belief that Isaac Stevens and James Douglas were negotiating with people who had no concept of property rights in land. Fisher, Barsh, and Rigsby maintain that the Northwest's native inhabitants did have a strong sense of proprietorship in the lands they ceded by treaty as well as the lands, fishing sites, and resources they reserved. However, Indians had long conceived of people's proprietary privileges and responsibilities in ways that probably prevented them from understanding a treaty cession as a sale of all right, title, and interest. Thus people of the Columbia Plateau, according to the anthropologist Rigsby, would not have expected the treaties to affect their access to and control of ancestors' graves and remains, even those in ceded territory.

Another discrepancy in the treaty parties' understandings—the subject of the essays by Fisher and Barsh—came to light when treaty Indians found themselves in competition with non-Indians at off-reservation fisheries. Contrary to the assumptions or assertions of federal lawyers responsible for defending Indians' right to fish, native people along the Columbia River and around Puget Sound traditionally regarded their fisheries as family property rather than the common resources of political entities that non-Indians called tribes. In pragmatic response to post-treaty developments, especially court rulings, the Indian treaty signers' descendants eventually embraced the notion of tribal rights and American conceptions of their tribes.

From the outset, however, Indian construction of the treaties did roughly correspond to American legal doctrine in one important sense: Indians understood that treaties acknowledged their status as distinct, self-governing peoples. In numerous instances that understanding has survived past efforts by the colonial governments to destroy self-governing tribal communities. It has also survived a plethora of changes in the nature and forms of indigenous political practices and institutions. Explaining such a resilient sense of group identity and desire for autonomy means, in part, knowing how indigenous people and their descendants have retained and transmitted historical memories of their treaties. It entails studying the content of Indian or First Nation histories and the multiple purposes those histories have served.

As several speakers at the University of Washington conference explained, the collective memories of native people have both reflected and influenced the state of interethnic relations. Keith Carlson, a historian at the University of Saskatchewan, analyzed a memory carefully preserved in the Sto:lo Nation of British Columbia, for which he formerly worked. An address by the Queen's deputy in 1864 led the Sto:lo to expect compensation for the lands they lost to settlers. Although Canadian politicians and historians have long ignored or discounted Indian accounts of that speech, Carlson found that "Sto:lo belief in the historical reality of the [so-called] Crown's Promise has shaped the way they have reacted to and interacted with western society over the past 140 years."[25] Other indigenous historical traditions figure prominently in the essays of Friday, Barsh, Rigsby, and historian Arthur Ray. Like Carlson, those contributors as well as de Costa suggest that airing and respecting indigenous historical traditions is an essential part of enabling treaties to achieve their goal of preventing or resolving conflict.

Although the descendants of indigenous people as well as the successors of colonial officials have preserved memories and tangible records of those treaties, their understandings and representations of the treaties have not remained static. That is apparent when Indians today insist on adherence to treaties their ancestors signed reluctantly. Likewise, the fact and ways that some modern non-Indian governments implement decades-old treaties would surprise the officials who drafted them. The meanings and effects of treaties have evolved over time as circumstances have changed, and there are studies in this book that track some particularly important adaptations.

The essays by Fisher and Barsh—the latter a lawyer with an extensive record of publication on ethnohistorical questions—describe an ironic shift in the nature of Indians' group affiliations and self-government, which they attribute to the Stevens treaties and judicial interpretations of those treaties. In Washington Territory, as elsewhere, the colonial officials who called treaty conferences and created the written treaty texts had conceptions of "Indian tribes" that did not correspond to indigenous peoples' actual sociopolitical organization. The treaties were instruments for creating—in Stevens's case, quite deliberately—new tribes that conformed to American notions of power and political allegiance.

Indian signers did not share and may not have understood Stevens's expectations, but they or their successors subsequently facilitated his creative effort, sometimes intentionally and sometimes not, when they asserted their treaty rights in colonial courts. They found themselves addressing people who were resistant or oblivious to conceiving of tribal identities as indigenous ancestors did. Although courts in the United States are supposed to construe treaties to meet the Indian signers' expectations if possible, judges and even lawyers for the Indians attributed Indians' treaty rights to political entities that resemble Isaac Stevens's notion of tribes more than aboriginal patterns of governance and social relations. According to Barsh, the effect has been to prompt Indians around Puget Sound to reformulate their group identities and embrace a competitive nationalism that gives rise to a way of allocating resources very different from the Aboriginal, kin-based system.[26] An implication of Barsh's analysis—that the change does not bode well for resource stewardship—contrasts with a more common view among scholars that emergent tribal governments have used the power flowing from the reaffirmed and clarified treaty rights to protect cherished resources from overexploitation by other stakeholders.[27]

INDIAN TREATIES, OLD AND NEW,
IN CONTEMPORARY FORUMS

Courtrooms are among the most important public forums where people have described memories related to Indian treaties. Tribe members versed in treaty history have sometimes gained a hearing there, but not always a respectful hearing or one that had the result they desired. And in the noisy world outside the courts, including the halls of academia where litigants find many of the experts who testify regarding history, non-Indian voices have long been louder and commanded more respect than Indian voices. Arthur Ray's essay in this volume concerns the power of colonial courts to declare whose histories of treaty relations are authoritative. Ray touches on an intriguing paradox and tension in U.S. and Canadian treaty relations with indigenous peoples. The hegemony of colonial law is indisputable; otherwise, Indians and First Nations people would not find themselves in federal, state, and provincial courts asserting or defending their rights. And yet colonial law has developed rules that require the courts to consider and even in some instances defer to Indian or Aboriginal interpretations of treaties and treaty history.

Ray shows that such rules are hard to fulfill when indigenous historical traditions—the events that indigenous people deem significant, their tests of authenticity, their ways of depicting the past—differ substantially from Euro-American or Euro-Canadian traditions. Judges and juries, even those imbued with the modern ethos of respect for cultural diversity, are often unable to transcend some biases that come with their socialization in a non-Indian culture. Instead, they hew tenaciously to their own culture's criteria for determining the credibility of stories about the past. For example, judges may give little or no credence to Indian testimony that incorporates orally transmitted history yet grant considerable weight to an anthropologist's account that is based on interviews with some of the same Indians.[28]

Ray offers reasons to doubt that courts are satisfactory forums for resolving differences in the stories that native and non-native people tell about the past or the meanings they assign to those stories. When courts in Canada or the United States entertain claims based on treaties (or the lack of treaties), the decisions turn on interpretations of historical information. But the persons who are called on to provide that information at trial may find themselves talking to an audience with limited interest in or basis for comprehending history told as scholars or native elders think proper. Ray, who has testified as an expert on history in several such lawsuits, entertainingly explains why it has been difficult to teach judges, even with all their formal education, about the complex histories and unfamiliar cultures of indigenous people. The challenges he describes also trouble contributor Bruce Rigsby. Rigsby specifically laments the courts' adherence to rulings in cases from years ago, when the witnesses were anthropologists whose data, models, and methodologies seem inadequate or erroneous to modern heirs.

Are there government bodies that offer native people better opportunities to tell their stories and better odds of swaying colonial decision makers than courts do? Contributors de Costa and Anderson do not give optimistic answers to that question. They look at occasions when native people have applied to politicians and government agents other than judges for justice. Ravi de Costa considers an ongoing treaty process in British Columbia and concludes that it does not sufficiently account for changes in the nature of the negotiating entities since the nineteenth century. He fears that new treaties will not resolve tensions unless they rest on thorough reviews of the parties' history and agreements about how to depict that history. The negotiators hope to settle longstanding grievances, but because change will continue, de Costa believes, finality should not be the goal of the modern negotiations.

Robert Anderson's essay analyzes modern negotiations in the United States that have led to agreements he calls treaty substitutes. He finds native people—outmatched by the powerful federal government—accepting problematic terms much as their nineteenth-century predecessors did. One case in point is Alaska Natives' campaign for federal legislation to settle their land claims. The result—the Alaska Native Claims Settlement Act of 1971—was ultimately a disappointment in several respects, including its creation of Native institutions that embodied American political and economic values rather than indigenous values. In the other case that Anderson discusses, rights guaranteed by a Stevens treaty gave the Nez Perce Tribe crucial leverage as it managed its engagement with the U.S. legal system in a water-rights contest; but the rules of that system imposed unsatisfactory limits on what the tribe could hope to achieve.

Like Anderson and Ray, many of the contributors to this volume have at some time served as advocates or expert witnesses on behalf of native people seeking to redeem treaty promises. All of the scholars represented in this book are acutely conscious that the subjects they write about are far from academic. Research and writing about treaties with indigenous peoples always has potential practical ramifications—in many cases very significant economic and political ramifications. It is not just that judges may read and rely on relevant articles in law journals or historical monographs; it is not just that historians or anthropologists, testifying in trials where the meanings of treaties are at issue, may have to defend every word of their previous publications on the subject. In fact, the repercussions of scholars' work are not limited to litigation, important as that is. Stories about treaties are modern origin stories, and origin stories are vital ingredients of all peoples' status and identities. Interrogate and dispute such a story, and you may threaten a people's understanding of who they are; affirm and disseminate that story, and you may give the same people reason for hope, confidence, or righteous anger. That is one message, articulated in various ways, of the essays by Raibmon, Friday, and Ray. The significance of treaties with indigenous peoples is ultimately dependent on the power to tell stories about those treaties that move listeners to take desired action.

Because people continue to tell treaty stories that have important practical consequences, Friday refers to treaties with indigenous peoples as "living" documents. In doing so, he echoes the declarations of many American Indians, and some of those declarations came as Indians prepared to observe the 150th anniversary of the treaties made in Washington Territory. Three men helping to plan a twenty-tribe sesquicentennial commemoration spoke to an Associated Press reporter of their strong sense that the treaties are a dynamic force in their tribes' continuing struggle for survival. At the same time they revealed that the treaties' modern significance for that struggle is a matter of ongoing debate:

"Even some of our tribal members look at the treaty as a piece of paper that identifies defeat," said Arlen Washines, a Yakama Nation officer and chairman of the planning committee. "But conquering nations do not sign treaties with those they overpower. This was no defeat." Carl Sampson, descendant of a Walla Walla treaty signer, said he preferred to see the sesquicentennial observance as a celebration of his ancestors' courage and foresight and an opportunity to give thanks for the tribes' endurance. "Much of what we're doing today," he told the reporter, "is to preserve this information and knowledge for the future, so that as we train the next generation of leaders, we're confident they have this knowledge." Antone Minthorn, chairman of the Confederated Tribes of the Umatilla Reservation, concurred. "The very treaties that forced Indians onto reservations," Minthorn insisted, "promise them rights that help to secure their futures."[29] Minthorn's words give vivid meaning to the assertion that the papers Indians signed long ago are "living documents."

The pledges exchanged and recorded at solemn nineteenth-century negotiations between Indian and American leaders reflected the promise makers' assessments and predictions of the two peoples' relative power. Since then, those promises have drawn power of their own from the expectations, needs, memories, anger, remorse, humanitarian concerns, principles, and actions of the promise makers and their heirs. History suggests that the life force of those promises will not be snuffed out as long as people still live who are conscious of the legacy bequeathed by the treaty makers.

NOTES

1. I use the same spelling for the aboriginal camping place as is used for the town now located on the site. In the United States record of the treaty signed there, the name appears as "muckl-te-oh." 12 *United States Statutes* 927. According to *HistoryLink.org: The Online Encyclopedia of Washington State History*, the name means "good camping place." See http://www.historylink.org/essays/output.cfm? file_id=5705, accessed February 4, 2006.

2. "Boston" is a Chinook trade jargon term that identified Americans by the principal port from which the first ones came to the Northwest on trading ships. The native people pronounced this word "pah-studs." "Siwash" is also Chinook jargon, derived from the French term "sauvage."

3. This and the following excerpts appear in "Record of the Proceedings of the Commission to Hold Treaties with the Indian Tribes in Washington Territory and the Blackfoot Country," Records of the Washington Superintendency of Indian Affairs, microform copy in the University of Washington Library, Mic A-171, Roll 26, Seattle.

4. Treaty with the Dwamish, Suquamish, etc., 1855, 12 *United States Statutes* 927.

5. Scholarly works that consider North American Indian treaties as a collective historical phenomenon include Francis Paul Prucha, *American Indian Treaties: The History of a Political Anomaly* (Berkeley: University of California Press, 1994); Jill

St. Germain, *Indian Treaty-Making Policy in the United States and Canada, 1867–1877* (Toronto: University of Toronto Press, 2001); and Bruce E. Johansen, ed., *Enduring Legacies: Native American Treaties and Contemporary Controversies* (Westport, Conn.: Praeger, 2004). Documentation of public controversy about Indian treaties in the United States is abundant. For example, see C. Herb Williams and Walt Neubrech, *Indian Treaties: American Nightmare* (Seattle: Outdoor Empire Publishing, 1976); Scott Kerr, "The New Indian Wars," *The Progressive* 54 (April 1990): 20; Jeffrey R. Dudas, "In the Name of Equal Rights: 'Special Rights' and the Politics of Resentment in Post–Civil Rights America," *Law and Society Review* 39 (December 2005): 723–57; and "Facts about Indian Law," *Everett* [Washington] *Herald*, October 23, 2006, 1.

6. "Record of the Proceedings of the Commission to Hold Treaties with the Indian Tribes in Washington Territory and the Blackfoot Country"; and Kent Richards, "The Stevens Treaties of 1854–1855: An Introduction," *Oregon Historical Quarterly* 106, no. 3 (fall 2005): 347.

7. Treaty with the Nisqualli, Puyallup, etc., 10 *United States Statutes* 1132; Treaty with the S'Klallam, 12 *United States Statutes* 933; Treaty with the Makah, 12 *United States Statutes* 939; Treaty with the Wallawalla, Cayuse, etc., 12 *United States Statutes* 945; Treaty with the Yakama, 12 *United States Statutes* 951; Treaty with the Nez Perces, 12 *United States Statutes* 957; Treaty with the Quinaielt, etc., 12 *United States Statutes* 971; Treaty with the Flatheads, etc., 12 *United States Statutes* 975; and Treaty with the Blackfeet, 11 *United States Statutes* 657.

8. Fronda Woods, "Who's in Charge of Fishing?" *Oregon Historical Quarterly* 160, no. 3 (fall 2005): 426–30.

9. Shannon Dininny, "Tribes Commemorate 150th Anniversary of 1855 Treaty," Associated Press State & Local Wire, May 28, 2005.

10. In the first U.S. treaty with Indians, leaders of the ongoing war for independence from England secured permission from Delaware chiefs to build forts in that Indian nation. Treaty with the Delawares, 1778, 7 *United States Statutes* 13.

11. Frederick E. Hoxie, "Why Treaties?" in *Buried Roots and Indestructible Seeds: The Survival of American Indian Life in Story, History, and Spirit*, edited by Mark A. Lindquist and Martin Zanger (Madison: University of Wisconsin Press, 1994), 85–105. There is no evidence that Indians in Washington Territory had experience making comparable treaties with non-Indians before 1854, although fur trade companies installed trading posts in the region as early as 1811 and apparently in most cases secured the consent of the people whose land they used. But the indigenous societies of the Pacific Northwest did have generations of experience negotiating and symbolizing the terms of relations between distinct communities, including territorial prerogatives. See, for example, Wayne Suttles, "Affinal Ties, Subsistence, and Prestige among the Coast Salish," *Coast Salish Essays* (Seattle: University of Washington Press, 1987), 23–24; and Ronald L. Trosper, "Northwest Coast Indigenous Institutions That Supported Resilience and Sustainability," *Ecological Economics* 41 (2002): 329–44.

12. Prucha, *American Indian Treaties*, 362; *Williams v. Lee*, 358 U.S. 217 (1959); *Puyallup Tribe v. Washington Department of Game*, 391 U.S. 392 (1968); and *Washington v. Washington State Commercial Passenger Fishing Vessel Association*, 443 U.S. 658 (1979).

13. Historian Michael J. Witgen has argued that a vast area straddling the U.S.-Canada border remained indigenous space into the early 1800s. England, France, and the United States had made little headway by then in their efforts to impose an imperial geography on native peoples' dynamic webs of kinship and alliances. See Witgen, "An Infinity of Nations: How Indians, Empires, and Western Migration Shaped National Identity in North America," Ph.D. dissertation, University of Washington, 2004.

14. David Thelen, "The Nation and Beyond: Transnational Perspectives on United States History," *Journal of American History* 86 (December 1999): 965. Also see Joy Porter, "Imagining Indians: Differing Perspectives on Native American History," in *The State of U.S. History*, edited by Melvyn Stokes (Oxford: Berg, 2001), 357; and Melissa L. Meyer and Kerwin Lee Klein, "Native American Studies and the End of Ethnohistory," in *Studying Native America: Problems and Prospects*, edited by Russell Thornton (Madison: University of Wisconsin Press, 1998), 198. Studies of nationalism and ethnicity that consider peoples in several locales around the globe include Benedict Anderson, *Imagined Communities: Reflections on the Origin and Spread of Nationalism* (London: Verso, 1983); Fredrik Barth, *Ethnic Groups and Boundaries* (Boston: Little, Brown, 1969); Manning Nash, *The Cauldron of Ethnicity in the Modern World* (Chicago: University of Chicago Press, 1989); and Eugeen E. Roosens, *Creating Ethnicity: The Process of Ethnogenesis* (Newbury Park, Calif.: Sage Publications, 1989).

15. John Wunder's publications include *"Retained by the People": A History of American Indians and the Bill of Rights* (New York: Oxford University Press, 1994); *Native Americans and the Law: Contemporary and Historical Perspectives on American Indian Rights, Freedoms, and Sovereignty* (New York: Routledge Press [previously Garland Publishing], 1996), 6 vols.; "'Merciless Indian Savages' and the Declaration of Independence: North Americans Translate the Ecunnaunuxulgee Documents," *American Indian Law Review* 25 (fall 2000): 1–28; "Indigenous Peoples, Identity, History, and Law: The United States and Australian Experience," *Law*Text*Culture* 4 (fall 1998): 81–114; and "'Looking after the Country Properly': A Comparative History of Indigenous Peoples and Australian and American National Parks," *Indigenous Law Journal* 2 (fall 2003): 27–62.

16. J. R. (Jim) Miller, "The Multiple Meanings of Canada's Indian Treaties: A Presentation to the 'Pacific Northwest Indian Treaties in National and International Perspective' Conference," University of Washington, Seattle, May 14, 2005, 1.

17. Surprisingly, there is no single publication that meets this need. Readers can find citations to most of the sources on this subject in a special issue of the *Oregon Historical Quarterly* 106 (fall 2005), entitled "The Isaac I. Stevens and Joel Palmer Treaties, 1855–2005."

18. For a few of the many comments on this problematic terminology, see James Taylor Carson, "American Historians and Indians," *The Historical Journal* 49 (September 2006): 921–34; Hillary N. Weaver, "Indigenous Identity: What Is It and Who Really Has It?" *American Indian Quarterly* 25 (spring 2001): 240–57; Patricia Doyle-Bedwell and Fay G. Cohen, "Aboriginal Peoples in Canada: Their Role in Shaping Environmental Trends in the Twenty-first Century," in *Governing the Environment: Persistent Challenges, Uncertain Innovations*, edited by Edward Anthony Parson (Toronto: University of Toronto Press, 2001), 196n3; Joane Nagel, *American Indian Ethnic Renewal: Red Power and the Resurgence of Identity and Culture* (New York: Oxford University Press, 1996), xi–xiii; and Alexandra Harmon, "Lines in Sand: Shifting Boundaries between Indians and Non-Indians in the Puget Sound Region," *Western Historical Quarterly* 26 (winter 1995): 429–53.

19. This paragraph and subsequent references to John Borrows draw on the contents of a draft paper he wrote and provided in advance of the conference under the title "Treaties as a Grant of Rights from the Indians: The Douglas and Stevens Treaties of the Pacific North-West." Professor Borrows is Anishinabe, a member of the Chippewa of the Nawash First Nation.

20. Prucha, *American Indian Treaties*, 5, 9.

21. Sources on the history summarized here include Francis Paul Prucha, *The Great Father*, 2 vols. (Lincoln: University of Nebraska Press, 1984); Richards, "Stevens Treaties of 1854–1855"; and Alexandra Harmon, *Indians in the Making: Ethnic Relations and Indian Identities around Puget Sound* (Berkeley: University of California Press, 1998), 78–79, and sources cited there.

22. I have argued elsewhere that decades of give-and-take passed before most such Indians lost confidence in their powers to turn relations with Americans to their advantage. Harmon, *Indians in the Making*.

23. Harris, Foster, and Grove also remind us that officials sanctioned the colonization of mainland British Columbia in the absence of treaties. Their essays differ from Raibmon's, however, in implying that laws and policies—and more specifically treaties—have made important practical differences in the places and communities they affected.

24. Hoxie, "Why Treaties?" 102–3.

25. Keith Thor Carlson, "The Clash of Histories: Salish Canadian Memories of Treaty Agreements That the Government Says Never Occurred," draft speaking notes in author's possession, May 2005.

26. Rigsby's essay alludes to a different way that legal developments have effectively changed the meaning of a treaty. Although Rigsby considers it important that the tribes of the Umatilla Reservation did not sign a treaty explicitly relinquishing their access and right to their ancestors' mortal remains, he concedes that the tribes may effectively have lost that ancient right when the U.S. Congress adopted and the federal courts interpreted the Native American Graves Protection and Repatriation Act of 1990.

27. Charles F. Wilkinson, *Messages from Frank's Landing: A Story of Salmon, Treaties, and the Indian Way* (Seattle: University of Washington Press, 2000);

Charles F. Wilkinson, *Blood Struggle: The Rise of Modern Indian Nations* (New York: Norton, 2005), chapters 7, 11, 12; Alexander V. Hayes, "The Nez Perce Water Rights Settlement and the Revolution in Indian Country," *Environmental Law* 36 (summer 2006): 869–99; and Evelyn W. Pinkerton, "Translating Legal Rights into Management Practice, Overcoming Barriers to the Exercise of Co-Management," *Human Organization* 51 (winter 1992): 330–41.

28. Sasha Harmon, "Writing History by Litigation: The Legacy and Limitations of Northwest Indian Rights Cases," *Columbia, the Magazine of Northwest History* (winter 1990–91): 5–15.

29. Dininny, "Tribes Commemorate 150th Anniversary of 1855 Treaty."

PART I

COLONIAL CONCEITS

1 Negotiated Sovereignty

INDIAN TREATIES AND THE ACQUISITION OF

AMERICAN AND CANADIAN TERRITORIAL RIGHTS

IN THE PACIFIC NORTHWEST

Kent McNeil

Indian treaties figure prominently in the history of American expansion into the Pacific Northwest. In British Columbia they are less important historically, as the Douglas Treaties on Vancouver Island in the 1850s and Treaty 8 in 1899, affecting the northeastern corner of the province, were the only treaties negotiated there. The absence of treaties in most of the Canadian Pacific Northwest has, however, given rise to legal and political issues that even today are largely outstanding.[1] The matter of unresolved Indian land claims in the region—specifically the claims of the Nisga'a Nation—came before the Supreme Court of Canada in 1973 in the case of *Calder v. Attorney-General of British Columbia*, in which the Court acknowledged the existence of Indian title but split evenly on whether it had been legislatively extinguished.[2] While inconclusive in result, that decision nonetheless prompted the Canadian government to rethink its attitude toward contemporary treaty making and formulate a policy for the negotiation of treaties in parts of Canada outside the geographical scope of the historical treaties.[3] The new policy eventually led to the resolution of the Nisga'a claim by a modern-day treaty ratified in 2000.[4] Reluctantly, the province of British Columbia in the early 1990s finally accepted the necessity of negotiating treaties as well. B.C. not only participated in the Nisga'a Treaty, but also set up the British Columbia

Treaty Commission to assist in the process of negotiating other land claims.[5]

Although the historical treaties in both the United States and Canada, and the contemporary treaty process in British Columbia,[6] involve lands and natural resources, they are also about sovereignty.[7] For a long time the United States Supreme Court has recognized that the Indian tribes negotiated treaties with the American government as sovereign nations and that they retained their sovereign status within the United States after the treaties were concluded.[8] In Canada, the Supreme Court has also acknowledged that France and Britain regarded the Indian nations as "independent nations" with whom "treaties of alliance or neutrality" were negotiated in the period prior to the cession of New France to Britain in 1763,[9] but it has yet to recognize the continuing sovereignty of the Indian nations after the treaties.[10] Nonetheless, in *Campbell v. British Columbia* the British Columbia Supreme Court upheld the constitutional validity of self-government provisions in the Nisga'a Treaty on the ground that the Nisga'a Nation's inherent right to govern itself had *not* been taken away by British colonization and the creation of Canada, and so the nature and extent of that right could be defined by a contemporary treaty.[11] The governments of British Columbia and Canada obviously supported this position, as they were parties to the treaty and argued in favor of its validity in *Campbell*.

However, Indian treaties, both historical and contemporary, are only part of the legal history of European and American colonization of the Pacific Northwest. They are not the only treaties of interest to indigenous peoples and scholars of indigenous / colonizer relations. In addition to dealing with the Indian nations by treaty, European governments and the United States engaged in wars and diplomatic relations and entered into treaties with one another, whereby they purported to divide up North America with scant regard for the Indian nations who occupied the territories being distributed. This process was taking place well before the Pacific Northwest became a region seriously contested by Spain, Russia, Britain, and later the United States. For example, by the 1763 Treaty of Paris, France ceded its North American possessions east of the Mississippi River to Britain. This treaty is generally regarded as establishing the boundary between British North America and the Louisiana Territory (secretly ceded by France to Spain in 1762 by the Treaty of Fontainebleau and reacquired by France in 1800 in the Treaty of San Ildefonso).

Similarly, the 1783 Treaty of Paris that acknowledged the independence of the United States set the northern boundary between the new republic and British North America from the Atlantic to the Lake of the Woods. In 1803, Thomas Jefferson purchased the Louisiana Territory from France, placing the United States in a geographical position to enter into the contest for the Pacific Northwest. The disputed boundary between the Louisiana Territory and the Spanish territories to the southwest was defined in 1819 by the Adams-Onís Treaty. On the northern plains the Convention of 1818 between Britain and the United States established the forty-ninth parallel as the boundary between their respective territories from the Lake of the Woods to the Rocky Mountains, but this agreement left the Oregon country free and open to the subjects and citizens of both nations for ten years. (This provision for joint access was renewed for an indefinite period in 1827.) Russia then renounced its claims in the Pacific Northwest south of 54'40" north latitude by an 1824 agreement with the United States and defined the extent of its claim to Alaska in a convention with Britain in 1825. Finally, the dispute over the region between Britain and the United States that almost resulted in war was settled in 1846, when the boundary between their respective territories was extended along the forty-ninth parallel from the Rocky Mountains to the Strait of Georgia and through the Strait of Juan de Fuca to the Pacific by the Oregon Boundary or Washington Treaty.[12]

These international treaties are generally accepted by historians and geographers as having accomplished what they set out to do—namely, delineate the geographical extent of the territorial rights of European nations and the United States in North America.[13] What then is one to make of the fact that Britain, the United States, and later Canada negotiated treaties with Indian nations that also dealt with territorial rights in these same geographical areas? The answer cannot be, as has too often been assumed in Canada, that the Euro-American treaties were concerned with territorial sovereignty, whereas the Indian treaties were concerned with property rights in lands and resources. That simplistic answer belies Indian understandings of what the treaty process was about,[14] and conflicts with American jurisprudence acknowledging the sovereign status of the Indian tribes.[15]

Instead, I think the answer lies in understanding sovereignty as a relative rather than an absolute matter. If this is correct, the Euro-American treaties effectively delineated the territorial sovereignty of the European parties and the United States as among themselves, but did not determine territorial sovereignty in relation to the Indian nations. Insofar as those nations are concerned, treaties had to be negotiated with them in order for the European powers, the United States, and Canada to acquire territorial sovereignty legitimately. In the absence of Indian treaties, American and Canadian claims to sovereignty over the territories of the Indian nations therefore lack legitimacy vis-à-vis those nations. This understanding adds significance to the treaty process that is currently under way in British Columbia, as it confirms that what is at stake is not just lands and resources but also sovereignty.[16] It also calls into question the decision of the U.S. Congress in 1871 not to enter into any more Indian treaties, leaving some Indian tribes in the Pacific Northwest and elsewhere without treaty relationships with the United States.[17]

My essay approaches this matter of the relativity of sovereignty in North America in a general way by identifying and evaluating some broad principles that could be applied to assess the validity of European, American, and Canadian territorial claims. This requires an examination of the law of nations (today known as international law) and an assessment of its applicability to the Indian nations. Using the Oregon boundary dispute between Britain and the United States as a case study, I discuss the problems with relying on the law of nations and international treaties as determinative of rights to territorial sovereignty vis-à-vis the Indian nations. I conclude that a more appropriate basis for assessing those rights involves examination of the relations between the Indian nations and the colonizing powers, based on mutually developed protocols and norms and expressed in the form of treaties.

TERRITORIAL SOVEREIGNTY AND THE LAW OF NATIONS

European nations and the United States purported to divide North America among themselves by entering into international treaties that essentially drew lines on maps, sometimes through areas where the European or American presence was practically or completely nonexistent. It is important to be aware that an international treaty, like any agreement, is binding only on the parties that enter into it.[18] So while the Treaty of Paris of 1783, for example, bound the United States and Britain to the agreed-on boundary from the Atlantic to the Lake of the Woods, it could not affect claims that other nation-states might make to the same territory. More important, for the purposes of this chapter, it could not affect the territorial rights of the Indian nations who inhabited the region in question, especially those whose territories were intersected by this new boundary.[19] As against nations that were not parties to the treaty, British and American claims would therefore have to be based on something other than the treaty. They would clearly require factual and normative foundations beyond the piece of paper on which the treaty was written.

What then were the factual and normative foundations for European and American claims to territorial sovereignty over areas of North America that were inhabited by indigenous nations? Remarkably, there is no clear answer to this question. From the time Columbus first arrived in America in 1492, the European nations relied on a variety of methods to assert their territorial claims. These included discovery, papal grants, symbolic acts of possession, colonial charters, and physical occupation by settlement. There was, however, no agreement among Europeans over the effectiveness of these various acts.[20] While Spain and Portugal favored discovery and papal grants because it was generally in their interest to do so, France and Britain relied more on symbolic acts, colonial charters, and occupation. So even when the factual basis for a claim was clear (and often it was not), no legal resolution was possible in the absence of agreement among the contending European powers on the juridical effect of the acts relied upon.

Moreover, even if the European nations had agreed on what was necessary to acquire territorial sovereignty in the Americas, such an agreement would suffer from the same limitation as bilateral international treaties: it would be binding only on the parties to the agreement, and so it could not affect the rights of other nations—especially the Indian nations of North America—who did not participate in it. This was recognized in the famous case of *Worcester v. Georgia*, where Chief Justice John Marshall acknowledged the independence of the Indian nations and questioned the value of discovery as a means of acquiring territorial sovereignty in North America: "America, separated from Europe by a wide ocean, was inhabited by a distinct people, divided into separate nations, independent of each other and of the rest of the world, having institutions of their own, and governing themselves by their own laws. It is difficult to comprehend the proposition that the inhabitants of either quarter of the globe could have rightful original claims over the inhabitants of the other, or over the lands they occupied; or that the discovery of either by the other should give the discoverer rights in the country discovered which annulled the pre-existing rights of its ancient possessors."[21]

Marshall was not, however, prepared to discard the doctrine of discovery he had formulated nine years earlier in the case of *Johnson v. M'Intosh*, where he had said "that discovery gave title to the government by whose subjects, or by whose authority, it was made, against all other European governments, which title might be consummated by possession."[22] Instead, he emphasized that the principle applied only to the European nations who, he thought (contrary to the historical evidence assembled more recently[23]), had agreed to it: "It was an exclusive principle which shut out the right of competition among those who had agreed to it; not one which could annul the previous rights of those who had not agreed to it. It regulated the right given by discovery among the European discoverers, but could not affect the rights of those already in possession, either as aboriginal occupants, or as occupants by virtue of a discovery made before the memory of man."[24]

For the preexisting rights of the Indians as independent nations to be affected, the title by discovery effective against other European nations had to be consummated by possession of the territory. This, Marshall said, could take place by conquest of the Indian nations, but more commonly the American government entered into treaties for incorporation of them into the United States as "domestic dependent nations"[25] and acquisition of portions of their territories. These treaties, he acknowledged, had international dimensions: "The words 'treaty' and 'nation' are words of our own language, selected in our diplomatic and legislative proceedings, by ourselves, having each a definite and well understood meaning. We have applied them to Indians, as we have applied them to the other nations of the earth. They are applied to all in the same sense."[26]

The composite picture that emerges from Chief Justice Marshall's opinions in *Johnson v. M'Intosh* and *Worcester v. Georgia* can be summed up as follows: Any agreement the European nations reached on acquisition of territorial sovereignty in the Americas applied only among themselves, not to the Indian nations that were not parties thereto. Discovery gave the discovering European nation an inchoate title against other European nations but had no effect on the preexisting sovereignty and territorial rights of the Indian nations, other than excluding other

European nations from dealing with them.[27] This inchoate title by discovery could be consummated by possession, which could be acquired by conquering or treating with the Indian nations. Until that occurred, the Indian nations remained sovereign and independent in their own territories. After conquest or treaty, they could be subject to the territorial sovereignty of the conquering or treating nation, but they retained any sovereign authority over their internal affairs that they did not explicitly relinquish.

Europeans jurists, however, had another way of assessing the validity of their nations' assertions of territorial sovereignty in North America. Instead of basing the rules for acquisition of territory on an agreement among the European nations, as Marshall had, some jurists opined that the so-called law of nations contained universally applicable rules governing this matter. Prior to the predominance of positivist thinking in the nineteenth century, jurists generally thought there was a "natural law" basis for the norms of nations,[28] which included rules for the acquisition of territorial sovereignty.[29] But although one might invoke a universal principle, such as first possession, to justify acquisition of vacant territories,[30] can one seriously suggest a natural law basis for rules permitting Europeans to acquire and convert into colonies territories that were already inhabited by indigenous peoples?[31] The self-serving motivation for such rules would obviously disqualify them as natural law, which should be rooted in ethical norms and principles of fundamental justice that are genuinely universal.[32] The legitimacy and universality of rules justifying colonialism would surely have been challenged by indigenous peoples themselves, thus undermining any claim those rules might have to universality or support by natural law.[33]

Jurists in the late eighteenth and nineteenth centuries relied more on positivist sources for the law of nations, or international law as it came to be known during this period.[34] They looked to convention, which is based on treaties and other agreements, and custom, which is based on state practice.[35] We have already seen that rules based on convention would bind only the parties and therefore could not be universal in the absence of unanimous agreement. Custom is subject to an equivalent limitation because the practices of European nations, even if universal among themselves, could not generate norms that would be binding on nations that neither participated in nor agreed to the creation of those norms.[36]

This is not to say that European conventions and customs are of no assistance in assessing claims to territorial sovereignty in North America. My argument is that, to the extent that the European nations had developed rules in this regard, those rules would have been binding only on the European powers and their successors, such as the United States and Mexico. The rules would not bind the Indian nations in North America and so could not be used to assess the validity of their claims to territory. In other words European norms would apply and could be used to assess the validity of territorial claims among Spain, France, Britain, Russia, the United States, and Mexico, but could not legitimately be applied to assess the relative claims of those nations vis-à-vis the Indian nations. In the latter context one has to look for other sets of norms.

The main problem, therefore, with relying on international law to determine the validity of European and American territorial claims is that that law was not universal at the time the claims were being made.[37] Just as it is an error to regard the Treaty of Paris of 1783, for example, as determining rights to territory vis-à-vis any nations other than Britain and the United States, it is erroneous to rely on so-called international law to determine rights to territory against nations that were not part of the European and Euro-American diplomatic and legal spheres. Consequently, we should not take European and American treaties and principles of international law as determinative of territorial rights in North America. We need to be aware of the relativity and limited application of those sources of rights, instead of regarding them as universal and absolute.

If the conventional and customary international law developed by the European powers did not apply to their relations with Indian nations, was there any body of norms governing these relationships? I reject the notion that there was a universal set of rules applicable in this context. That would not be in keeping with the diversity of cultures, political systems, and protocols of the indigenous peoples of North America. Instead, I think unique, relationship-specific rules were developed out of particular contacts between the Europeans and Americans on the one hand and the Indian nations on the other.[38] Often the nature of these relationships was negotiated in intersocietal exchanges and sometimes formalized in treaties that were governed by protocols and norms arising out of the particular cross-cultural context.[39]

Keeping in mind the relativity of territorial sovereignty, and the need to identify which normative systems apply to whom when assessing the validity of territorial claims in North America, let us now examine the Oregon boundary dispute between Britain and the United States.

THE OREGON BOUNDARY DISPUTE
AND INDIAN SOVEREIGNTY

Standard accounts of the dispute over the Oregon country tend to focus on the history of the controversy among would-be colonizers and the diplomatic efforts to resolve it.[40] Originally, this dispute involved Spain and Russia as well as Britain and the United States. However, Spain renounced its claims north of the forty-second parallel (now the boundary between the states of California and Oregon) by the Adams-Onís treaty with the United States in 1819,[41] and Russia gave up its claims south of the 54'40" north latitude in an 1824 agreement with the United States and defined the limits of Alaska in an 1825 convention with Britain.[42]

The American claim to the Oregon country, which can be defined for present purposes as the territory west of the Rocky Mountains between the forty-second parallel and 54'40" north latitude,[43] was based partly on the Adams-Onís Treaty. That treaty, the United States argued, together with the 1824 agreement with Russia, gave it territorial title to the region. However, because American claims to the Oregon country under those treaties would be no better than the dubious claims of Spain and Russia, the United States asserted an original claim as well. In diplomatic exchanges with Great Britain the United States contended that its territorial title had been established with the discovery of the mouth of the Columbia River by the American captain Robert Gray in 1792, the expedition of Lewis and Clark to the Pacific from 1804 through 1806, and the construction by John Jacob Astor of the fur-trading post of Astoria near the mouth of the Columbia in 1811.[44] Britain, however, relied on its own subjects' discoveries and explorations, principally by Captain James Cook, Captain George Vancouver, and Sir Alexander Mackenzie. It contended as well that its title by discovery had been consolidated with the presence of the North West Company and the Hudson's Bay Company in the region.[45]

As previously mentioned, in 1818 Britain and the United States had agreed on joint access to the territory, without prejudice to the claims of either. In the 1820s and 1830s, nonetheless, British physical presence prevailed through the activities of the Hudson's Bay Company, which absorbed the North West Company in 1821.[46] By the mid-1830s, though, American missionaries began to arrive in the Willamette Valley, and by the mid-1840s streams of American settlers were arriving each year over the Oregon Trail.[47] The growing number of Americans in the Oregon country in the 1840s strengthened U.S. claims in the southern part of the territory. This was probably a factor that persuaded Britain to accept the forty-ninth parallel as the boundary in 1846, when the Washington Treaty was signed.[48]

Accounts of the Oregon boundary dispute that focus on the relative strengths of the British and American claims generally assess those claims from the perspective of the international law of the time.[49] The presence of the numerous Indian nations inhabiting the region is generally not considered in these assessments because they were not regarded as having international status and therefore were thought not to count. There are at least two problems with this approach.

First, we have seen that from the time Columbus arrived in the Caribbean until at least the middle of the eighteenth century, there was no agreement among European nations and jurists over what acts were sufficient to acquire territorial sovereignty in the Americas.[50] But as positivist thinking began to influence European jurists, a consensus started to emerge in the second half of the eighteenth century, and gained currency in the nineteenth and early twentieth centuries, that acquisition of territorial sovereignty depends on effective occupation, involving physical presence of some permanence and, in more recent formulations, the exercise of jurisdiction.[51] This view has since been endorsed by international tribunals, which appear to have pushed its application back to at least the eighteenth century.[52] If effective occupation was the international law standard from the latter half of the eighteenth century, then neither Britain nor the United States could have had a valid claim to territorial sovereignty over parts of the Oregon country that were effectively occupied by Indian nations.[53] So even if one accepts the application of international law to the Oregon country, all the 1846 Washington Treaty accomplished legally was the division of the territories effectively occupied by Britain and the United States at the time.

During the Oregon boundary dispute the United States nonetheless argued that discovery of the Columbia River by Captain Gray, combined with the explorations of Lewis and Clark and the establishment of the fur-trading post of Astoria near the river's mouth, gave it territorial sovereignty over the whole of the Columbia drainage basin.[54] In international law the doctrine the United States was relying on here is usually known as the contiguity doctrine. Its application to the Columbia watershed was, however, rejected by Britain. Moreover, international jurists, while accepting the validity of the doctrine and its application in situations where the occupation of a coastline resulted in control over access to the interior up to the crest of a nearby range of mountains, generally denied its applicability to the vast watershed of the Columbia, which could be accessed from the interior as well as from the coast.[55]

The second major problem with the standard approach to analysis of the Oregon boundary dispute is closely related to the first. The Eurocentric nature of international law in the nineteenth century led jurists and other commentators to misconstrue the effect of that law. As in other North American contexts where boundaries were disputed and determined, not only did government officials and jurists tend to think that the actions of European nations and the United States were all that mattered,[56] but those actions were taken to give rise to territorial rights that were effective against everyone else in the world.[57] This is erroneous because, as we have seen, the international law of the time was not universal in its application and so could not give rise to universal rights. To use a modern-day analogy, it would be as though the European Union developed law that purported to govern rights to minerals located under the high seas. Although that law would probably be effective to determine seabed rights among the members of the European Union, any claim that it would be effective to determine rights vis-à-vis other nation-states such as Brazil, China, or the United States would likely be met with derision. And yet this is precisely what the European nations and the United States purported to do when they applied the international law they had developed to validate their own territorial claims in North America.

So although international law could properly be applied to determine territorial rights between Britain and the United States in the Oregon country, it could not determine territorial rights between those nations and the Indian nations. Nor can one point to the Washington Treaty of 1846 as resolving this matter of territorial sovereignty where the Indian nations are concerned.[58] As we have seen, that treaty would have no binding effect on them because they were not parties to it. Other norms and other treaties are therefore required to determine U.S. and Canadian territorial rights vis-à-vis the Indian nations.

INDIAN TREATIES AND NEGOTIATED SOVEREIGNTY

It is not my intention in this essay to identify or describe the norms and treaties that would be applicable in this context. As stated earlier, I do not think any set of norms would be universally applicable to determine Indian and European territorial rights in North America. Instead, a complex patchwork of norms would have been operative, depending on cultural, political, military, geographical, and other factors. Norms of the affected indigenous peoples must be included in this patchwork.

I nonetheless think a general approach to this matter can be outlined for application in specific contexts. The main thing to consider is the history of relations between a particular Indian nation and Britain or the United States, starting from the time of contact and inquiring specifically whether the relationship reflected a mutual understanding about relative territorial sovereignties. In some circumstances the relationship may have been primarily economic, mediated by the activities of the Hudson's Bay Company or other traders.[59] In other instances there may have been informal agreements creating diplomatic or political relations (for example, between sea captains or explorers and Indian nations).[60] Less significant contacts would have been with individual British subjects or American citizens who had no official status or trading license, such as missionaries and settlers.

Formal treaties were made on behalf of the British Crown in the 1850s with a few of the Indian nations on Vancouver Island and on behalf of the U.S. government after the Washington Treaty with some Indian nations south of the forty-ninth parallel.[61] Those treaties would be the primary sources for determining the nature of the relationship between the parties from the time they were negotiated. In some cases they may have included recognition of British or American territorial sovereignty, or possibly joint or shared sovereignty. That would depend on a proper assessment of the parties' understanding of the treaty relationship. But the essential point is that, relative to the Indian nations, the legitimacy and nature of the territorial rights of Britain and the United States would depend on these treaties and the protocols and norms governing their negotiation and interpretation, rather than on the Convention of 1818, the Washington Treaty of 1846, and the diplomatic protocols and norms of international law.

This approach raises a fundamental issue regarding those areas of the Pacific Northwest where Indian treaties were not negotiated. As mentioned earlier, this includes most of present-day British Columbia and parts of the U.S. Pacific Northwest. It would no doubt be unrealistic today to deny that the Crown in right of Canada has de facto sovereignty over the whole of British Columbia, or that the United States has de facto sovereignty over Oregon, Washington, Idaho, and western Montana. But if international law and the Washington Treaty of 1846 were ineffective to give the British Crown and the United States sovereignty relative to the Indian nations who live there, was that sovereignty acquired legitimately and, if so, how and when did that occur? International law may have an answer to this question—namely prescription.[62] Basically, prescription applies in situations where a nation-state has effectively occupied and exercised jurisdiction over a territory for an extended period of time, and other nation-states by their actions have explicitly or implicitly acknowledged that nation-state's sovereignty.[63]

While Canada's claim to British Columbia and the American claim to the Pacific Northwest south of the forty-ninth parallel may meet the requirements for a prescriptive title in international law,[64] the problems with the application of that law to the Indian nations remain unresolved. So although the exercise of sovereign authority in those territories by the Canadian and U.S. governments is an obvious fact, the legitimacy of that authority with respect to the Indian nations, especially those who have never entered into treaties, is questionable. Unless treaties are entered into whereby the Indian nations acknowledge the sovereignty of Canada and the United States, this cloud on Canadian and American claims to sovereignty will continue to cast a shadow on the validity of their territorial rights.

As pointed out earlier, the governments of Canada and of British Columbia are currently engaged in negotiations with many of the Indian nations in the province who have not yet entered into treaties. Although these treaty talks are often referred to as "land claims negotiations," there is obviously more at stake than property rights. Part of the purpose of this essay has thus been to show that the legitimacy of Canada's claim to sovereignty over the territory known as British Columbia is a fundamental aspect of these negotiations. As in the United States, where the nineteenth-century treaties generally resulted in mutual recognition of the sovereign status and shared jurisdiction of the Indian nations and the United States, the treaty process in British Columbia is also about sovereignty and the shared jurisdiction that is entailed by the concept of self-government.

Let me end this essay with an appeal to historians, geographers, and jurists to question the effect of international treaties like the Washington Treaty of 1846. Academics, lawyers, and judges should not simply accept the carving up of North America by the European powers and the United States without considering the political and moral legitimacy—as well as the legal validity—of that process. If we take the actions of these nation-states at face value and disregard the independent status of the Indian nations and their role in negotiating sovereignty, we risk becoming accomplices in a colonial process that many of us deplore.

NOTES

1. See Paul Tennant, *Aboriginal Peoples and Politics: The Indian Land Question in British Columbia, 1849–1989* (Vancouver: UBC Press, 1990); Robin Fisher, *Contact and Conflict: Indian-European Relations in British Columbia, 1774–1890*, 2d ed. (Vancouver: UBC Press, 1992); and Hamar Foster, "Letting Go the Bone: The Idea of Indian Title in British Columbia," in *Essays in the History of Canadian Law: British Columbia and the Yukon*, vol. 6 in the Osgoode Society Series, edited by Hamar Foster and John McLaren (Toronto: University of Toronto Press, 1995), 28.

2. *Calder v. Attorney-General of British Columbia* [1973] *Supreme Court Reports* (SCR) 313. See Hamar Foster, Heather Raven, and Jeremy Webber, eds., *Let Right Be Done: Aboriginal Title, the* Calder *Case, and the Future of Indigenous Rights* (Vancouver: UBC Press, 2007).

3. See Canada, *Comprehensive Land Claims Policy* (Ottawa: Indian and Northern Affairs Canada, 1987).

4. Nisga'a Nation of British Columbia, *Nisga'a Final Agreement*, initialled 4 August 1998. See *The Nisga'a Treaty, BC Studies*, no. 120 (winter 1998–99); and Tom Molloy, *The World Is Our Witness: The Historic Journey of the Nisga'a into Canada* (Calgary: Fifth House, 2000).

5. See Christopher McKee, *Treaty Talks in British Columbia: Negotiating a Mutually Beneficial Future* (Vancouver: UBC Press, 1996).

6. Although the United States did not sign treaties with all the tribes in the Pacific Northwest, it does not have a contemporary treaty-making process, in part because the U.S. Congress in 1871 legislatively terminated the negotiation of Indian treaties. See Francis Paul Prucha, *American Indian Treaties: The History of a Political*

Anomaly (Berkeley: University of California Press, 1994), 287–310; and Jill St. Germain, *Indian Treaty-Making Policy in the United States and Canada, 1867–1877* (Toronto: University of Toronto Press, 2001), 150–53.

7. See generally Prucha, *American Indian Treaties*; and Vine Deloria Jr., *Behind the Trail of Broken Treaties: An Indian Declaration of Independence* (Austin: University of Texas Press, 1985). On earlier treaties and sovereignty, see Robert A. Williams Jr., *Linking Arms Together: American Indian Treaty Visions of Law and Peace, 1600–1800* (New York: Oxford University Press, 1997).

8. For example, see *Worcester v. Georgia*, 31 U.S. (6 Pet.) 515 (1832); *United States v. Wheeler*, 435 U.S. 313 (1978); and *United States v. Lara*, 541 U.S. 193 (2004). For discussion, see Vine Deloria Jr., and Clifford Lytle, *The Nations Within: The Past and Future of American Indian Sovereignty* (New York: Pantheon Books, 1984); Charles F. Wilkinson, *American Indians, Time, and the Law: Native Societies in a Modern Constitutional Democracy* (New Haven, Conn.: Yale University Press, 1987); and David E. Wilkins and K. Tsianina Lomawaima, *Uneven Ground: American Indian Sovereignty and Federal Law* (Norman: University of Oklahoma Press, 2001).

9. *R. v. Sioui*, [1990] 1 SCR 1025 at 1052–53.

10. See Kent McNeil, "Judicial Approaches to Self-Government since *Calder*: Searching for Doctrinal Coherence," in *Let Right Be Done*, edited by Foster, Raven, and Webber, 129.

11. *Campbell v. British Columbia* [2000] 4 *Canadian Native Law Reporter* (CNLR) 1. As this decision was not appealed, it is the law in British Columbia.

12. For general accounts see Bruce Hutchison, *The Struggle for the Border* (Don Mills, Ontario: Longman Canada, 1970); Norman L. Nicholson, *The Boundaries of the Canadian Confederation* (Toronto: Macmillan of Canada, 1979); D. W. Meinig, *The Shaping of America: A Geographical Perspective on 500 Years of History* (1986; reprint, New Haven, Conn.: Yale University Press, 1993), vols. 1 and 2; Richard White, *"It's Your Misfortune and None of My Own": A New History of the American West* (Norman: University of Oklahoma Press, 1991); Clyde A. Milner II, Carol A. O'Connor, and Martha A. Sandweiss, eds., *The Oxford History of the American West* (New York: Oxford University Press, 1994); and Donald A. Rakestraw, *For Honour or Destiny: The Anglo-American Crisis over the Oregon Territory* (New York: Peter Lang, 1995).

13. See the works cited above, in note 12.

14. See Deloria, *Behind the Trail of Broken Treaties*; Williams, *Linking Arms Together*; James [Sákéj] Youngblood Henderson, "Empowering Treaty Federalism," (1994) 58 *Saskatchewan Law Review* 241; John Borrows, "Wampum at Niagara: The Royal Proclamation, Canadian Legal History, and Self-Government," in *Aboriginal and Treaty Rights in Canada: Essays on Law, Equality, and Respect for Difference*, edited by Michael Asch (Vancouver: UBC Press, 1997), 155; and Harold Cardinal and Walter Hildebrandt, *Treaty Elders of Saskatchewan: Our Dream Is That Our Peoples Will One Day Be Clearly Recognized as Nations* (Calgary: University of Calgary Press, 2000).

15. See the cases cited in note 8, especially *Worcester v. Georgia*, which has also been relied on by the Supreme Court of Canada in, for example, *R. v. Sioui*, cited in note 9.

16. This is evident from the judicial treatment of the Nisga'a Treaty in *Campbell v. British Columbia*, cited in note 11, although the court conceptualized the matter in terms of self-government rather than sovereignty.

17. See note 6.

18. *Direct United States Cable Company v. Anglo-American Telegraph Company* (1877), 2 Appeal Cases 394 (P.C.), 421; *Clipperton Island Case* (1932) 26 *American Journal of International Law* (AJIL), 390 at 394; Lord [Arnold Duncan] McNair, *The Law of Treaties* (Oxford: Clarendon Press, 1961), 309–21; Charles G. Fenwick, *International Law*, 4th ed. (New York: Appleton-Century-Crofts, 1965), 412; and Ian Brownlie, *Principles of Public International Law*, 6th ed. (Oxford: Oxford University Press, 2003), 598–600.

19. On relations between these nations and Britain before the American War of Independence, see Howard R. Berman, "Perspectives on American Indian Sovereignty and International Law, 1600 to 1776," in *Exiled in the Land of the Free: Democracy, Indian Nations, and the U.S. Constitution*, by Oren Lyons et al. (Santa Fe, N.Mex.: Clear Light Publishers, 1992), 125.

20. See L. Oppenheim, *International Law: A Treatise* (London: Longmans, Green, 1905), vol. 1, 265; M. F. Lindley, *The Acquisition and Government of Backward Territory in International Law* (London: Longmans, Green, 1926); Friedrich August Freiherr von der Heydte, "Discovery, Symbolic Annexation and Virtual Effectiveness in International Law" (1935) 29 AJIL 448; Julius Goebel Jr., *The Struggle for the Falkland Islands: A Study in Legal and Diplomatic History* (1927; reprint, Port Washington, N.Y.: Kennikat Press, 1971), 47–119; John Thomas Juricek, "English Claims in North America to 1660: A Study in Legal and Constitutional History," Ph.D. dissertation, University of Chicago Department of History, 1970; Brian Slattery, *French Claims in North America, 1500–59* (Saskatoon: University of Saskatchewan Native Law Centre, 1980); Brian Slattery, "Paper Empires: The Legal Dimensions of French and English Ventures in North America," in *Despotic Dominion: Property Rights in British Settler Societies*, edited by John McLaren, A. R. Buck, and Nancy E. Wright (Vancouver: UBC Press, 2005), 50; and Patricia Seed, *Ceremonies of Possession in European Conquest of the New World, 1492–1640* (Cambridge: Cambridge University Press, 1995). Compare Arthur S. Keller, Oliver J. Lissitzyn, and Frederick J. Mann, *Creation of Rights of Sovereignty through Symbolic Acts, 1400–1800* (New York: Columbia University Press, 1938).

21. *Worcester v. Georgia*, 542–43.

22. 21 U.S. (8 Wheat.) 543 (1823) at 573, quoted in *Worcester v. Georgia*, 543–44. For critiques of Chief Justice Marshall's doctrine of discovery, see Deloria, *Behind the Trail of Broken Treaties*, 85–111; and Wilkins and Lomawaima, *Uneven Ground*, 19–63. Compare Robert J. Miller, *Native America, Discovered and Conquered: Thomas Jefferson, Lewis & Clark, and Manifest Destiny* (Westport, Conn.: Praeger Publishers, 2006).

23. See the works cited in note 20. Fenwick, *International Law*, 405, observed that "Chief Justice Marshall doubtless went too far" in his declaration of the doctrine of discovery in *Johnson v. M'Intosh*.

24. *Worcester v. Georgia*, 544.

25. *Cherokee Nation v. Georgia*, 30 U.S. (5 Pet.) 1 (1831), 17.

26. *Worcester v. Georgia*, 559–60.

27. This exclusion, it needs to be emphasized, resulted from the agreement among the European nations, not from any limitation on the sovereignty of the Indian nations.

28. See G. F. de Martens, *Summary of the Law of Nations, Founded on the Treaties and Customs of the Modern Nations of Europe*, translated by William Cobbett (Philadelphia: Thomas Bradford, 1795), 2, and more generally E. B. F. Midgley, *The Natural Law Tradition and the Theory of International Relations* (New York: Barnes and Noble, 1975).

29. For example, see Francisco de Vitoria, *De Indus et de ivre belli relectiones* (1532), translated by J. P. Bate (Washington, D.C.: Carnegie Institution of Washington, 1917); Hugo Grotius, *The Law of War and Peace* (1625), translation of the 1646 edition by Francis W. Kelsey (Oxford: Clarendon Press, 1925); and Emmerich D. Vattel, *The Law of Nations, or the Principles of Natural Law*, translation of the 1758 edition by Charles G. Fenwick (Washington, D.C.: Carnegie Institution of Washington, 1916). Although such authors sometimes drew on practices and norms from outside the European sphere, their intellectual and cultural formation, and the focus of their attention, were clearly European: see J. H. W. Verzijl, *International Law in Historical Perspective* (Leiden, Netherlands: A. W. Sijthoff, 1968), 435–36; R. P. Anand, *Confrontation or Cooperation? International Law and the Developing Countries* (Dordrecht, Netherlands: Martinus Nijhoff, 1987), 2–17; and S. James Anaya, *Indigenous Peoples in International Law*, 2d ed. (New York: Oxford University Press, 2004), 16–19. See also Antony Anghie, "Francisco de Vitoria and the Colonial Origins of International Law" (1996) 5 *Social & Legal Studies* 321; and Michel Morin, *L'Usurpation de la souveraineté autochtone: Le cas des peuples de la Nouvelle-France et des colonies anglaises de l'Amérique du Nord* (Montreal: Boréal, 1997), 31–62.

30. For example, in *Geary v. Barecroft* (1667), 1 *Siderfin's Reports* 346 (K.B.), it was said that the law of occupancy is based on the law of nature, and so the first persons to inhabit and possess a new country acquire title to it.

31. This was forcefully questioned by William Blackstone, *Commentaries on the Laws of England* (Oxford: Clarendon Press, 1765–69), vol. 2, 7, where he wrote that "so long as it was confined to flocking and cultivation of desart uninhabited countries, it kept strictly within the limits of the law of nature. But how far the seising on countries already peopled, and driving out or massacring the innocent and defenceless natives, merely because they differed from their invaders in language, in religion, in customs, in government, or in colour; how far such a conduct was consonant to nature, to reason, or to christianity, deserved well to be considered by those, who have rendered their names immortal by thus civilizing

mankind." Chief Justice Marshall raised similar questions in *Worcester v. Georgia*, 543.

32. See Lon L. Fuller, *The Morality of Law* (New Haven, Conn.: Yale University Press, 1964); John Finnis, *Natural Law and Natural Rights* (Oxford: Clarendon Press, 1980); and Ellen Frankel Paul, Fred D. Miller Jr., and Jeffrey Paul, eds., *Natural Law and Modern Moral Philosophy* (Cambridge: Cambridge University Press, 2001).

33. For example, see Robert A. Williams Jr., *The American Indian in Western Legal Thought: The Discourses of Conquest* (New York: Oxford University Press, 1990); and Sharon Helen Venne, *Our Elders Understand Our Rights: Evolving International Law Regarding Indigenous Rights* (Penticton, British Columbia: Theytus Books, 1998), 1–27.

34. See Thomas Alfred Walker, *A History of the Law of Nations* (Cambridge: Cambridge University Press, 1899), vol.1, 1.

35. For example, see de Martens, *Summary of the Law of Nations*, especially 2–5; Henry Wheaton, *Elements of International Law*, edited by Richard Henry Dana (Boston: Little, Brown, 1866); Sir Robert Phillimore, *Commentaries upon International Law*, 3d ed. (London: Butterworths, 1879); William Edward Hall, *International Law* (Oxford: Clarendon Press, 1880); and Sir Travers Twiss, *The Law of Nations Considered as Independent Political Communities*, new edition (Oxford: Clarendon Press, 1884). See also Anaya, *Indigenous Peoples in International Law*, 26–30.

36. See T. J. Lawrence, *The Principles of International Law*, 4th ed. (London: Macmillan, 1911), 160: "Occupation gives a valid title under it [international law]; but the title can be valid only as between the states who are subjects of the law." Compare this positivist viewpoint with the natural law perspective expressed in *Geary v. Barecroft*, cited in note 30. But instead of concluding from this that international law cannot confer rights as against indigenous peoples who are not subject to it, Lawrence adopted the typical Eurocentric view of the nineteenth-century positivists that those peoples have only moral claims, not rights, because they are not organized as "states."

37. For further criticism of international law's claims to universality, see Anand, *Confrontation or Cooperation?*; Surya Prakash Sinha, *Legal Polycentricity and International Law* (Durham, N.C.: Carolina Academic Press, 1996); and Antony Anghie, "Finding the Peripheries: Sovereignty and Colonialism in Nineteenth-Century International Law" (1999) 40 *Harvard International Law Journal* 1.

38. For a specific example, see Janna Promislow, "Toward a Legal History of the Fur Trade: Looking for Law at York Factory, 1714–1763," master of laws thesis, York University, Toronto, 2005. More generally, see Richard White, *The Middle Ground: Indians, Empires, and Republics in the Great Lakes Region, 1650–1815* (Cambridge: Cambridge University Press, 1991); and Jeremy Webber, "Relations of Force and Relations of Justice: The Emergence of Normative Community between Colonists and Aboriginal Peoples" (1995) 33 *Osgoode Hall Law Journal* 623.

39. See Williams, *Linking Arms Together*; Henderson, "Empowering Treaty

Federalism"; Cardinal and Hildebrandt, *Treaty Elders of Saskatchewan*; and Berman, "Perspectives on American Indian Sovereignty and International Law."

40. For example, see Frederick Merk, *The Oregon Question: Essays in Anglo-American Diplomacy and Politics* (Cambridge: Harvard University Press, 1967); and Rakestraw, *For Honour or Destiny*. For a refreshing new examination that does take the presence of the Indian nations into account, see Miller, *Native America, Discovered and Conquered*.

41. See Thomas Maitland Marshall, *A History of the Western Boundary of the Louisiana Purchase, 1819–1841* (Berkeley: University of California Press, 1914); and Philip Coolidge Brooks, *Diplomacy and the Borderlands: The Adams-Onís Treaty of 1819* (Berkeley: University of California Press, 1939).

42. See Wheaton, *Elements of International Law*, 245–50; Nicholson, *Boundaries of the Canadian Confederation*, 43–45; and Rakestraw, *For Honour or Destiny*, 16.

43. This corresponds with standard descriptions of the disputed territory: for example, see Rakestraw, *For Honour or Destiny*, especially the map on 15.

44. See J. C. Calhoun, American Plenipotentiary, to R. Pakenham, British Plenipotentiary, 3 September 1844, in *Oregon: The Claim of the United States to Oregon, as Stated in the Letters of the Hon. J.C. Calhoun and the Hon. J. Buchanan* (London: Wiley and Putnam, 1846), 3 at 4–7. See also Travers Twiss, *The Oregon Territory: Its History and Discovery* (New York: D. Appelton & Co., 1846); Frederick Merk, *History of the Western Movement* (New York: Alfred A. Knopf, 1978), 310; and Rakestraw, *For Honour or Destiny*, 5–26, especially 24.

45. See R. Pakenham to J. C. Calhoun, 12 September 1844, in *Oregon: The Claim of the United States to Oregon*, cited in note 44, App. 2 at 6. See also Rakestraw, *For Honour or Destiny*, 5–26, especially 24; and Twiss, *Oregon Territory*.

46. See David Lavender, *Land of Giants: The Drive to the Pacific Northwest, 1750–1950* (Edison, N.J.: Castle Books, 2001), 53–139; and John Phillip Reid, *Contested Empire: Peter Skene Ogden and the Snake River Expeditions* (Norman: University of Oklahoma Press, 2002).

47. See David Lavender, *Westward Vision: The Story of the Oregon Trail* (New York: McGraw-Hill, 1963); William A. Bowen, *The Willamette Valley: Migration and Settlement on the Oregon Frontier* (Seattle: University of Washington Press, 1978); and John D. Unruh Jr., *The Plains Across: The Overland Emigrants and the Trans-Mississippi West, 1840–60* (Urbana: University of Illinois Press, 1993).

48. Compare Merk, *History of the Western Movement*, 327–29.

49. The most complete treatment is Twiss, *Oregon Territory*. See also Wheaton, *Elements of International Law*, 242–55; Fenwick, *International Law*, 409–10; and William Edward Hall, *A Treatise on International Law*, 8th ed., edited by A. Pearce Higgins (Oxford: Clarendon Press, 1924), 134–36.

50. See the works cited in note 20.

51. Vattel, *Law of Nations*, especially 85, and de Martens, *Summary of the Law of Nations*, 67–68, appear to have been eighteenth-century proponents of this view. For nineteenth- and twentieth-century support for it, see Gerard de Rayneval,

Institutions du droit de la nature et des gens, nouvelle édition publiée en 1832 (Paris: August Durand, 1851), 291–92; Phillimore, *Commentaries upon International Law*, vol. 1, 349–50; Hall, *International Law*, 87–90; Twiss, *Law of Nations Considered*, 196–210; Lindley, *Acquisition and Government of Backward Territory*, 139–59; von der Heydte, "Discovery, Symbolic Annexation, and Virtual Effectiveness"; Brownlie, *Principles of Public International Law*, 133–38; John Westlake, *International Law*, Part I, *Peace*, 2d ed. (Cambridge: Cambridge University Press, 1910), 101–5; and C. H. M. Waldock, "Disputed Sovereignty in the Falkland Islands Dependencies" (1948) 25 *British Yearbook of International Law* 311, especially 315–17, 334–37.

52. See "Island of Palmas Case" (1928) 2 *Reports of International Arbitral Awards* (RIAA) 829; "Legal Status of Eastern Greenland Case" (1933) 2 *Permanent Court of International Justice* (PCIJ), Series A / B, No. 43; and "Minquiers and Ecrehos Case" 1953 *International Court of Justice Reports* (ICJR) 47.

53. In negotiations over their respective claims east of the Mississippi in 1761, both France and Britain acknowledged that the presence of the Indian nations had to be taken into account. On the one hand, France regarded the Indian nations living between French Canada and Louisiana and between Virginia and Louisiana as "neutral nations, independent of the sovereignty of the two Crowns, and serv[ing] as a barrier between them." See *An Historical Memorial of the Negotiation of France and England, from the 26th of March, 1761, to the 20th of September of the Same Year*, in Charles Jenkinson, *A Collection of All the Treaties of Peace, Alliance, and Commerce, between Great-Britain and Other Powers* (London: J. Debrett, 1785), vol. 3, 80 at 134. Britain, on the other hand, regarded the Indian nations situated "between the British settlements and the Mississippi" as "reputed to be under the protection" of the British Crown (see ibid., 149). Twiss, *Oregon Territory*, 213–14, and Westlake, *International Law*, 115, both acknowledged the relevance of France's views on this to the Oregon dispute.

54. See James Buchanan, American Secretary of State, to R. Pakenham, 12 July 1845, in *Oregon: The Claim of the United States to Oregon*, 20 at 27–28. See also Twiss, *Oregon Territory*; Westlake, *International Law*, 114–16; Hall (1924), *Treatise on International Law*, 134–35; and Fenwick, *International Law*, 409.

55. See Westlake, *International Law*, 114–18; Lawrence, *Principles of International Law*, 157; Hall, *Treatise on International Law*, 129–36; and Fenwick, *International Law*, 409–10.

56. State practice, however, did not always support this Eurocentric view. For examples, see note 53 as well as discussions of the relations between Britain and France and the Indian nations in *Worcester v. Georgia* and *R. v. Sioui*. Moreover, in its Advisory Opinion in the "Western Sahara Case" 1975 ICJR 12, the International Court of Justice rejected the notion that territories occupied by indigenous peoples who were socially and politically organized were *terra nullius*. Relying on state practice in the latter half of the nineteenth century, the Court concluded that those territories could not be acquired by the original mode of occupation, but only by a derivative mode such as cession by treaty.

57. See works cited in note 49.

58. Compare *Delgamuukw v. British Columbia*, [1997] 3 SCR 1010, at paragraph 145, where Chief Justice Antonio Lamer relied on the trial judge's finding (not disputed on appeal) "that British sovereignty over British Columbia was conclusively established by the Oregon Boundary Treaty of 1846."

59. For example, see Reid, *Contested Empire*, and, regarding other times and places, Arthur J. Ray, *Indians in the Fur Trade: Their Role as Hunters, Trappers and Middlemen in the Lands Southwest of Hudson Bay, 1660–1870* (Toronto: University of Toronto Press, 1974); Arthur J. Ray, *"Give Us Good Measure": An Economic Analysis of Relations between the Indians and the Hudson's Bay Company before 1763* (Toronto: University of Toronto Press, 1978); Daniel Frances and Toby Morantz, *Partners in Furs: A History of the Fur Trade in Eastern James Bay, 1600–1870* (Montreal: McGill-Queen's University Press, 1983); and Promislow, "Toward a Legal History of the Fur Trade."

60. Lewis and Clark, for example, entered into diplomatic relations with numerous Indian nations on their trek to the Pacific and back. See James P. Ronda, *Lewis and Clark among the Indians* (Lincoln: University of Nebraska Press, 1984). See also White, *Middle Ground*; and Webber, "Relations of Force and Relations of Justice."

61. See Dennis F. K. Madill, *British Columbia Treaties in Historical Perspective* (Ottawa: Research Branch, Corporate Policy, Department of Indian and Northern Affairs, 1981); Fay G. Cohen, *Treaties on Trial: The Continuing Controversy over Northwest Indian Fishing Rights* (Seattle: University of Washington Press, 1986), especially 35–39; Terence O'Donnell, *An Arrow in the Earth: General Joel Palmer and the Indians of Oregon* (Portland: Oregon Historical Society Press, 1991); and Prucha, *American Indian Treaties*, 246–55.

62. Some jurists, however, have rejected prescription as a source of rights in international law: for example, see de Martens, *Summary of the Law of Nations*, 63–66.

63. See Phillimore, *Commentaries upon International Law*, vol. 1, 353–68; Hall (1924), *Treatise on International Law*, 143–44; Lindley, *Acquisition and Government of Backward Territory*, 178–80; Fenwick, *International Law*, 420–22; I. C. MacGibbon, "Scope of Acquiescence in International Law" (1954) 31 *British Yearbook of International Law* 143 at 152–67; D.H.N. Johnson, "Consolidation as a Root of Title in International Law" [1955] *Cambridge Law Journal* 215; R. Y. Jennings, *The Acquisition of Territory in International Law* (Manchester: Manchester University Press, 1963), 20–23; Yehuda Z. Blum, *Historic Titles in International Law* (The Hague: Martinus Nijhoff, 1965), 6–37; and Surya P. Sharma, *Territorial Acquisition, Disputes and International Law* (The Hague: Martinus Nijhoff Publishers, 1997), 107–19, 167–70.

64. Note, however, that these requirements are not certain, especially insofar as the period of time and degree of acquiescence necessary for a prescriptive title are concerned. See the works cited in note 63.

2 Unmaking Native Space

A GENEALOGY OF INDIAN POLICY, SETTLER PRACTICE,

AND THE MICROTECHNIQUES OF DISPOSSESSION

Paige Raibmon

PRE-SCRIPT

In 1791 the fur trader and U.S. ship captain Robert Gray sailed into Tla-o-qui-aht territory on the west coast of Vancouver Island. His visit would prove memorable for generations to come because before he left, he kidnapped the son of Chief Wickaninnish and ordered the torching of two hundred houses at the village of Opitsaht. More than two centuries later, on a sunny July afternoon in 2005, three canoes carrying Gray's descendants pulled ashore at this same village. They came to apologize. The family spokesperson, William Twombly, announced to the assembled crowd: "We are sorry for the abduction and insult to your chief and his great family and for the burning of Opitsaht."[1] It was a remarkable step for Gray's descendants to take. Gray's actions at Opitsaht do not seem like the sort of family story typically resurrected at family reunions. Yet these people knew the story and had traveled thousands of miles from Oregon, Texas, New Hampshire, Massachusetts, and London, England, to acknowledge their ancestor's behavior. They had come, they announced, "in peace to offer ourselves in good spirit to suggest that we'd like forgiveness and we'd like to honour our ancestral connection and honour your people."[2] The Tla-o-qui-aht appreciated the gesture and accepted it with grace and hospitality. They returned the respect shown by Gray's descendants, treating them as honored potlatch guests.

What were these hosts and guests doing when they mutually honored their ancestral connection, a connection born of violence, dispossession, and the colonial imbalance of power? Surely Twombly and his family did not consider themselves, nor did the Tla-o-qui-aht consider them, literally to blame for the acts of their long-dead ancestor. Yet all seemed to agree that Twombly and his fellow canoe-mates were in some fashion responsible. In what other context could an "apology" make sense? What follows in this essay is an extended meditation on these questions. Those present on the beach at Opitsaht in 2005 understood something about colonial genealogies and thus have something important to teach us. They came together that day as the result of a literal family connection, but we can usefully read their example as analogous to a much broader family tree—a figurative genealogy of colonialism. Current residents of settler societies like British Columbia do not need to be direct bloodline descendants of men like Captain Gray to have inadvertently reaped the results of the colonial work they helped to initiate. I urge readers to consider what it might mean if *all* the inheritors of colonial legacies (whether literal descendants or not) understood their relationship to the past and their responsibilities in the present in a manner akin to the Twombly family.

FAMILY TIES

If these metaphorical family ties of colonialism seem counterintuitive or difficult to trace, it is partly due to historiographical convention. Under settler colonialism the displacement of original inhabitants and the arrival of new ones are mutually reinforcing projects. Yet historians have long treated colonization and immigration—the twin histories of indigenous lands and settler lands—as separate topics.[3] Rectifying this requires not only initiating dialogue between existing fields but also bringing the history of settler practice into greater focus. Although settler policies have been amply studied, settler practices have not.[4]

Ultimately, my interest lies in the place where practices of settlement and the experiences of Aboriginal people intersect. From the vantage of this intersection we can illuminate the context for the production of what I call "settlement lands." I use the term in a dual sense to refer both to lands required for the settlement of Aboriginal claims and lands claimed by settler society and its descendants. It is practically a truism in British

Columbia today that the available supply of such lands is exhausted. Many people assert that the land required to settle Aboriginal claims in the province was (some admit, regrettably) appropriated by colonial society far too long ago to make repatriation of indigenous land feasible.[5] They ascribe natural and irrevocable status to the designation "private property" and thus conclude that the problem of "settlement lands" is deadlocked.

Colonial representatives have consistently treated private property and its approximations (that is, preemption) as sacrosanct designations. Given this, closer attention is warranted to the precise mechanisms for transforming land into these hallowed categories, for transforming Aboriginal territory into settlement lands. The historical geographer Cole Harris has fruitfully used the term "making Native space" to refer to the creation of small, scattered Indian reserves.[6] But "making Native space" was about more than creating Indian enclaves; it was about making private property too. Reserves were not Native spaces made anew; they were radically diminished refashionings of precolonial Native spaces. Indian policy mandated reserves. But it was the deployment of colonial land policy by colonizers that transformed traditional Aboriginal territories into colonial jurisdictions. Settler and developer practices of land appropriation shrank Native space from its hereditary territorial boundaries to the confines of Indian reserves. Native space had to be unmade as much as it had to be made. That is, the indigenousness of hereditary territories had to be undone before the colonial reserve geography could gain purchase. This unmaking was accomplished by the mundane processes that comprised settler life even when Aboriginal people themselves were out of settlers' sight and, by extension, out of settlers' minds. Over time, settler practices and Indian policy combined in a mutually sustaining dialectic to do the work of colonialism.

The meticulous attention required to track this dialectic demands a form of history that we can usefully regard as genealogical. This is not the same thing as literally tracing family trees, but the metaphor is useful, because we need to map "family connections" not only between people but among an array of past practices, policies, and even accidents. Genealogy in this sense, notes the French writer Michel Foucault, "is gray, meticulous, and patiently documentary."[7] It seeks to represent the discrete and disparate processes of the past in all their rawness before they are cooked in "the long baking process of history."[8] History, continues Foucault, is "fabricated in a piecemeal fashion from alien forms," an insight that is obscured when we focus on the final product (the boundaries of modern reserves, for example) at the expense of the constitutive ingredients (multifarious settler practices, for example).[9] Apparent absences, disconnects, and non sequiturs are crucial to such an endeavor. To extend Foucault's baking metaphor, the yeast in a baked loaf of bread may be tasteless, but it is still responsible for the bread's rising. Genealogy requires that we suspend our tendency toward teleology while we examine the myriad makings of dispossession in all their confusion and complexity.

Genealogy overlaps with microhistory insofar as it tracks local practices as they occurred on the ground over time. But it differs from microhistory insofar as its ultimate interest lies less with specific locales or events than with connections between disparate people and practices. Only once the initial shortening of our vision has brought the relevant actors and elements within purview can we cast our eyes out over the entire array and feel, as critic Walter Benjamin put it, "the full force of the panorama opening out" before us.[10] It is then that the connections between widely disparate events and practices become powerfully apparent.

Attending to the relationship between Indian land policy and settler practice can be seen as genealogical in at least a threefold sense. First, charting the close ties between these policies and practices would produce a fuller and more dynamic picture of colonial geography than we are used to seeing. It would lend geographically and historically specific context to the belief that settlement lands are perennially in short supply. Reserves themselves were not static; rather, they grew and, more often, shrank over time. Preemptions, too, had a checkered existence; some were conveyed into fee-simple land while many others lapsed only to be preempted again or revert to the Crown. The precise timing of these changes in relation to the movements and practices of colonizers was often crucial in shaping the future of Aboriginal communities.

Second, investigating the intersection of Indian policy and settler practice can help refine our conceptualization of colonial processes themselves. By illuminating the genealogical roots that colonial practices put down across the land, we clarify the mechanisms of dispossession. We are able to identify the individuals who laid down those roots, and we can then map the familial relationships of these individuals. Sometimes the relationships were literal. Legal scholars Hamar Foster and Alan Grove have made this point effectively when they take note of the extensive social ties and intermarriage among families of high-ranking judicial and government officials throughout the region sometimes dubbed Cascadia.[11] These literal kinships were not always framed by clear racial markers. The frequency of relationships between immigrant men and Indigenous or mixed-heritage women means that the colonial family tree cannot be easily categorized using binary racial labels.

Just as important, the genealogical method I advocate unearths figurative kinships between diverse and distant practices that even those attentive to literal genealogies can overlook. As the historian Victoria Freeman has noted: "The colonization of North America has been the result of millions of actions, or non-actions, great and small, by thousands, even millions, of people over hundreds of years."[12] Such acts are connected, and it is genealogy's task to show us how.

There is inevitably some overlap between figurative and literal genealogies. As Foster and Grove show in their case, for example, literal family ties are diagnostic of broader intellectual kinship among practices of law and treaty making in what became Alaska, British Columbia, Washington, and Oregon.[13] The resultant "family tree" is a representation of colonialism that is extremely precise and simultaneously disengaged from questions of intention. Identification of relationships and the assignment of responsibility replace the overly simplistic search for blame. Such a conceptualization of dispossession reminds us of the great uncertainty and historical contingency that Aboriginal people faced under colonialism. Only then can we comprehend the logic by which colonizers persuaded themselves and their descendants (that is, us) that they had succeeded in diminishing Native space from vast indigenous territories to minute colonial reserves. Only then can we make sense of the process through which reserves became Native spaces, not only in colonial eyes but in Aboriginal ones as well.

Finally, reflecting on the work that settler practice did, and more specifically on many scholars' own lack of attention to that work, tells us something about the genealogical ties that bind us as scholars to the colonial past we narrate. Our individual choices as scholars do not align by accident. We would do well to investigate the sources and implications of our own narrative commonalities.

This genealogical approach has intellectual promise for studying a diversity of colonial contexts. Whether or not they agreed to treaties with colonial governments, Aboriginal people lost land and resources as a result of multiple, diverse, and cumulative acts of dispossession by a variety of newcomers, many of whom were not policy makers, government administrators, or Indian haters. In treaty jurisdictions such as Washington State a genealogical history would encompass diverse practices over time beyond the formal sphere of treaty negotiations and thus help explain why treaties provided inadequate protection of Aboriginal rights to land and resources. In jurisdictions such as British Columbia, where most Aboriginal homelands remain unceded, a genealogical analysis can show how, in the absence of treaties, land was alienated from Aboriginal title-holders in practice.

Regardless of the jurisdiction under consideration, this analysis provides a framework through which non-Aboriginal citizens today can understand their relationship to colonial settlers and authorities of the past. In a place like British Columbia this entails accepting kinship with those who enacted alienation of land and resources on the ground even as they refused to formalize the process through treaty. In a place like Washington it means understanding both that historical treaty obligations ought to be honored today and that so doing requires the maintenance or restoration of ancillary conditions to ensure the spirit and not just the letter of the treaty is meaningfully honored. To build this sort of genealogy, we must invert the usual family tree. Instead of starting with ourselves at the "crown of a branching family tree and trac[ing] our ancestors back to a single trunk of sturdy and supposedly pure stock," we must be willing, as the historian Claudio Saunt has suggested, "to place us at the base of the tree and follow the branches of our ancestors back in time as they divide and subdivide."[14]

GENEALOGIES OF LAND ALIENATION

There is a paradox at the center of the conviction we have inherited about the short supply of settlement lands. Much like the nostalgic figure of the nineteenth-century "vanishing Indian," settlement lands are positioned as always vanishing, yet they never disappear. The supply of settlement lands has ostensibly been short, practically endangered, since the first generation of settler society arrived in British Columbia. Much as their inheritors do today, the first generation of newcomers shielded themselves from Aboriginal land claims by proclaiming that it was always already too late to restore the land to Indigenous claimants.

As early as 1878, efforts of the Indian Reserve Commissioner Gilbert Malcolm Sproat to satisfy Aboriginal land claims were stymied by the prior accretion of immigrant land titles.[15] Throughout the 1880s and 1890s the Indian Reserve Commissioner Peter O'Reilly lacked the mandate to interfere with the property rights of settlers.[16] And by 1913 members of the McKenna-McBride Royal Commission were telling an old story when they advised Aboriginal people that land for them was unavailable because of its prior alienation from the Crown.[17] The colonial state afforded Aboriginal people in British Columbia one more formal opportunity to express their need for a land base during the Ditchburn-Clark inquiry in the early 1920s. But J. W. Clark and W. E. Ditchburn were no more willing to entertain requests for land claimed by colonists than their predecessors had been.[18] And not until the latter half of the twentieth century would Aboriginal claimants in British Columbia regain the government's ear even to this limited extent. The colonial division of land between Natives and newcomers was thus largely set by the 1920s.[19]

Expressed as an abstract principle, this practice of noninterference with settler title sounds straightforward and authoritative. It might even sound fair. But upon reflection the authority we grant these stories about settler title, preemption, and private property begins to seem counterintuitive. Except, arguably, in the limited areas covered by the treaties that James Douglas had negotiated and under Treaty 8, the land in question had never been legally alienated from its Aboriginal owners—a fact that was not lost on the Aboriginal complainants, even if it went unnoticed by successive commissioners. Notions of property, as the geographer Nicholas Blomley has recently reminded us, are simply stories that we tell ourselves. Within colonial contexts stories about land and property were (and still are) freighted with particular power. But powerful as such stories were and are, it is worth remembering that they are just that: stories.[20] Narratives stressing the inviolate nature of non-Native title fit easily with teleological notions of progress and civilization. Such narratives conflated the imposition of a common law property regime with the civilization of both land and people.[21] And they suggested that this imposition took place according to the principles of law and order. But it did no such thing.

In the crucial decades when authorities worked to impose their notion of a civilized landscape, dispossessing Aboriginal people in the process, they repeatedly betrayed the logic of their own self-proclaimed law and order. Examples of this abound as soon as we shift our focus from the names and dates of government commissions and zoom in on the micro-techniques of dispossession across settlement lands. Such breaches of British logic and law took a range of forms, including simple illegalities, conflicts of interest, and more subtle practices that worked at cross-purposes with the quite separate Indian policy being deployed over the bureaucratic fence in other government departments.

In British Columbia the Crown officially made land available to settlers through the Land Ordinance of 1861. Settlers could preempt any Crown-claimed land that was not an Indian reserve and did not contain "Indian improvements," as long as they improved the land and resided on the land permanently without being absent for more than two months. Significantly, the majority of land was unsurveyed at the time of preemption. In such instances the would-be settler simply wrote a description and sketched a map of the selected land and submitted both to the surveyor general in Victoria for registration. Other than a small administrative fee, no payment was required until the land was surveyed, at which point four shillings and two pence per acres was due. For preemptors these conditions amounted, at least at the outset, to free land.[22] Since this all operated on an honor system, it is not surprising to find that settlers frequently breached the preemption laws and that registrations were often inaccurate.

There are many instances in which settlers preempted land that did contain Indian improvements. Aboriginal families would return from seasonal labor and find settlers occupying their houses. In the early twentieth century, for example, more than one Ahousaht family came home to find a White man occupying their home.[23] On the Sunshine Coast a settler named Alfred Jeffries took proactive steps to create the conditions that would make the land he desired eligible for preemption: he simply destroyed the "Indian improvements," burning down the house and fruit trees of a Sechelt man, Charlie Roberts. When questioned about whether his preemption had in fact contained Indian improvements, Jeffries offered the lame excuse that he had been temporarily hard of hearing at the time the affidavit stating that the land contained no improvements was read to him.[24] A preemption that took in Indian houses, clearing, and a well was likewise granted in Pender Harbour.[25] Up the coast in

Malaspina Inlet settler Barnard Nelson accomplished the same feat at the expense of Domonic Tom, a Sliammon man.[26] And farther north William Thompson, who came to the Homalco community at Church-house as the schoolteacher, went on to preempt land that encompassed eight residences, the schoolhouse, the church, and cemeteries.[27]

Settlers had good reason to covet preemptions that came complete with house and clearing. Logging the dense rainforest of the West Coast was no simple task. Even with dynamite the removal of stumps could take a man and horse four hundred hours of labor per acre.[28] As William Thompson said in his own defense: "The land around here, as you will see, is mountainous and covered with heavy and thick timber, and a man my age, well it is simply impossible for me to do any hard work such as that would entail."[29] Similar practices characterized the settlement even where land clearance did not pose the same obstacle. In the interior ranchers preempted land cultivated by Aboriginal people, and Chinese miners worked land that encompassed Indian settlements.[30]

In other instances settlers violently displaced Aboriginal people from their homes without even the formality of filing a preemption. White squatters in places as far-flung as the Cowichan and Nass valleys attempted to drive Cowichan and Nisga'a inhabitants from their land at gunpoint.[31] Indigenous people along the west coast of Vancouver Island had similar experiences. An Ahousaht man, Joe Didian Sr., faced threats first from a White settler and later from the Indian agent, who told him that settlers were coming to burn down his house.[32] Kelsomaht chief Charlie Johnnie's community fled a village of thirteen houses when the Indian agent came and told them their houses would be set alight.[33] Set-tlers destroyed Muchalaht houses along the Gold River, and settlers in Haida Gwaii used Haida houses for firewood.[34] Indian agents pled impo-tence in such situations, leaving the dispossessed to fend for themselves.[35] Preemptions may well have followed in the wake of these violent dis-placements, since "Indian improvements" could be legally preempted if they had been "abandoned." The law said nothing about the conditions that precipitated such "abandonment." Whether individuals perpetrated violence with the calculated intent to preempt the newly "abandoned" land themselves, as Alfred Jeffries had done, or whether they simply cleared the way for subsequent preemptors to do so matters less than the powerful momentum generated by the ongoing dialectic of practice and policy.

Settlers also breached preemption requirements related to residency and improvements. This is clear from historian Ruth Sandwell's study of Salt Spring Island between 1859 and 1891. Most settlers on Salt Spring neither fulfilled nor shared the agrarian ideal that was supposed to justify colonial usurpation of indigenous lands. Financially unable to subsist on their land year-round, many settlers relied on intervals of off-island wage-earning. In so doing, they violated the preemption policy's residency requirements. Moreover, most preemptors on Salt Spring never purchased their claim outright. Instead, they manipulated colonial regulations, and the lack of enforcement thereof, to turn the preemption system into one that gave them perpetual access to free land and the franchise. Some even found ingenious ways to pass their never-purchased preemptions on to their heirs.[36]

Sandwell convincingly interprets such behavior as evidence of the flexibility of settler practice and of the distance between that practice and the goals of the colonial elite. But this is only half the story. These creative settler practices were irrevocably bound to microtechniques of dispossession across the colonies and later the province. The accumulation of individual settler acts had acute outcomes for Aboriginal people, who were told by royal commissioners and Indian agents that the notion of property embodied by the settler and his preemption was inviolate. Colonial officials simply deemed lands covered by Crown grants or timber licenses "unavailable" to Indigenous applicants.[37] Many settlers would over time allow their preemptions to revert back to the Crown. But even then it was unlikely that such land would be restored to Indigenous applicants if the reversion occurred after reserves had been allotted and surveyed.

The precise geography and timing of such incidents could be crucial. In 1881, for example, several properties near Pemberton Meadows lay abandoned with back taxes owing. Even though faced with a directly competing Aboriginal need for arable land, the province still did not enforce the land laws and instead bent over backward to allow the preemptors additional time in which to perfect their claims. In this fashion the last agriculturally viable land in the area was alienated from the Crown and lost to the Pemberton band.[38] As it played out on the ground, even the rights of settlers who flouted land laws took precedence over Aboriginal claims.

Conflicts of interest characterized other preemption claims, and in these cases, too, timing was everything. In 1859, for example, the assistant land commissioner, after being instructed to reserve lands for Aboriginal people at Lytton, instead purchased the land and recorded the water rights for himself. The legality of this purchase was questioned, after which point the land was still not gazetted as a reserve but passed into the hands of other settlers. By 1878, when Indian Reserve Commissioner Sproat arrived to allot lands, his intent to remedy past injustices mattered little: a boulder field was all that remained for him to reserve.[39]

These examples of colonial law bent or broken reinforce a number of important points. First, they remind us that the powerful stories about the rational, coherent, and just nature of British law were riddled with contradictions at the time of their telling. In and of itself this is no indictment. The stories we live by are inevitably marbled with contradictions. But we might begin to think more deeply about the consequences of particular contradictions at particular places and times. Which contradictions have been tolerated to the point of invisibility, while others have been called up as evidence of an impoverished or inaccurate story?[40]

Second, the examples of settler practice here at hand further remind us that stories about yeoman farmers, private property, and the concomitant civilization of land and people were not so much "British stories" or "settler stories" in general but stories told by a particular group of newcomers—elite, literate, urban, and those least likely to get their hands dirty trying to uproot ancient trees in the name of an agricultural dream. The stories were not widely shared colonial truths; rather, they were selective rhetorical gestures belied by the practices of others at the same time. Settlers themselves were driven less by a blind desire for privately owned patches of their own Arcadia than by the practical exigencies of clearing land, growing crops, and feeding families.[41] In the end it was practice and rhetoric combined that effected dispossession.

Aside from settler activities that directly flouted colonial law, there is another and arguably larger category of settler practice that deserves close scrutiny. Numerous regulations and practices, quite legal in nature and on their face affecting only settlers, often had critically important impacts on Aboriginal communities. The Indian reserves, limited in size, were hemmed in through various colonial techniques that further undermined the already marginal quality of reserve land. In the interior of British Columbia, for example, one of the most obvious and widespread examples of this was the taking of water records. Settlers acquired water rights without regard to the needs of the reserves so that by the 1870s farms and ranches on reserves found themselves without necessary water.[42] Similarly, reserves that commissioners had allocated as fishing stations came, through various means, to be deprived of fish.[43]

Nearly a century later, similar practices persisted: at the mouth of the Gold River on the western coast of Vancouver Island, for example, lessees filled a water lot, the province built a highway, and the Crown sold a piece of land. Individually, none of these activities even involved Aboriginal people; combined, however, they eliminated the riparian access of the Mowachaht / Muchalaht village that had stood on saltwater for thousands of years. The name of the place, Ahaminaquus, still indicated that that it was beach (*quus*), but now it was beach in name only. The fill became provincial Crown land, which the Crown conveyed to the multinational corporation that had filled the water lot in the first place. Ahaminaquus has still not regained its beach.[44] The Sliammon reserve of Toh Kwon_non, an important fishing site, was also amputated from its most important purpose when timber companies acquired Crown land on the steep hills above the reserve. In the 1960s the companies logged and constructed roads without regard to the consequences of erosion on the downhill site. In the 1990s a landslide that predictably originated on the logged-out Crown land swept down to devastate the reserve and destroy the salmon habitat and spawning grounds. The reserve lost its purpose, and the people lost the enormous chum salmon found only at Toh Kwon_non.[45]

As the historical geographer Cole Harris has stressed, the cross-purposes of provincial and dominion agendas greatly contributed to such outcomes in the nineteenth and early twentieth centuries.[46] No doubt a similar lack of reconciliation between levels of government played a role later on too. In a larger sense, however, it is the cross-purposes of settler society and indigenous claims—the basic conundrum of settlement lands —that is responsible. Breaches of the spirit and letter of colonial laws were not so much colonial anomalies as they were constituent elements of colonialism. Only after taking close note of the multiplicity of discrete practices on the ground can we step back and see their interlocking and contradictory relationships to one another. We can thus map the precise workings of land transfer and transformation, appropriation and alienation. We are afforded a clearer view of how Native space was simultaneously made and unmade. Then perhaps we can begin to make sense of how it can be that 94 percent of the land base in British Columbia remains provincial Crown land at the same time as the perceived shortage of settlement lands endures.

GENEALOGIES OF COLONIALISM I

Revealing the dialectic between policy and practice can elucidate the nature of colonialism and dispossession more broadly. The presumed separation of Indian policy, settler policy, and settler practice is historically entrenched, and we live with (and through) it still. "Indian land" is neatly segregated from "non-Indian land." The separation is palpably present in the stranding of reserve lands across British Columbia: farms without irrigation, "beaches" without water access, fishing stations without fish. Settler policies and practices worked in concert with Indian policy to produce this landscape of the absurd. Policy makers and settlers may not have cooperated knowingly, but their lives were part of a common colonial lineage. Like members of an extended family, they were related even as they operated largely independently of one another. Not all family members were on speaking terms, but this did not erase their common family ties.

Historian Duane Thomson's work on the Okanagan can be used to illustrate this point. In 1861 the Okanagan reserved lands for themselves that encompassed most of the good bottomland in the Penticton region. But in 1865 a justice of the peace ordered these reserves be reduced to an eighth of their original size because the tracts were, in his estimation, too large for "semi-nomadic" people. In fact, "Penticton," which means "people always there," was quite probably occupied year-round historically. In 1877, Okanagan protests helped persuade the Indian Reserve Commission to restore some land to the reserves based on the number of head of livestock held. At first glance this seems an instance where colonizers righted their own wrongs. But in the years between 1865 and 1877 settler stockholders had preempted the fertile bottomland that was previously part of the reserve, and that land would not be restored to the reserve. Over the same period many Okanagan families, suffering from the lack of adequate rangeland and water, must also have lost heads of livestock, which reduced the acreage to which they were entitled in 1877. Throughout the 1890s settler practices eroded the Okanagan land base further. The reserve's river frontage was fraudulently appropriated, compromising riparian access of reserve residents. The Crown sold off land adjacent to the reserves, eliminating Okanagan right-of-way to Crown lands that lay beyond. Then, in the early twentieth century, international property developers began to turn land in the region toward fruit production, siphoning off ever greater proportions of the scarce water resources.[47] Settlers and developers and investors came and went. Whether they thought about Aboriginal people in the process made little difference to the outcome: the Okanagan people ended up with marginal land and without the water rights necessary to improve that land. Okanagan families watched as orchards sprang up around their parched communities. Their reserves became desert isles surrounded by fresh water seas of irrigation. Generations of settlers, developers, administrators, and reformers were partnered, whether they knew it or not, in a common choreography of dispossession.

Chinese immigrants, themselves victims of discrimination under colonial policies, were likewise members of this colonial troupe. In 1884 the legislature passed an act denying Chinese the right to preempt land or divert water.[48] Legally their status became more similar to Indians than ever before. But in practice this legislation did little to forge alliances between Chinese and Aboriginal people. Instead, it increased the likelihood of Chinese trespasses on the small portion of lands that were being remade as "Native space." Legally shut out from land and water rights, Chinese settlers looked to lands reserved for people similarly reviled by colonial authorities. Chinese prospectors or farmers might have anticipated that White authorities would be slow to correct transgressions committed against Aboriginal people. Some Chinese had found this to be the case even before the 1884 restriction.[49] By placing Chinese and Indians on similar legal footing, White authorities diverted Chinese ambitions away from the land desired by Whites and toward reserve land. At the same time Chinese preemptions that predated 1884 became obvious targets for Indians whose meager reserve allocations were too small to support them. Under such circumstances conflicts over land and water between Indians and Chinese were almost inevitable.

By indirectly engineering such conflicts, elites also generated increased measures of Indian acquiescence to colonial hegemony. Faced with Chinese encroachments, Aboriginal people were more likely to turn for help to federal Indian agents (who had no jurisdiction over provincial matters of preemption) or to White neighbors (who could afford to act benevo-lently with their racial privilege safely swaddled). When Whites inter-vened (as they sometimes did) to rectify illegal action taken by Chinese against Aboriginal people, they simultaneously solidified their authority and power over Aboriginal people. Mapping these complex intercon-nections on the ground would tell us new things about the racialized production of hegemonic consent that facilitated dispossession in places like the interior of British Columbia, where treaties were never signed.[50]

Elsewhere, where treaties *were* signed, the contours of colonialism's figurative genealogies appear remarkably similar. Here, too, the micro-techniques of dispossession that transformed indigenous territory into settlement lands were crucial in determining the historical meaning and efficacy of treaty provisions over time. The treaties in Washington Ter-ritory (1854–56) and the Douglas treaties in British Columbia (1850–54) all contained articles guaranteeing the signatories the right to hunt and/or fish in the customary manner on unoccupied ceded land. Article 5 of the Treaty of Point Elliott (1855), for example, which encompassed Island County, Washington, promised both the "right of taking fish at usual and accustomed grounds and stations" and "the privilege of hunt-ing and gathering roots and berries on open and unclaimed lands."[51]

The interrelated land practices that would nullify this clause in prac-tice, if not on paper, take us back before 1855. "Gathering roots" referred to the cultivated bracken and camas that were staples of the Coast Salish diet. Yet bracken and camas grew on the same prairie land coveted and seized by the first generation of White settlers to Island County. A macro view of Island County history tells us that White pop-ulation growth was minimal—only 294 by 1860—and might mislead us to believe that Article 5 protected indigenous subsistence and usufruct rights. But the micro view offers a more telling story: The wave of set-tlers who arrived between 1852 and 1853 settled "almost entirely on prairie land," with the result that by the spring of 1853 "open and unclaimed" prairie was practically nonexistent.[52] Thus, two years before the Treaty of Point Elliott, it was already impossible to protect the prairie land ecology of the Kikiallus of Island County. The promise to do so in 1855 was hollow; by that time the Kikiallus were already dispossessed from this key element of their economy.

Having acquired the most fertile land in the county, early prairie set-tlers and their heirs stayed and prospered. They created successful farms on land that increased a hundredfold in value over twenty years; the farmers who followed would not come close to matching the prosperity of this first generation.[53] The Kikiallus, displaced from the agricultural elements of their traditional economy, became farm laborers. Laboring in order to feed their families, they further subsidized the prosperity of early settlers. (The first subsidy, of course, had been the land itself.) In the mid-1870s mechanization began to push the Kikiallus out of farm labor.[54] After the loss of the prairie, this was the second economic displacement that they experienced in less than a generation.

Kikiallus access to hunting grounds likewise eroded. Through the 1860s White men cut timber for their personal use and for sale to mills even though, in the words of the historian Richard White, they "did not have a shadow of title to it."[55] Fraud and theft were ordinary practices in the woods. Mill companies bought their own land but delayed logging it as long as logs from rogue operators were available. The Kikiallus were doubly denied: they had access to unsurrendered but logged-over land, and they lacked access to forested but alienated land. At the same time speculators were able to purchase and hang on to large tracts of the county despite nonpayment of taxes.[56] The Kikiallus hunting territory in Island County shrank piecemeal.

Eventually, in the 1890s these economic displacements were followed by full physical displacement when the Kikiallus began at last to acquiesce to the prospect of moving to the reservations that had been set out in the 1855 treaty. Reservation residents might have hoped to make use of Article 5 when they returned to Island County to fish seasonally, but in this, too, they would be stymied. In the first decades of the twentieth century non-Indian-owned fish traps encircled Whidbey Island, effectively barring Kikiallus access to fish there.[57] Had they been compensated for that valuable prairie land decades earlier, the Kikiallus might have had the capital to invest in fish traps of their own. Newcomers' guarantee of usufruct rights on paper and their breach of that guarantee in practice worked in concert to dispossess the Kikiallus.[58]

The succession of newcomers to places like Island County, Salt Spring Island, and the Okanagan Valley included farmers, speculators, loggers, and fishers. These groups were riven by class differences; they worked largely independently of each other. Some of them were probably hostile toward Aboriginal people; others were no doubt sympathetic toward those they viewed as "vanishing Indians"; and others still surely formed meaningful and nuanced relationships across the divides of culture and power. Assessing the intentions of different members of the colonial family does not bring us closer to understanding the mechanisms of dispossession on the ground. For that we need to examine the relationships between the practices of colonizers of different stripes. We need to zoom in to map the microtechniques of dispossession on the ground, and we then need to stand back to view the constellation of these techniques as the product of colonialism.

GENEALOGIES OF COLONIALISM II

Members of the colonial family tree were diverse by class, ideology, and personal idiosyncracy. We would be seriously remiss, however, to overlook the additional diversity of ancestries that we conceptualize as "race." Marriage among early pioneers was not only, or even primarily, among White immigrants. In late nineteenth-century British Columbia and Washington, for example, more than a thousand pioneer families originated in households where an Aboriginal woman partnered with a non-Aboriginal man.[59] In the case of rural British Columbia this means, as the historian Jean Barman has pointed out, that "somewhere between one in every ten to twenty non-Aboriginal men lived with an Aboriginal woman, and another larger proportion with a woman of mixed race."[60] These women of Aboriginal and mixed ancestry were pioneers too, although they have not generally been recognized as such.[61] The mix of non-Aboriginal and Aboriginal heritage in these pioneer households must surely complicate the figurative genealogies of colonial practice discussed earlier. What does it mean that the elite men who made land policy and the working-class men who labored on the land were often married to Aboriginal women?

Instead of assigning blame for Aboriginal dispossession to one member of a mixed-heritage family, it is more useful to consider the general questions of relationship and responsibility that these genealogies raise. Colonialism's network of laws, attitudes, and practices placed these families and their offspring at the center of the transformation and transfer of lands. In British Columbia, children of combined Aboriginal and non-Aboriginal descent often found themselves doubly denied. In Canada, the federal Indian Act of 1876 imposed a patrilineal definition of "Indian," denying Indian status to Aboriginal women who had children with non-Aboriginal men. The children were likewise denied Indian status. Mothers and children alike were forbidden from residing on reserves. Denying these children access to their mothers' extended families propelled them into the social and economic milieu of immigrant society. The consequences of this in turn were gender specific. Lacking social and material capital, the boys usually grew up to be laborers in the colonial economy, subsidizing the primitive accumulation of early immigrant pioneers. This was an experience they shared with the Kikiallus of Island County and with their Aboriginal kin in general. The young men were denied both the white privilege of their fathers and the Aboriginal rights of their mothers. Daughters of dual heritage had more opportunities to integrate into the social milieu of their fathers but usually at the cost of their Aboriginal identity. Many of these women in turn bequeathed a genealogical amnesia to their children, choosing not to tell them about their Aboriginal lineage.[62]

In practice, then, thousands of descendants of Aboriginal mothers were effectively cut off from their indigenous roots. Families were cleaved in two, often never to be reconnected. The outcome of this deracination was certainly social, but it was also political and economic. When assimilationist practices bled off members of Aboriginal families, the number of people with demonstrable links to indigenous political structures shrank drastically. At the same time assimilationist practices and pressures reduced the pool of people who could challenge the ongoing transfer of British Columbia's capital (that is, land and resources) from indigenous hands to nonindigenous control. If what Marx ironically termed the "secret of so-called primitive accumulation" was to remain a secret, colonizers were well advised to limit the number of people who were in on it.[63]

Since the first days of European arrival in North America, intermarriage with Indigenous peoples had been a survival strategy for newcomers. This practice is usually seen as ending with the fur trade era. In places like rural British Columbia, however, intermarriage between immigrants and Aboriginal women continued well past the fur trade period. Immigrant settlers to Salt Spring Island in the second half of the nineteenth century, for example, gained access to and knowledge about local resources from their Aboriginal friends and relatives. Historian Ruth Sandwell has stressed that the economies and lifestyles of non-Aboriginal settlers had a great deal in common with those of Aboriginal

people on reserve, some of whom were their in-laws.[64] These commonalities in practice are crucial, in part because they enrich our understanding of social history. More broadly, they matter because they
masked the simultaneous transformations at the political and economic
levels as massive amounts of wealth were siphoned off from Aboriginal
communities.

Aboriginal people who built log houses on Salt Spring Island knew
that their right to land had a different derivation than that of settlers
who built similar structures. They pointed to this difference when they
explained that they had "always" used the island's land and resources,
a historically entrenched claim that they supported with the physical evidence of ancestral graves.[65] Working-class immigrants to Salt Spring
Island had likely never owned the means of production, but their Aboriginal friends, neighbors, and relatives had until quite recently. The
extent to which rural settler and reserve economies resembled one
another by the end of the nineteenth century is a measure of the extent
to which Aboriginal people had already been dispossessed in practice,
although not in law, of their capital.

Sandwell reads the similarities between Aboriginal and non-Aboriginal
rural life as a challenge to "the very notion of a coherent white-settler
society that could be understood as the colonizing 'other' of nineteenth-
century British Columbia."[66] The point is not simply that there existed
no single unified monolith of "colonial society," although this is true
enough. What deserves our attention is that a "coherent white-settler
society" was not *required* in order to colonize and dispossess Indigenous
peoples of their land and resources. The fractures and fissures in that fiction of "white-settler society" cannot be said to have curbed the process
of colonization in any straightforward manner. And in fact, they may
have facilitated colonization's success. After all, one is unlikely to mount
resistance against in-laws and neighbors who lead lives much like one's
own. Regardless of personal intentions, feelings, or affiliations, the practices of pioneer families on the ground were what fashioned British
Columbia out of indigenous territory. If Indian policy was an iron fist,
intermarried pioneer men were sometimes the velvet glove.

The White men who raised families with women of Aboriginal
descent may have done colonialism's work, but they received neither
reward nor recognition for their acts. Instead, the White men who partnered with Aboriginal women lived against the grain of colonial dis-

course that reviled their choices. Charged with undermining racial supremacy, compromising civilization, and threatening the stability of empire, these men had little reason to see themselves on the same side as the elite urban missionaries, politicians, and rhetoriticians who judged them.[67] Yet the de facto result of their marriages was the deracination of their wives from their Aboriginal families and patrimony.

And what of the Aboriginal and mixed-heritage wives? How are we to understand their precarious position in colonialism's sprawling genealogy? We know little about their motivation for marrying immigrant men, although we might well assume that they did what they believed best for themselves and their families.[68] At the level of individual instances this may have turned out to be the case in the short and even long terms. Evidence of relationships that endured over time, that were marked by affection, or that provided secure homes for women and their families is important and should not be dismissed. At the same time such evidence should not, as historian Adele Perry has noted, "obscure . . . the coercive details and larger brutality of colonialism."[69] The disparate practices of colonialism shaped the broader impact of these women's individual spousal choices. The combined effect was to earn these women places on the colonial family tree.

Such genealogical connections do not ascribe blame; they do point to the opacity of the colonial context when viewed from the ground. They remind us that in the long run the broader ramifications of our daily actions are utterly unpredictable. They remind us that direct causal connections are not necessary to achieve consequential outcomes. The result can be equally forceful, as Perry notes, when phenomena are "inextricably and largely accidentally bound by chronology."[70] Such is the central insight of genealogy.

GENEALOGIES OF SCHOLARSHIP

There is precious little work that takes up the perspective I have advocated throughout this essay. Sources are part of the problem. Tracing the history of land practices is not nearly as simple as tracing the history of land policies. Sources are much scarcer for such an endeavor, if they exist at all. Getting at most land practices requires sources of rural rather than urban origin. Given the low literacy rates among many rural residents in the nineteenth-century North American West, such sources are rare. It is sometimes possible to cross-reference land records to trace the history of specific pieces of land, as Ruth Sandwell has done, but this is time-consuming, demanding, and must be meticulously done. Such is to be expected of a genealogical approach, which, as Foucault noted, "requires patience and a knowledge of details, and . . . depends on a vast accumulation of source material."[71] The most obvious reason there has been so little of this sort of research is simple: it is hard work.

Yet if academics have devoted little genealogical attention to settler practice, the same cannot be said of the teams of researchers who work for First Nations. First Nations attention to settler practice is not simply of scholarly interest; rather, it is central to their efforts to gain restitution, whether at the treaty table or in the courtroom. Lawyers, judges, bureaucrats, and officials of today demand a close and precise accounting of settlers' actual practices on the land over time. The historical genealogy of land practice across British Columbia is not impossible to retrieve. In fact, it is accumulating day by day in the databases and filing cabinets of band and treaty offices. The barriers between academic and applied research are such that many academic scholars may be entirely unaware of these growing collections of historical knowledge. Those who are aware cannot even hope to gain access to the research until after the cases have been tried. And even then, First Nations may decide not to release the research for academic purposes. Yet as the legal stakes increase, so do the caches of research. Genealogical method not only produces a conceptually more satisfying framework for understanding colonialism, it also provides a more usable framework for dealing with its legacy.

Why, then, have academic scholars been slow to focus research on settler practice? Conceptual blinders, inherited from our scholarly forebears, have certainly played a role, and these deserve our scrutiny. The scholarly tendency to privilege policy over practice suggests one of the ways in which colonial tropes continue to shadow our narrative and interpretive choices. Our scholarship no longer celebrates the colonial past, yet our choice of historical protagonists, heroes, and villains remains diagnostic. We have become comfortable laying responsibility for our modern-day "Indian problem" at the feet of politicians and Indian affairs bureaucrats of days gone by. We have had studies of Indian affairs bureaucrats at the federal and agency levels.[72] The scholarship on British Columbia, in particular, has long been characterized by debates over the personalities, policies, and intentions of men in official positions such as James Douglas and Joseph Trutch, with Gilbert Malcolm Sproat recently being added to the cast.[73] These policy makers of the past are easily othered—that is, they are not us. This tendency is only accentuated by today's general cynicism toward politicians and bureaucrats.

We are less comfortable, it seems, dealing with the mundane practices of colonialism and dispossession as they were deployed by so-called regular folk. Sandwell's microhistory of Salt Spring Island, for example, offers an impressively intimate view of settler practices on the ground over time. Having taken great care to distinguish between urban-based rhetoric and rural-based practice, Sandwell's instinct is to stress settler and Aboriginal agency in its resistance to dominant rhetoric rather than to locate that agency within its genealogical context. This leaves broader questions of power unaddressed and implicitly suggests that similarities between Aboriginal and non-Aboriginal lifestyles somehow distanced nineteenth-century working class immigrants from the colonial project.[74] My point is not to single out Sandwell but rather to urge reflection on the contours of our collective scholarly choices. To a greater extent than we often admit, our scholarly "choices" continue to be shaped by those who came before us. In a practical sense we can see this in the sources we have inherited. Documents about "Indians" reside in different record groups than documents about immigrants. Bureaucratic distinctions have become archival distinctions and these in turn historiographical ones. In a broader discursive sense we have likewise inherited ideological baggage packed within colonial categories. As scholars today we disown the historiographical traditions that uncritically celebrated pioneer heroes and mourned vanishing Indian victims. But we have not brought our correctives to these two traditions into conversation with one another. And it is here that our scholarly choices may betray us. Scholarship's segregation of immigrant pioneers from the work of dispossession suggests that at some level we continue to lionize hardworking pioneers. In Canada in particular the exceptionalist myth that frontier settlement followed in the wake of British law and order has furthered tendencies to see settlers as hapless bystanders rather than full participants in colonialism. Likewise, scholarly work that removes indigenous actions from their colonial context continues to deny full agency to Aboriginal people. Indigenous people participated in colonialism but, to paraphrase Marx, not under circumstances of their own making. They were victims but they were not *only* victims.[75] The colonial family tree is gargantuan, and it is hung heavy with contradictions and inequalities among its members.

YOU DON'T PICK YOUR FAMILY

Whether or not individuals carried heavy consciences for acts perpetrated by their colonial relations, they enjoyed the subsidy of free land and bequeathed it to their heirs. This is something for which they cannot personally be blamed but for which they are nonetheless surely responsible. The specter of mass reparations haunts any discussion such as this, of course. But we have plenty of precedent for this sense of responsibility in our society. In both legal and moral terms we accept that people are often responsible for outcomes they did not intend. Intention plays a role in the distinction between manslaughter and murder, for example, but it does not absolve the perpetrator or bring back the victim. We are similarly accustomed to holding institutions responsible for actions committed in the past under the auspices of the corporation, church, government, or military as the case may be. The same can be said more broadly of society. The ancestors of our society, even if not our biological ancestors, made treaties that we are responsible for honoring, and they committed depredations—including the refusal to negotiate treaties—that we are responsible for rectifying.[76]

"Responsibility" also has another, more positive connotation that is helpful here. We should remember that being considered a "responsible person" is a positive trait in our society and that we appreciate those who live up to their responsibilities. Following the work of historian Victoria Freeman, we might attempt "the acknowledgement of the destruction we have wrought—not for the purposes of assigning blame and guilt, but as a necessary foundation for trust."[77] With this in mind we might feel less threatened by, and thus more open to, the reconfiguration of colonial genealogy that encompasses us all.

Every non-Aboriginal person in British Columbia today is a living beneficiary of the original sin of dispossession. This hidden subsidy keeps our quality of life afloat. And it is the unspoken secret of this subsidy that causes a collective shudder when the reallocation of settlement lands is proposed. We did not pick our colonial family, but we have inherited its assets and are responsible for its debts. Ninety-four percent of land in British Columbia remains Crown land, much of which can still be leased or purchased in fee simple, yet paying our long-overdue debt to the original landowners seems to many an impossible feat. Our past is heavy with the accumulated multigenerational weight of these microtechniques of dispossession, these intimate interactions between policies and practices over time. Our past may be heavy with them, but they only comprise our history if we choose to shoulder our family responsibility and narrate them as our history.

POSTSCRIPT

This takes us, finally, back to the beach at Opitsaht. The Twombly family took a brave step when they returned to accept their inheritance of Captain Robert Gray's legacy. The "ancestral connection" they honored that day was neither easy nor pleasant. But it was an acknowledgment of a shared past, and in this acknowledgment the seeds of trust could be sown. Not all of us can trace our literal roots to early colonization, but we are nonetheless all rooted to this past. We all have a spot on this colonial genealogy. This is a difficult fact with which to reckon, particularly for residents of British Columbia today. It was perhaps no accident that the supplicants on that summer's day came from afar. For British Columbians to engage in a comparable act would be fraught not only with personal tensions and pain but with material stakes as well. The Twomblys, after all, did not occupy British Columbia, and whatever land they occupy today is not the land that the Tla-o-qui-aht want back. Joe Martin of the Tla-o-qui-aht First Nation seemed to understand this well when he spoke to a reporter about why the apology was so significant to his community: "Because . . . this has never been done anywhere else in Canada as far as I know. . . . These people are from the U.S of A. and we've never had the government come here . . . the government of *Canada* come here to apologize, to apologize to our people for taking out all these resources from under our feet and so on that belong to us, they rightly, rightfully belong to our people. People are very . . . happy about it and then of course a lot of them are being educated by it."[78]

We can all be educated by the exchange that took place on the beach that day. The Twomblys did not pick their family, but they accepted their inheritance all the same. It would have been more difficult for them to take such steps at home in Texas, Massachusetts, New Hampshire, or Oregon, just as it will be more difficult for British Columbians to do so in British Columbia. It is a harrowing task to dig down where we live and expose the roots that tie us to the colonial past, but it is also imperative.

NOTES

I would like to thank the organizers and participants of the conference "Pacific Northwest Indian Treaties in National and International Historical Perspective," held in May 2005, where I first had the opportunity to present this essay. My appreciation for commentary, critique, and assistance also goes to Courtney Booker, Hart Caplan, Glen Coulthard, Dara Culhane, Linda Dorricott, Alexandra Harmon, Doug Harris, Harmony Johnson, Loraine Littlefield, Elsie Paul, Susan Roy, Ruth Sandwell, Claudio Saunt, Sheila Savey, Dan Smith, and the Mowachaht/Muchalaht First Nation. Funding for this research came from the Social Sciences and Humanities Research Council of Canada.

1. Kevin Drews, "Descendants of U.S. Fur Trader Apologizes to Natives Near Tofino, B.C," *Canadian Press*, 19 July 2005, available online at http://www.aptn.ca/forums/index.php?showtopic=521 (accessed 23 September 2005).

2. "Historic Apology to First Nation," 18 July 2005, available online at http://vancouver.cbc.ca/regional/servlet/View?filename=bc_tofino-apology20050718 (accessed 25 July 2005).

3. Adele Perry, *On the Edge of Empire: Gender, Race, and the Making of British Columbia, 1849–1871* (Toronto: University of Toronto Press, 2001), 19, 196.

4. Ruth Sandwell, *Contesting Rural Space: Land Policy and the Practices of Resettlement on Saltspring Island, 1859–1891* (Montreal: McGill-Queen's University Press, 2005), 5.

5. I hear this sentiment expressed by students in my classrooms, by liberal-minded middle-class families around the dinner table, and by pundits in their editorials. This notion persists, although 94 percent of land in British Columbia is still Crown land. Available online at http://www.lwbc.bc.ca/o2land/index.html (accessed 21 October 2005).

6. Cole Harris, *Making Native Space: Colonialism, Resistance, and Reserves in British Columbia* (Vancouver: UBC Press, 2002).

7. Michel Foucault, "Nietzsche, Genealogy, History," in *The Foucault Reader*, edited by Paul Rabinow (New York: Pantheon Books, 1984), 76–77.

8. Ibid., 79.

9. Ibid., 78.

10. Choosing a different metaphor, Walter Benjamin likens this method to climbing a ladder "rung by rung, according as chance would offer a narrow foothold," never allowing oneself "a moment to look around" until the final

moment. Benjamin, *The Arcades Project*, translated by Howard Eiland and Kevin McLaughlin (Cambridge, Mass.: Belknap Press of Harvard University Press, 1999), 460nn2 and 4.

11. Hamar Foster and Alan Grove, "'Trespassers on the Soil': *United States v. Tom* and a New Perspective on the Short History of Treaty Making in Nineteenth-Century British Columbia," chapter 3, this volume.

12. Victoria Freeman, *Distant Relations: How My Ancestors Colonized North America* (Toronto: McLelland and Stewart, 2000), 452.

13. Foster and Grove, "'Trespassers on the Soil,'" chapter 3, this volume.

14. Claudio Saunt, *Black, White, and Indian: Race and the Unmaking of an American Family* (New York: Oxford University Press, 2005), 29.

15. Harris, *Making Native Space*, 138, 140–41.

16. Ibid., 177–78.

17. See, for example, *Evidence Submitted to the Royal Commission on Indian Affairs for the Province of British Columbia: New Westminster Agency Transcripts, Part I* (Victoria, B.C.: The Commission, 1913–16), 254–55, 278; *Evidence Submitted to the Royal Commission on Indian Affairs for the Province of British Columbia: New Westminster Agency Transcripts, Part II* (Victoria: The Commission, 1913–16), 330; and Harris, *Making Native Space*, 248.

18. Harris, *Making Native Space*, 253.

19. Ibid., chapter 8.

20. Of course, we might argue from this that story or not, these were the truths through which historical actors created meaning, and we treat those actors unfairly, not to mention ahistorically, if we assess them by today's stories instead of their own. Such a relativistic stance, however, obscures at least one crucial fact: these historical stories of property were never that straightforward.

21. The history of this conflation dates at least to the seventeenth century. The absence of private property was one of the traits of the Hobbesean "war of all against all." John Locke's subsequent work on property stressed the notion of "improvement" of land and did much to influence the progressive narrative about property that continues to hold so much sway. See Nicholas Blomley, *Unsettling the City* (New York: Routledge, 2004), 85–86 and 115–16, for commentary on Locke. See also Harris, *Making Native Space*, 46–56.

22. Robert Cail, *Land, Man, and the Law: The Disposal of Crown Land in British Columbia, 1871–1913* (Vancouver: UBC Press, 1974), 15; and Sandwell, *Contesting Rural Space*, 69–70. If the preemption had already been surveyed, the preemptor had three years' grace in which to make payment. The 1861 Ordinance provided that a single man could claim 150 acres, and a married man could claim 200 acres with an additional 10 acres per child under eighteen. Cail, *Land, Man, and the Law*, 15. See Harris, *Making Native Space*, 76–78, for examples of the "slips of paper" that substantiated preemptions. Settlers similarly preceded surveyors in Washington. See Richard White, *Land Use, Environment, and Social Change* (Seattle: University of Washington Press, 1980), 38.

23. *Evidence Submitted to the Royal Commission on Indian Affairs for the Province of British Columbia: West Coast Agency Transcripts* (Victoria: The Commission, 1913–16), 107–8, 116–17.

24. *Evidence Submitted to the Royal Commission on Indian Affairs for the Province of British Columbia: New Westminster Agency Transcripts, Part I*, 280–82; *Evidence Submitted to the Royal Commission on Indian Affairs for the Province of British Columbia: New Westminster Agency Transcripts, Part II*, 439–40, 446, 666–67; and J. Laverock, Land Surveyor, to G. H. Dawson, Surveyor General, 27 November 1915, file 520b, volume 11020, RG10, Department of Indian Affairs.

25. *Evidence Submitted to the Royal Commission on Indian Affairs for the Province of British Columbia: New Westminster Agency Transcripts, Part I*, 272–73.

26. Ibid., 298; [?] to Royal Commission, 11 August 1915, file 520b, volume 11020, RG10, Department of Indian Affairs.

27. *Evidence Submitted to the Royal Commission on Indian Affairs for the Province of British Columbia: New Westminster Agency Transcripts, Part I*, 312–13, 323–26.

28. Richard White, *Land Use, Environment, and Social Change*, 56. On the difficulty of clearing land, see also Sandwell, "Negotiating Rural," in *Beyond the City Limits*, edited by Ruth Sandwell (Vancouver: UBC Press, 1999), 96; and Richard Mackie, "Cougars, Colonists, and the Rural Settlement of Vancouver Island," in *Beyond the City Limits*, 133.

29. *Evidence Submitted to the Royal Commission on Indian Affairs for the Province of British Columbia: New Westminster Agency Transcripts, Part I*, 324.

30. Harris, *Making Native Space*, 140, 144.

31. *Evidence Submitted to the Royal Commission on Indian Affairs for the Province of British Columbia: Nass Agency Transcripts* (Victoria: The Commission, 1913–16), 176–77; *Evidence Submitted to the Royal Commission on Indian Affairs for the Province of British Columbia: Cowichan Agency Transcripts, Part I*, 46.

32. *Evidence Submitted to the Royal Commission on Indian Affairs for the Province of British Columbia: West Coast Agency Transcripts*, 112.

33. Ibid., 97–98.

34. Ibid., 159–60, 161, 162; *Evidence Submitted to the Royal Commission on Indian Affairs for the Province of British Columbia: Queen Charlotte Agency Transcripts* (Victoria: The Commission, 1913–16), 43.

35. *Evidence Submitted to the Royal Commission on Indian Affairs for the Province of British Columbia: West Coast Agency Transcripts*, 97–98, 112.

36. Sandwell, *Contesting Rural Space*, 73–75, 85–121, 128, 226–28; and Sandwell, "Negotiating Rural," 91–95, 98–100.

37. See, for example, "New Westminster Agency—Applications for Land—Land Improvements," file 520b, volume 11010, RG10, Department of Indian Affairs; and *Evidence Submitted to the Royal Commission on Indian Affairs for the Province of British Columbia: New Westminster Agency Transcripts, Part II*, 451–679.

38. Harris, *Making Native Space*, 182.

39. Ibid., 141.

40. See J. Edward Chamberlain, *If This Is Your Land, Where Are Your Stories?: Finding Common Ground* (Toronto: Vintage Canada, 2004).

41. Sandwell, *Contesting Rural Space*, 225–31; Sandwell, "Negotiating Rural"; and White, *Land Use, Environment, and Social Change*, 56–59, 67.

42. Harris, *Making Native Space*, 140–44.

43. On fishing and reserves in British Columbia, see Douglas C. Harris, *Landing Native Fisheries: Indian Reserves and Fishing Rights in British Columbia, 1849–1925* (Vancouver: UBC Press, 2008).

44. R. J. Sparke to Regional Land Use Officer, 2 June 1971, J. Woodard File 1664.5.12.1969–1973; R. J. Sparke to Land Registry Office, 20 February 1973, J. Woodard File 1664.5.12.1969-1973; "Leases and Legal Problems Facing the Nootka Band," 3 January 1974, J. Woodard File 1664.7.10; R. J. Sparke to Chief & Council, Mowachaht Band, 23 May 1975, J. Woodward file 1664.7.03; R. J. Sparke to Lewis Wong, 24 June 1975, J. Woodard File 1664.5.12.1974-76; and Meeting Minutes, "Book E," 15 February 1980, J. Woodard File 1664.5.18.00 (Ledgers). All files property of the Mowachaht/Muchalaht First Nation.

45. Davis McKenzie, "Righting Past Wrongs: Restoring Toh Kwon_non," *Neh Motl*, 1 September 2005, 1–2; personal communication with Elsie Paul, Sliammon, B.C., 29 March 2005. In the fall of 2005, the Sliammon were working to restore the reserve and salmon habitat at Toh Kwon_non.

46. Harris, *Making Native Space*, especially part 2.

47. Duane Thomson, "The Reponses of Okanagan Indians," *BC Studies* 101 (spring 1994): 102–4, 108, 109.

48. Cail, *Land, Man, and the Law*, 36.

49. See, for example, Harris, *Making Native Space*, 144.

50. I am indebted for these insights to conversations with Tao-Yee Lau, an honors student in the history department at the University of British Columbia. She explores examples of Chinese-Aboriginal interaction in her research paper for History 429, "Indigenous Inhabitants and Alien Migrants: Chinese Intrusion onto Native Land in 1870s–1890s British Columbia," December 2004.

51. "Treaty of Point Elliott, 1855," *HistoryLink.org: The Online Encyclopedia of Washington State History,* available online at http://www.historylink.org/essays /output.cfm?file_id=2629 (accessed 23 September 2005).

52. White, *Land Use, Environment, and Social Change*, 21, 37.

53. Ibid., 55, 59. Early arrival gave White, but not Black, settlers on Salt Spring Island a similar "edge" over later arrivals. Sandwell, *Contesting Rural Space*, 187, 227.

54. White, *Land Use, Environment, and Social Change*, 72.

55. Ibid., 80.

56. Ibid., 58–59, 77, 83.

57. Ibid., 72.

58. This dual phenomenon had deep historical roots that extended back to seventeenth-century New England, where it had similarly helped accomplish indigenous dispossession. See Freeman, *Distant Relations*, 440–41.

59. Jean Barman, "What a Difference a Border Makes," *Journal of the West*, 28, no. 3 (July 1999): 16.

60. Jean Barman, "Invisible Women: Aboriginal Mothers and Mixed-Race Daughters in Rural Pioneer British Columbia," in *Beyond the City Limits*, 160.

61. Ibid., 159–60.

62. Ibid., 173–77.

63. On the effect of thus reducing the number of individuals who could claim "Indian" status, see Bonita Lawrence, *"Real" Indians and Others: Mixed-Blood Urban Native People and Indigenous Nationhood* (Vancouver: UBC Press, 2004). The concept of the "secret of primitive accumulation" comes from Karl Marx, *Capital, Volume One (1867)* (Toronto: Vintage Books, 1977), chapter 26. Quite different implications remain to be explored south of the border in Washington, where mixed-heritage families were far more likely to be identified as "Indians." Barman, "What a Difference a Border Makes," 14–20.

64. Sandwell, *Contesting Rural Space*, 5, 134–37. See also Barman, "Invisible Women," 160; Perry, *On the Edge of Empire*, 58–61; and Jay Nelson, "'A Strange Revolution in the Manners of the Country': Aboriginal-Settler Intermarriage in Nineteenth-Century British Columbia," in *Regulating Lives: Historical Essays on the State, Society, the Individual and the Law*, edited by John Mclaren, Robert Menzies, and Dorothy E. Chunn (Vancouver: UBC Press, 2002), 50.

65. G. H. Richards, Rear Admiral and Commander in Chief, to James Douglas, Governor, 10 April 1860, File 1213, GR1372, British Columbia Archives.

66. Sandwell, *Contesting Rural Space*, 5.

67. Perry, *On the Edge of Empire*, 69–74.

68. As Barman notes, the relative lack of historical understanding of Aboriginal women results from the gendering of both historical sources and of historiography. Barman, "Invisible Women," 163.

69. Perry, *On the Edge of Empire*, 62.

70. Ibid., 75.

71. Foucault, "Nietzsche, Genealogy, History," 76–77.

72. E. Brian Titley, *Narrow Vision: Duncan Campbell Scott and the Administration of Indian Affairs in Canada* (Vancouver: UBC Press, 1986; E. Brian Titley, *The Frontier World of Edgar Dewdney* (Vancouver: UBC Press, 1999); and Robin Jarvis Brownlie, *A Fatherly Eye: Indian Agents, Government Power, and Aboriginal Resistance in Ontario, 1918–1939* (Don Mills, Ontario: Oxford University Press, 2003).

73. Robin Fisher, *Contact and Conflict: Indian-European Relations in British Columbia, 1774–1890*, 2d edition (Vancouver: UBC Press, 1992); Paul Tennant, *Aboriginal Peoples and Politics: The Indian Land Question in British Columbia, 1849–1989* (Vancouver: UBC Press, 1990); and Harris, *Making Native Space*.

74. Although Cole Harris offers a certain corrective to this tendency, he errs in another direction. Harris does not shy away from implicating settlers, and instead affords settler attitudes significant explanatory power in the processes of dispossession. Yet he accomplishes this by transposing metropolitan rhetoric about settler

ideology onto "settler society" at large. This is the same conflation of rhetoric and practice that Sandwell so convincingly demonstrates requires deconstruction; this is the conflation that the logic of genealogy challenges. See, for example, Harris, *Making Native Space*, 46–56.

75. Freeman, *Distant Relations*, 462.

76. Ibid., 445, 452, 455.

77. Ibid., 458.

78. Emphasis in original. "B.C. Almanac's Mark Forsythe Speaks with CBC TV Reporter Duncan McCue," 18 July 2005, audio clip: bc_tofino050718.ram, available online at http://vancouver.cbc.ca/regional/servlet/View?filename=bc_tofinoapology 20050718 (accessed 25 July 2005).

PART II

CROSS-BORDER INFLUENCES

3 "Trespassers on the Soil"

UNITED STATES V. TOM AND A NEW PERSPECTIVE

ON THE SHORT HISTORY OF TREATY MAKING IN

NINETEENTH-CENTURY BRITISH COLUMBIA

Hamar Foster and Alan Grove

> The insatiable greed of the white man leads him to desire to obtain
> all that the Indian has, and if he cannot get it without law, he will
> have a law enacted which will enable him to get it.—*Missionary
> William Duncan of Metlakatla, 1886*

T he British Columbia "Indian Land Question" has been an issue
since the 1860s. Until 1927, when Parliament imposed legal
restrictions, Aboriginal groups lobbied, petitioned, and protested
in support of their land rights.[1] The campaign for title resumed when
these restrictions were dropped in the 1950s, and since the 1973 *Calder
v. AGBC* decision, British Columbia has produced most of the Supreme
Court of Canada's leading Aboriginal rights decisions.[2] The province
has even had its own unique tripartite treaty process since 1993.[3]

This exceptionalism is largely because treaty making ceased after a
number were made on Vancouver Island in the 1850s and no more were
completed until—with one exception—the Nisga'a Treaty was finalized
in 2000.[4] As a result, land in the province was sold to or preempted by
settlers without extinguishing the Aboriginal title, a practice that hampered the efforts of reserve commissioners from the 1870s on.[5] It also
created a cloud on title that today "has grown to lower" over most of the
province.[6] Prior to the renewal of treaty making prompted by the *Calder*
case, land cession treaties in Canada were either never made (as in

Québec and the Atlantic provinces) or treaty making, once commenced, was pursued to completion (as in Ontario and on the prairies). Only in what is now British Columbia did the process end almost as soon as it had begun. When the legality of this was eventually challenged, the province managed—until relatively recently—to keep the issue out of the courts. But why treaty making was terminated remains something of a mystery.

To put the matter more concretely, why did Judge Matthew Baillie Begbie—who admonished Governor James Douglas in 1860 that it was imperative that the Indian title be extinguished—"inexplicably" change his mind?[7] In our view part of the answer to this question may be found in the years that Douglas and other colonial officials spent in Oregon, where federal Indian law required treaties; in a deviation from that law developed by the courts in Oregon and applied in Alaska; and in the close ties between the administrative and judicial elites of British Columbia, Oregon, and Washington. In short, we think that although British and American territories on the West Coast were separate and very different national jurisdictions after 1846, a similar, albeit legally heterodox, attitude toward Aboriginal land rights thrived in both.[8] We attempt to make this case in this essay. But first we cast a brief glance at treaty making on colonial Vancouver Island.

I. THE DOUGLAS TREATIES

In 1850, pursuant to instructions from the Hudson's Bay Company (HBC) and the Colonial Office, James Douglas began to make agreements with the indigenous people of Vancouver Island to purchase their land.[9] It was his responsibility because he was the senior local official of the HBC, the body to whom the Crown had conveyed the Island and charged with extinguishing the Indian title.[10] By 1854 fourteen treaties had been made: eleven with the Coast Salish peoples of southern Vancouver Island, two with the Wakashan peoples at the northeastern end of the Island, and one with the Coast Salish at Nanaimo.[11] The text used in these transactions was taken from New Zealand precedents for purchasing Maori land.[12]

The "Douglas treaties" are basically deeds of conveyance in which land is transferred to "the white people forever" in return for a monetary consideration, paid largely in blankets. Probably neither party spoke the other's language very well, and none of the chiefs would have understood the concept of land as a transferable commodity. It seems more likely that they regarded the agreements as temporary measures designed to secure peace until more permanent arrangements could be worked out.[13] Although the text is therefore an uncertain guide to what they thought had occurred, the oral and written guarantees that were made, rather than the blankets, are probably why these documents were signed —and why they are properly regarded as treaties. In addition to reserving village sites and enclosed fields, the signatories were solemnly assured that they and their descendants would be "at liberty to hunt over the unoccupied lands, and to carry on their fisheries as formerly." To a fishing people, a promise that their fisheries would remain undisturbed would have been a significant inducement indeed.[14]

After the Nanaimo treaty of 1854, no more of these agreements were formally recorded. Instead, the colony began to sell land without purchasing the Indian title. But the Cowichan, who were the first to have their lands dealt with in this manner, strongly resisted incursions into their territory, frustrating anxious purchasers who had been waiting months, some even years, to take possession.[15] Apparently unwilling to use the monies received from these sales to extinguish the Indian title, Douglas attempted in 1861 to pry funds out of the imperial treasury instead. And because he was supposed to have been extinguishing the Indian title *before* selling land to settlers, he advised the secretary of state for the colonies that "until 1859" it had been his practice to do just that.[16]

Douglas thought he could look to Britain for funds because title to Vancouver Island was to revert to the Crown in 1859, thus ending the HBC's responsibility. But he would not have helped his case by acknowledging that he had made no treaties between 1854 and 1859, when the HBC was supposed to be paying to extinguish the Indian title. Nor, one presumes, would he have been inclined to reveal that he had permitted Indian land to be sold to settlers before the Aboriginal title had been extinguished.[17] It was much more effective to present the problem in the way that he did: a diligent HBC had done its duty until 1859, and now the imperial parliament should do the same. But the secretary of state for the colonies was not buying. The Duke of Newcastle informed Douglas that responsibility for extinguishing the Indian title had moved from the HBC to the colony, not to the imperial treasury. And the relatively small sums involved, he added, were quite within the means of colonial taxpayers, particularly for a purpose that was, as both Douglas and the Assembly had acknowledged, so "essential to the interests of the people of Vancouver Island."[18]

Essential or not, the history books do not record a treaty at Cowichan or anywhere else after 1854. One writer has suggested that the reason for this is simple: the colonial elite, including Judge Begbie, invested heavily in real estate and came to see Indian title as a threat to their financial interests.[19] Another proffered explanation is also financial: Douglas ran out of money. On this view the Colonial Office decreed that funds to extinguish the Indian title had to be raised locally, the colony balked, and that was that.[20] But as political scientist Paul Tennant has pointed out, this account does not square with the facts. Not only did the legislature vote funds for buying Indian land, but for a while editorial opinion seems to have been in favour of it as well.[21] Douglas, moreover, was also governor of the mainland colony, where he ran up a considerable public debt on other projects. The Cariboo wagon road alone cost many times what would have been necessary to extinguish Indian title along the way, and funds were found, or at least borrowed, for that.[22] Even more telling: soon after Douglas retired, the two colonies probably spent in excess of one hundred thousand dollars in capturing and executing the chiefs responsible for the Chilcotin war—a sum that would probably have been sufficient at that time to extinguish Indian title throughout B.C.[23] Therefore the money explanation, although part of the story, fails to satisfy.

According to Tennant, what really happened is that, quite apart from financial considerations, Douglas decided that negotiating payment for Indian land was difficult and that even completed treaties did not make adequate provision for the Indians' economic security and social development. In September of 1853 he therefore advised his HBC superiors that he would not attempt to reopen negotiations at Nanaimo until he felt it was "safe and prudent to do so," adding that the question of Indian rights "always give[s] rise to troublesome excitements, and has on every occasion been productive of serious disturbances."[24] So he resolved on a different approach.

The details of what Tennant has called the "system" that Douglas developed to replace treaties need not detain us. Suffice it to say that he clearly preferred to avoid the turmoil of treaty talks and debates about compensation. He proposed instead to guarantee Aboriginal people special hunting, fishing, and education rights, as well as reserves of land adequate to support them in adapting to the new social and economic reality. Douglas also took the position—rather remarkably, given the tenor of the times—that in every other respect Indians would have the same legal rights as non-Indians.[25] His successors, however, reduced the reserves and were clearly of the view that Indians should not have the same rights as settlers. Instead, they enacted legislation restricting such rights. And they certainly did not make treaties.

Tennant's theory is a useful corrective to the view that it was only a lack of funds that ended treaty making in B.C., and this seems closer to the truth. So does a more detailed variation on this theory that historical geographer Cole Harris has recently developed. Harris argues that Douglas did not really change his mind about treaties. Rather, he simply made them when he thought it made sense to do so, but not otherwise, stopping on Vancouver Island when to continue would have involved acquiring more land than he could protect. On the mainland he made no treaties because there were too many different bands there and not the same expectations. The Colonial Office, moreover, was fast losing its enthusiasm for liberal humanitarianism and was not pressing him. "There was a jumble of Native land policies around the empire," Harris notes, arguing that although the idea of Indian title "remained in the air" in the 1850s, the Colonial Office "no longer quite knew what to do with it." For his part, Douglas was a practical man, not a theorist. He may never have taken seriously the idea that treaties were legally necessary. In the end he appears to have decided that the cost—including the administrative effort, time, and money that would have to be devoted to negotiating them— was not worth it. It was better to allocate generous reserves and to ensure that Indians enjoyed all the rights that colonists did.[26]

There is surely much truth in this. But it submerges law in policy, obliterating the difference—however tenuous that difference may sometimes be—between the two. It also appears to assume that Douglas and his successors either did not know or did not care that the idea of Indian title had spawned a body of law that by the 1850s was generating treaties in Canada and the United States, including right next door in Washington and Oregon. Yet only twenty years later, B.C.'s continuing refusal to acknowledge Aboriginal land rights after confederation clearly surprised the dominion government, which was just embarking on a major treaty-making project of its own.[27]

In fact, even in B.C. the treaty process did not end abruptly at Nanaimo in 1854, although it was certainly suspended. This is an impression fostered by twentieth-century court decisions that have classified only fourteen of a number of events as treaties, partly because Douglas was insufficiently diligent when it came to completing and recording his decisions regarding Indian lands.[28] The Nanaimo treaty, for example, has no text. There are simply signatures ("X's"), and a notation in the register that the "conveyance" by the Sallequun tribe at Nanaimo in 1854 was "similar" to the rest.[29] There is an indistinct line between this sort of informality and transactions with no signatures—in other words, oral promises—that can be misunderstood or misrepresented and, if necessary, denied.

Thus in 1860, Douglas reported to the Colonial Office that he had promised the tribes of the Okanagan that the magistrates would reserve as much land as they needed, and that the tribes were "delighted" with this proposal. But the Okanagan seem to have expected more negotiations and compensation for the lands they were giving up.[30] When this did not happen, they felt betrayed—a sentiment that nearly led to warfare in the 1870s. The Shuswap people took a similar view of promises made to them. Government officials, they said years later, had assured them that a "very large reservation would be staked off for us," and that the government would buy "all the tribal lands outside this reservation" that were required for white settlement.[31] This is also what the Cowichan said about the events that followed Douglas's rebuff by the Duke of Newcastle.

II. THE COWICHAN "TREATY"

In the early 1850s the Cowichan had expressed interest in a treaty but Douglas was unwilling: little was known about their territory, and the land was not needed for settlement. By 1859, however, the situation had changed in at least two ways. First, military expeditions in 1853 and 1856—expeditions that had ended in executions and some bitterness—had revealed the agricultural potential of the Cowichan Valley, and the Fraser Gold Rush had brought new settlers. Second, Aboriginal people knew what was going on south of the international border. As we discuss in section III, below, by 1853 warfare and a much harsher treaty process were replacing the relatively benign treaty making of the early

1850s. This probably contributed not only to the problems Douglas had in negotiating the Nanaimo treaty, but also changed many Cowichan minds as well. Douglas then soured relations further by selling off their land without treaty or payment.[32] As the House of Assembly put it in 1861, the Cowichan were aware of the compensation that had been paid "in the earlier settled districts of Vancouver Island [and] the neighbouring territory of Washington, and strenuously oppose[d] the occupation of settlers of lands deemed their own."[33] The denial of Douglas's request for imperial funds to resolve this problem therefore left the purchasers of land at Cowichan in a tight spot, as many of them must have been persons of modest means who had risked everything in coming to Vancouver Island.

Finally, it seems, patience ran out. In August of 1862 a group of nearly eighty settlers set out for Cowichan on board the HMS *Hecate*. As one contemporary observer put it, they were determined to go ahead even though "the Indians [were] unwilling to sell, still less to be ousted from their land."[34] It no doubt helped that the *Hecate* was a ship of the Royal Navy: this served to remind the Cowichan of the naval expeditions that had been mounted against them. It is also interesting that the gallows for the executions at Nanaimo in 1853 appear to have been constructed near the coal mines that those treaty negotiations were intended to secure, and that when the treaty was finally made in 1854, the formalities took place at Gallows Point.[35] Neither the Cowichan nor the Nanaimo could have missed the significance of this, nor forgotten it by 1862.

Douglas himself accompanied the *Hecate*, in order "to prevent the Indians from objecting" to the settlement.[36] He apparently meant to do this by paying for the land, because a contemporary newspaper account of what occurred describes a scene straight out of the treaty process of the early 1850s. The Indians, according to the *British Colonist*, were promised that "compensation for the lands taken up would be made *as previously established.*"[37] But it wasn't. At least there is no real evidence that it was. And Douglas did not make a formal record of the transaction. If he had, it might have made its way into the books as the fifteenth Douglas treaty.

Even before the *Hecate* sailed, there were those who questioned what was going on. Lieutenant Edmund Hope Verney, commander of the gunboat *Grappler*, had been in the area a few days before and expressed a concern that there might have been "some underhand dealing among the officials in this matter."[38] What he meant is not clear. But the Cowichan were not happy, and they complained. In 1866, for example, a Cowichan delegation went to see the new governor to tell him that they "wanted to be paid for the lands taken by the white men."[39] Other tribes, they said, "have had Indian claims allowed, why not we? The lands we occupy we do not wish to give up: for the rest we wish to be paid."[40] But by then there was not only a new governor. There was a new regime entirely.

The commissioner of lands and works, in particular, was unsympathetic. Joseph William Trutch was committed to a policy of taking Indian lands without compensation, even lands in reserves that had been formally laid out and guaranteed by the Douglas administration.[41] Responding to repeated complaints to Governor Anthony Musgrave by the Cowichan and their supporters, Trutch reported in late 1869 that he could find "no record of any promise having been made to these Indians that they should be paid for the lands in the Cowichan Valley, nor can I learn that any such promise has ever been made." (Apparently then, as today, one cannot believe everything that one reads in the newspapers— even the *British Colonist*.) Trutch conceded that the Cowichan may have expected to be paid, as other tribes had been. He also conceded that it was likely that Douglas had intended to pay "gratuities."[42] But he maintained that there had been no promise, notwithstanding Governor Douglas's acknowledged "intention."[43] The fact that the government had already acted on Trutch's advice and unilaterally reduced reserves without paying compensation may help to explain why Musgrave pronounced himself satisfied with this rather doctored account of events at Cowichan—that and the fact that Trutch was his brother-in-law.

A decade later Reserve Commissioner Gilbert Malcolm Sproat investigated what had happened and, typically, left a lengthy memorandum on the subject.[44] Pretty much everything he unearthed supports the Cowichan version of events, including a letter written in 1865 by the Reverend A. C. Garrett to the surveyor general. According to Garrett, Governor Douglas had made "definite promises" to the Indians at Cowichan in 1862. In particular, he said, Douglas had assured them that he would return in the autumn, "have a gathering of all their tribes, and make them suitable presents. This promise was never fulfilled." Sproat concludes that in 1869 Trutch knew most of these facts, "except perhaps Sir James Douglas' alleged unfulfilled promise."[45] The "perhaps" is interesting and rather takes the shine off what would have otherwise been a most charitable concession.

In light of this, we conclude that although the Nanaimo treaty in 1854 is the last one acknowledged in the history books, a treaty of sorts was made at Cowichan in 1862. It was not formally recorded, nor apparently was it honoured. But then the Nanaimo treaty was only a set of marks, with no text. Did the same sort of thing happen in the Okanagan and the Shuswap? Who knows? But a good case can be made that although Douglas abandoned the treaty process after 1854, circumstances obliged him to revive it—or at least part of it—at Cowichan.

To most colonists, the issue was a practical not a legal one. Whether treaties were *legally* required was rarely debated, and Aboriginal people in the mid-nineteenth century had neither the technical knowledge nor the resources to go to court to debate it. Nor was a test case, whereby the legal status of Aboriginal title might be raised in litigation between settlers, ever brought in colonial British Columbia.[46] However, if Douglas and his successors thought that there was no legal obligation to extinguish Indian title before settlement, there was little support for such complacency in imperial law. Only two years before the colony of Vancouver Island was established, the Supreme Court of New Zealand had ruled that native title in the British Empire existed at common law whether acknowledged by treaty or not.[47] And between 1787 and 1835 both the Congress and the Supreme Court of the United States, relying on British practice and the Royal Proclamation of 1763, had confirmed the legal status of Indian title.[48] It is possible that Douglas did not know about any of this. But if he did know, why would he think that he could dispense with treaties?[49]

The line between law and policy in the common law system is admittedly indistinct. At the time there was also the calculated indifference of the Colonial Office. By the 1850s enthusiasm for humanitarian causes in far-away possessions was waning in Britain, and the Indian Mutiny in 1857 and the Maori Wars of the 1860s served only to emphasize the ingratitude of the indigenous inhabitants of the empire. No one therefore was keeping too close a watch on how careful Douglas and his successors were being about Aboriginal title.[50] But no one in the imperial government told them that they could ignore it, either. In fact, in 1859 the Colonial Office told Douglas that whenever Indian lands were required for settlement, "His Majesty's Government earnestly wish that . . .

measures of liberality and justice may be adopted *for compensating [the Indians] for the surrender of the territory which they have been taught to regard as their own.*"[51] Yet that very year Douglas sold land at Cowichan without paying for it. Then a year later Begbie informed him that Indian title on the mainland "was by no means extinguished" and that "separate provision must be made for it, and soon."[52] Why was this not done? Partly, no doubt, because a wish is not a command, however earnest. And in politics if one can get away without doing something onerous, one usually will. But again, we think that a piece of the puzzle may be missing—a piece that Begbie, who did not arrive in the colony until late 1858, may not have become familiar with until later.

III. THE TRUE INTERESTS OF A WHITE POPULATION: *UNITED STATES V. TOM*

In 1846 the Treaty of Washington fixed the international boundary west of the Rockies at the forty-ninth parallel.[53] This meant that formal colonization could now proceed, so in 1849 Great Britain created the colony of Vancouver Island, which had been confirmed as British even though it extended south of forty-nine degrees. A year earlier Congress had transformed the provisional government organized by the settlers by creating the federal territory of Oregon, which until 1853 included what is now the state of Washington. But the new territorial administration was immediately faced with a problem: although the provisional government had legally committed itself to respecting Indian land, no treaties extinguishing the Indian title had been made.[54] As delegate Samuel R. Thurston told the U.S. Congress in February 1850, two months before Douglas began negotiating his Fort Victoria treaties, "although the white population in Oregon [is] about fifteen thousand . . . the Indian title . . . in that territory has never been extinguished." As a result, he concluded, "no man owns a foot of land in Oregon; but all of us are trespassers on the soil."[55]

What Thurston meant was that extinguishment by treaty had been British and U.S. policy for at least a century. It had, moreover, been given the force of law through the Royal Proclamation of 1763 and, in the United States, the Northwest Ordinance of 1787 and the Indian Trade and Intercourse Acts of 1790 and 1834. In the 1834 act Congress had specifically required treaty making in the "Indian country," which was defined as including "all that part of the United States west of the Mississippi, and not within the states of Missouri and Louisiana, or the territory of Arkansas."[56] So when the Treaty of Washington confirmed in 1846 that Oregon was part of the United States, the new territory was "Indian country" as defined by the 1834 act and subject to federal Indian law.

Accordingly, in June 1850 Congress passed a statute authorizing the appointment of a treaty commission for Oregon and providing that the "law regulating the trade and intercourse with the Indian tribes east of the Rocky Mountains, or such provisions of the same as may be applicable, be extended over the Indian tribes in the Territory of Oregon." This confirmed that Oregon was subject to the special laws and obligations contained in the 1834 act.[57] A few months later Congress also enacted the Donation Land Claims Act, which provided for free land grants.[58] The way was now clear to make treaties and confirm the settlers' land titles.

And that is what happened. An assortment of officials, including the federal Indian superintendent Anson Dart, negotiated and signed at least nineteen treaties with the tribes. By the time the amended version of the Donation Land Act had expired in 1855, title to more than 2.5 million acres of the surrendered land had been formally transferred, gratis, to nearly seventy-five hundred non-Aboriginal homesteaders. These treaties, however, were not popular in the settler community. They were seen as too generous to the tribes, and they did not provide for removal of the Indians to large reservations. The U.S. Senate therefore refused to ratify them.[59] This left putative owners—whose land grants had been legally confirmed because everyone thought that the Indian title was being disposed of—in a somewhat awkward position. If Oregon was Indian country, their land grants were subject to the requirement in the Indian Trade and Intercourse Act of 1834 that the Indian title be extinguished by federally sanctioned treaty. Oregonians were thus in much the same position as the settlers at Cowichan would be a decade later. They had taken title to land before the Indian title had been extinguished. The difference was that Oregon, unlike Vancouver Island, was subject to U.S. law, and in particular to the 1850 statute regarding treaty making. It was also subject to a federal government that had exclusive authority over Indian matters and that was committed—for its own reasons—to enforcing federal Indian law. Thus in Oregon treaty making had to, and did, continue.

Something rather interesting happened before the process was complete, however. In December 1853 the Oregon Supreme Court decided the case of *United States v. Tom*, in which "Tom, an Indian," was indicted pursuant to section 20 of the Indian Trade and Intercourse Act of 1834 for selling a gill of brandy worth twenty-five cents to another Indian.[60] The case was not as ordinary as it might sound. First, Tom had a lawyer.[61] Even more unusually, the defence moved to quash the indictment on the ground that Oregon was not "Indian country," which meant that federal Indian law, including the 1834 act, did not apply. In ruling on the motion, the court began by noting that the act of 1850 appeared to make the 1834 act effective in Oregon only insofar as local circumstances made its various provisions "applicable"—a common statutory provision. The judges therefore decided that whether the earlier act met this test was for them to decide, and they went on to hold that insofar as the liquor prohibition was concerned, Oregon was Indian country.[62] "Defenceless white persons, women and children, who are exposed to violence of drunken savages" were said to need the protection of section 20. Crude as this statement may be, it was all they needed to say to decide the case on its facts.[63]

The court went on to state that although Oregon was "generally supposed to be part of the Indian country named by Congress" in the 1834 act, in fact it was not. Chief Justice George H. Williams explained that in 1834 the United States and Great Britain had jointly occupied Oregon, which stretched from Spanish California in the south to Russian Alaska in the north, so it was not part of the United States at that time. Oregon therefore could not have been subject to the act and was not Indian country.[64] Moreover, he added, "much of the act of 1834 is clearly unsuited to the present condition of the country." How then was one to tell which provisions of federal Indian law applied and which did not? According to the chief justice, "all which tends to prevent immigration [and] the free occupation and use of the country by whites must be considered repealed." The proper test for deciding what portions of the act applied in Oregon was therefore a simple one: "Whatever militates against the true interests of a white population is inapplicable."[65]

This forthright way of putting the matter is remarkable, because these are words that could have been spoken by almost any settler, politician, or land-jobber west of the Rockies whether north or south of forty-nine degrees. They are, however, the words of a federally appointed chief justice. Certainly judges in British colonies might think along similar lines, but they would have had sense enough to disguise it in legal language.[66] So far as the Oregon Supreme Court was concerned, Oregon was not subject to most of the federal Indian laws that applied elsewhere in the United States; and until Congress said otherwise, any law that was not in "the true interests of a white population" was quite simply not law.[67] The *Tom* decision therefore looked very much like a signal to Washington that not only the settlers but their judiciary thought that the Pacific Northwest was special, and that any treaty making that took place there should reflect this.

In 1855 the commissioner of Indian affairs requested U.S. Attorney General Caleb Cushing to respond to *Tom*. Cushing described its reasoning as "strange" and "untenable" and subjected the decision to a lengthy and scathing criticism. Whether the test for applicability was the rights of the white population or their interests, he wrote, the decision violated the United States Constitution because it gave Oregon instead of Congress jurisdiction over commerce with the Indian tribes.[68] The attorney general concluded by stating that "a white settler has the same right . . . to oust the Indians as he has to oust white men, and no more: that is, the right to substitute robbery for purchase, and violence for law."[69] So federal law, in this case the combination of the acts of 1834 and 1850, prevailed. But Chief Justice Williams and his court were not simply rattling their swords: they were telling Congress that it was the Indians, not the whites, who were the trespassers, and they were setting the tone for the new treaties.

What happened to Tom is unclear because once the point about Indian country had been made, his fate was of interest only to him. Because the indictment based on the liquor prohibition in the 1834 act was upheld, there was nothing for the U.S. attorney general to appeal. There was also little if any prospect that Tom, who no doubt was convicted, could find the resources to do so.[70] The Oregon Supreme Court's ruling on Indian country was therefore never reviewed by a higher court. In Oregon it survives only as a particularly unattractive, albeit forthright, curial statement of the *grundnorm* of the settler state. But its spirit clearly informed the new, less generous process that would soon provide substitutes for the failed treaties. The result was warfare, Aboriginal displacement, and defeat.[71]

To take one example, the treaty at Medicine Creek in Washington

Territory forced the Nisqually and Puyallup tribes onto reservations and took away prime farmland. The war that ensued ended in defeat for the tribes and after two trials the conviction of Leschi, a prominent chief, for murder. The first jury could not reach a verdict because two of the jurors concluded that the killing was part of an act of war. Governor Isaac Stevens, to whom history has not been kind, therefore arranged to have the trial moved to a more compliant venue. The second jury convicted.[72] Justice Obadiah B. McFadden, who had participated in the *Tom* decision, wrote the opinion denying the appeal, and Leschi was hanged on February 19, 1858.[73]

Now, James Douglas was not delicate about executions. But neither was he a fan of American Indian policy, the evil effects of which quickly became known to the tribes north of the international boundary.[74] He was particularly opposed to the large-scale removals in the new treaties, and it is likely that the wars in Washington and Oregon helped to persuade him that treaty making of any sort was increasingly ill advised. If so, after 1853 he could look to *Tom* as authority for the proposition that Oregon, which until 1846 included British Columbia, was not Indian country. In other words a man who was already skeptical about treaties might see certain advantages in a decision that legally treaties did not have to be made in the Pacific Northwest unless clearly mandated by a legislature with jurisdiction to do so.

The decision in *United States v. Tom* was of course not a binding precedent north of the border, which was now a completely separate national jurisdiction. Nonetheless, in 1849 the imperial parliament had specifically withdrawn Vancouver Island from the Indian territories,[75] and U.S. law on Indian title was a much more tangible presence in British Columbia than the Royal Proclamation of 1763 or the New Zealand Supreme Court.[76] Another consideration is the notion that the whole coast, from northern California to Alaska, was really a single region ("Cascadia," as some would have it) requiring compatible policies. This sentiment may even have contributed to a decision of Federal District Court judge Matthew P. Deady in the case of the *United States v. Seveloff*, which also involved the sale of liquor to Indians. Sitting in Portland, Deady relied on *Tom* to rule in 1872 that Alaska, too, was not Indian country.[77]

We return to this part of the story in section V, below. For now the point is that the land question in Alaska, like the land question in British

Columbia, was left unaddressed until the 1970s, when a century after *Seveloff* the U.S. Congress passed the Alaska Native Claims Settlement Act.[78] So although the *Tom* decision may have been something of a judicial comet in Oregon, flaming out soon after it appeared, its progeny lived on in Alaska. It is not difficult to see how a British official who was becoming disenchanted with treaty making might find its conclusions comforting.

IV. THE OREGON CONNECTION

Was Douglas comforted? Did he even know about the *Tom* decision? There is reason to believe that he did. He had been a justice of the peace for the Indian Territories since the 1830s, and he had lived and worked in Oregon for nearly twenty years before permanently transferring to Fort Victoria in 1849. During this period he had become increasingly involved in civil governance and with issues regarding land. He also collected newspaper articles, including ones on law, and as early as 1837 he began compiling detailed notes on preemption rights and on various departments of the U.S. government.[79] The HBC and its officers were prominent landowners in Oregon, so it would have been their business to inform themselves in this way, especially when the trickle of land-hungry American pioneers coming over the Oregon Trail became a flood.

President John Tyler sent the first federal Indian agent, Dr. Elijah White, to Oregon in 1842, and Douglas and Chief Factor John McLoughlin supplied White with men, food, and weapons. They also sent along Thomas McKay, McLoughlin's stepson and a man with a formidable reputation among the tribes, as White's escort—a move that gave his initiatives the imprimatur of the HBC.[80] These initiatives consisted primarily of a series of "treaties of amity" to regulate trade and intercourse among the tribes, the HBC, and American economic migrants. The tribes agreed to punish any of their members who violated these treaties, and in return White agreed to pay them compensation for allowing Americans to pass through their territories. He also urged Washington to "save [the Indians] from being forcibly ejected from the lands and graves of their forefathers."[81]

Foremost among White's treaties was the "civil compact" that the HBC had helped him negotiate with the Nez Percé, an arrangement that the Indians viewed as a declaration of good faith on behalf of the whites generally.[82] This impression can only have been strengthened when in 1844 the recently established Oregon provisional government passed "an Act in relation to Indians" stating that "such vacant land as [the Indians] occupy with their villages or other improvements, and such fisheries as they have heretofore used," should be protected.[83] It was this government that Douglas and McLaughlin joined in 1845, after the region north of the Columbia was constituted a separate county. When the Organic Act was passed in 1848 to establish Oregon as a federal territory, it provided that nothing should affect Indian rights "so long as such rights remain unextinguished by treaty between the United States and such Indians." It also extended the Northwest Ordinance of 1787 to Oregon, notably the provision that the "utmost good faith shall always be observed towards the Indians [and] their lands and property shall never be taken away from them without their consent."[84]

Soon after Oregon was divided into counties, Douglas was elected to a three-year term as senior judge of the County Court for Vancouver, the region north of the Columbia that the HBC expected to be confirmed as British. The position involved extensive administrative as well as judicial responsibilities.[85] Douglas therefore would have known that the Indians of the Pacific Northwest expected treaties. He would have known that the provisional government had acknowledged that some sort of legal obligation in this regard existed. And he would have known that the immediate source of this obligation was U.S. federal Indian law. When he settled on Vancouver Island, Douglas learned something else: the Indians there were, if anything, even more jealous of their property rights than those in Oregon.[86]

Douglas's connection with Oregon and Washington did not end when he moved north. He remained in contact with the governors of both territories and with HBC people who had stayed south of the forty-ninth parallel to retire or to manage the company's remaining operations.[87] He also continued to oversee these operations, notably those of the Puget Sound Agricultural Company, an HBC subsidiary. Moreover, others who had been involved with the Oregon provisional government went on to hold the sort of office that he would. Peter H. Burnett, for example, who had been a member of the Oregon legislature and a judge, moved to California and became its first governor. In his gubernatorial message for 1851 he opined that "a war of extermination will continue to be waged between the two races until the Indian race becomes extinct." Burnett regretted this, but felt that it was "beyond the power and wisdom of man to avert."[88] Douglas would have been appalled at such a vision. But what about the suggestion in the *Tom* case that the law of Indian title did not apply in the West as it did in the East?

Even if he had never heard of the Royal Proclamation of 1763, Douglas must have arrived on Vancouver Island in 1849 knowing that U.S. law, which was based on British law and practice, required that Indian title be extinguished. So the instructions he received to purchase the Indian title on Vancouver Island before allowing settlement would not have come as a surprise. But he found negotiating treaties increasingly arduous, and in December 1853 the highest court west of the Rockies proclaimed that treating before settlement was not required unless compelled by statute.[89] A year later, in December 1854, Douglas concluded the treaty at Nanaimo, and even if he did not find *Tom*'s racially based reasoning appealing, it could have encouraged him to think that he was not legally obliged to make any more (see the chronology at the end of this chapter).[90] It would of course have been difficult to refuse to complete the negotiations at Nanaimo: the company wanted the coal and expectations had been raised. But it was his last recognized treaty, and the timing is, to say the least, interesting.

It is true that eight years after the *Tom* decision, Douglas sought imperial funding to make a treaty at Cowichan. As scholars such as Tennant and Harris have pointed out, Douglas was a practical man who sought practical solutions: in 1861 a treaty may have seemed the only option. But he resisted as long as he could. When he realized that he could weather the Cowichan crisis without formalizing these proceedings or paying for the land, the idea was dropped, even though the written and oral records suggest that a treaty of some sort was made. This was seen to be in the interests of the white population at the time, and it set an important precedent—one that Trutch would soon follow.

Douglas could change course like this because of the difference between Oregon and British Columbia in the 1850s and 1860s that we have already noted. Treaty making could not be abandoned in Oregon because there was a federal government in that country that was determined to enforce federal law, however compromised the treaties that resulted might be.[91] Until 1871 there was no such law or federal authority in the British possessions to the north.[92] There was only a distant

Colonial Office that by 1860 had relinquished its management of Indian affairs in Canada and had no intention of assuming real responsibility for such matters in its colonies on the Pacific coast. As a result, there was no Caleb Cushing to tell Douglas that selling land at Cowichan without extinguishing the Indian title was theft. So if Douglas decided that *Tom* was a green light, and that he could permit settlement before extinguishing the Indian title, he would have been correct in thinking that there was really no one to gainsay him. Even if he thought that a generous reservation policy was a fair equivalent, his successors took a rather different view of what "generous" meant. And until union with Canada in 1871, there would be no one to challenge them, either.[93]

There is admittedly no direct evidence that the *Tom* decision played a role in this, or even that Douglas knew about it. But as a former judge and land manager in Oregon, with many sources of information south of the forty-ninth parallel, he must have known. Even if he did not, the American influence was even more important later on, when the last "Douglas treaty" was slipping into history and a different breed of man came to dominate the colonial government.

V. THE SPIRIT OF *TOM*

Joseph William Trutch, viewed by many as the architect of the policy denying Indian title in B.C., lived and worked in Oregon as a young man. The territorial surveyor general, John Bower Preston, had hired Trutch in 1852 as an assistant surveyor, and he was there in 1853 when *Tom* was decided. Trutch was by all accounts a man intent on making the right connections. He soon married Preston's sister-in-law and after several years in Oregon and Illinois he went to B.C., where he displayed a similar determination to prosper. From 1859 to early 1864 he worked as an engineer and surveyor, enjoying a series of lucrative government contracts. He was elected to the Vancouver Island House of Assembly in 1861. Trutch's long and successful public career really began, however, when Douglas, in one of his last official acts, made this former Oregonian B.C.'s commissioner of lands and works in April 1864.

By then Trutch was already a well-connected member of the colonial elite. In 1863 his sister had married Peter O'Reilly, who in 1880 would become B.C.'s Indian reserve commissioner. Trutch's position would be further consolidated in 1870, when his brother John married Zoe Musgrave, the sister of Anthony Musgrave, the governor who shepherded B.C. into confederation with Canada.[94] Trutch was also a friend of Judge Begbie and Attorney General (later Justice) Henry Pering Pellew Crease. More important for present purposes, his many friends and correspondents included Judge Mathew P. Deady of the Oregon District Court, who is important to an understanding of the subsequent career of *Tom*. Deady had been a judge since 1853 and regularly sat on the Ninth Circuit with Circuit Court Judge Lorenzo Sawyer of San Francisco and U.S. Supreme Court Justice Stephen Field. This would be unremarkable were it not for the fact that in 1870 Field's brother, David Dudley Field, became the father-in-law of Governor Musgrave—who was of course also related by marriage to Trutch.[95] Cascadia was a small world.

Trutch's surviving letters to Deady deal mainly with personal and business matters, including letters of introduction for various family members and business associates.[96] Would further research reveal letters that discuss Indian title? Even if it would not, it is clear from legal historian John McLaren's work that Canadian and American judges west of the Rockies consulted one another on other legal matters, notably those affecting the status of the Chinese.[97] Is it not likely that they also discussed the law of Indian title? And came to a common view? Certainly there was no doubt in Trutch's mind that such title was a chimera. As he said in a letter to Prime Minister John A. Macdonald in 1872, just as Canada was embarking on treaty making in the Northwest, British Columbia had never "bought out any Indian claims to land" and to start now would be to "go back of all that has been done here for 30 years past."[98] By the 1880s Begbie, who had once urged Douglas to extinguish the Indian title on the mainland as soon as possible, was adding a judicial gloss to this theme in a decision on Indian title that preceded the case known as *Calder v. AGBC* by nearly a century.

The occasion was the spectacular clash between missionary William Duncan and the Church Missionary Society, and one of the issues was the ownership of two acres of land at Metlakatla. Duncan's supporters relied on Indian title, but in his ruling, Begbie wrote that before reserves are laid out, Indians "have no rights whatever except such as the grace and intelligent benevolence of the Crown may allow." To be sure, British law was never as clear on the point as it might have been. But these sentiments do not sound like the Begbie of 1860.[99]

Whether the *Tom* decision influenced Douglas and his successors or not, the view that treaties were unnecessary prevailed not only in British Columbia but in Alaska, notwithstanding that they were being made east of the Rockies and south of the border in Washington and Oregon. Why? If there is, as we suggest, a legal dimension to this question, the key to answering it is Deady, whose first judicial appointment was to the territorial supreme court when the chief justice of that court was George Williams. Deady did not sit on the bench that decided *Tom*, but he and Williams were friends and "political allies" from the 1850s until Deady's death in 1892.[100] In 1859, when Oregon became a state, President James Buchanan appointed Deady a federal district judge, and in 1864, Williams was elected to the U.S. Senate. In 1872, President Ulysses S. Grant made Williams U.S. attorney general.[101] In that same year, and only two months after Trutch advised Prime Minister Macdonald that it would be to "go back on" all that had been done in B.C. if treaties were made, Deady decided the first of his Alaska "Indian Country" cases.[102]

The facts of *United States v. Seveloff* are basically those of *Tom*.[103] Ferveta Seveloff, a "Sitka Creole," had been charged with selling liquor to "one John Doe, an Indian," and sent south to Portland to be tried by Deady.[104] Because the statute under which Seveloff had been charged was the 1834 Indian Trade and Intercourse Act, the defence made the same objection to the indictment that defence counsel in *Tom* had made, but with more success. Deady acquitted Seveloff and ruled that Alaska —like Oregon—was not part of the United States in 1834 and was therefore not Indian country.[105]

Deady would use *Tom* and what we have called the "spirit" of *Tom* in three more decisions to confirm his conclusion that unless the U.S. Congress explicitly legislated otherwise, Alaska was not Indian country. He did this even after the U.S. Supreme Court ruled in the landmark case of *Ex Parte Crow Dog* that all the territory described in the 1834 act as Indian country "remains Indian country so long as Indians retain their original title to the soil." If that were not clear enough, the Court added that the definition in the 1834 act "now applies to all the country to which the Indian title has not been extinguished within the limits of the United States, even when not within a reservation expressly set apart for the exclusive occupancy of Indians, although much of it has been acquired since the passage of the Act of 1834."[106] Yet, in the case of *Kie v. United States*, Deady suggested that the "anomalous condition of

Alaska was probably not considered by the [Supreme] Court." He ruled that because Russia had not made treaties and the United States had purchased Alaska from the Russians, this act extinguished the Indian title. In other words he stuck to his guns: Alaska was *not* Indian country.[107] Deady's view prevailed: no treaties were made.

The provincial authorities in British Columbia during this period were likewise convinced of the anomalous condition of their province, and they did little to prevent settlers from preempting Indian lands before the reserve commission could allot reserves. They also never tired of asserting B.C.'s uniqueness when Ottawa complained about its heterodox Indian policy.[108] As a consequence, in both Alaska and British Columbia the law of Aboriginal title was suspended. Indeed, the debate about whether the Indian Trade and Intercourse Act of 1834 automatically applied in newly acquired territory such as Oregon and Alaska strikingly resembles the debate in Canada over whether the Royal Proclamation of 1763 "followed the flag" to British Columbia.[109] It is true that dominion politicians and officials often grumbled about the intransigence of the B.C. government and muttered occasionally about making treaties or at least submitting the issue to court. But it in the end the dominion government did neither.[110] Nor did it do what the U.S. Congress had done in Oregon—that is, pass a statute requiring that treaties be made.[111] Canada's fragile confederation was not about to be imperiled over an issue such as Indian title.

The fact is that legally B.C. was surrounded: it had *Tom* to the south of it and *Seveloff* to the north, both stating that in the absence of contrary legislation Cascadia was not Indian country. Thus if we are correct in thinking that the spirit of *Tom* was influential, it seems reasonable to wonder whether B.C.'s rogue Indian policy might represent "the farthest extension of US Indian law into Canada."[112] Certainly the settler population and their representatives were sympathetic to the sort of views expressed by the judges in *Tom*, and insofar as Aboriginal title was concerned, these views became in effect the law of British Columbia for more than a hundred years. As a result, there were no treaties extinguishing the Indian title, and reserve allotments could not be adequately carried out because so much land came into the hands of settlers before the reserve commissioners could act. The question of title was deferred and denied until by the 1990s it could no longer be avoided.

Trutch was a man likely to be attracted by the idea, first expressed in *Tom* and but given important legal force in *Seveloff*, that whatever militated against the interests of a white population could not be law. Did he tell Douglas that land could be sold to settlers without worrying about extinguishing the Indian title? Or did Douglas, who presided over just such a process at Cowichan, reach that conclusion on his own? It would not have been difficult. According to the *Tom* decision, Oregon was not Indian country, and by 1858 not only Vancouver Island but also the mainland had been withdrawn from the "Indian territories" as defined by the imperial parliament.[113] And what did Begbie mean when he said at Douglas's retirement dinner that he had disagreed with the governor "in almost every point of public policy"?[114] Did these disagreements include the fact that in 1860 he had advised Douglas to extinguish the Indian title on the mainland, and this had not been done? If so, Begbie eventually came on side.

In the absence of documentation establishing that colonial authorities were aware of and impressed by cases such as *Tom*, the influence of Oregon law on the premature end of treaty making on Vancouver Island— and its complete absence on the mainland—can only be guessed at. But it seems almost inconceivable that Douglas and Trutch, with their strong Oregon connections, would not have known about these developments. And it is, at the very least, interesting that the last recognized Douglas treaty was signed within a year of the decision in *Tom*, and that by the 1870s, Judge Deady and Lieutenant Governor Trutch were applying similar reasoning to Alaska and British Columbia.

It is certainly true that there were other factors at work. Before the gold rushes the number of settlers in the area was disappointing, and Douglas was always reluctant to buy Indian land too far in advance of settlement because he believed that the Indians would not regard such arrangements as binding. Eventually, it seems, he decided that he did not have to buy the land at all. It may be that this was simply pragmatism. But if this experienced property manager and former county court judge was aware of U.S. federal Indian law and its roots in British law and practice, perhaps he saw in *Tom* an exception that applied in B.C.— whatever the situation might be in Oregon.

Even if *Tom* did not have an immediate effect on Indian policy in B.C., what about later on? In 1872, when Judge Deady invoked the case as a precedent for deciding that Alaska was not Indian country, Ottawa was just discovering that its brand-new province was not about to let reserve allocation interfere with white immigration. Nor would B.C. countenance any revival of the treaty process: Trutch told Macdonald this in 1872, and B.C. politicians kept repeating it until 1990. By 1886, Judge Begbie was even proclaiming in his Metlakatla decision that "no proposition . . . could be more decisively or clearly consistently established than this, that . . . Indians (not being enfranchised) had no rights to the land" other than occupation "at the will of the Crown."[115] He stated that this was also the law in the United States— "whose law is founded on ours." But he declined to cite any U.S. precedents, and counsel for the defendants apparently had fewer than twenty-four hours to prepare.[116] So the decision was hardly a well-considered one.

Brushing aside the contrary opinions of the dominion minister of justice, the governor general, and a prominent local cleric as political and mischievous "all round," Begbie concluded that it was the right of every civilized power . . . to occupy and settle in a country utterly barbarous."[117] The following year, missionary William Duncan and his Tsimshian followers left Metlakatla and moved across the line to establish New Metlakatla in Alaska. Of course, Alaska wasn't "Indian country," either; Deady had seen to that. But there were very few settlers there, and the Americans were prepared to give Duncan the land he wanted.[118] Was Begbie's view of U.S. law influenced by Deady?

The fact is that by the 1870s and 1880s relations between the elites in B.C. and the western United States were even closer than they had been in the 1850s. As we have already argued, Trutch and Deady are key figures. Trutch had been in Oregon when the legal test of "the true interests of a white population" was first promulgated in 1853, and he remained at the center of B.C.'s Indian Land Question until he retired in 1889. He was chief commissioner of lands and works from 1864 until confederation and B.C.'s first lieutenant governor from 1871 to 1876. In 1880 he became the dominion's agent in B.C., with particular responsibility for the railway. Trutch also advised on Indian land matters, kept in touch with Deady, and even influenced the appointment of his brother-in-law, Peter O'Reilly, as Indian reserve commissioner.

For his part, Deady was acquainted with many prominent British Columbians. In 1873 he visited Victoria and met with Dr. William Fraser Tolmie, whom he knew from his Oregon days.[119] In 1880 he decided that it was time to see Alaska, the territory over which his court had exercised jurisdiction since 1868, and on his way he stopped again in Victoria, where he met with Trutch, O'Reilly, and Justice John Hamilton Gray. Deady also went to see coal baron Robert Dunsmuir at Nanaimo before proceeding to Sitka.[120] On the return journey he stopped again, playing billiards at the Union Club with Justice Gray and Chief Justice Begbie and traveling to New Westminster with Trutch. He also went to church with Begbie and watched him play cricket at Beacon Hill Park. Over dinner with Mr. and Mrs. Trutch, who had visited him in Portland in the summer of 1876, Deady and his hosts "went over all the old people of Oregon."[121] He socialized with various other members of B.C.'s ruling elite during this visit, and there was one particularly evocative moment when Deady met Begbie and Justice Henry Pering Pellew Crease at their chambers in the courthouse. As he records in his diary, "I [put] on the latter's gown and wig and sat in the [Chief Justice's] seat and was much complimented on my judicial appearance."[122] He then made at short tour of the interior with Trutch, and visited Victoria at least once more, in 1890, when he met with Trutch and Begbie for what was probably the last time.[123]

Of course, none of this proves a direct link between Deady's jurisprudence and B.C. Indian land policy. People can know each other and share views without conspiring together, particularly when the law of Indian title in British North America was unsettled. Equally, what lawyers and judges believe the law to be may not always be as important as what the public, the media, and government officials think it is, especially when any appeal to higher authority is unlikely. But surely it is not unreasonable to suggest that these men discussed Indian title and commiserated about what they saw as ill-advised federal Indian policy in both their countries.[124] They may not have agreed on everything, but as McLaren has argued in the context of the anti-Chinese discrimination cases, "the commonality of belief and perception" among the B.C. and Oregon judges is striking.[125] Perhaps they also sought a common approach to

Indian title in Alaska and British Columbia, where the turmoil at Metla-katla—and on the Nass and Skeena rivers—could not be contained by a flimsy international border. Old and New Metlakatla are after all only seventy miles apart.

The approach that Begbie and Deady adopted may have sat uneasily with the law laid down elsewhere—most explicitly in U.S. Supreme Court jurisprudence—but it managed to stop just short of openly confronting it. Deady justified his rulings by distinguishing such cases as *Crow Dog*.[126] Begbie simply did not refer to contrary precedent, and his Met-lakatla decision is unreported, even today. Both judges also benefited from the fact that, at least for the time being, the possibility of an appeal with respect to Indian title was slim to nil.[127] And, as B.C.'s confedera-tion debates reveal, by the 1870s there was a marked official reluctance to discuss the details of Indian policy in public, a reluctance that may possibly have contributed to the elusive record on this point.[128] The result, as we have suggested, is that B.C., like Alaska, went its own way.

There is no better illustration of this point than the *Calder* case itself. When it came before the Court of Appeal in 1971, one of the justices made it clear that whatever the law in New Zealand or the United States might be, it was not the law in British Columbia. And another unwit-tingly turned delegate Samuel Thurston's proposition on its head. Not-withstanding the absence of treaties extinguishing Aboriginal title in the province, he said, it was not the settlers but the Indians who in law were trespassers on the soil.[129] Two years later Canada's Supreme Court Jus-tice Emmett Hall described this as "a proposition which reason itself repudiates."[130] But it was nonetheless an accurate summary of a century of law and policy. Had he been aware of *United States v. Tom*, Hall could have added that it was a proposition that found its first judicial expression on the West Coast in 1853.

Until now, the question of why the treaty process ended so prema-turely in British Columbia has been addressed in terms of finances and policy. The role of the law has been neglected or discounted, and most Canadian scholars have proceeded as if the neighbouring U.S. territories and legal developments there are not particularly relevant to what hap-pened in Canada. In this essay we have endeavored to show that they are relevant, and that whether our speculations are close to the mark or not, the need to look beyond Canada's borders in such matters is clear.

1763 The Royal Proclamation (King George III) (United Kingdom)
1787 The Northwest Ordinance (United States)
1818 The Treaty of Joint Occupation (United States and Great Britain)
1834 The Indian Trade and Intercourse Act (United States)
1843 The Oregon Provisional Government is formed, and Fort Victoria is established.
1844 An Act in Relation to Indians (Oregon Provisional Government)
1845 James Douglas is elected to the Vancouver County Court in Oregon.
1846 The Treaty of Washington ends the joint occupation of Oregon.

	Washington, Oregon, Alaska	*Vancouver Island, B.C.*
1848	The Oregon Territory is established.	The colony of Vancouver Island is established.
1850	The U.S. Congress enacts the Donation Act, extends the 1834 act to Oregon, and treaty making begins.	Douglas makes nine treaties.
		Douglas makes two treaties.
1853	Indian wars in Oregon; Washington Territory is carved out of Oregon; *United States v. Tom* is decided.	
1854	Indian wars in Oregon	Last recorded treaty at Nanaimo
1855	Indian wars in Washington and Oregon	
1856	Indian wars in Washington and Oregon	
1858	Indian wars in eastern Washington	The colony of British Columbia is established.
1860		Begbie advises Douglas that Indian title must be extinguished.
1862	The United States purchases Alaska from Russia.	The Cowichan "treaty" is made.
1872	*United States v. Seveloff* (Deady) is decided.	Trutch advises Ottawa that treaties should not be made in British Columbia.
1886	*Kie v. United States* (Deady) is decided.	*AG and Nash v. Tait* (Begbie)

NOTES

This chapter is a slightly modified version of an essay with the same title that first appeared in *BC Studies* in 2003. The 1886 quotation from Missionary William Duncan of Metlakatla is from Peter Murray, *The Devil and Mr. Duncan: A History of the Two Metlakatlas* (Victoria, B.C.: Sono Nis Press 1985), 191.

1. *Statutes of Canada* (SC) 1927, c. 32, s. 149A, which criminalized land claims unless the government approved. See also the Criminal Code offences in *Revised Statutes of Canada* (RSC) 1906, ss.109–10.

2. See, for example, *Calder v. AGBC* (1973), 34 *Dominion Law Reports* (DLR), 3d, 145; *Guerin v. The Queen* [1984] 2 *Supreme Court Reports* (SCR) 335; *R. v. Sparrow* (1990), 56 *Canadian Criminal Cases* (CCC), 3d, 263; and of course *Delgamuukw v. BC* (1997), 153 DLR, 4th, 193.

3. For an early look at this process, see Hamar Foster and Alan Grove, "Looking behind the Masks: A Land Claims Discussion Paper for Researchers, Lawyers, and Their Employers" (1993), 27 *University of British Columbia Law Review* 213.

4. The exception is Treaty 8 in 1899, discussed in Arthur J. Ray, "Treaty 8: A British Columbia Anomaly," *BC Studies* 123 (1999): 5.

5. See Cole Harris's recent and excellent account of this process in *Making Native Space: Colonialism, Resistance, and Reserves in British Columbia* (Vancouver: UBC Press, 2002).

6. Per Justice of Appeal Southin, in *Skeetchestn Indian Band v. British Columbia* (2000), 80 *British Columbia Law Reports* (BCLR), 3d, 233 at 239.

7. See David R. Williams, "The Man for a New Country" (Sidney: Gray's Publishing 1977), 105, comparing Begbie to Douglas, 30 April 1860, *British Columbia Archives and Records Services* (BCARS), microfiche file 142c at 20, with *A. G. and I. B. Nash v. John Tait* (Begbie Bench Books) 8 BCARS (28 October 1886), 446.

8. An early plea for comparative analysis is Earl S. Pomeroy, "Toward a Reorientation of Western History: Continuity and Environment," *Mississippi Valley Historical Review* 41 (March 1955): 579. For the Pacific Northwest see, inter alia, W. J. Trimble, "The Indian Policy of the Colony of British Columbia in Comparison with That of the Adjacent American Territories," *Proceedings of the Mississippi Valley Historical Association* 4 (1913): 11; F. W. Howay, W. N. Sage, and H. F. Angus, *British Columbia and the United States: The North Pacific Slope from the Fur Trade to Aviation* (Toronto: Ryerson Press, 1942); Robin Fisher, "Indian Warfare and Two Frontiers: A Comparison of British Columbia and Washington Territory during the Early Years of Settlement," *Pacific Historical Review* 50 (1981): 31; Barry Gough, "The Indian Policies of Great Britain and the United States in the Pacific Northwest in the Mid-Nineteenth Century," *Canadian Journal of Native Studies* 2, no. 2 (1982): 321; and Hamar Foster, "Law Enforcement in Nineteenth Century British Columbia: A Brief and Comparative Overview" *BC Studies* 63 (1984): 3. But only the last of these deals with the law in any detail.

9. See, inter alia, Harris, *Making Native Space*, 18–19. One confidential Colonial Office memorandum in 1849 stated that "in parting with the land of [Vancouver's] Island, Her Majesty parts only with her own right therein, and . . . whatever measures she was bound to take in order to extinguish the Indian title are equally obligatory on the [Hudson's Bay] Company" (Public Records Office [PRO] [now the National Archives in London], Colonial Office [CO] 305, no. 1, 324–28).

10. In 1851, Douglas also became governor, replacing the unhappy Richard Blanshard, who had discovered that he had little real authority in a colony so dominated by the fur company.

11. Reproduced in *Papers Connected with the Indian Land Question* (1875, Victoria, B.C.: Government Printer; reprint, Victoria: Queen's Printer for British Columbia, 1987) and Dennis Madill, *British Columbia Indian Treaties in Historical Perspective* (Ottawa: Research Branch Corporate Policy, Indian and Northern Affairs Canada, 1981). The southern treaties are discussed in Wilson Duff, "The Fort Victoria Treaties," 3 *BC Studies* (1969): 3–57.

12 For the New Zealand connection see Hamar Foster, "The Saanichton Bay Marina Case: Imperial Law, Colonial History, and Competing Theories of Aboriginal Title" (1989), 23 *University of British Columbia Law Review* 629.

13. See Janet Poth, ed., *Saltwater People, As Told by Dave Elliott Sr.* (Saanich School District 63, 2d ed., 1990), 69–72, and Fisher, "Indian Warfare and Two Frontiers," 39.

14. This promise was soon being systematically violated. See Douglas Harris, *Law, Fish, and Colonialism: The Legal Capture of Salmon in British Columbia* (Toronto: University of Toronto Press, 2001).

15. According to Joseph William Trutch, "portions of the Cowichan Valley were surveyed by Government and sold in 1859" (Enclosure in Musgrave to Granville, 19 January 1870, in *Papers Connected with the Indian Land Question*, at 11 of the supplement).

16. See Douglas to Newcastle, 25 March 1861, ibid., 19, where he states that he had until 1859 "made it a practice . . . to purchase the native rights in the land, in every case, *prior to* the settlement of any district" (emphasis added).

17. Although he advised Newcastle that, except for Cowichan, Chemainus, and Barclay Sound, all of the "settled districts" in the colony had been bought from the Indians, he gives the impression that he is classifying them as settled simply because colonists have gone there. He says nothing about having sold land in those districts before extinguishing the Indian title. See Douglas to Newcastle, ibid. But a decade later Trutch (see note 15, above) let the cat out of the bag.

18. Newcastle to Douglas, 19 October 1861 (see note 16, above), 20 (referring to a petition from the Assembly that Douglas had included in his dispatch). During George Grey's first term as governor of New Zealand, he received more than £73,000 in parliamentary grants-in-aid, primarily to buy Maori land and ensure security. See John Miller, *Early Victorian New Zealand: A Study of Racial Tension and Social Attitudes, 1839–1852* (Oxford: Oxford University Press, 1958), 92. But

this was exceptional: by 1861 the colonial office was in no mood to repeat such largesse on Vancouver Island.

19. Peter Murray, *The Devil and Mr. Duncan: A History of the Two Metlakatlas* (Victoria, B.C.: Sono Nis Press, 1985), 121.

20. See, for example, George Edgar Shankel, "The Development of Indian Policy in British Columbia," Ph.D. dissertation, University of Washington, 1946, 43–45; Robin Fisher, *Contact and Conflict*, 2d ed. (Vancouver: UBC Press, 1992), 153; and Gilbert Malcolm Sproat in an 1876 memorandum to the dominion minister of the interior: BCARS, Add MSS 257, vol. 15, file 15, 34.

21. Paul Tennant, *Aboriginal People and Politics: The Indian Land Question in British Columbia, 1849–1989* (Vancouver: UBC Press, 1990), 23–24.

22. Ibid., 26. Douglas's authority on the mainland—as opposed to the Island, which had a representative assembly—was so ample as to be almost unprecedented, and the colonial office cautioned him not to abuse it. He stepped down as governor after the imperial parliament enacted a new, and less authoritarian, constitution for the colony.

23. Shankel, "Development of Indian Policy in British Columbia," 74.

24. Douglas to Barclay, 3 September 1853, quoted in Madill, *British Columbia Indian Treaties*, 21. Douglas was probably referring to the fact that the Nanaimo people were beginning to appreciate the value of the coal deposits that the company wanted. But he may also have been mindful of feelings aroused by recent executions there. See Hamar Foster, " 'The Queen's Law Is Better Than Yours': International Homicide in British Columbia," in *Essays in the History of Canadian Law: Vol. 5, Crime and Criminal Justice*, edited by Jim Phillips et al. (Toronto: The Osgoode Society, 1994), 41 at 61–63.

25. See also Harris, *Making Native Space*, chapter 2, and note that Douglas had personal reasons for favouring racial equality; see notes 80 and 90, below.

26. Ibid., chapter 1, 15; chapter 2.

27. In 1875 the dominion temporarily suspended B.C.'s land laws because they made no provision for Indian title. See "Report of the Honourable the Minister of Justice, Approved . . . on the 23rd January, 1875," in *Special Committees of the Senate and House of Commons . . . to Inquire into the Claims of the Allied Indian Tribes of British Columbia* (Ottawa: Printed by Order of Parliament at Ottawa by F. A. Acland, printer to the King's Most Excellent Majesty, 1927), Appendix B, 39–44. But Ottawa was never prepared to force the issue.

28. Chapter 4 of Thomas R. Berger, *One Man's Justice* (Vancouver: Douglas & McIntyre 2002), reveals how unclear these matters were prior to the decision in *Regina v. White and Bob* (1965), 52 DLR, 2d, 481 (SCC). Berger was counsel for the defendants. On Douglas's methods see, inter alia, Harris, *Making Native Space*, 25–26 and 43–44.

29. *Papers Connected with the Land Question*, 11, and see Berger, *One Man's Justice*, 93.

30. Duane Thomson, "The Response of Okanagan Indians to European Settle-

ment," *BC Studies* 101 (1994): 96 at 101–2. See also Harris, *Making Native Space*, 344n87.

31. "Memorial to Sir Wilfrid Laurier . . . from the Chiefs of the Shuswap, Okanagan and Couteau Tribes of British Columbia Presented at Kamloops, B.C., August 25, 1910." Chief Bonnie Leonard of the Kamloops Indian band most kindly provided a copy of this document.

32. Foster, "'The Queen's Law Is Better Than Yours,'" and Shankel, "Development of Indian Policy in British Columbia," 47–48, 79. Funds originally earmarked for treaties may have been used to mount these expeditions. In the assembly Dr. William F. Tolmie, an old HBC colleague from Oregon, asserted that the reason Douglas had deferred paying the Cowichan was their conduct, specifically the murder of white men.

33. Petition by the House of Assembly to the Duke of Newcastle in 1861, quoted in "Statement of Facts and Claims on Behalf of the Indians of British Columbia," compiled by J. M. Clark, KC, in 1910, BCARS, NWp 970.5 C593s. This is the petition that Douglas sent to Newcastle (see note 18, above).

34. R.C. Mayne, *Four Years in British Columbia and Vancouver Island* (London: John Murray, 1862), 152. Cowichan oral history is even more emphatic: see Daniel P. Marshall, *Those Who Fell from the Sky: A History of the Cowichan Peoples* (Duncan, British Columbia: Cowichan Tribes, 1999), and Chris Arnett, *The Terror of the Coast* (Burnaby, British Columbia: Talonbooks, 1999).

35. One of the condemned hanged at Nanaimo was Cowichan. For more detail regarding this aspect of Cowichan history, see Arnett, *Terror of the Coast*, and Graham Brazier, "How the Queen's Law Came to Cowichan," *The Beaver* 81, no. 6 (2002): 31.

36. Gilbert Malcolm Sproat, "Rough Memorandum on Cowichan Reserve," February 1878, NAC, RG10, Vol. 3662, File 9756, Pt. 1.

37. *British Colonist*, 22 August 1862, emphasis added. The events at Cowichan in 1862 are also discussed in Hamar Foster, "Letting Go the Bone: The Idea of Indian Title in Nineteenth Century British Columbia," in *Essays in the History of Canadian Law*, Vol. 6: *British Columbia and the Yukon*, edited by Hamar Foster and John McLaren (Toronto: The Osgoode Society 1995), 28 at 44–46.

38. Arnett, *Terror of the Coast*, 104, citing Allan Pritchard, ed., *Vancouver Island Letters of Edmund Hope Verney, 1862–65* (Vancouver: UBC Press, 1996), 82.

39. The new governor was Frederick Seymour, the second since Douglas. William Young, the acting administrator during the transition, advised Seymour in a memorandum dated 19 November 1866 that payment for Cowichan lands should not be delayed "one day longer than is absolutely necessary" because "the faith of the Indian in the white man had been severely tried" (Shankel, "Development of Indian Policy in British Columbia," 80).

40. Remarks of Comiaken chief Soucahlelzup, from notes by Bishop Hills of the "Speeches of Indian Chiefs, Nov. 14th 1866 (about their lands), copy sent to Gov.

Seymour, Dec. 10.66." We are grateful to Mrs. Mavis Gillie for providing us with a copy of these notes from the Anglican Diocesan Archives, Victoria, British Columbia.

41. Enclosure in J. W. Trutch to the acting colonial secretary, 28 August 1867, in *Papers Connected to the Land Question*, 41–43, referring to reserves on the lower Fraser River, at Kamloops and in the Shuswap. See also note 49, below.

42. The Saanich people had received 41.13s. 4d pounds in goods and blankets, marked up 300 percent, as the HBC usually did when selling goods to nonemployees. The real amount was therefore closer to 14 pounds. In applying this markup, Douglas had in mind that the HBC was entitled to be reimbursed for money spent on colonization when its grant expired.

43. *Papers Connected to the Land Question*, at 10 of the supplement, enclosure in Musgrave to Granville, 29 January 1870.

44. See note 36, above.

45. Ibid., quoting Garrett to the surveyor general, 10 March 1865. Garrett was at the Indian Mission in Victoria but visited other locales, including Cowichan: see Frank A. Peake, *The Anglican Church in British Columbia* (Vancouver: Mitchell Press, 1959), 60, 63. The attitude of the *British Colonist* in December 1862 had been that "the Indians have a right to be paid for their lands. If the Government has made any agreement with them they should in honour fulfill it" (quoted in Arnett, *Terror of the Coast*, 97).

46. For New Zealand and U.S. examples of such cases, see *The Queen v. Symonds* (1847), [1840–1932] *New Zealand Privy Council Cases* (NZPCC) 387 (NZSC) and *Johnson v. McIntosh*, 21 U.S. (8 Wheat.) 543 (1823).

47. *The Queen v. Symonds*.

48. See the cases discussed in Hamar Foster, "Forgotten Arguments: Aboriginal Title and Sovereignty in *Canada Jurisdiction Act* Cases" (1992) 21 *Manitoba Law Journal* 343 at 355–63, and the statutes discussed in section III of this essay.

49. Perhaps he thought that these legal principles did not apply in B.C., or that telling the tribes that they could keep whatever land they wanted constituted sufficient compliance. If so, it was a policy that his successors quickly reversed. As a Musqueam chief reported in 1913: "Since these [survey] posts were put down by Sir James Douglas . . . the land has been lessened twice. The Indians were not notified or consulted . . . and after that three persons came . . . and told some of the Indians that the posts . . . meant nothing at all." Quoted in Cole Harris, *The Resettlement of British Columbia* (Vancouver: UBC Press, 1997), 91.

50. Harris, *Making Native Space*, 24, and see also chapters 1 and 3.

51. Lord Carnarvon to Douglas, 11 April 1859, in *Papers Connected with the Indian Land Question*, at 18, emphasis added.

52. See note 7, above.

53. For the background to this treaty, see Norman A. Graebner, "The Northwest Coast in World Diplomacy, 1790–1846," in *The Changing Pacific Northwest: Interpreting the Past*, edited by David H. Stratton and George A. Frykman (Pullman: Washington State University Press, 1988), 3–22.

54. The dominion government was faced with a similar problem after B.C. joined Canada in 1871.

55. The *Oregon Spectator*, 11 July 1850.

56. Section 1 of *An Act to Regulate Trade and Intercourse with the Indian Tribes, etc.* (1834), reproduced in Francis Paul Prucha, ed., *Documents of United States Indian Policy*, 2d ed. (Lincoln: University of Nebraska Press, 1990), 64–68. (Article 1, section 8, clause 3 of the U.S. Constitution assigns authority to regulate commerce with the Indian tribes to Congress.)

57. *An Act Authorizing the Negotiation of Treaties with the Indian Tribes in the Territory of Oregon, for the Extinguishment of Their Claims to the Lands Lying West of the Cascade Mountains, and for Other Purposes* (1850), in Prucha, *Documents of United States Indian Policy*, 80–81.

58. 31st Congress, Sess. I., ch. 76 (1850). Free land in Oregon made the colonization of Vancouver Island even more challenging.

59. S. F. Dicken and E. F. Dicken, *The Making of Oregon: A Study in Historical Geography* (Portland: Oregon Historical Society, 1979), at 18; C. F. Coan, "The First Stage of the Federal Indian Policy in the Pacific Northwest, 1849–52," *Oregon Historical Quarterly* 22 (1921): 55 at 63; Fisher, "Indian Warfare and Two Frontiers," 43; and Cesare Maring, "History of Western Washington since 1846," in *Handbook of North American Indians, Vol. 7: Northwest Coast*, edited by Wayne Suttles (Washington, D.C.: Smithsonian Institution, 1990), 169. A list of the unratified treaties is contained in Stephen Dow Beckham, "History of Western Oregon since 1846," *Handbook of North American Indians*, 181. Notwithstanding his earlier rhetoric, Thurston was instrumental in opposing ratification of these treaties.

60. *United States v. Tom*, 1 Oregon 26 (1853).

61. A few months earlier Siam-a-sit and Squ-eath had been hanged at Nanaimo for murder, and they had no lawyer. There were none on Vancouver Island in 1853.

62. One of the three members of the Oregon Supreme Court who heard the defence motion was somewhat uncomfortable with the broad discretion that he purported to believe the U.S. Congress had conferred upon his court: *United States v. Tom*, at 29, per Justice McFadden.

63. *United States v. Tom*, at 28 and 30, per Chief Justice Williams and Justice McFadden, who added that the law was also necessary to protect the Indians themselves.

64. Technically, Justice McFadden did not actually rule on whether Oregon was Indian country. Although he stated that he doubted that it was, he thought that the question did not need to be decided.

65. *United States v. Tom*, at 27, per Chief Justice Williams.

66. Justice Olney preferred to say that any conflict between federal law and the "*rights* of the whites" had to be resolved in favour of the latter. He stated that in making "the true interests of the white population" the test, the chief justice meant "*his* ideas of what is *expedient* for them" (emphasis in original).

67. For a critique of the reasoning in *United States v. Tom*, see Deborah Niedermeyer, " 'The True Interests of a White Population': The Alaskan Indian Coun-

try Decisions of Judge Mathew P. Deady," *International Law and Politics* 21 (1988): 195–253.

68. Cushing may overstate somewhat here. Although the chief justice did say that Oregon was not Indian country, he did not deny the authority of Congress to so declare; he simply said, rather disingenuously, that they had not done so clearly enough in the acts of 1834 and 1850.

69. Honorable Caleb Cushing to the Secretary of the Interior, 22 June 1855, 7 *Ops. Attorneys General* 293 at 294, 298, 299.

70. In the 1850s the only possible appeal would presumably have been a prohibitively expensive one to the U.S. Supreme Court.

71. See C. F. Coan, "Adoption of the Reservation Policy in the Pacific Northwest, 1853–55," *Oregon Historical Quarterly* 23 (1922): 1–38, and Beckham, "History of Western Oregon since 1846," and Maring, "History of Western Washington since 1846."

72. Remarkably, one of the prosecutors switched to the defence for the second trial: Janice Schuetz, *Episodes in the Rhetoric of Government-Indian Relations* (Westport, Conn.: Praeger Publishers, 2002), chapter 1.

73. *Leschi v. Washington Territory*, 1 *Washington Territory Reports* 13 (1857), reprinted in Book 40 of the *Pacific State Reports*.

74. See Harris, *Making Native Space*, 35, and Fisher, "Indian Warfare and Two Frontiers," 42–43. Douglas's colleague Dr. William F. Tolmie had testified for the defence in the Leschi case, and after the jury's verdict Tolmie unsuccessfully urged the authorities to commute the death sentence.

75. (1849) 12 & 13 Vict., c. 48 (UK). All of what is now B.C. was part of the "Indian territories" pursuant to (1803) 43 George III, c. 138 (UK) and (1821) 1 & 2 George IV, c.66 (UK). The mainland was withdrawn from these territories when it became a Crown colony in 1858: (1858) 21 & 22 Vict., c.99 (UK).

76. Or the theories of such colonial officials as Herman Merivale. See David T. McNab, "Herman Merivale and Colonial Office Indian Policy in the Mid-Nineteenth Century," *Canadian Journal of Native Studies* 1, no. 2 (1981): 277–302, and Harris, *Making Native Space*, 6–9, 13–14.

77. Because Alaska, like Oregon, was not part of the United States in 1834: *United States v. Seveloff*, 27 (Fed. Cas.) 1021. The *Seveloff* case is discussed by Niedermeyer, "'The True Interests of a White Population,'" and Sidney L. Harring, "The Incorporation of Alaskan Natives under American Law: United States and Tlingit Sovereignty, 1867–1900" (1989) 31 *Arizona Law Review* 279 at 284–87. After the United States purchased Alaska in 1867, the military officer sent to govern the new territory was ordered to stop at Victoria and consult with Governor Seymour "with the object of cordial cooperation on our part toward securing" peace between Indians and whites: see Major General H. W. Hallbeck, Headquarters, Military Division of the Pacific, San Francisco, to Lieutenant Colonel R. N. Scott, 3 September 1867, and Lieutenant Colonel R. N. Scott to Governor Seymour, Victoria, B.C., 24 September 1867, both in BCARS, GR 1392, Box, 1, File 3.

78. 43 U.S. Code Annotated (USCA), sections 1601–28 (1971). Because of its

climate and location, there was "little pressure to settle" Alaska until it became a state in 1958 and oil was discovered: David H. Getches and Charles F. Wilkinson, *Cases and Materials on Federal Indian Law*, 2d ed. (St. Paul, Minn.: West Publishing Co., 1986), 775.

79. "James Douglas, Miscellaneous Notes and Clippings, 1837," BCARS, Add. MSS 678, Vol. 2. We are grateful to John Adams, author of *Old Square-Toes and His Lady: The Life of James and Amelia Douglas* (Victoria, B.C.: Horsdal & Shubart, 2001), for providing us with the archival file number for this source.

80. In 1871, Judge Deady ruled that because McKay had been a British subject and his wife was Chinook, his son was not a U.S. citizen and therefore could not vote: *McKay v. Campbell*, 16 Fed. Cas. 161 (Oregon District Court), commented on in Malcolm Clark Jr., *The Diary of Judge Matthew P. Deady 1871–1892: Pharisee among Philistines*, 2 vols. (Portland: Oregon Historical Society, 1975), vol. 1, 115. It may have been the prospect of laws and rulings like this that influenced Douglas's decision to leave Oregon: see note 90, below.

81. See "Elijah White, Sub-Agent Indian Affairs, WRM, Willamette Valley, Oregon to Hon. JM Porter, Secretary of War, Washington, DC," 15 November 1843, reprinted in A. J. Allen, *Ten Years in Oregon: Travels and Adventures of Doctor EJ White and Lady, West of the Rocky Mountains* (Ithaca, N.Y.: 1850), 213–15.

82. Ibid., at 215. However, as one writer has remarked, pacts such as the one with the Nez Percé "were helpful in that they postponed hostilities until the white population had increased." See Ray H. Glassley, *Indian Wars of the Pacific Northwest* (1953; reprint, Portland, Ore.: Binfords & Mort, 1972), 3.

83. "An Act in Relation to Indians," 23 December 1844, cited in Theodore Stern, *Chiefs and Change in the Oregon Country: Indian Relations at Fort Nez Percés, 1818–1855* (Corvallis: Oregon State University Press, 1996), vol. 2, 234. The wording is similar to that of the treaties Douglas began making on Vancouver Island six years later, and probably reflects the views of the Swiss jurist Emer de Vattel, whose writings were especially influential among mid-nineteenth-century colonizers.

84. 9 *U.S. Statutes* 323, cited in Beckham, "History of Western Oregon since 1846," 180.

85. Victor John Town, "Comparison and Contrast of the Territorial Government of Washington and the Colonial Government of British Columbia," M.A. thesis, University of British Columbia, 1940, 38. See also Stern, *Chiefs and Change in the Oregon Country*, vol. 2, 120. By 1846 two HBC men (including Douglas) were county court judges and two (including Tolmie) were members of the legislature. When Oregon was ceded to the United States in 1846, four of its senior elected officials were therefore British subjects.

86. In his dispatch to Newcastle of March 1861 (see note 16, above), Douglas states that "the native Indian population . . . have distinct ideas of property in land . . . and would not fail to regard the occupation [of their lands] by white settlers, unless with the full consent of the proprietary tribes, as national wrongs."

87. Douglas remained quite close to his old boss, John McLoughlin, and in their respective jurisdictions both men became wealthy landowners. On the latter, see

W. R. Sampson, *John McLoughlin's Business Correspondence, 1867–48* (Seattle: University of Washington Press, 1973), and B. B. Baker, *The Financial Papers of Dr. John McLoughlin* (Portland: Oregon Historical Society, 1949).

88. Quoted in Robert F. Heizer and Alan J. Almquist, *The Other Californians: Prejudice and Discrimination under Spain, Mexico, and the United States to 1920* (Berkeley: University of California Press, 1971), 26. Governor Stevens is alleged to have said something similar: see Albert Furtwanger, *Answering Chief Seattle* (Seattle: University of Washington Press, 1997), 113n.

89. In this connection it may be worth noting that the only courts in Vancouver Island in the 1850s were lay magistrates and a superior court with one judge, also a layman, who was Douglas's brother-in-law. But Douglas himself, notwithstanding his occasional protestations that he knew little about law (see, for example, Douglas to Labouchere, *British Parliamentary Papers*, vol. 21, 392), was hardly a neophyte.

90. Douglas would not have found the reasoning attractive because his mother was Creole, and his wife, Amelia, was the daughter of Chief Factor William Connolly and a Cree woman: see *Connolly v. Woolrich and Johnson et al.* (1867), 11 LC Journal 197, and *Johnstone et al. v. Connolly* (1869), 17 *Rapports judiciaires revisés de la Province de Québec* (RJRQ) 266. His children were therefore of mixed blood, and some "half-breeds" as well as Indians were discriminated against in Oregon: see note 80, above. This may be one of the reasons why Douglas's policy provided for equal rights for all. The prohibition against "aborigines" preempting land in B.C. was not enacted until after he retired.

91. See, for example, *Worcester v. Georgia*, 31 U.S. (6 Pet. 515) (1832), which confirmed that the U.S. Constitution conferred exclusive jurisdiction over Indians and their lands upon Congress, and the *Crow Dog* case, discussed in the text accompanying note 106, below.

92. Apart from the Royal Proclamation of 1763, of which Douglas may have been unaware and which appeared on its face to apply only in the East.

93. In fairness, it should be noted that Arthur Kennedy, who succeeded Douglas as governor of Vancouver Island, believed that "the growing difficulties with the Indians would continue to increase as long as the extent of their land was left undefined and their just claims not liquidated." But his bad relations with the elected assembly ensured that he would make little progress on this front, and the assembly demanded instead that the reserves at Cowichan and elsewhere be made available for sale or lease to settlers: see Shankel, "Development of Indian Policy in British Columbia," 75–79.

94. *Dictionary of Canadian Biography*, vol. 13 (Toronto: University of Toronto Press, 1994), 1034.

95. For years the Ninth Circuit was made up of Sawyer, Field, and a district court judge, often Deady: Niedermeyer, "'The True Interests of a White Population,'" 211. See also *Diary of Judge Matthew P. Deady*, vol. 1, 315.

96. In 1883, for example, Deady sent Trutch an article on juries that Trutch promised to give to "our Judges here." He added that he "heartily" concurred with

the views that Deady had "so forcibly expressed" and regretted that he had missed Mrs. Deady when she passed through from Alaska a few days earlier. In another letter he introduces George Preston, a son of Oregon's surveyor general in the 1850s, "whom I am sure you remember." Trutch to Deady, 13 August 1882 and 29 August 1883, Deady, Matthew Paul Papers, MSS 48, Oregon Historical Society Research Library, Portland. The younger Preston's visit is also recorded in Deady's diary, vol. 2, 399–400.

97. See, for example, Begbie to Deady, 18 February 1886, in which Begbie sent Deady a newspaper clipping that showed, as he put it, that he had "been following your example (and indeed citing your authority) for quashing by-laws against Chinamen." This letter is cited in John McLaren, "The Early British Columbia Judges, the Rule of Law, and the 'Chinese Question': The California and Oregon Connection," in *Law for the Elephant, Law for the Beaver: Essays in the Legal History of the North American West*, edited by John McLaren, Hamar Foster, and Chet Orloff (Pasadena, Calif., and Regina, Saskatchewan: Ninth Judicial Circuit Historical Society and Canadian Plains Research Centre, 1992), 237 at 263.

98. Trutch to Macdonald, 14 October 1872, reproduced in Robert E. Cail, *Land, Man, and the Law: The Disposal of Crown Lands in British Columbia, 1871–1913* (Vancouver: UBC Press 1974), 297–99. Thirty years was an exaggeration—and the Douglas treaties, which Trutch dismissed, had been made barely twenty years earlier.

99. See note 7, above.

100. Niedermeyer, "'The True Interests of a White Population,'" 210. Deady did not sit on *Tom* because of "Whig chicanery." A mistake in the documents invalidated his appointment, and Obadiah McFadden took his place. However, when Washington was made a separate territory, McFadden went to that court and Deady was reinstated to the Oregon court: *Diary of Judge Matthew P. Deady*, vol. 1, xxxv.

101. In 1873, President Grant nominated Williams to be chief justice of the U.S. Supreme Court. There were concerns about his qualifications, however, as well as a whiff of scandal, and the president subsequently withdrew the nomination: Sidney Tesier, "The Life of George H. Williams: Almost Chief Justice," *Oregon Historical Quarterly* 47 (1946): 255, and *Diary of Judge Matthew P. Deady*, vol. 1, 142, 155–56.

102. Deady's court had been assigned jurisdiction over Alaska in 1868: Niedermeyer, "'The True Interests of a White Population,'" 210–11. On Deady's judicial record see Ralph James Mooney, "Formalism and Fairness: Matthew Deady and Federal Public Land Law in the Early West," 63 *Washington Law Review* (1988): 317–70, and "Matthew Deady and the Federal Judicial Response to Racism in the Early West," 63 *Oregon Law Review* (1984): 561–637.

103. *United States v. Seveloff* (see note 77, above) was decided on 10 December 1872.

104. A "Creole" in Alaska was a person of mixed Russian and native ancestry: see Harring, "The Incorporation of Alaskan Natives under American Law," 284.

105. There was no statute in force in Alaska comparable to the 1850 law in Oregon, so Deady could not pick and choose which provisions of the 1834 act might apply. Congress subsequently extended the liquor prohibition in the Indian Trade and Intercourse Act to Alaska.

106. 109 U.S. 556 (1883), 561.

107. 27 *Federal Reporter* (F.) 351 (CCD Or. 1886), 353–54. The Alaska court had jurisdiction to try the case under another federal statute, however. For a discussion of *United States v. Kie*, see Harring, "The Incorporation of Alaskan Natives under American Law," 289–93, and Niedermeyer " 'The True Interests of a White Population,' " 241–45. The ramifications of Alaska not being "Indian country" continue today: see David M. Blurton, "*John v. Baker* and the Jurisdiction of Tribal Sovereigns without Territorial Reach" (2003) 20 *Alaska Law Review*, no. 1, 1.

108. As historian and archivist R. E. Gosnell put it, B.C. "had interests which are *sui generis* in a degree greater perhaps than is true of any other province in Canada." See "British Columbia and British International Relations," *Annals of the American Academy of Political and Social Science* 45 (1913): 2, cited in Allan Smith, "The Writing of British Columbia History," in *British Columbia: Historical Readings*, edited by W. Peter Ward and Robert A. J. Macdonald (Vancouver: Douglas & McIntyre, 1981), 10.

109. See, inter alia, *Calder v. A.G.B.C.* and *Delgamuukw* (cited in note 2, above) at trial and in the B.C. Court of Appeal. The latter court was especially clear in *Calder*, reported (1971) at 13 DLR, 3d, 64: the Royal Proclamation of 1763 did not apply because B.C. was after-acquired territory, and in the absence of such legislation, there could be no aboriginal title.

110. See Foster, "Letting Go the Bone," and Hamar Foster, "A Romance of the Lost: Tom MacInnes' Role in the History of the B.C. Indian Land Question," in *Essays in the History of Canadian Law, Vol. 8: In Honour of D.C.B. Risk*, edited by G. B. Baker and J. Phillips (Toronto: Osgoode Society for Canadian Legal History and University of Toronto Press, 1999), 171–212.

111. Although in 1875 it may have come close: see the report of the dominion minister of justice referred to in note 27, above.

112. The phrase is Sid Harring's, in a personal communication to the authors. Professor Harring was kind enough to read and comment on a draft of this essay.

113. See note 75, above, and the accompanying text.

114. Quoted in Williams, "Man for a New Country," 155–56 and 197. As Williams points out, this was a strange remark because the two men not only had similar styles—authoritarian—but in fact agreed on most issues. Begbie may have had too much to drink.

115. *A.G. and I.B. Nash v. John Tait* (see note 7, above).

116. The case was an application for an injunction to restrain Duncan's people from trespassing on land that was claimed by the Church Missionary Society. Begbie had adjourned the proceedings for a day to see if counsel could be obtained for the "poor savages," and although described as appearing for Duncan, Theodore Davie made submissions in support of the defence. Davie did not, however, refer to

the *Symonds* case (see note 47, above): see Jennifer Harry, "What Happened to Sir Matthew Baillie Begbie?" unpublished paper, University of Victoria, Law 362, 1989.

Begbie's failure to cite U.S. authority in support of his view is interesting. If he was aware of such cases as *Tom* and *Seveloff*, was it because they were difficult to reconcile with the leading U.S. Supreme Court decisions? The only legal authority he refers to is the trial court decision in *Regina v. St. Catherine's Milling and Lumber Company* (1885) 10 *Ontario Reports* 196, which had rejected the notion of Indian title and therefore clearly supported Begbie's conclusion. Two years later, however, the Judicial Committee of the Privy Council ruled on appeal that Indian title *is* an interest in land protected by section 109 of the British North America Act, now the Constitution Act, 1867: see [1888] 14 AC 46.

117. The report of the dominion minister of justice that Begbie dismissed as a product of "compulsion of politics" is the report referred to in note 27, above.

118. Accounts of the events leading to Duncan's departure for Alaska may be found in Murray, *Devil and Mr. Duncan*, chapters 15 and 16, and in Jean Usher, *William Duncan of Metlakatla: A Victorian Missionary in British Columbia*, Publications in History, No. 5 (Ottawa: National Museums of Canada, 1974), chapters 6 and 7.

119. *Diary of Judge Matthew P. Deady*, vol. 1, 137–38.

120. Ibid., 309–10. On Dunsmuir's subsequent history with the courts and the issue of Chinese labour in the mines, see Alan Grove and Ross Lambertson, "Pawns of the Powerful: The Politics of Litigation in the Union Colliery Case," *BC Studies* 103 (fall 1994): 3.

121. *Diary of Judge Matthew P. Deady*, 313–15. It seems that the Trutch family also retained property in Oregon: see *Trutch v. Bunnell* (1883) 588, *The Pacific Reporter* 5.

122. *Diary of Judge Matthew P. Deady*, 313.

123. Ibid., 315–18, and vol. 2, 601.

124. Begbie's attitude toward dominion Indian policy may be gleaned from an 1885 decision in which he stated that this policy was one where "every Indian . . . is fed by the eleemosynary daily bounty of the state." He concluded such an approach "may fit a mass of state-fed hereditary paupers educated with habitual idleness," but not "a race of laborious independent workers" such as the Indians of B.C.: quoted in Williams, "Man for a New Country," above note 7, 102. The case was probably *Caskane et al. v. Findlay and McLellan* (BCARS, Begbie Benchbooks, vol. 13, 127), which involved the Songhees Indian reserve in Victoria.

125. McLaren, "Early British Columbia Judges," 244.

126. And his views triumphed, in a way, years later in the U.S. Supreme Court: see *Tee-Hit-Ton Indians v. United States*, 348 U.S. 272 (1955).

127. As Harring ("The Incorporation of Alaskan Natives under American Law," 326) puts it, "none of Deady's [Alaska] rulings was ever appealed to the United States Supreme Court. No Alaska native had either the resources or sufficient confidence in American legal institutions to do so." Indeed, in *Crow Dog's Case: Amer-*

ican Indian Sovereignty, Tribal Law, and United States Law in the Nineteenth Century (Cambridge University Press 1994), 220, Harring suggests that Deady "mooted" his decision in *United States v. Kie* to prevent an appeal by remanding the case to the trial court on the ground that the sentence had been miscalculated.

128. Foster, "Letting Go the Bone," 57–58.

129. (1971), 13 DLR, 3d, 64 at 94 (BCCA), per Justice of Appeal Tysoe: "As a result of [colonial land legislation] the Indians of the Colony of British Columbia became in law trespassers on and liable to ejectment from lands in the Colony other than those set aside as reserves for the use of the Indians."

130. (1973), 34 DLR, 3d, 145 at 217 (SCC).

4 The Boldt Decision in Canada

ABORIGINAL TREATY RIGHTS TO FISH ON THE PACIFIC

Douglas C. Harris

The Oregon Treaty of 1846 established the forty-ninth parallel as the boundary between British and American interests in western North America. Described in treaty text and drawn on a map in a distant capital, this international border severed Aboriginal worlds that at the time were largely oblivious to the remote geopolitical maneuverings of two imperial powers. Eventually the border would constrain the movement of people whose lives spanned it, in some cases restricting or eliminating access to important resource procurement and village sites, and also to markets on its other side.[1] More immediately, after 1846 those to the north of the border negotiated with the British Crown the terms of their coexistence with incoming settlers, those to its south with the United States. As a result, while some of the Coast Salish and Kwak'waka'wakw peoples in what would become British Columbia concluded treaties between 1850 and 1854 with the Crown's representative, James Douglas, the tribes in the United States settled with the governor of the Washington territory, Isaac I. Stevens, in 1854 and 1855.

In the Douglas and the Stevens treaties, as the agreements came to be known, Britain and the United States sought to extinguish Aboriginal rights and title and to replace them with a defined set of treaty rights. These treaty rights included monetary payment and guarantees of reserved land, hunting rights, and fishing rights.[2] The fisheries provisions in the written text of the treaties were short. The Douglas treaties reserved to Aboriginal peoples the right to "their fisheries as formerly";[3] the Stevens treaties provided that "the right of taking fish at usual and accustomed grounds and stations is further secured to said Indians in common with all citizens of the Territory."[4]

This essay focuses on the relationship between U.S. and Canadian judicial interpretations of these treaty rights to fish. In the first two sections the essay describes the rulings in *United States v. Washington* (known as "the Boldt decision")[5] and *Washington v. Washington State Commercial Passenger Fishing Vessel Association* (*Passenger Fishing Vessel*).[6] It then explores the impact of these two cases from the United States on the general development of Aboriginal and treaty rights in Canada. Although not widely cited in Canadian courts, the U.S. decisions have had a profound influence on Canadian Aboriginal law.[7] In particular, the priority that Canadian courts accord to conservation and then to the Aboriginal food fisheries, before commercial and sport fisheries, is closely correlated with the fishing rights framework established in the Boldt decision. In addition, the idea that treaty rights to fish entail a right to a moderate livelihood, now well established in Canada, comes directly from the U.S. Supreme Court's interpretation of the Stevens treaties in *Passenger Fishing Vessel*.

The third part of the essay considers the historical evidence pertaining to fishing rights in the Douglas treaties and suggests various interpretations. Finally, it turns to the Boldt decision and away from *Passenger Fishing Vessel* to offer the outlines of a reasonable judicial determination of treaty rights to fish in British Columbia. The question remains whether these U.S. decisions provide useful guidance for the interpretation of the fishing rights provision in the Douglas treaties. The difference in legal jurisdictions certainly limits their applicability, but Canadian courts are more inclined to consider decisions from other jurisdictions than are their U.S. counterparts. In the area of Aboriginal law Canadian courts frequently refer to U.S. Supreme Court Chief Justice John Marshall's nineteenth-century trilogy and many later Indian and treaty rights cases as well.[8]

Beyond case law, the fact that many fish—including salmon, halibut, and herring—traverse the international boundary suggests that courts should pay some attention to judicial pronouncements from its other side. Moreover, except for the two treaties with the Kwak'waka'wakw at the north end of Vancouver Island, the fisheries covered by the Douglas treaties are in Coast Salish territory, as are the Stevens treaties around Puget Sound. Douglas and Stevens negotiated with peoples who shared a cultural heritage and an economic base in the fisheries that long preceded the Canada-U.S. border in western North America.[9] They also share a broadly similar history of lost access to their fisheries, at least until the Boldt decision.[10] For these reasons, and for the simple fact that the fishing rights under the Stevens treaties have received more legal and scholarly attention than the fishing rights under the Douglas treaties, the U.S. decisions are a relevant and important resource in determining the division and management of the fisheries in British Columbia.

UNITED STATES V. WASHINGTON (THE BOLDT DECISION)

In 1970 the U.S. government and several tribal governments sued the State of Washington for its repeated harassment of Indian fishers and its disregard for the fishing rights in the Stevens treaties. The treaties provided that "the right of taking fish at usual and accustomed grounds and stations is further secured to said Indians in common with all citizens of the Territory."[11] From the advent of an industrial commercial fishery on the Pacific Coast in the last quarter of the nineteenth century, the state, which has jurisdiction over fisheries in state waters, maintained that the treaties did little more than permit tribe members to participate individually in the fisheries on the same terms as the rest of the public. The federal government disagreed. It presented extensive historical and anthropological evidence to the court to establish that although the tribes had ceded land under the treaties, they had reserved to themselves extensive off-reservation fishing rights, including the right to a substantial share of the fish that returned to the tribes' "usual and accustomed" fishing places.[12] Given this divergence of opinion, all the parties understood *U.S. v. Washington* to be an important test case, meant to settle issues unresolved after several earlier judicial interpretations of treaty fishing rights.[13]

The principal rulings in the ensuing decision, released on February 12, 1974, involved the allocation and management of the fisheries. First, Judge George Boldt held that the treaty right to fish "in common" amounted to a right to catch up to 50 percent of the harvestable anadromous fish (salmon and steelhead) at "usual and accustomed" tribal fisheries: "'In common with' means *sharing equally* the opportunity to take fish at 'usual and accustomed grounds and stations'; therefore, non-treaty fishermen shall have the opportunity to take up to 50% of the harvestable number of fish that may be taken by all fishermen at usual and accustomed grounds and stations and treaty right fishermen shall have the opportunity to take up to the same percentage of harvestable fish."[14] By "harvestable" Judge Boldt meant *commercially* harvestable; the fisheries were to be divided equally after accounting for conservation requirements and the needs of the Indian ceremonial and subsistence fishery. Ceremonial and subsistence fishing, he wrote, had "a special treaty significance distinct from and superior to the taking of fish for commercial purposes."[15]

Judge Boldt also held that the tribes had the right to manage their off-reservation fisheries, and he set out the terms under which that responsibility might be assumed. Two tribes—the Quinault and the Yakima—could assume jurisdiction immediately because of their existing fisheries management experience, the others when they had established the capacity to do so. The state had the right to regulate the off-reservation treaty right to fish but only to the extent necessary to ensure the preservation of the species: "The fishing right was reserved by the Indians and cannot be qualified by the state. The state has police power to regulate off reservation fishing *only to the extent reasonable and necessary for conservation of the resource.* For this purpose, conservation is defined to mean perpetuation of the fisheries species. Additionally the state must not discriminate against the Indians, and must meet appropriate due process standards."[16] In other words the treaty right to fish had priority over the state's right to manage the fishery, with the one exception that the state might limit the treaty right in order to preserve and sustain the fisheries. However, the state had to achieve its conservation objectives legitimately and fairly; it could not discriminate against the Indians by imposing conservation burdens so that others might fish.

The Boldt decision outraged many non-Aboriginal fishers, who turned to protest and civil disobedience but also to the state courts.[17] In 1977 the Washington Supreme Court held that Judge Boldt's interpretation of the treaties, by allocating the right to catch up to half of the commercial fisheries to a small proportion of the population (treaty Indians), violated the equal rights protection in the U.S. Constitution.[18] In this context of legal and political turmoil, Judge Boldt assumed continuing oversight of the implementation of his ruling.

Then in 1979, on appeal from the cases in the state courts, the U.S. Supreme Court largely confirmed the Boldt decision. However, in *Passenger Fishing Vessel* the Supreme Court altered the original decision in two ways: it held that the 50 percent allocation was to include the tribal ceremonial and subsistence fishery (rather than calculated after accounting for that fishery) and 50 percent was the maximum allocation (not the minimum). If the ability of tribal members to secure a "moderate living" from the fishery required fewer fish, then the treaty right could be honored with an allocation of less than 50 percent. The Supreme Court offered no legal or historical basis for limiting the right to a level that supported a "moderate livelihood"—a ruling that has not been widely adopted in U.S. Indian treaty interpretation[19] but, according to the Court, was central to the decision:

> The central principle here must be that Indian treaty rights to a natural resource that once was thoroughly and exclusively exploited by the Indians *secures so much as, but no more than, is necessary to provide the Indians with a livelihood—that is to say, a moderate living.* Accordingly, while the maximum possible allocation to the Indians is fixed at 50%, the minimum is not; the latter will . . . be modified in response to changing circumstances. If, for example, a tribe should dwindle to just a few members, or if it should find other sources of support that lead it to abandon its fisheries, a 45% or 50% allocation of an entire run that passes through its customary fishing grounds would be manifestly inappropriate because *the livelihood of the tribe* under these circumstances could not reasonably require an allotment of a large number of fish.[20]

Although measures to implement the treaty rights were contested after the Supreme Court decision, the basic parameters had been established. Under the Stevens treaties Indian tribes had a right to catch up to 50 percent of the harvestable fish at usual and accustomed places in order to secure for their members a "moderate living"; if that could be achieved with fewer fish, then the entitlement would be reduced. Once they had demonstrated the capacity to manage the fisheries, Indian tribes were to assume jurisdiction over their fisheries. The Washington Fisheries and Game departments had the capacity to limit the treaty right, but only for the purpose of ensuring the continuing viability of the resource. Conservation measures could not discriminate against Indians.

FROM THE BOLDT DECISION TO *JACK*, *SPARROW*, *GLADSTONE*, AND *MARSHALL*

Within three weeks after the U.S. Supreme Court's 1979 decision in *Passenger Fishing Vessel*, the Supreme Court of Canada released its decision in *Regina v. Jack*.[21] It was the first foray of that Court into Aboriginal fishing rights in British Columbia, although the members of the Cowichan Tribes who were charged with *Fisheries Act* offenses did not raise an Aboriginal or treaty rights defense. The Cowichan, a Coast Salish community on eastern Vancouver Island, were not party to the Douglas treaties, and the entrenchment of Aboriginal and treaty rights in the Canadian constitution was still three years away.[22] The Cowichan therefore relied on the colonial policy not to interfere with Aboriginal fisheries and on the federal government's commitment in the terms of union with British Columbia, when it assumed responsibility for Indians and fisheries in British Columbia in 1871, that it would continue "a policy as liberal as that hitherto pursued by the British Columbia government" in its management of Indian affairs.[23]

The *Jack* decision turned on the details of Canadian federalism, whereas the Boldt decision involved an interpretation of treaty rights in Washington State. It is hardly surprising therefore that the Supreme Court of Canada did not refer to the U.S. case. However, two basic principles outlined in the Boldt decision—that the government with jurisdiction over the fisheries might limit the exercise of the treaty right to fish only for conservation purposes, and that the Indian food and ceremonial fishery had priority over other fisheries—reappeared in the Canadian decision. The majority dismissed the Cowichan defense, rejecting the argument that the terms of union inhibited or limited Canada's jurisdiction over Aboriginal fisheries. Justice Brian Dickson concurred in the result, although for very different reasons.

Justice Dickson found that "the colony [of British Columbia] *gave priority to the Indian fishery* as an appropriate pursuit for the coastal Indians, primarily for food purposes and, to a lesser extent, for barter purposes with white residents."[24] Therefore, because the federal government assumed responsibility for Indians and fisheries in British

Columbia and undertook to treat the former as liberally as the colonial government had done, it had to recognize the priority of the Indian fisheries. However, this priority was subject to the overriding goal of conservation, and Justice Dickson adopted the following priority scheme: "(i) conservation; (ii) Indian fishing; (iii) non-Indian commercial fishing, or (iv) non-Indian sports fishing." The priority of the Indian fishery, he continued, "is at its strongest when we speak of Indian fishing for food purposes, but somewhat weaker when we come to local commercial purposes. If there are to be limitations upon the taking of salmon here, then those limitations must not bear more heavily upon the Indian fishery than the other forms of the fishery."[25] The proposition that an Indian food fishery had priority and that the federal Department of Fisheries might have to justify its regulation of the Indian fisheries on the basis of conservation were important developments—ones that bore a distinct resemblance to the ruling in the Boldt decision.

Eleven years later the Supreme Court of Canada, then led by Chief Justice Dickson, would develop this priority scheme in *Regina v. Sparrow*, the case that would become the cornerstone in the interpretation of Aboriginal rights in Canada.[26] In *Sparrow* the Court held that the Musqueam, a Coast Salish community at the mouth of the Fraser River and not party to the Douglas treaties, had an "aboriginal right to fish for food and social and ceremonial purposes."[27] Chief Justice Dickson and Justice Gérard La Forest then applied the priority scheme first outlined in *Jack* to infuse the right with content. In practice, the right provided that "if, in a given year, conservation needs required a reduction in the number of fish to be caught such that the number equalled the number required for food by the Indians, then all the fish available after conservation would go to the Indians according to the constitutional nature of their fishing right. If, more realistically, there were still fish after the Indian food requirements were met, then the brunt of conservation measures would be borne by the practices of sport and commercial fishing."[28] Thus, after conservation the Indian food fishery had priority. But conservation was, in the Court's words, a "compelling and substantial" objective that would justify the federal government's infringement of an Aboriginal right to fish.[29] To this extent, the judgment mirrored the Boldt decision without citing it.

However, Canada's Supreme Court went further, suggesting that the federal government might have other objectives, such as the prevention of harm, that might justify infringing an Aboriginal right. The standard was high; the "public interest," for example, was too vague and uncertain an objective to justify limiting a constitutional right.[30] This constraint on the Crown's capacity to infringe Aboriginal and treaty rights marks an important difference between Canadian and U.S. law. While federal power to abrogate Indian treaty rights in the United States is nearly unconstrained,[31] if seldom exercised, in Canada the federal government's capacity to limit Aboriginal and treaty rights has been reduced since those rights were entrenched in the constitution in 1982. As a result, in *Sparrow* the Supreme Court held that the federal government must justify its infringement of an Aboriginal right by establishing a compelling and substantial objective (such as conservation), and that its actions in pursuing that objective reflect the honor of the Crown in its relationship with Aboriginal peoples.[32]

In *Sparrow* the Supreme Court did not address the priority of an Aboriginal right to a commercial fishery. Justice Dickson had hinted in *Jack* that it would be less secure, and the Court confirmed this approach six years later in the case of *Regina v. Gladstone*.[33] In that case Chief Justice Antonio Lamer, writing for the majority, concluded that the Heiltsuk had an Aboriginal right to a commercial herring-spawn-on-kelp fishery. This right, he continued, conferred priority but not exclusivity.[34] As a result, the federal government might justifiably infringe the right to a commercial fishery not only for conservation purposes, but also to pursue policies of "economic and regional fairness" or to recognize "the historical reliance upon, and participation in, the fishery by non-aboriginal groups."[35]

These objectives were too broad for some members of the Court. Justice Beverley McLachlin replied in *Regina v. Vander Peet*, a decision the Supreme Court released with *Gladstone*, that Chief Justice Lamer's test, which required a balancing of social policy objectives against constitutional rights, was "indeterminate and ultimately more political than legal."[36] In rejecting Chief Justice Lamer's approach, Justice McLachlin defined the right to a commercial fishery much less expansively, suggesting that "the Aboriginal right to trade in herring spawn on kelp from the Bella Bella region is limited to such trade as secures *the modern equivalent of sustenance*: the basics of food, clothing and housing, supplemented by a few amenities."[37] Similarly, in her dissenting opinion in *Vander Peet*, Justice Claire L'Heureux-Dubé constructed the commercial fishing right as "an Aboriginal right to sell, trade and barter fish for *liveli-hood, support and sustenance purposes.*"[38] These dissenting opinions defined the right more narrowly and thus avoided Chief Justice Lamer's expansive understanding of what might justify infringing an Aboriginal right. However, the basis for this narrower interpretation is unclear. Chief Justice Lamer responded that "the evidence in this case [*Gladstone*] does not justify limiting the right to harvest herring spawn on kelp on a commercial basis to, for example, the sale of herring spawn on kelp for the purposes of obtaining a 'moderate livelihood.'"[39]

The definitions in the dissenting opinions of Justices McLachlin and L'Heureux-Dubé of Aboriginal rights to commercial fisheries as securing the "modern equivalent of sustenance" or "livelihood, support and sus-tenance" were new developments in the Supreme Court of Canada. They derive from the U.S. Supreme Court's decision in *Passenger Fishing Ves-sel*, although through reference to the dissenting opinion of Justice Doug-las Lambert in the British Columbia Court of Appeal rather than to the U.S. cases themselves. In *Vander Peet* Justice Lambert described the Abo-riginal right to the salmon fishery fish as securing the right to "a mod-erate livelihood" from that fishery, and he acknowledged *Passenger Fishing Vessel* as his source.[40]

In the context of Aboriginal rights, therefore, the right to fish for food is broadly established following *Sparrow*. However, each First Nation must establish the right to a commercial fishery independently. Where established (and to this point only the Heiltsuk in *Gladstone* have suc-cessfully established such a right, and only for their herring spawn-on-kelp fishery), the commercial right is expansive, although subject to broad federal powers to infringe that right. The dissenting approach—to define the rights in terms of a moderate livelihood—has not been adopted.

In the context of treaty rights (as distinct from Aboriginal rights) to fish, however, the moderate livelihood standard is well established in Canada. Again, although the Canadian rulings have not included direct citations, it is plain that this understanding originates in the U.S. Supreme Court's interpretation of the Stevens treaties in *Passenger Fish-ing Vessel*. In *Regina v. Marshall*, for example, the Mi'kmaq of Nova Scotia contested a prosecution on the grounds that they had a treaty right to fish derived from an eighteenth-century agreement with the British. The Supreme Court of Canada agreed in 1999 but limited the commercial right to fish to that which secured the *"equivalent to a moderate livelihood"*; the right did "not extend to the open-ended accumulation of wealth."[41] Justice Ian Binnie, who wrote for the majority, tracked the lineage of the "moderate livelihood" definition of the right from Justice Lambert in the B.C. Court of Appeal to Justices McLachlin and L'Heureux Dubé in *Gladstone* and *Vander Peet*.[42] He did not cite the American antecedents, but their incorporation through Justice Lambert, who dealt with them at length, seems clear.[43]

In sum, the principles articulated in the interpretation of the Stevens treaties are a significant presence in the interpretation of Aboriginal and treaty rights to fish in Canada, even if the U.S. decisions are seldom cited. Given the importance of fishing rights to the articulation of Aboriginal and treaty rights in general, the impact of these principles has been pervasive. With this legal framework established, the question remains how the courts will interpret the fisheries clause in the Douglas treaties. That will turn, at least in part, on the historical evidence.

"FISHERIES AS FORMERLY"

The agreements known as the Douglas treaties are the fourteen land purchases from Aboriginal peoples on Vancouver Island made between 1850 and 1854 by James Douglas, the Hudson's Bay Company's (HBC) chief trader and eventual governor of the colonies of Vancouver Island and mainland British Columbia. They followed the British grant in 1849 of Vancouver Island to the HBC as a proprietary colony for the purposes of settlement. The purchases were limited to the land around the fort at Victoria, the Saanich Peninsula, the future townsite of Nanaimo midway up the island, and land around Fort Rupert near the island's north eastern end. (See map 4.1.) With the exception in 1899 of Treaty 8 covering the northeast corner of British Columbia, the Douglas treaties marked the beginning and the end of a treaty process and of the formal recognition of Aboriginal title in the province until the 1990s.

Much has been written about why Douglas undertook these purchases on Vancouver Island and why he did not continue them. It seems that recognition of a legal requirement to extinguish Aboriginal title was an important part of his motivation for beginning the process, but ebbing enthusiasm for treaties in the Colonial Office in London reduced the incentive to continue the process when other interests intervened.

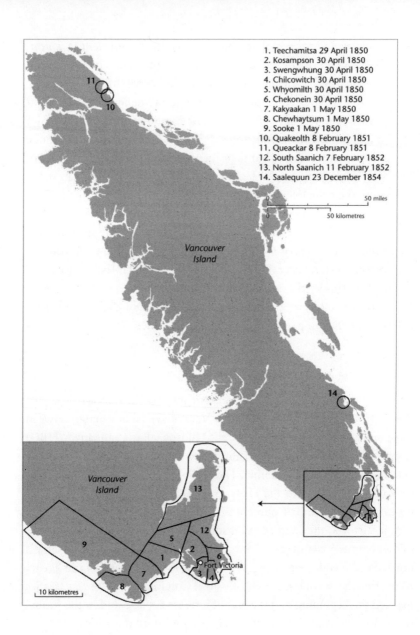

1. Teechamitsa 29 April 1850
2. Kosampson 30 April 1850
3. Swengwhung 30 April 1850
4. Chilcowitch 30 April 1850
5. Whyomilth 30 April 1850
6. Chekonein 30 April 1850
7. Kakyaakan 1 May 1850
8. Chewhaytsum 1 May 1850
9. Sooke 1 May 1850
10. Quakeolth 8 February 1851
11. Queackar 8 February 1851
12. South Saanich 7 February 1852
13. North Saanich 11 February 1852
14. Saalequun 23 December 1854

MAP 4.1 *Boundaries of the Douglas Treaties, 1850–54. The treaty process did not continue beyond 1854, leaving the issue of Native title unresolved on the rest of Vancouver Island and throughout most of the mainland colony of British Columbia.* SOURCE: *The treaty boundaries were adapted from information available in the Government of Canada's Directory of Federal Real Property (http://www.tbs-sct.gc.ca/dfrp-rbif/treaty-traite.asp?Language=EN).*

Historical geographer Cole Harris has emphasized Douglas's pragmatism, born of a lifetime in the fur trade, suggesting that he was less concerned about theories of Indian land policy and even of the law of Aboriginal title than about finding workable solutions for Native and European coexistence.[44] Legal historians Hamar Foster and Alan Grove speculate that the decision of an Oregon court to deny the existence of Aboriginal title, discredited in Oregon and Washington but picked up later in Alaska, may also have influenced Douglas and his successor in the formation of colonial land policy, Commissioner of Lands Joseph Trutch, who was openly hostile to the idea of Aboriginal title.[45]

The legal standing of Aboriginal title may have been fragile enough in the mid-nineteenth century that colonial authorities were prepared to ignore it, but there was less doubt about the existence of specific Aboriginal rights, particularly rights to hunt and fish. Moreover, protecting these rights, on which Aboriginal economies depended, fit Douglas's pragmatism. Aboriginal peoples' hunting could coexist with non-Aboriginal ownership, if not use and occupation, of the land, and the fishery could be secured without much impact on the land available for incoming settlers. In anticipation of the treaties, Douglas wrote to the HBC that he "would strongly recommend, equally as a matter of justice, and from regard to the future peace of the colony, that the Indians Fishere's [sic], Village Sitis [sic] and Fields, should be reserved for their benifit [sic] and fully secured to them by law."[46] HBC secretary Archibald Barclay, in setting out the company's obligations and policy toward Aboriginal peoples on Vancouver Island, instructed Douglas that the "right of fishing and hunting will be continued to them."[47]

On the basis of these instructions, Douglas entered negotiations with the tribes on southern Vancouver Island. After minimal discussions (of which no minutes were kept), Douglas asked the chiefs to place X's on blank sheets of paper. Following the conclusion of the first nine agreements at Fort Victoria between April 29 and May 1, 1850, Douglas wrote to the HBC to explain his understanding of what had transpired: "I informed the natives that they would not be disturbed in the possession of their Village sites and enclosed fields, which are of small extent, and that they were at liberty to hunt over unoccupied lands, and *to carry on their fisheries with the same freedom as when they were the sole occupants of the country*."[48] He forwarded the "signatures" of the chiefs and asked that the HBC supply the proper conveyancing instrument to which the signatures could be attached. Several months later Barclay replied, approving the agreements and sending a template, based on New Zealand precedents, that would become the text of the Douglas treaties.[49] The first paragraph would provide a description of the lands that were covered by the treaty; the second described the terms as follows:

> The condition of or understanding of this sale is this, that our [Indian] village sites and enclosed fields are to be kept for our own use, for the use of our children, and for those who may follow after us; and the land shall be properly surveyed, hereafter. It is understood, however, that the land itself becomes the entire property of the white people for ever; it is also understood that we are at liberty to hunt over the unoccupied lands, and *to carry on our fisheries as formerly*.[50]

Although the structure and content of Barclay's template emulated the New Zealand deeds, the final clause setting out the hunting and fishing rights was new. The guarantee that the tribes were "at liberty . . . to carry on our fisheries as formerly" appears to be an abbreviated version of the agreement Douglas described several months earlier when he wrote that the Native peoples "were at liberty . . . to carry on their fisheries with the same freedom as when they were the sole occupants of the country."

Given this sequence of events, the treaties are best understood as oral agreements between Douglas and the chiefs. The written texts, based on imperial precedent, drafted by someone not present at the negotiations and supplied months afterwards, should be considered as evidence of the terms of those agreements, not as the agreements themselves.[51] As evidence, the written texts probably provide reasonable indication of what the HBC thought it needed to do and of how Douglas understood the treaties. The anthropologist Wilson Duff considered the texts to be "the white man's conception (or at least his rationalization) of the situation as it was and of the transaction that took place."[52] They provide little or highly qualified evidence at best of how the Aboriginal participants understood the agreements and should not be considered the full texts of what were oral agreements. However, given the thin documentary and oral history record surrounding the treaties, the written texts assume particular importance.

Even the terms of the written texts are not self-evident.[53] It is clear, however, that "fisheries" were important parts of the agreements. A "fishery" (or its plural, "fisheries") refers not only to the act of fishing but also to the places where it occurs. In reserving "fisheries," therefore, the Douglas treaties reserved the right to fish in the places where Aboriginal people fished. It was the same approach that Governor Stevens and the tribes in the Washington Territory would adopt in reserving the "right of taking fish at usual and accustomed grounds and stations."[54] In neither case, however, were the boundaries of the right carefully drawn. An abundance of fish was assumed in the 1850s, and there was little non-Aboriginal interest in the fisheries. Even so, the fisheries were not an afterthought. The HBC had deployed some of its workers to the fisheries of the Fraser River in the 1840s but had realized that it was more efficient and effective to purchase fish from Aboriginal fishers. Those fish, which the HBC had been barrelling and salting on the Fraser since the late 1820s, had become one of its principal exports from the Pacific Coast of North America.[55] Thus the treaties were concluded in a context of well-established and ongoing commercial fishing involving the HBC and Aboriginal peoples. Douglas believed that this would continue and hoped it would grow.

There is no evidence that either Douglas or the Aboriginal parties understood their agreements as limited to food fishing. Several years after concluding the last of the treaties, Douglas informed the Vancouver Island House of Assembly that Aboriginal peoples "were to be protected in their original right of fishing on the coast and in the bays of the Colony."[56] In describing the fishing right as "original," Douglas meant that it preceded the British assertion of sovereignty and therefore derived from sources other than the British Crown, not that it was limited to a food fishery. In fact, the category of "Indian food fishing" was not yet a way of thinking about Aboriginal fishing in British Columbia. Established in Canadian fisheries regulations in the late nineteenth century, it would become an important part of fisheries management and an effective way of diminishing Aboriginal peoples access to the fish, but it was not part of the framework in which the treaties were negotiated.[57] Rather, the treaties emerged in the context of a long-established commercial relationship. The parties would have understood that the right to "fisheries as formerly" included a continuing commercial fishery.

How expansive, then, was the understanding of the commercial aspect of the treaty right to fish? At one end of a spectrum of possible mean-ings, the treaty right might have been intended to protect only commerce between Aboriginal peoples. This is not likely. In fact, given the context and the wording of the written text it is highly implausible that the Abo-riginal peoples who participated in the negotiations understood they had conceded anything in respect of their fisheries. Instead, the text suggests that the Aboriginal signatories could continue their fisheries without any non-Aboriginal restriction—that is, "as formerly." At the other end of the spectrum, therefore, the right could be interpreted literally as secur-ing the fisheries exclusively to Aboriginal peoples. When the treaties were concluded, Aboriginal peoples worked and managed the fisheries exclu-sively. Moreover, the laws of many First Nations established certain fish-eries as the exclusive property of one family or house-group.

However, Douglas certainly did not intend to preclude non-Aboriginal fishing. He believed that the long-term prosperity of the colony depended on attracting immigrants and that the fisheries would be one of its prin-cipal draws. The HBC had sought control of the fisheries as part of the Crown grant of Vancouver Island, but the Crown appears to have with-drawn this provision, which was in an early draft, in the midst of wide-spread public disapproval of the HBC in London.[58] As a result, the HBC prospectus for the colonization of Vancouver Island informed prospec-tive settlers that "*every freeholder shall enjoy the right of fishing* all sorts of fish in the seas, bays, and inlets of, or surrounding, the said Island."[59] With respect to tidal waters, then, the prospectus asserted the right of the landowning public to fish as indeed the common law doctrine of the pub-lic right to fish established it for the public at large.

Is it possible to reconcile previously exclusive Aboriginal fisheries with the colonial public's right to fish? In English law the Crown could not limit the public right to fish in tidal waters (except with the sanction of Parliament), but the common law doctrine did not affect exclusive fish-eries that preexisted the British assertion of sovereignty and thus preex-isted the common law in British Columbia.[60] Such preexisting fisheries would include exclusive Aboriginal fisheries. Under Aboriginal law some fisheries were understood as exclusive property, but others were public, at least in the sense that allies and trading partners were welcome to par-ticipate.[61] As a result, where Aboriginal peoples held what they under-stood to be exclusive fishing rights, the Douglas treaties did not interfere with those rights. In fact, the text confirms that existing fisheries were to be protected "as formerly." Where they did not have exclusive fisheries —areas that were understood as public fisheries—the treaties provided the basis for non-Aboriginal participation.

Just as some areas of land under the treaties were to remain for the exclusive use of Aboriginal peoples (village sites and fields), so some Aboriginal fisheries in tidal and nontidal waters were also to remain exclusively for Aboriginal peoples. But whereas most of the land was to be opened for non-Aboriginal settlement and the reserved parcels were small, the opposite was true in the fisheries. The treaties provided expansive protection for the Aboriginal fisheries, with the prospect that non-Aboriginal fishers could participate where they could do so without interfering with these fisheries. Similarly, just as Aboriginal peoples had the right to continue hunting in a manner that did not interfere with non-Aboriginal occupation of lands (the right "to hunt over the unoccupied lands"), so non-Aboriginal fishers had a right to fish so long as they did not hinder the existing Aboriginal fisheries.[62] In sum, the right to "fisheries as formerly" is best understood as protecting the Aboriginal fisheries, including the rights to catch fish and manage the fisheries in the places where they conducted their fishing and the right to dispose of fish for whatever purpose, but also as securing for the Crown the right to grant settler access to fisheries that were not exclusive before the treaties.

This was a satisfactory resolution in the 1850s, when abundance was assumed and there was little prospect that non-Aboriginal fishing would interfere with the Aboriginal fisheries. However, beginning in the 1870s, many Aboriginal fisheries would come under great strain when, with the introduction of an industrial fishery, cannery boats worked by Aboriginal and non-Aboriginal fishers occupied owned fishing grounds, and cannery fleets radically diminished the upriver fisheries on which many Aboriginal peoples relied. At that point the federal Department of Marine and Fisheries largely ignored the existing treaties and the province, with federal acquiescence, refused to negotiate others. Indian Reserve Commissioner Gilbert Malcolm Sproat, while working to allot Indian reserves along the Fraser River as part of an Indian land policy in the absence of treaties, wrote that "if the Crown had ever met the Indians of this Province in council with a view to obtain the surrender of their lands for purposes of settlement, the Indians would in the first place have made stipulations about their rights to get salmon to supply their particular requirements."[63]

Instead of negotiating treaties, the two levels of government imposed an Indian land policy that was premised on continuing Indian access to their fisheries. The small and scattered Indian reserves allotted under treaty or by the reserve commissions were intended primarily to provide points of access to the fisheries that would support viable local economies. Without the fisheries the Indian reserve geography in British Columbia provided little prospect for other commercial activity and made little sense except as a means of clearing Aboriginal peoples from the land.[64] In this context the Aboriginal fisheries ought to have been, in the words of James Douglas, "fully secured to them by law." Those who were parties to the Douglas treaties reasonably believed that they had been.

JUDICIAL INTERPRETATION OF "FISHERIES AS FORMERLY"

As of 2007, Canada's courts had yet to provide a definitive judicial interpretation of the right to "fisheries as formerly" in the Douglas treaties. The British Columbia Court of Appeal's 1989 decision in *Saanichton Marina Ltd. v. Tsawout Indian Band* remained the principal judicial statement of the treaty right to fish.[65] In that case the Tsawout presented evidence that Saanichton Bay, where they and their ancestors lived, "provided a wide variety of fish, shellfish, sea mammals and waterfowl important in the economy and diet of the Saanich people."[66] They claimed a continuing treaty right to fish and argued that a proposed marina development in the bay infringed this right. The court agreed, concluding that "the effect of the treaty is to afford to the Indians an independent source of protection of their right to carry on their fisheries as formerly,"[67] and that in this case the "construction of the marina will derogate from the right of the Indians to carry on their fisheries as formerly in the area of Saanichton Bay which is protected by the treaty."[68] Although the court was not explicit, the decision seemed to imply a right to participate in determining what activities might coexist with their fisheries. In other words the treaty recognized the Tsawout right to access and manage their fisheries.

After that decision the courts struggled to define the treaty right to fish more precisely. It seemed clear that the treaties protect and give priority to a food fishery, a category that was firmly entrenched in Canadian law by then. In *Regina v. Ellsworth*, a case involving charges against a member of the Tsartlip First Nation who was fishing coho and chinook salmon in the Goldstream River for food purposes, Justice Murphy of the British Columbia Supreme Court defined the right broadly to include "fishing, conservation and the use of fish by the Indian people for whatever purpose the fish were used by the signatories to the treaty. One of these purposes was for food obviously."[69] In this view the treaty recognized the priority of the Native fishery, at least but not limited to a food fishery, as well as a right to participate in the conservation or management of the fish stocks.

Justice Harvey Groberman, also of the British Columbia Supreme Court, described a similar set of treaty rights, including priority to the fishery and management rights, in *Snuueymuxw First Nation v. British Columbia*. In that case the Snuueymuxw (Nanaimo) First Nation sought an interlocutory injunction to remove log booms from the Nanaimo River estuary on the basis that they damaged fish habitat and infringed the treaty right to fish. Justice Groberman held: "The contours of the right to 'carry on fisheries as formerly' have not been fully articulated by the courts. The treaty would seem, at the very least, to entitle the First Nation to priority over the fish stocks that exist. It also places responsibilities on the Crown and vests the First Nation with powers to manage the fishery in such a manner as not to jeopardize the constitutionally protected rights of the Douglas Treaty First Nations."[70] The nature of the priority, including the question of whether priority extends to a commercial fishery, remained undeveloped. In *Regina v. Hunt*, Justice Brian Saunderson of the British Columbia Provincial Court held that the treaty right does not include either a commercial fishery or a deep-water fishery because the Kwakiutl had not established, to his satisfaction, that either activity was integral to the distinctive culture of the Kwakiutl.[71]

The Kwakiutl did not appeal Justice Saunderson's decision, but they subsequently brought a treaty fishing rights case on their terms. In *Hunt v. Canada* they sued Canada and the province for a declaration that their treaty right to fish in their territory includes "a priority right to harvest the aquatic resources . . . and to the commercial sale of a reasonable quantity of fish *to meet their livelihood needs*" and "a right to manage and conserve the aquatic resources . . . exercisable together with Canada's power to manage the fishery."[72] These pleadings, which frame the right to a fishery in terms of "livelihood needs," reveal how central that approach has become to the interpretation of treaty fishing rights. The Kwakiutl did not append "moderate" to their claim, but the term "livelihood needs" suggests that they recognize some limit on their treaty right beyond conservation. And rather than claiming jurisdiction over the fisheries, the Kwakiutl sought a declaration of joint management. The pleadings are an indication of what some First Nations believe to be possible within the parameters of Canadian law.

Although the fisheries certainly supported Aboriginal peoples' livelihoods, there is no evidence that the Douglas treaty right was limited to fisheries that supported "moderate" livelihoods. Where this limitation has been imposed, as in *Passenger Fishing Vessel* and *Marshall*, it is a later construct designed to establish some grounds for those without treaty rights to participate in the fishery. Although the aim is legitimate, the "moderate livelihood" standard is flawed. Beyond the fact that there may be no historical evidence for such a standard, it is inherently vague and changeable, and not something that courts are equipped to determine. Moreover, the building of a moderate livelihood, if its meaning can be determined, depends on so much more than access to a resource that it seems peculiar to establish the level of access on the basis of that standard. A clear division of the fisheries along the lines of the Boldt decision, which provides certainty and is broadly if not unanimously perceived as a fair interpretation of the treaty, is eminently preferable to all those working in the fisheries, and to the sustainability of the fisheries themselves.

CONCLUSION

In attempting to account for the Boldt decision, legal scholar Fay Cohen has suggested that by the early 1970s the state of the law on Indian treaty rights to fish was such that "a definitive ruling could hardly have been avoided."[73] Perhaps so. Perhaps thirty years later Aboriginal and treaty rights to fish in British Columbia are at a similar point, and perhaps a case such as *Hunt v. Canada* will provide a definitive ruling. However, unlike Washington State, where most of the tribes hold rights to fish under treaties with virtually identical fisheries provisions, in British Columbia in 2007 there is a patchwork of arrangements that include historical treaties, one modern treaty, two final agreements in the process of ratification, and several agreements-in-principle, all with different fisheries provisions. For most of the province there are no treaty rights but, instead, ill-defined Aboriginal rights to fish or rights to fisheries as an incidence of claimed but not-yet-recognized Aboriginal title. In this context a single definitive ruling seems unlikely. A clear ruling from the courts on the meaning of the fisheries provision in the Douglas treaties will not resolve the continuing conflict over fish, but it might hasten a resolution.

The recognition of Aboriginal and treaty rights to fish in Canada has been building slowly since they were entrenched in the Canadian constitution. Steps to enhance Aboriginal peoples' access to the fisheries, following decisions such as *Sparrow* and *Marshall*, have produced determined opposition from many in the commercial fleet, including court cases based on the proposition that privileging Aboriginal fishers violates the equality guarantee in the Canadian Charter of Rights and Freedoms.[74] In this there are important similarities to the reaction against the Boldt decision in Washington. However, judicial recognition of substantial treaty rights to fish in British Columbia, should it occur, could hardly shock the fishers and fisheries managers in the province to the same degree that it did those in Washington.

Although a small number of Aboriginal peoples are parties to the Douglas treaties, a fuller judicial interpretation of the right to "fisheries as formerly" will be important across the province. It will establish the extent to which the tribes reserved their fisheries to themselves when they granted to the Hudson's Bay Company the right to occupy certain areas of their traditional territories. Understood as reserved rights instead of granted rights (rights that the treaty tribes reserved to themselves rather than received from the Crown), the treaty rights would represent, at a minimum, the fishing rights that nontreaty nations still retain. As a result, the impact of a judicial interpretation of the fisheries clause in the Douglas treaties has the potential to extend across most of the province, building on the basic platform of fishing rights that the Supreme Court of Canada established in the *Sparrow* decision.

Given the continuing conflict over the fisheries in British Columbia and the great difficulty in reaching negotiated settlements, a court-directed interpretation of the fisheries provision in the Douglas treaties seems inevitable. That interpretation, when it occurs, will be based on the text of the treaty and the surrounding circumstances at the time each treaty was negotiated. It is hard to imagine that the interpretation of the

Stevens treaties in Washington State will not also have some impact on the outcome. In a dissenting opinion in the British Columbia Court of Appeal on a commercial fishing rights case, Justice Lambert suggested that the interpretations of the Stevens treaties certainly ought to be considered. He thought it "of great importance to try to achieve harmony between the recognition of aboriginal rights in British Columbia and the recognition of aboriginal rights in Washington State, where the Indians are closely related to the Indians of British Columbia and where they share many of the same customs, traditions, and practices."[75]

The holding in the Boldt decision that access to the commercial fishery should be divided evenly between Aboriginal and non-Aboriginal fishers may not be reproduced. That conclusion is perhaps too closely a product of the particular language in the Stevens treaties. However, the general conclusions that the treaties include rights to a substantial commercial fishery and to manage that fishery seem applicable and appropriate to the interpretation of the Douglas treaties. If a ruling fails to recognize that the treaties protected significant Aboriginal control of the fisheries, it will appear manifestly unjust.

NOTES

I thank Hamar Foster, Alexandra (Sasha) Harmon, Cole Harris, Joseph Taylor, and Michael Thoms for their comments on earlier versions of this essay; Barbara Lane, who served as an expert witness in many of the U.S. and Canadian cases discussed in this chapter, for numerous discussions about the cases and the historical evidence presented in them; Betsy Segal for her research assistance; and Eric Leinberger for drawing map 4.1. Any errors are entirely mine.

1. The Oregon Treaty of 1846, also referred to as the Treaty of Washington, is officially known as the *Treaty with Great Britain, in Regards to Limits Westward of the Rocky Mountains*, United States and United Kingdom, June 15, 1846, 9 *U.S. Statutes* 869. On the role of the border that cut through the middle of Coast Salish territory, see Lissa Wadewitz, "The Nature of Borders: Salmon and Boundaries in the Puget Sound/Georgia Basin," Ph.D. dissertation, University of California, Los Angeles, 2004.

2. The Stevens treaties also included the promise of agricultural and industrial schools, and of a doctor to provide medical care.

3. Copies of the treaties are contained in *Papers Connected with the Indian Land Question, 1850–1875, 1877* (Victoria, B.C.: Queen's Printer, 1987), 5–11.

4. This clause from the Treaty of Medicine Creek (December 26, 1854, 10 *U.S. Statutes* 1132) that Stevens concluded with the Nisqually and Puyallup on Decem-

ber 26, 1854, appears with some slight variations in each of the treaties along the Washington coast: Treaty of Point Elliott (January 22, 1855, 12 *U.S. Statutes* 927); Treaty of Point No Point (January 26, 1855, 12 *U.S. Statutes* 933); Treaty with the Makah (January 31, 1855, 12 *U.S. Statutes* 939); and Treaty of Olympia (July 1, 1855, 12 *U.S. Statutes* 971).

5. *United States v. Washington*, 384 *Federal Supplement* (F. Supp.) 312 (1974) (hereafter *U.S. v. Washington*.

6. *Washington v. Washington State Commercial Passenger Fishing Vessel Association*, 443 U.S. 658 (1979) (hereafter *Passenger Fishing Vessel*).

7. Of the two U.S. decisions, Canadian courts have referred to the Boldt decision more frequently. See *Regina v. Adolph*, [1982] 2 *Canadian Native Law Reporter* (CNLR) 149 (B.C. Prov. Ct.); *Regina v. Sparrow* (1986), 36 *Dominion Law Reports* (DLR) (4th) 246, at paragraphs 75–79, [1987] 1 CNLR 145 (British Columbia Court of Appeal [BCCA]); *Regina v. Vander Peet*, [1993] 5 *Western Weekly Reports* (WWR) 459, at paragraphs 115–17, [1993] 4 CNLR 221 (BCCA); *Regina v. N.T.C. Smokehouse*, [1993] 5 WWR 542, at paragraph 159, [1993] 4 CNLR 158 (BCC.A.); and *Regina v. Jack* (1995), 131 DLR (4th) 165, at paragraph 60, [1996] 2 CNLR 113 (BCCA); and *Kwakiutl Nation v. Canada*, 2006 British Columbia Supreme Court (BCSC) 368, at paragraph 8.

8. Christopher D. Jenkins, "John Marshall's Aboriginal Rights Theory and Its Treatment in Canadian Jurisprudence," (2001), 35 *University of British Columbia Law Review* (UBCLR), 1.

9. Wayne Suttles, "Central Coast Salish," in *The Handbook of North American Indians, Vol. 7: Northwest Coast*, edited by Suttles (Washington, D.C.: Smithsonian Institution, 1990); and Wayne Suttles, *Coast Salish Essays* (Vancouver: Talon Books, 1987).

10. See Daniel L. Boxberger, "Lightning Boldts and Sparrow Wings: A Comparison of Coast Salish Fishing Rights in British Columbia and Washington," *Native Studies Review* 9 (1993–94): 1. Although the history is broadly similar, U.S. courts interpreted the Stevens treaties to provide some protection for Indian fisheries in the late nineteenth and early twentieth centuries. The most important of these early cases is *United States v. Winans*, 198 U.S. 371 (1905). There are no contemporary Canadian counterparts. For histories of the Aboriginal fisheries in Washington State and British Columbia, see Daniel L. Boxberger, *To Fish in Common: The Ethnohistory of Lummi Indian Salmon Fishing* (Seattle: University of Washington Press, 1989; Dianne Newell, *Tangled Webs of History: Indians and the Law in Canada's Pacific Coast Fisheries* (Toronto: University of Toronto Press, 1993); and Douglas C. Harris, *Fish, Law, and Colonialism: The Legal Capture of Salmon in British Columbia* (Toronto: University of Toronto Press, 2001).

11. Treaty of Medicine Creek, Article 3.

12. See Barbara Lane, "Summary of Anthropological Report in *U.S. v. Washington*," expert report submitted at trial, November 30, 1972. Lane also produced individual reports for each tribe involved in the litigation.

13. Some of the immediately preceding decisions include *Puyallup Tribe v.*

Department of Game, 391 U.S. 392 (1968); *Sohappy v. Smith*, 302 F. Supp. 899 (D. Or. 1969) (hereafter, *Sohappy*); and *Department of Game v. Puyallup Tribe*, 414 U.S. 44 (1973). See also Alexandra Harmon, *Indians in the Making: Ethnic Relations and Indian Identities around Puget Sound* (Berkeley: University of California Press, 1998), 227–36.

14. *U.S. v. Washington*, at 343, emphasis in original (citation omitted).

15. Ibid.

16. Ibid., emphasis added. See also *Sohappy*, at 908 (cited in *U.S. v. Washington*, at 346): "It [the state] may use its police power only to the extent necessary to prevent the exercise of that right in a manner that will imperil the continued existence of the fish resource."

17. See Fay G. Cohen, *Treaties on Trial: The Continuing Controversy over Northwest Indian Fishing Rights* (Seattle: University of Washington Press, 1986); and Boxberger, *To Fish in Common*.

18. *Washington State Commercial Passenger Fishing Vessel Ass'n v. Tollefson*, 571 P.2d 1373 (Wash. 1977). See also *Puget Sound Gillnetters Ass'n v. Moos*, 565 P.2d 1151 (Wash. 1977). For commentary see Shannon Bentley, "Indians' Right to Fish: The Background, Impact, and Legacy of *United States v. Washington*," (1992) 17 *American Indian Law Review* 1.

19. See Jack Landau, "Empty Victories: Indian Treaty Fishing Rights in the Pacific Northwest," (1979–1980) 10 *Environmental Law* 413, at 450–52; Dana Johnson, "Native American Treaty Rights to Scarce Natural Resources," (1995–96) 43 *UCLA Law Review* 547.

20. *Passenger Fishing Vessel*, 686–87, emphasis added (citation omitted).

21. *Regina v. Jack* (1979), [1980] 1 Supreme Court Reports (SCR) 294, [1979] 2 CNLR 25 (hereafter, *Jack*).

22. Aboriginal and treaty rights are protected under section 35 of the *Constitution Act, 1982*, being Schedule B to the *Canada Act 1982* (UK), 1982, c.11. Although the Cowichan are not one of the Douglas treaty tribes, Hamar Foster and Alan Grove (in their contribution to this volume, "'Trespassers on the Soil': *United States v. Tom* and a New Perspective on the Short History of Treaty Making in Nineteenth-Century British Columbia") adduce the evidence for an unrecorded treaty with the Cowichan.

23. Under term 13 of the *British Columbia Terms of Union*, RSC, 1985, appendix II, No. 10, the federal government covenanted in 1871 to continue "a policy as liberal as that hitherto pursued by the British Columbia government" toward the Indians in the province. Under the *British North America Act, 1867*, sections 91(12) and 91(24), the federal government assumed responsibility over "Seacoast and Inland Fisheries" and "Indians and Lands Reserved for Indians."

24. *Jack*, at paragraph 37 (emphasis added).

25. *Jack*, at paragraph 43.

26. *Regina v. Sparrow*, [1990] 1 SCR 1075, [1990] CNLR 160 (hereafter, *Sparrow*).

27. Ibid., at paragraph 45.

28. Ibid., at paragraph 78.

29. Ibid., at paragraph 71.

30. Ibid., at paragraph 72.

31. *Lone Wolf v. Hitchcock* 187 U.S. 553 (1903).

32. In recent decisions the Supreme Court of Canada has clarified how the honor of the Crown gives rise to duties to consult with Aboriginal peoples where an infringement occurs and, so far as possible, to accommodate the Aboriginal or treaty rights. For a review of these developments, see Gordon Christie, "Developing Case Law: The Future of Consultation and Accommodation" (2006) 39 UBCLR 139.

33. *Regina v. Gladstone*, [1996] 2 SCR 723, [1996] 4 CNLR 65 (hereafter, *Gladstone*).

34. In *U.S. v. Washington*, at page 401, Justice Boldt wrote: "Neither the Indians nor the non-Indians may fish in a manner so as to destroy the resource or preempt it totally."

35. *Gladstone*, at paragraph 75.

36. *Regina v. Vander Peet*, [1996] 2 SCR 507, at paragraph 302, [1996] 4 CNLR 177 (hereafter, *Vander Peet*).

37. *Gladstone*, at paragraph 165 (emphasis added).

38. *Vander Peet*, at paragraph 221 (emphasis added). In *Regina v. Horseman*, [1990] 1 SCR 901, at paragraphs 8–31, [1990] 3 CNLR 95, Justice Wilson (in dissent) interpreted Treaty 8 and the Natural Resources Transfer Agreement to recognize a right to hunt for "livelihood" purposes as opposed to hunting both for personal consumption only and for commercial purposes.

39. *Gladstone*, at paragraph 57.

40. *Vander Peet* (BCCA), at paragraphs 168–74 (emphasis added).

41. *Regina v. Marshall*, [1999] 3 SCR 456, at paragraph 7 (emphasis added), [1999] 4 CNLR 161 (hereafter, *Marshall*).

42. *Marhsall*, at paragraphs 57–61. In the SCC's ruling on a motion for a rehearing and a stay of decision in *Marshall*, it adopted the expansive justifications for the infringement of Aboriginal rights found in *Gladstone* to the treaty rights context: *Regina v. Marshall*, [1999] 3 SCR 533, at paragraph 41, [1999] 4 CNLR 301.

43. If Canadian courts borrowed the moderate livelihood approach from the U.S. Supreme Court, then it is much less clear where the U.S. Court drew its inspiration. The approach does not appear to rest on historical evidence or established legal doctrine.

44. Cole Harris, *Making Native Space: Colonialism, Resistance, and Reserves in British Columbia* (Vancouver: UBC Press, 2002). See also Paul Tennant, *Aboriginal People and Politics: The Indian Land Question in British Columbia, 1849–1989* (Vancouver: UBC Press, 1990); and Chris Arnett, *The Terror of the Coast: Land Alienation and Colonial War on Vancouver Island and the Gulf Islands, 1849–1863* (Burnaby, B.C.: Talon Books, 1999).

45. Foster and Grove, "Trespassers on the Soil" (in this volume).

46. Hartwell Bowsfield, ed., *Fort Victoria Letters: 1846–1852* (Winnipeg, Manitoba: Hudson's Bay Record Society, 1979), 43, Douglas to Archibald Barclay, HBC Secretary, September 3, 1849.

47. Hudson's Bay Company Archives, A.6/28 fos. 90d-92, Archibald Barclay to James Douglas, December 17, 1849.

48. Bowsfield, *Fort Victoria Letters*, 96, Douglas to A. Barclay, May 16, 1850 (emphasis added).

49. B.C. Archives, AC 20, Vi7 M430, A. Barclay to Douglas, August 16, 1850. On the New Zealand connection and understandings of Native title, see Hamar Foster, "The Saanichton Bay Marina Case: Imperial Law, Colonial History, and Competing Theories of Aboriginal Title," (1989) 23 UBCLR 629.

50. *Papers Connected with the Indian Land Question*, 5–11 (emphasis added).

51. The Supreme Court of Canada appears to have adopted this approach in the hunting rights case of *Regina v. Morris*, 2006 SCC 59, [2007] 1 CNLR 303. Justices Deschamps and Abella (for the majority) wrote: "The Douglas Treaties were the reflections of oral agreements reduced to writing by agents of the Crown" (at paragraph 19). The capitalized "Douglas Treaties" in this sentence appears to refer to the written text, but several paragraphs later Justices Deschamps and Abella wrote: "The oral promises made when the treaty was agreed to are as much a part of the treaty as the written words" (at paragraph 24). For a similar approach to understanding the treaties between the British and the Mi'kmaq, see William C. Wicken, *Mi'Kmaq Treaties on Trial: History, Land, and Donald Marshall Junior* (Toronto: University of Toronto Press, 2002). See also Brian Slattery, "Making Sense of Aboriginal and Treaty Rights" (2000) 79 *Canadian Bar Review* 196, at paragraph 208.

52. Wilson Duff, "The Fort Victoria Treaties," (1969) 3 *BC Studies* 4. See a Tsartlip account of the treaties in David Elliot Sr., *Salt Water People* (Saanich, B.C.: School District No. 63, 1983), 45–50.

53. On the possible meanings of "village sites," for example, see Harris, *Making Native Space*, 25–26.

54. There is some evidence that the Douglas treaties influenced Stevens. He had visited Vancouver Island in 1854 and thought that the emerging land policy, based on small reserves and access to the fisheries, might also work in Washington. Records of the Washington Superintendent of Indian Affairs, roll 1, frame 0100, Stevens to Manypenny, February 1, 1854. Thanks to Sasha Harmon and Kent Richards for bringing this to my attention.

55. See Richard Mackie, *Trading beyond the Mountains: The British Fur Trade on the Pacific, 1763–1843* (Vancouver: UBC Press, 1996).

56. House of Assembly Correspondence Book, August 12, 1856, to July 6, 1859 (Victoria, B.C.: 1918), Douglas to House of Assembly, February 5, 1859.

57. On the construction of an "Indian food fishery," see Douglas C. Harris, *Landing Native Fisheries: Indian Reserves and Fishing Rights in British Columbia, 1849–1925* (Vancouver: UBC Press, 2008), chapter 6.

58. In correspondence over the application of the Reciprocity Treaty with the United States to the inhabitants of Vancouver Island, Herman Merivale (permanent undersecretary of the Colonial Office) wrote that the Crown grant of Vancouver Island to the HBC "not only omits the fisheries, but these were specifically and deliberately omitted." British Columbia Archives (BCA), Colonial Office Cor-

respondence, CO 305/6, 237, Merivale annotations to a letter from E. Hammond to H. Merivale, June 13, 1855.

59. *Prospectus for the Colonization of Vancouver Island* (London, 1849) (emphasis added).

60. Harris, *Landing Native Fisheries*, chapter 4.

61. Harris, *Fish, Law, and Colonialism*, 18–27, 61–65.

62. Historian Michael Thoms has argued that in the treaties of the late eighteenth and early nineteenth centuries in Upper Canada (now southern Ontario), the Ojibwa and the Crown constructed a divided ecology: the Ojibwa secured the lowlands to protect their fisheries; the Crown acquired the right to open the uplands to non-Ojibwa settlers who were interested principally in farming. See Thoms, "Ojibwa Fishing Grounds: A History on Ontario Fisheries Law, Science, and the Sportsmen's Challenge to Ojibwa Treaty Rights, 1650–1900," Ph.D. dissertation, University of British Columbia, 2004.

63. Federal Collection of Minutes of Decision, Correspondence, and Sketches (copy held by Department of Indian Affairs and Northern Development, Vancouver Regional Office), Volume 1, Letterbook No. 2, Joint Indian Reserve Commission to Sproat, March 1878 to January 1879, 193–97, Sproat to E. A. Meredith, July 30, 1878.

64. Harris, *Landing Native Fisheries*.

65. *Saanichton Marina Ltd. v. Tsawout Indian Band* (1989), 57 DLR (4th) 161, [1989] 3 CNLR 46 (BCCA) (hereafter, *Saanichton Marina*). See Foster, "Saanichton Bay Marina." Thanks to Clo Ostrove of Mandell Pinder for providing access to the appeal books in this case.

66. *Saanichton Marina*, at paragraph 7.

67. Ibid., at paragraph 46.

68. Ibid., at paragraph 52.

69. *Regina v. Ellsworth*, [1992] 4 CNLR 89, at paragraph 13, [1992] *British Columbia Weekly Law Digest* 1004.

70. *Snuueymuxw First Nation v. British Columbia* (2004) BCSC 205, 26 *British Columbia Law Reports* (BCLR) (4th) 360, at paragraph 20.

71. *Regina v. Hunt*, [1995] 3 CNLR 135. This test, drawn from an early variant of the test in *Vander Peet* to establish Aboriginal rights to commercial fisheries, has not been adopted to interpret treaty rights.

72. *Hunt v. Canada*, (Vancouver Registry No. S013414), Second Further Amended Statement of Claim (June 30, 2004), 7–8 (emphasis added). This case is slowly working its way toward trial. See *Kwakiutl Nation v. Canada (Attorney General)* (2006) BCSC 1368.

73. Cohen, *Treaties on Trial*, 16.

74. *Regina v. Kapp*, 2006 BCCA 277, 56 BCLR (4th) 11, [2006] CNLR 282, leave to appeal to SCC granted.

75. *Regina v. N.T.C. Smokehouse Ltd.* (1993), 80 BCLR (2nd) 158, [1993] 4 CNLR 158, (BCCA), at paragraph 179.

PART III

INDIGENOUS INTERPRETATIONS
AND RESPONSES

5 Performing Treaties

THE CULTURE AND POLITICS OF TREATY REMEMBRANCE
AND CELEBRATION

Chris Friday

On Martin Luther King Jr. Day in March 1999, three Lummi
Nation representatives sat at a table before an audience of
Whatcom Community College students and faculty in Bellingham, Washington. Salted here and there in the audience were visitors to
the campus,both Indian and non-Indian. The title of the panel, organized
by the college and the Whatcom County Human Rights Task Force, was
"Cultural Genocide: Native Treaty Rights." The elder on the panel,
Lummi Tribal Council member Vernon Lane, spoke first. He highlighted
the consequences of a long history of cultural repression and forced-
assimilation programs foisted on Lummi tribal members and Puget
Sound–area Indians in general. The other panelists—Juanita Jefferson (a
member of the Lummi Nation) and Darrell Hillaire (a member of the
Lummi Indian Business Council)—reinforced Lane's message.

Yet Lane took the discussion of repression further than the others: he
connected it to a history of broken treaty promises. The repression, he
declared, meant that Indians lost sight of the power and import of the
Treaty of Point Elliott until the tribes rediscovered it in the 1950s as an
empowering document. Since then, Lane told the audience, the tribe had
tried to use the treaty, with mixed success, to protect its resource base
and the regional environment. We "hope we can get it beautiful again,"
he explained, by using the treaty provisions to bring an Indian cultural

157

sensibility to bear on land management. He reminded the audience that the Lummi could not do this alone and needed allies: "We need people to support our treaty."[1]

Contrary to what Lane said about lost culture and lost knowledge of the treaty, however, the Lummi and other Indians in the Puget Sound region have a long history of using the so-called Stevens treaties (which include the treaties of Medicine Creek, Point Elliott, and Point No Point) in public forums, much as Lane did in 1999. During the first hundred years of life under the treaties of the 1850s, tribal members articulated their understanding of the treaties multiple times in order to protect reservation lands, secure Indian access to economic resources, and ensure their ability to continue customary practices. To be fair to Lane, one should note that there were transformations over time in how Indians acted upon, or performed, those treaty rights. The fact that Lane came of age in the 1950s might provide a partial explanation for his perspective: treaty performances were undergoing a change in that era. A more complete explanation might also include Lane's possible awareness that the political tactic of playing the victim can have a powerful impact on certain audiences.[2]

By examining the history of Indians performing treaties—that is, publicly articulating and negotiating the meaning and application of treaties —historians can contribute to an assessment of treaties as "transcripts" of power and resistance. Scholars over the past several decades have recognized that oppressed people can and do resist, but that often such resistance is subtle and scarcely recognizable by the oppressors. Culturally coded meanings in everyday speech and songs, as well as petty acts of violence and disobedience, can reveal "hidden transcripts" that are messages commonly understood and recognized within the oppressed group. Sometimes these acts of resistance erupt into the open, and these formerly hidden transcripts become part of a larger public discourse and even rebellion.[3] Treaties, however, were not (and are not) hidden transcripts. Over the past century and a half treaties like that negotiated at Point Elliott have been the very scripts that Indians and non-Indians have employed in a series of contests.[4] An examination of how Puget Sound Indians have used the treaties in public contestations engages a broader discussion of the relationship between power and resistance.

The many Indian performances of treaties also illustrate continuities and innovations in the application of treaty rights. They show how people using "inventive strategies" adapted their portrayals of the treaties to the political, social, and economic contexts of different historical eras.[5] Thus history demonstrates that treaties were and are living documents, not stale artifacts locked in museum cases or legal relics whose modern significance is limited to the narrow confines of ostensible original intent. Public performances or expressions of the meanings that Indians have given to treaties can yield insights into power relationships among Indians, between Indians and the federal government, or between Indians and non-Indians in general. The study of treaty performances is also central to American Indian studies because it concerns the nature and extent of resistance and the meaning of dependency as well as questions of authenticity, identity, and innovation within tradition.[6]

A survey of the ways that Indians of Western Washington have staged public performances of their treaties, especially the Treaty of Point Elliott, is an excellent way to demonstrate these points. In the existing scholarly literature, several authors have described the treaty performances, yet no one has analyzed them as a group, across a long span of time, for the purpose I have described in this essay.[7]

PERFORMANCE AT THE TREATY COUNCIL

Any analysis of the Western Washington treaty councils and the performances surrounding them should begin with recognition that the settler society in 1855 was still weak relative to the large indigenous population, whose basis for understanding events was very different from that of American negotiators. Washington Territory governor Isaac I. Stevens intended the treaties as confirmation of Americans' dominance in Indian-white relations, and he was a man "in a hurry" to prove his fitness for leadership, as Stevens's biographer has maintained.[8] But he could not blithely dictate to assembled Indians because he did not have sufficient power to enforce terms from which Indians expected no benefit. Furthermore, although Stevens had orders to "leave no question open, out of which difficulties may hereafter arise," he did leave a great many details of treaty application open or, at best, implied because the Indians had the power to reject the treaties outright.[9]

Thanks to Indians' relative strength, as the historian Alexandra Harmon has aptly noted, treaty councils in the Puget Sound area were as much ceremonies by and for American Indians as they were occasions for

Stevens to deliver and dictate terms of coexistence to Indians. As early American settlers recognized, Indians gained status in their societies "by hosting feasts and giveaways," often called "potlatches."[10] And most members of the Indian bands, Harmon surmises, "probably expected the treaty councils to have the same kinds of social repercussions as their own potlatches."[11] Later testimony tends to support this inference. In the late 1920s, for example, eighty-five-year-old Puyallup tribe member Lucy Gurand said her family members had understood at the treaty councils that "the Government [was] giving them free gift of some goods."[12] Sixty-eight-year-old Augustus Kautz, also Puyallup, made the comparison with traditional giveaways more explicit. In recounting a meeting that likely took place not long after the treaty, he explained: "My mother tells me of coming from the Nisqually to the mouth of the Puyallup River to what they called the potlatch of the Government— they called it a potlatch—she got a piece of calico."[13]

Students of the treaty negotiations have had to rely primarily on minutes kept by Isaac Stevens's associates at the councils and, as anthropologist Barbara Lane and coresearcher Robert Brockstedt Lane have argued, those are only "a partial record of what happened."[14] Still, a careful examination of the minutes and other sources, contemporary and subsequent to the treaty, provides evidence of Indian perspectives. Much care must be taken with such a reconstruction, but it is possible to infer some aspects of Indian understanding that are necessary for a satisfactory analysis of those events. In particular, a close look at the negotiators' recorded speeches and their context reveals that the treaty council was an important moment for specific Indian individuals to enhance their power or status. Indian performances at the time said as much about power relationships among Indians as about the relationship between Indians and whites.

Instead of focusing solely on the iconic and misunderstood man named Seattle or Sealth, whom Stevens anointed as "principal chief" for Indians at the Point Elliott council, it pays to look at other "players" in the treaty negotiations. Consider Chowitsut (also known as Chowitshoot), for example. Identified on the Treaty of Point Elliott itself as "Chief of the Lummi and other tribes," Chowitsut was one of the four major chiefs at the council and one of fourteen men who signed the treaty on behalf of the Lummi and related bands in northwest interior Washington.[15] He was the lone Lummi to give a recorded speech. The minutes indicate only that he said: "I work on the ground (raise pota-toes) and build houses. But I will stop building if you wish and move to Chah-chou-sen."[16] A deeper meaning of this seemingly simple statement is apparent when one reconstructs the context in which it was spoken.

The treaty tribe called Lummi was a group of loosely affiliated bands and complex lineages linked by marriages and grouped around various headmen who established large, multifamily houses in portions of the San Juan Islands and the Bellingham Bay area.[17] Between 1780 and 1830 or so, the growing fur trade, deaths from diseases introduced by Europeans, and increased conflict with northern raiding tribes (most likely Haida or Tlingit, but possibly also Kwakwaka'wakw, also known as Kwakiutl), forced Coast Salish peoples like the Lummi to consolidate and sometimes fortify their villages. While the Lummi continued to move seasonally to camps and villages throughout the San Juan and Southern Gulf islands, on Vancouver Island, and at mainland sites on both sides of what would become the U.S.-Canada border, the Lummi Peninsula increasingly emerged as a central geographical focus of group life, with several of the larger seasonal encampments and winter villages located there.[18]

By 1850 one of the major settlements consisted of the large (four-hundred-feet-long) multifamily house built by the emerging headman Chowitsut at a place known as "The Portage" on the tip of the penin-sula. (Chowitsut had also sponsored the building of houses at other, lesser sites.[19]) Longstanding Lummi custom meant that house construc-tion, which was a cooperative endeavor, resulted both in private own-ership and land occupancy rights for the sponsor of a lodge and in a sense of collective ownership on the part of those who contributed labor and materials.[20] It was clear, however, that Chowitsut was a leading fig-ure among the Lummi, thanks to his immense wealth, social as well as economic.[21]

In 1852 and 1853, when land speculators and entrepreneurs Henry Roeder and J. E. Peabody sailed into Bellingham Bay seeking a location with the timber and falling water needed to operate a lumber mill, they found Chowitsut waiting for them.[22] Later accounts hold that Roeder and Peabody traveled to the large Lummi village at The Portage—a site on the mainland between Portage Island and the southwestern tip of the Lummi Peninsula. There, according to early local chronicler Lottie Roeder Roth, "Chief Chowitsut not only gave them the Falls and the land surrounding it, but promised to send some of his men to help raise the mill."²³ A different reading of events in context suggests Roeder understood that Chowitsut simply "invited" him to stay in the area as a "guest."

More recent Indian oral accounts support the interpretation that Chowitsut hoped to incorporate members of the Roeder and Peabody mill community into the political economy of the immediate area. The establishment of European American activities in Lummi territory would give him access to trade goods and resources previously available only through trade with the British at Fort Langley to the north or Victoria to the southwest. Chowitsut may also have calculated the value that Roeder and Peabody offered as allies against Indians from the northern coastal stretches of British Columbia, who periodically raided Coast Salish villages and encampments, including those of the Lummi.²⁴ Furthermore, given the calculus of house-building among Coast Salish peoples, Chowitsut must have figured that the contribution of Lummi labor gave him at least a partial interest in the mill that Roeder and Peabody erected, notwithstanding notions of property held by the two Americans.²⁵

Chowitsut's activities in regional politics and diplomacy during the early and mid-1850s provide additional evidence of his growing power and ambition. At roughly the same time as the Point Elliott Treaty negotiations, Chowitsut acted as an intermediary in the diplomatic marriage between early Bellingham Bay settler Edmund C. Fitzhugh and the "Samish noblewoman" E-yow-alth. E-yow-alth was the daughter of the headman S'ya-whom (Sihome), who lived across Bellingham Bay from the Lummi Peninsula and himself had married in an alliance with a S'Klallam family.²⁶ Such diplomatic relations were not new to Chowitsut. On February 11, 1852, he had signed the South Saanich Treaty on Vancouver Island as one of 118 individuals. That treaty was the eleventh of fourteen negotiated from 1850 to 1854 between First Nations peoples and Sir James Douglas, then chief factor of the Hudson's Bay Company and governor of the British colony.²⁷ Exactly how and why Chowitsut came to be involved in that treaty remains unclear. Saanich bands like the Pacquachin and the Tseycum shared fishing sites and camps near Point Roberts (particularly rich fishing grounds for sockeye salmon migrating to the Fraser River). It is likely that Chowitsut's ties to the Saanich came through such contacts. The frequency of contact and fluidity of movement among Salish peoples in the area meant that a host of complex lineage affiliations and other ties linked them together.[28] Chowitsut's signing of the Saanich treaty is thus intriguing but not surprising.

It is no wonder then that early in 1854 the powerful Chowitsut made certain to meet with Governor Stevens when the latter toured the region to visit tribal leaders before negotiating the treaties. According to Lummi oral history, Stevens and Chowitsut went together to the bluff near the mouth of the Nooksack River and Chowitsut "stood . . . with his arms outstretched (one toward Lummi [or Portage] Island and one toward Cherry Point) [while] he explained to Stevens that that was the territory the Lummi desired for their reservation."[29] By the time Chowitsut traveled to the Point Elliott Treaty Council in late January 1855, he surely had his own understanding of what the treaty would mean for him. His involvement in the council was part of a long-term and ongoing effort on his part to consolidate his influence or prestige, and the treaty speech and signing was his public proclamation of the advantageous arrangements he had already made. Chowitsut's willingness to "stop building" in places other than the Lummi Peninsula, where the reservation was to be located, was not simply an act of submission to the Americans. It also confirmed that he had consolidated considerable personal power. By standing at the council and delivering that short speech, he was able to solidify the social status he had already attained among Indians. His household would be one of the two principal village sites on the reservation designated for Lummis, and it would remain so until after his death and the establishment of a new "Lummi village" near the mouth of the Nooksack River in 1861. (The latter settlement coalesced around another headman who rose to power with Chowitsut's passing.)

Chowitsut's speech and subsequent treaty signing was therefore not merely some resignation to a lesser evil, nor was it clearly and singularly a concession to an inevitable European American dominance. Although Chowitsut could not fully redefine the "rules of engagement," he did use the treaty negotiations to perform and potentially enhance his social rank and status. Thus close examination of circumstances behind an Indian treaty oration helps us begin to fathom how individuals and bands used the treaties as prospective opportunities in specific historical moments.[30]

Except for the Treaty of Medicine Creek—the first of the treaties negotiated by Isaac Stevens—treaties with Indians around the Puget Sound did not enjoy immediate ratification by the U.S. Congress. In the period between the negotiation of the Treaty of Point Elliott on January 22, 1855, and ratification on March 8, 1859, Indians of the region grew increasingly unhappy with the delay.[31] In May of 1858 the local superintendent of Indian affairs, M. T. Simmons, met with tribes to mollify their discontent by distributing gifts and hearing their complaints regarding the Senate's failure to ratify the treaties. In each of these meetings, hundreds of people gathered and witnessed Simmons's attempt to communicate federal goodwill to Native leaders, who responded with forthright calls for ratification. At Fort Kitsap, Simmons met with some four hundred people, including Chief Seattle, who vividly described his people's illness and poverty and then asked: "Why don't our papers come back? . . . I fear we are forgotten, or that we are to be cheated out of our land. . . . I should like to be paid for my land before I die."[32] Pushing harder, Chief Seattle pointed out that his people "were ashamed" that the parties to the only treaty yet ratified, the Nisqually and Puyallup, had risen up in open, armed rebellion against American settlers. Why, he asked, do "the Puyallups have their papers . . . , while we . . . get nothing?"[33]

Headmen in other parts of the Puget Sound not only adopted a rhetorical and oratorical strategy similar to Seattle's but also hit the same themes: the federal government had been dishonest, Indian reserved lands were in jeopardy, they should be compensated for ceded lands, and they were bitterly frustrated to see the Puyallup and Nisqually rewarded for rebellion with a ratified treaty and the protected land base and annuities that it promised. For example, Hetley Kanim of the Snoqualamie asked Simmons in front of nearly 750 people when the "Great Father" was "going to send our papers back? Four summers have now passed since you and Governor Stevens told us we would get pay for our land. . . . [O]ur hearts are very sick because you do not do as you promised. We saw the Nisqually and Puyallups get their annuity paid them last year, and our hearts were sick because we could get nothing."[34]

Kanim was interested in how he might use the treaties as more than just paper acknowledgments of Indians' rights and promises of money.

He wanted the treaty provisions to preserve and extend his people's economic base: "We consider it good to have white people among us. Our young women can gather berries and clams, and our young men can fish and hunt, and sell what they get to the whites. We are willing that the whites shall take the timber, but we want the game and fish, and want our reserves where there is plenty of deer and fish, and good land for potatoes."[35] Kanim believed the treaties could provide the basis for a robust economic strategy so that Puget Sound Indians could expand their role in the region's newly emerging economic order.

When considered in light of the fact that Puget Sound Indians' economic strategy combined traditional subsistence activities with economic pursuits made possible by non-Indian settlement, the 1858 performances by Seattle and Kanim, along with other similar evidence, confirm that Indians used such moments of public discourse to push for the ratification of treaties because they believed the documents could provide leverage for a broad community good; they could be more than a defense against non-Indian encroachments. In this respect the treaties were "offensive" weaponry. The chiefs' calls for their "papers" to be sent back also show that they were cognizant of the stock Americans put in written records of their promises. Indian leaders were comfortable enough with the power and meaning of written documents to use them to their advantage. Orality and the written words were therefore not mutually exclusive; both modes of communication had meaning within their communities as well as in their relations with non-Indians.

PERFORMING THE TREATY'S PURPOSE

By spring of 1859 the Treaty of Point Elliott and Treaty of Point No Point had been ratified in the U.S. Senate. During the 1860s and early 1870s executive orders clarified and modified boundaries of the treaty reservations and established some additional reservations.[36] For the most part Indians who settled on the reservations and federal officials assigned to oversee them spent much of the 1860s absorbed with the details of administering those enclaves. They also witnessed the emergence of new leaders alongside the older generation of headmen, many of whom had signed the treaties.

By the early 1870s uncertainty about how the reservations would be administered and the treaty provisions carried out came to a head when railroad construction threatened the integrity of reservation lands. Records of a visit to the Puget Sound by the chairman of the influential Board of Indian Commissioners Affairs, Felix R. Brunot, illustrate how Indians took what federal representatives hoped to accomplish and bent it to their own ends. In 1871, Brunot held a series of special councils at select reservations in Oregon and Washington Territory, including the Lummi Reservation. Heading the agenda was a potential survey of the reservations and the possibility of consolidating several reservations.[37] Brunot preached about the desirability of "civilization" and the problems that arose when Indians continued with their "wild ways." His was a program of racial uplift and assimilation that required Indians to become "civilized" (but not white) by taking up agriculture, individual land ownership, and Christianity.

While Brunot recited his prepared lines at each stop on his tour with remarkable consistency, he ran into Indian leaders who did not hesitate to tell him what they believed the treaties meant. At the Lummi Reservation, for example, the headmen who had succeeded Chowitsut were quite forceful. They made it clear that they wanted precise boundaries for the reservation, they must have access to tools and supplies in order to succeed in the new market agriculture economy, the treaty was central to their remaining self-sufficient, and the treaty required an ongoing commitment from the federal government to preserve reservation lands and the reservation economy for future generations.

David Crockett was the most vocal of the Lummi speakers. Crockett was a "traditional" headman as well as Catholic lay leader in the community. His role in helping build the Catholic church at the Lummi Village was comparable to the power embodied in Chowitsut's house at The Portage. At the meeting with Brunot, Crockett told the assembled crowd:

> I know what Governor Stevens said when the treaty was made; half the Indians put a wrong construction on it, and it fooled them. Governor Stevens gave us to understand that we were to have half of all this country, and the whites the other half. We thought the reservation took in both sides of the river, but then the surveyor changed the boundary from what we thought it was. I want you to assist us in defining the boundary line of the reservation, so that the whites and others will know just where it is, and there may never be any trouble about it. My people are increasing in number, and we want

much land for them, and we want the line so fixed that the whites will not encroach on us, and our children may inherit the land. . . . I want my people to be like white men, have cattle and horses, and imitate the good whites . . . ; all I want is this land secured to my children, and the implements necessary to cultivate it, that my children may cultivate it when I am dead. This is all that is on my mind; that my children may have a home after I am dead. . . . [W]e want the reservation surveyed . . . that all may have lands, and know what is theirs.[38]

At the same meeting Crockett also explained that the first agent assigned to the reservation had "furnished lumber for the buildings on the reservation, of which we are proud" along with "cattle . . . , two horses and a wagon; also plows, oxen, and yokes." Crockett's role in the acquisition and distribution of such items, implied in his statement, would have helped consolidate his social status within the tribe. Although it seemed that "we got all that belonged to us at the time" of the treaty, Crockett said, it had been a number of years since anything more had come to the tribe. Those early gifts, he urged, "are becoming old and worn out; the wagon is old and not fit for much service; it is the same with the plows and the tools."[39] He also explained to Brunot that even more of the reservation land could be opened for cultivation if Lummi had the means to dike and drain the marshlands. Of the land near Old Lummi Village, Crockett stated that it "overflows, and we cannot cultivate it; if we had tools we would ditch it, and have much good land."[40] Without those instruments at hand, he argued, neither his generation nor the next could develop the reservation's potential.

Brunot's reply to Crockett revealed that his conception of the reservation's future was not so different from Crockett's. Brunot told Crockett and the assembled crowd: "I am going to ask the President to make out the lines on the reservation . . . [and] then each man, when he builds a house, may build it on his own land, and no one can ever take it from him. . . . The rest would belong to all of you, and when a boy grows up and gets married, and goes to work, you could give him a farm."[41] The exchange between Crockett and Brunot demonstrates that federal officials and a Lummi tribal member agreed that the reservation created by treaty was to be a permanent fixture, even if some of the land was to be held individually while other land was still held by "all of you" and managed for the well-being of that generation and future generations of

Indians. The reservation was to be a homeland for industrious, self-supporting Indians. Thus leading Indian men cited the treaties when trying to define the boundaries of the reservations and give Indian residents access to vital resources. This meant that some measure of economic well-being was tied to the treaties, and the management of the treaties for those purposes brought power to the headmen who insisted on their fulfillment.[42]

Although it is possible to read this insistence as Indian "dependency," in that the tribes' economic and political viability depended on Americans fulfilling the treaty, it is clear that individuals like Crockett could articulate a "transcript" of resistance and manipulate it to meet their individual, family, and tribal needs while appearing to conform to demands of the federal government. In such moments Indians' exercise of power was syncretic and an "innovation within tradition" or an improvisation on the basic official script that was the treaty.[43] Indians supplemented their orality—their tradition of spoken and performed agreements—with literacy and appeals to legality in order to achieve a decidedly Indian geography and political economy of the reservation.

PERFORMANCE, ORALITY, AND POWER
FOR SUBSEQUENT GENERATIONS

By the 1870s federal officials had started, informally, to assign tracts of reservation land to individuals according to treaty provisions.[44] With those assignments came new proposals from a range of federal representatives to close or consolidate some reservations while perhaps expanding others. Such actions prompted further Indian articulations of what the treaties meant to them. In 1877 the special agent for Indians of the Tulalip Agency, Edmond Mallet, offered an important glimpse into these Indian understandings. He reported that the Indians said: "The reservations were reserved by themselves as the permanent homes of themselves and children, and . . . the cession was of their lands other than the reservations. They therefore claim that the reservation lands belong to them absolutely, and it need not be added that the proposition to consolidate them with other tribes at another agency does not meet with their [approbation]."[45] Mallet's report indicates a shift in how Indians understood the results of the treaty negotiations, or at least a shift in the meanings of the treaty that they emphasized. Up through the

1870s most Indian performances of the treaties stressed Indian desires for fulfillment of the promises of annuity payments and schools. This focus shifted subtly but significantly in ensuing decades.

Prior to about 1880, Puget Sound Indians remained largely self-sufficient economically. To ancient subsistence practices, many individuals added seasonal paid work—mining, logging, selling fish to canneries, farm labor, and occasional transport services. During the late 1870s and 1880s, however, a surge in the capitalist transformation of the region brought new levels of resource extraction and waves of migrants (and immigrants). Those demographic and economic developments in turn brought escalating assaults on Indian treaty rights, which prompted Indians to pay greater attention to two aspects of the treaties —their reservation of exclusive Indian lands and their promise of continuing access to resources on and off the reservations.

Complicating the issue was the aging and passing of the generation of Indians who had witnessed the treaty councils. The exit of that generation from the stage was gradual. Even in the late 1920s a few tribal members could still claim a direct connection to the treaty-making process. For those individuals, having been there was a basis of legitimacy and authority. Snoqualmie tribal member William Kanim was eighty-seven years old in 1927, and he had only to state "I am going to tell you what Governor Stevens and John Taylor [the Indian interpreter] said" in order to establish that his was an authentic account of the Point Elliott Treaty Council.[46] Such exact knowledge of the treaties and an ability to mobilize it became markers of leadership. August Martin of the Lummi recalled how his father-in-law, Chief Henry Kwina, had swayed a legal case that followed the arrest of several Lummi tribal members for off-reservation fishing in the 1910s. Martin explained that Kwina told the judge "all he knowed about the treaty": "When he came through telling all what he knowed about the treaty, the judge or the lawyer opened the book and he find this was correct, what he was saying. They don't bother the rest of the men that was called, when they find out this Chief Henry Kwina he hit it right, he hit every word correct on that book, on the treaty book."[47]

Although older tribal members could use their direct experience to assert what the treaties meant, those from younger generations could not because, as James Nimrod of the Muckleshoot said, they "did not hear the promise."[48] Like Nimrod, Richard Squi-Qui of the Lower

Skagit seemed to lament Indians' need to rely on the oral transmission of knowledge about the treaties. "That was the only thing Indians had," Squi-Qui told lawyers taking testimony for a Court of Claims case about alleged breaches of the treaty. "They didn't have anything—didn't know how to read and write the same as white people do."[49]

However, this and other testimony from litigation in the late 1920s reveals that the Indians had ways of preserving knowledge orally, including significant facts about the treaties. Many younger people recounted how a grandfather, grandmother, father, uncle, or mother had instructed them not only in aspects of culture and subsistence, but also explicitly in the meaning of the treaties. Jimmy Jones of the Upper Skagit explained: "Every tribe . . . [has] maybe one or two of what you might call an instructor, instructing the younger generation or younger people as to what . . . happened here in the past as their custom, and it is abided by the parties that were instructed."[50] And August Martin of the Lummi told how his father-in-law "and all the rest of his friends, brothers, and uncles, when we gather uplike [sic] this, he always told about the treaty. . . . That is why we all know . . . and that is why it is coming down . . . from generation to generation. That is why we can not say we don't know nothing about the treaty."[51]

In contrast to the written word, which is so often treated as immutable from its moment of creation, treaty teachings based in orality could be mobilized at any time, not just at formal proceedings, where the writing was on display. When Indian families traveled around the Puget Sound for work or pleasure, elders consistently used the opportunity to instruct the young in the history of places and customary practices. Talking about clamming beds, camas fields, potato plots, fishing sites, and house locations invariably invoked some discussion of treaty rights (and losses). Jennie Davis of the Duwamish recounted that her "grandfather used to often talk" about house and village locations "because we used to go along in that lake there and all these places there it was shown; I could see it."[52] Agnes Sigo of the Suquamish simply stated that the treaty "was common talk among the people."[53] In all cases children were expected and required to listen and learn.[54]

Occasionally a treaty-centered teaching moment exposed doubts among Indians about the information being passed down. In 1880 or 1881, for example, a "council of chiefs . . . who had signed the treaty" of Point Elliott gathered on the Tulalip reservation.[55] The accounts differ as to why. In one version John Sam of the Snoqualmie recalled that Snohomish band member John Taylor called the meeting to explain what he "understood at the time when . . . [he] was interpreting" from Chinook jargon to local languages at the Point Elliott treaty negotiations.[56] Sam explained: "I remember that John Taylor told the people, to be sure to don't forget to remember what was promised them—the elk, deer, bears, berries, clams, and fish."[57]

Another version of Taylor's public proclamation cites the arrival of a government "inspector" who had called the chiefs together to hear grievances. As remembered by Josie Celestie, a Snohomish band member and Taylor's nephew, the situation was rife with conflict. After several rounds of heated exchanges between the chiefs and the inspector, Chief Clubshelton abruptly said: "You, John Taylor, who was interpreting this treaty, step up here now and tell this white man what you understood. We have disputed you and we have been thinking that you hadn't interpreted this treaty right."[58] According to Celestie, Taylor's careful recitation of unfulfilled treaty obligations mollified Clubshelton, but the incident reveals that not all performances of the treaties were conflict free. Celestie recounted that Taylor had explained the treaty "at many council meetings," but none appeared to have been as overtly contentious as that early 1880s meeting at Tulalip.[59]

By the 1920s decades of discussions among Indians and occasional public declarations to wider audiences about the meaning of the Stevens treaties came to a head in a Court of Claims case entitled *Duwamish et al. v. United States.* Testimony in the case, taken in 1927, was a grand performance of orality as well as evidence of the shifting emphasis on specific treaty rights. A full recounting of the case and its subtleties lies well beyond the scope of this essay, but even a cursory glance at the testimony demonstrates how Puget Sound Indians had blended orality and the written words of the treaties to gain points of leverage for their economic, political, and social well-being.[60] On the surface, however, the Duwamish and twenty-three other named "tribes" sought compensation for U.S. failure to create a "big general reservation," which Indians believed Stevens had promised at the treaty negotiations.[61] (There was much variety in testimony about where this reservation was to have been located, but most witnesses seemed to hold that the larger reservation was to have been near their original reservation.) The tribes also sought payments for the loss of "improvements" to the lands from which they had moved—a provision of Article 7 of the Treaty of Point Elliott.[62] The improvements described included root and berry grounds, "marketable" timber, houses (which settlers had frequently appropriated as part of their homesteads and burned), and fishing and hunting grounds.[63]

The courtroom testimony was tightly bound by the scripting of legal counsel on both sides and by the requirement that Indians place a dollar value on lost goods, resources, and properties, be they tribal or individual. Nevertheless, Puget Sound Indians proved unruly actors in the case. One reason their testimony was so cacophonous was that they saw the case as an opportunity to compensate for the dual impact of downturns in commercial fishing and on-reservation agriculture. The fisheries were clearly an area of contention. In his examination of Lummi salmon fishing, ethnohistorian Daniel L. Boxberger has explained that fisheries were an uncontested resource for the Lummi before about 1880. With non-Indians' commercialization and capitalization of the salmon fisheries, which included large mechanized processing plants and huge, stationary, corporate salmon traps, Indian fishers like the Lummi found themselves at the margins of the fishing economy within two generations. Because they could not raise the capital necessary to compete in the commercial fisheries and because the courts would not uphold Indian rights to specific fish trap locations, the transition left them in a state of economic and political dependency.[64]

The fisheries were not the only factor pushing Indians of the region toward dependency. Conditions for Indian farmers had also grown worse since the nineteenth century, when several of the area reservations and especially the Lummi Reservation had held substantial agricultural prospects, which some Indian residents had tried to exploit. Hay, root crops, berries, and dairy and poultry items had yielded significant returns that benefited the community, not just individuals. Early-twentieth-century "working bees" suggest that individual and tribal resources were intimately connected, even after land allotment. In 1903, George Bremner, a schoolteacher on the Lummi Reservation who temporarily took on the tasks of the government agent in charge there, complained to the superintendent at Tulalip: "It is the common practice in clearing land, and even in plowing and planting, to have working 'bees,' which result in much feasting with little work poorly done. Each time that a death occurs the Indians all, or many of them, congregate at the home of the bereaved and feast and gossip for three or four days at the expense of the near relatives of the deceased. These and other foolish customs consume an amount of valuable time that, if used advantageously, would in a few years transform the reservation into a veritable garden spot."[65] Bremner's response was typical of federal agents, who perceived profligate waste in anything that smacked as "tribal," especially when they believed it distracted Indians from agricultural pursuits.[66] Yet the "working bees" on the Lummi Reservation demonstrate that tribal practices persisted amid what otherwise might appear to be purely individual efforts. The good of the community depended on the cooperation of various individuals and families in many economic activities, including agriculture.

In the twentieth century the host of problems that confronted small-scale American farmers hit Puget Sound Indians, and peculiarly "Indian" issues amplified the pain.[67] Indians contended with fractured ownership of inherited land allotments, lack of access to capital, and federal officials' application of various "technologies of power" to control the distribution of seeds, tools, livestock, and machinery. As if those discouraging circumstances were not enough, Lummi farmers were hit with fees to finance a diking district that was supposed to reduce floods and open marshlands to agricultural production. As a consequence, many faced bankruptcy and the alienation of reservation lands accelerated. Like the fishermen, Indian agriculturalists found themselves in a state of economic dependency by the late 1920s and early 1930s.[68]

Given the loss of income and control in commercial fishing and in agriculture, it is no wonder that witness after witness in the Court of Claims emphasized losses of land, houses, and other economic resources that went well beyond the scope of the legal courtroom script. The breadth of the *Duwamish* testimony was markedly different from those performances that had come before it, and it presaged many of those that would follow in the next century. By the last decade of the twentieth century and the first decade of the twenty-first, battles for treaty-reserved resources would even extend beyond the quantifiable losses emphasized in the *Duwamish* case to hunting rights, access to clam beds, and even groundwater rights.[69]

TREATY REMEMBRANCE AND PERFORMANCE

In 1910, Tulalip agency superintendent Charles Buchanan initiated a new practice—an annual celebration of the 1855 signing of the Treaty of Point Elliott. In his official diaries of agency affairs, Buchanan noted that the first few years of "dinner speeches" along with "old time games, customs . . . , [and] old time songs and dances" made Treaty Day an impressive event. In sponsoring these activities, Buchanan hoped to use older Indians to show the younger ones just how far they had traveled down the path to "civilization" since the signing of the treaty. For the first several years Buchanan was effusive in his descriptions of successful Treaty Day celebrations. Limited vision initially prevented him from recognizing the Pandora's box that his action had opened.[70]

In 1927, William Shelton, whose service as a reservation policeman and judge had prompted Buchanan to laud him earlier as the model of a progressive modern Indian, recalled the first Treaty Day celebration as an event very different from that depicted by Buchanan. Shelton explained that the speakers included Tyee William, or Steh-shad, who said "that he would like to have the Government to come with the promise that they made; that he would like to get the government to settle up before he died; that he wants all the young Indians to listen to his talk, to remember that this promise must be fulfilled, even after he is dead. And that is just what happened."[71] Whether this "transcript" of protest and resistance went unrecognized by Buchanan, or Shelton and others projected their sentiments back onto that day, Shelton's testimony reveals that the meaning of Treaty Day performances and celebrations had slipped quickly from Buchanan's grasp.

Indeed, by 1915 and 1916 it became clear even to Buchanan that the Indians, under the guise of celebrating the treaty, had taken Treaty Day as an occasion for performing some of the old "pagan dances" at Tulalip and other reservations. In response Buchanan called an abrupt halt to the 1916 Treaty Day events and turned his energies toward promoting Indian agricultural fairs instead.[72] He could not stop the spread of Treaty Day celebrations to other locations, however, especially the Lummi and Swinomish reservations. By the end of the decade the public performance of Treaty Day and customary winter or spirit dances had become tightly interwoven, much to Buchanan's displeasure.[73] Buchanan used all means at his disposal—moral suasion, withholding individual money disbursements, community pressure, the Catholic Church, and federal orders stipulating fines and arrests—to squelch the multiday dances.[74] Yet despite such efforts, the dances continued unabated, and even the Nooksack, who had not signed the treaty, took the opportunity to link Treaty Day celebrations to the public performance of dance ceremonies.[75] Treaty Day had clearly taken on the characteristics of an open rebellion, not simply a resistance, to federal policies —all in the name of a document supposedly recording Indians' concession to federal power.

The strength and force of the resistance surprised Buchanan. Solomon Balch of the Lummi responded to Buchanan's threats with threats of his own, telling Buchanan: "I think if you stop and think over the matter, you would soon find the first reviver of this pagan dances: let us look back and ask the founder of the treaty day celebration, he's the reviver and influencer of all the custom practices. . . . [When we received allotments and patents] we was told . . . that all the people was called citizens . . . with all the rights and privileges as any other citizen of the united states; therefore I feel in liberty to go to any party or gathering or dinner party what ever it may be as such citizen."[76] Balch was in no mind to back down and was unafraid to exercise his right as a "citizen" to sidestep Buchanan's threat—a right he possessed by virtue of federal actions and treaty provisions.

A month later, farmer-in-charge and Lummi tribal member William McCluskey reported to Buchanan that he went to investigate dances at the ceremonial "Smokehouse" on the Lummi Reservation and take names. There Louis Washington, one of the dance leaders, announced to the crowd "that they need not fear in carrying out their own custom and that no white man's law can stop them from such practice."[77] Tom Squiqui, another dance leader, followed with an affirmation of Washington's proclamation and added that "Treaty matters and Church teachings" supported the legitimacy of their rights to perform the dances.[78] When the dances subsequently stopped, McCluskey admitted that he could not claim credit. He explained to Buchanan: "As far as I can understand the dancing is about ended but [I] can not say whether it is through warnings that they have stopped or that their dancing season is now over."[79]

McCluskey's second option was the correct explanation, for the next year the combination of Treaty Day celebrations and spirit dances returned despite continuing efforts to discourage them. In 1921, McCluskey noted, "Pagan Dances was held at Gooseberry Point this Reservation in full swing according to the old custom on the face [pretext] of holding a Treaty Day celebration."[80] When tribal member John

Alexis applied to the relatively new agency superintendent for permission to perform "our social dance," he cited connections to the treaty, Indians' ability to police themselves against "whiskey," and the fact that it was "nature of the north west red people to be . . . happy as the great spirit has given them enjoyment and pleasure."[81] Such frontal assaults on federal authority meant that any transcript of resistance was at best only partially hidden.

By the mid-1920s Treaty Day celebrations and the spirit dances were inextricably linked, and the two had become performative marks of Indian identity.[82] Yet the dances and Treaty Day as performances had room to grow and expand in meaning and purpose. In the late 1920s and 1930s Treaty Day became an occasion for leaders of the Northwestern Federation of American Indians—the same people who had organized the multi-tribal *Duwamish* case—to transact their business and plan political and legal strategies in a public forum of Indians from various tribes as well as whites.[83] During the 1930s Treaty Day celebrations at the Lummi and Swinomish reservations were large, multitribal and international events drawing relatives and representatives from British Columbia tribes as well as the greater Puget Sound region.[84]

That was also the character of Treaty Day celebrations in the 1940s and 1950s. At the same time the celebrations also took on new meanings of tribal power, first with the creation of new tribal constitutions and then with the subsequent shift to a federal policy of terminating U.S. protection for Indian tribes.[85] Throughout the 1970s and 1980s Treaty Day celebrations and dances continued to represent tribal strength. Lummi Tribal chairman Sam Cagey told local reporters in 1978 that "singing and dancing at the celebration represents a victory" for the tribes against missionaries and federal officials who attempted to destroy "our tradition and culture." Chief and tribal council vice president Jim McKay used the occasion to warn that "Congress is considering changing the treaties" and thus marked Treaty Day as a means to claim and maintain the Treaty of Point Elliott. Tellingly, Cagey followed with a comment regarding state fisheries closures as a violation of treaty fishing rights.[86] At the 1981 Treaty Day ceremonies, Joe Washington argued that it was not a "celebration" but a "recognition" of broken treaty promises, including the treaty fishing rights.[87] The statements by Cagey, McKay, and Washington reveal that in the last quarter of the twentieth century, Treaty Day had become not only a vehicle for "spiritual prayers, songs, dances, spiritual medicine, and a noon dinner," but also a venue for public proclamations of resource control through the exercise of treaty rights.

PERFORMANCES AS TRANSCRIPTS OF RESISTANCE

When Vernon Lane used his appearance at the 1999 Martin Luther King Jr. Day event to highlight broken treaty promises and recruit allies, his speech fit well into the long lineage of public performances of the treaty.[88] The variations over time in performances of the Stevens treaties by Indians of the Puget Sound region came about because Indians mobilized the treaties and their understandings of them for the purposes of the day. In doing that, Indians did not "rewrite" the treaty promises or invent new ones; rather, they elaborated creatively on the original promises and thus honored a tradition of invoking the treaties to achieve goals they defined. In the early years their struggle was to find ways to articulate an Indian understanding of treaty terms and persuasively urge the implementation of the treaty. Those who had been present to hear Stevens could claim an authority and legitimacy. As those generations passed and the focus shifted to teaching younger Indians about the treaties, however, there was a need to emphasize resource control because those resources were under increasing threat. By the twentieth century, public treaty performances expanded to include displays of the power of citizenship and religious freedom. The treaties also became increasingly politicized as their role in court claims grew. The court of public opinion took on more importance, and by the late twentieth century, treaties and treaty performances became bulwarks of defense against repression and dispossession.

Such transformations in the performance of treaties reveal how orality and the written word have evolved together, making treaties living documents. The treaties have been central to the struggle for power not only between Indians and non-Indians but also among Indians for the past century and a half and have served to bring much of Indian resistance into the open. Scholar Fran Lisa Buntman, in her study of prisoner resistance in apartheid-era South Africa, has noted that acts of public and private resistance are not mutually exclusive or absolute binaries, but instead are related to each other. Resistance is most important, she explains, when it "begins to appropriate power."[89] This links "hidden transcripts" of language and meaning, apparent only to those who share the same cultural context, to the public discourses of recognizable and understandable resistance for actors and audiences alike, especially in the case of the treaties, because Indians and non-Indians were simultaneously actors and audience members in the performances. The treaties were common scripts. The words in the treaties did not change, but Indians came together to challenge and redirect them even if they did not fully subvert the "authorized script."[90] While the historical evidence makes it clear that some of the messages in treaty performances are likely to remain "hidden transcripts" of resistance, understandable only from specific cultural perspectives, the same evidence demonstrates that Indians could also simultaneously translate performances meant for many other people's ears and eyes to convey messages, sometimes forcefully, to a variety of audiences.

NOTES

1. "'Cultural Genocide: Native Treaty Rights': A Conference in Honor of Martin Luther King, Jr., Day—Community Voices, Community Concerns," videotape, Whatcom County Human Rights Task Force and Whatcom Community College, Bellingham, Washington, 1999.

2. For discussions of the potential strengths and weaknesses of such "strategic essentialism," see Paige Raibmon, *Authentic Indians: Episodes of Encounter from the Late-Nineteenth-Century Northwest Coast* (Durham, N.C.: Duke University Press, 2005), 13, 216; and Claire Jean Kim, "Playing the Racial Trump Card: Asian Americans in Contemporary U.S. Politics," *Amerasia Journal* 26, no. 3 (2000–1): 35–65.

3. The literature on resistance is immense and complex. I draw here on a recent review and application by Fran Lisa Buntman, *Robben Island and Prisoner Resistance to Apartheid* (Cambridge: Cambridge University Press, 2003), who builds on a notion of "hidden transcripts" and resistance in work by James C. Scott, *Weapons of the Weak: Everyday Forms of Peasant Resistance* (New Haven, Conn.: Yale University Press, 1985) and *Domination and the Arts of Resistance: Hidden Transcripts* (New Haven, Conn.: Yale University Press, 1990). For additional guidance, see Nickolas B. Dirks, Geoff Eley, and Sherry B. Ortner, "Introduction," in *Culture/Power/History: A Reader in Contemporary Social Theory*, edited by Nickolas B. Dirks, Geoff Eley, and Sherry B. Ortner (Princeton, N.J. : Princeton University Press, 1994), 18–21; and Nickolas B. Dirks, "In Near Ruins: Cultural Theory at the End of the Century," in *In Near Ruins: Cultural Theory at the End of the Century*, edited by Nickolas B. Dirks (Minneapolis: University of Minnesota Press, 1998), 14–15.

4. For an example of how individuals and groups "invoke and enact legality," see Susan S. Silbey, "Everyday Life and the Constitution of Legality," in *The Blackwell Companion to the Sociology of Culture*, edited by Mark D. Jacobs and Nancy Weiss Hanrahan (Malden, Mass.: Blackwell Publishing, 2005), 335–37.

5. Ibid., 335.

6. Among significant studies to address these issues are Richard White, *The Roots of Dependency: Subsistence, Environment, and Social Change among the Choctaws, Pawnees, and Navajos* (Lincoln: University of Nebraska Press, 1983); Daniel L. Boxberger, *To Fish in Common: The Ethnohistory of Lummi Indian Salmon Fishing* (Seattle: University of Washington Press, 2000); Thomas Biolsi, *Organizing the Lakota: The Political Economy of the New Deal on the Pine Ridge and Rosebud Reservations* (Tucson: University of Arizona Press, 1992); Alexandra Harmon, *Indians in the Making: Ethnic Relations and Indian Identities around Puget Sound* (Berkeley: University of California Press, 1998); Frederick E. Hoxie, *Parading through History: The Making of the Crow Nation in America, 1805–1935* (Cambridge: Cambridge University Press, 1995); Philip J. Deloria, *Indians in Unexpected Places* (Lawrence: University Press of Kansas, 2004); and Elizabeth Vibert, *Traders' Tales: Narratives of Cultural Encounters in the Columbia Plateau, 1807–1846* (Norman: University of Oklahoma Press, 1997).

7. Kent D. Richards, *Isaac I. Stevens: Young Man in a Hurry* (Provo, Utah: Brigham Young University Press, 1979), provided the first substantial "modern" historical treatments of the treaty negotiations in his biography of Isaac Ingalls Stevens, but Richards focused almost exclusively on Stevens's motivations and actions, providing very little insight into Indians' views of treaty negotiations. Neither did Richards discuss Indian life under the treaties in subsequent years. Harmon, *Indians in the Making*, provides the best discussion of Indian life and identity formation over the past two centuries, noting how the original councils and later negotiations served ceremonial as well as political purposes. She argues persuasively that Indian discussions regarding treaties and their application were essential to the creation of various tribal identities as well as a larger "Indian" identity. Harmon's focus on such a large scope of time and the slippery topic of identity meant that she was not able to devote as much specific attention to treaty performances as is possible in this essay. Andrew H. Fisher, "'This I Know from the Old People': Yakama Indian Treaty Rights as Oral Tradition," *Montana* 49, no. 1 (1999): 2–17, relies on an application of arguments by Walter J. Ong, *Orality and Literacy: The Technologizing of the Word* (London: Methuen, 1982), to show how one might trace evolving syncretic interaction between oral and written traditions that have been part of an ongoing process as Indians negotiate and renegotiate treaty provisions.

8. Richards, *Isaac I. Stevens*.

9. Charles Mix to Isaac Stevens, August 30, 1854, Records of the Washington Superintendency of Indian Affairs, 1853–1874, File Microcopies in the National Archives, no. 5, roll 1, National Archives, Washington, D.C., 1945.

10. Harmon, *Indians in the Making*, 74.

11. Ibid., 79.

12. Lucy Gurand testimony, *Duwamish et al.*, Court of Claims of the United States, no. F-275, 647, Evidence for Plaintiff and Defendant, box 46, Northwest Ethnohistory Collection, Center for Pacific Northwest Studies, Western Washington University, Bellingham, Washington (hereafter cited as *Duwamish et al.*)

13. Augustus Kautz testimony, *Duwamish et al.*, 680.

14. Robert Brockstedt Lane and Barbara Lane, "Western Washington Treaty Proceedings" (1977), 3, box 34, Northwest Ethnohistory Collection, Western Washington University, Bellingham, Washington.

15. See Charles J. Kappler, "Treaty with the Dwamish, Suquamish, Etc., 1855," *Indian Affairs: Laws and Treaties, Vol. 2: Treaties* (Washington, D.C.: Government Printing Office, 1904), 669.

16. Gibbs Journal, Tuesday, January 16, 1855, Stevens 1855 Treaty Journal, box 17, Northwest Ethnohistory Collection, Center for Pacific Northwest Studies, Western Washington University, Bellingham, Washington. "Chah-chou-sen" refers to the "island" created by various channels of the Nooksack River and specified in the Treaty of Point Elliott as one of the designated reservation sites.

17. Wayne Suttles, *Coast Salish and Western Washington Indians: The Economic Life of the Coast Salish of Haro and Rosario Straits I* (New York: Garland Publishing, 1974), 30. For a debate as to the existence and nature of political leadership among Indians of the Puget Sound prior to and during the early stages of contact, see Daniel L. Boxberger and Bruce G. Miller, "Creating Chiefdoms: The Puget Sound Case," *Ethnohistory* 41, no. 2 (1994): 267–93; Kenneth D. Tollefson, "In Defense of a Snoqualmie Political Chiefdom Model," *Ethnohistory* 43, no. 1 (1996): 145–71; Daniel L. Boxberger and Bruce G. Miller, "Evolution or History? A Response to Tollefson," *Ethnohistory* 44, no. 1 (1997): 135–37; and Jay Miller, "Back to Basics: Chiefdoms in Puget Sound," *Ethnohistory* 44, no. 2 (1997): 375–87.

18. For general background see Barbara Lane, "Anthropological Report on the Identity, Treaty Status, and Fisheries of the Lummi Tribe of Indians," Lane Reports, box 19, Northwest Ethnohistory Collection, Center for Pacific Northwest Studies, Western Washington University, Bellingham, Washington; Wayne Suttles, "Post-Contact Culture Changes among the Lummi Indians," *British Columbia Historical Quarterly* 18, nos. 1–2 (1954): 29–102; David G. Tremaine, *Indian and Pioneer Settlement of the Nooksack Lowland, Washington to 1890* (Bellingham, Wash.: Center for Pacific Northwest Studies, Western Washington State College, 1975), 10–11; Bernard J. Stern, *The Lummi Indians of Northwest Washington* (New York: Columbia University Press, 1934), 101; and George Gibbs, "Tribes of Western Washington and Northwestern Oregon," in *Tribes of the Extreme Northwest*, edited by W. H. Dall (Washington, D.C.: Government Printing Office, 1877), 223.

19. Suttles, *Coast Salish and Western Washington Indians*, 38; Frank Hillaire testimony, *Duwamish et al.*, 486; and Daniel L. Boxberger, Chronology, "Lummi and Other NW," box 77, Northwest Ethnohistory Collection.

20. John Andrew Wilson testimony, *Duwamish et al.*, 471–72.

21. One Lummi informant recounted to an early anthropologist that ordinarily a house opening required three feasts but that Chowitsut's vision had directed him

to hold five for the opening of his house. The ability to hold five large, public feasts was a sign of immense wealth. See A. B. Reagan, "Note on Lummi-Nooksack Indians," *Kansas Academy of Science* (1921): 430–31.

22. Bellingham Bay provided the first site north of San Francisco not taken by other entrepreneurs. See Chris Friday, "Whatcom Creek: A History of a Place," for the Remembering Whatcom Creek exhibit, Center for Pacific Northwest Studies, Western Washington University, Bellingham, August 1999.

23. Lottie Roeder Roth, *History of Whatcom County*, vol. 1 (Chicago: Pioneer Historical Publishing Company, 1926), 18.

24. Friday, "Whatcom Creek: A History of a Place."

25. For a discussion of houses, house-building, and concepts of property ownership, see John Andrew Wilson testimony, *Duwamish et al.*, 471–72, and Suttles, *Coast Salish and Western Washington Indians*, 272–75.

26. Coll-Peter Thrush and Robert H. Keller Jr., "'I See What I Have Done': The Life and Murder of Xwelas, a S'Klallam Woman," *Western Historical Quarterly* 26, no. 2 (summer 1995): 172–74.

27. British Columbia, *Papers Connected with the Indian Land Question, 1850– 1875* (Victoria, B.C.: R. Wolfenden, 1875), 5–11, simply gives the text of the treaties, lists a few of the key individuals who signed, and indicates the number of "others" who also signed. Douglas later attached lists of names to the treaties. In the case of the South Saanich Treaty, this was the longest list of individuals, with the other treaties signed by as few as four people and as many as thirty-three. Chowitsut signed the South Saanich Treaty as the twenty-fourth individual (of thirty-seven) on a second sheet, probably as part of the Tseycum Band. Signature sheets in possession of the author and courtesy of Daniel L. Boxberger, Department of Anthropology, Western Washington University, Bellingham, Washington, December 5, 2006.

28. Suttles, *Coast Salish and Western Washington Indians*, 30.

29. Isaac I. Stevens to George W. Manypenny, February 1, 1854, Washington Superintendency Microfilm Roll 907, Records of the Bureau of Indian Affairs, RG 75; and D. L. Boxberger, "The Point Francis Question, June/July 1987," 17, box 6, Northwest Ethnohistory Collection, Center for Pacific Northwest Studies, Western Washington University, Bellingham.

30. Raibmon, *Authentic Indians*, 6–13, offers a fine discussion of how Indians negotiated the binaries inherent in colonial regimes.

31. Kappler, "Treaty with the Dwamish, Suquamish, Etc., 1855," 669; and Kappler, "Treaty with the S'Klallam," 674.

32. *Annual Report of the Commissioner of Indian Affairs 1858*, 228–29 (hereafter cited as *ARCIA*). For discussions of Sealth or Seattle and the many versions of his speeches, see Jerry L. Clark, "Thus Spoke Chief Seattle: The Story of an Undocumented Speech," *Prologue* 17, no. 1 (1985): 58–65; Denise Low, "Contemporary Reinvention of Chief Seattle: Variant Texts of Chief Seattle's 1854 Speech," *American Indian Quarterly* 19, no. 3 (1995): 407–21; Albert Furtwangler, *Answering Chief Seattle* (Seattle: University of Washington Press, 1997); and Crisca

Bierwert, "Remembering Chief Seattle: Reversing Cultural Studies of a Vanishing Native American," *American Indian Quarterly* 22, no. 3 (1998): 280–304.

33. *ARCIA 1858*, 229.

34. Ibid.

35. Ibid, 229–30.

36. For the Executive Order that solidified the boundaries of the Lummi Reservation, see Charles J. Kappler, "Lummi Reserve, November 22, 1873," *Indian Affairs: Laws and Treaties, Vol. 1: Laws, Part III — Executive Orders Relating to Indian Reserves* (Washington, D.C.: Government Printing Office, 1904), 917. For the order establishing the Muckleshoot Reservation, see "Muckleshoot Reserve, April 9, 1874," ibid., 918.

37. President Ulysses S. Grant had established the Board of Indian Commissioners as an advisory body, but its influence on American Indian policy in this era was immense. Francis Paul Prucha, *The Great Father: The United States Government and the American Indians*, vol. 1 (Lincoln: University of Nebraska Press, 1984), 506–7.

38. *ARCIA 1871*, 141–43.

39. Ibid, 142.

40. Ibid, 143.

41. Ibid., 142.

42. Biolsi, *Organizing the Lakota*, 5, 31–46, argues a similar point regarding the way in which the "three-fourths' majority rule" became "the *traditional* method of tribal decision making" by the twentieth century, and chiefs used it to represent themselves as spokesmen for the tribe.

43. For examples of "innovation within tradition," see Vibert, *Traders' Tales*, 63–67. For discussions of how individuals and groups can improvise and negotiate "scripts" generally, see Chris Barker, *Making Sense of Cultural Studies: Central Problems and Critical Debates* (London: Sage Publications, 2002), 42. For a more specific study, see Jeffrey C. Goldfarb, "The Autonomy of Culture and the Invention of the Politics of Small Things: 1968 Revisited," in *Blackwell Companion to the Sociology of Culture*, 432–39.

44. *ARCIA 1867*, 59; *ARCIA 1871*, 273; *ARCIA 1874*, 80; and C. C. Finkbonner to Father Chirouse, Annual Report, 1872, Microfilm Roll 2, Puget Sound Agency, RG 75, National Archives and Records Administration (NARA), Seattle.

45. *ARCIA 1877*, 198.

46. William Kanim testimony, *Duwamish et al.*, 189.

47. August Martin testimony, *Duwamish et al.*, 500.

48. James Nimrod testimony, *Duwamish et al.*, 176.

49. Richard Squi-Qui testimony, *Duwamish et al.*, 327.

50. Jimmy Jones testimony, *Duwamish et al.*, 380.

51. August Martin testimony, *Duwamish et al.*, 500.

52. Jennie Davis testimony, *Duwamish et al.*, 704.

53. Agnes Sigo testimony, *Duwamish et al.*, 408–9.

54. Richard Squi-Qui testimony, *Duwamish et al.*, 329.

55. John Sam testimony, *Duwamish et al.*, 203.

56. Ibid., 204.

57. Ibid., 205.

58. Josie Celestie testimony, *Duwamish et al.*, 242.

59. Ibid., 243, 244.

60. Harmon, *Indians in the Making*, demonstrates that it was essential in building a larger "Indian" identity beyond the newly formed tribal identities of Puget Sound Indians. Furthermore, both she and Boxberger, *To Fish in Common*, point out that the case had important political repercussions, including the formation of the Northwestern Federation of American Indians and, in the case of the Lummi, the creation of the new Tribal Business Council as the political representative of the various bands consolidated onto the Lummi Reservation.

61. Some 144 Indians with affiliations to twenty-four tribes or bands testified in the case. *Duwamish et al.*, 155–58.

62. Kappler, "Treaty with the Dwamish, Suquamish, Etc., 1855," 671.

63. *Duwamish et al.*, passim.

64. Boxberger, *To Fish in Common*, especially 35–102.

65. *ARCIA 1903*, 339.

66. David Rich Lewis, "Reservation Leadership and the Progressive-Traditional Dichotomy: William Wash and the Northern Utes, 1865–1928," *Ethnohistory* 38, no. 2 (1991): 124–48.

67. The literature on American family farmers is voluminous, but for some key examples, see Theodore Saloutos, *The American Farmer and the New Deal* (Ames: Iowa State University Press, 1982); Donald J. Pisani, *From the Family Farm to Agribusiness: The Irrigation Crusade in California and the West, 1850–1931* (Berkeley: University of California Press, 1984); and David Vaught, *Cultivating California: Growers, Specialty Crops, and Labor, 1875–1920* (Baltimore, Md.: Johns Hopkins University Press, 1999).

68. I have dealt with these issues extensively in an unpublished document prepared for the Department of Justice and the Department of Interior on behalf of the Lummi Nation. See Chris Friday, "Analysis and Documentation of Lummi History: Aboriginal, Prehistoric, Treaty, and Reservation Periods for the Lummi Peninsula Water Rights Case," prepared for Northwest Economic Associates, January 2003, in possession of the author.

69. For examples, see Danny Westneat, "Tribes to Start Clamming: '95 Ruling Allows Digging on Private Land," *Seattle Times*, July 24, 1996, B1; "Indian Loses Case over Right to Hunt," *Seattle Times*, February 22, 2000, B2; and Friday, "Analysis and Documentation of Lummi History." On the relationship between treaty obligations and off-reservation sites as part of the ongoing process of negotiation and renegotiation, also see Katrine Barber, *Death of Celilo Falls* (Seattle: University of Washington Press, 2005).

70. Harmon, *Indians in the Making*, 150; Diary of Superintendent from July 1, 1909, to November 30, 1912, box 310, Tulalip Agency, RG 75, NARA, Seattle. I am also indebted to Serena Sprungl for her award-winning seminar paper "Treaty

Days and 'Pagan Dances' among the Puget Sound Indians, 1910s to 1920s," stunningly researched and written as part of an undergraduate history seminar at Western Washington University, in Bellingham, in 2005.

71. William Shelton testimony, *Duwamish et al.*, 254.

72. Charles Buchanan to William McCluskey, February 8, 1915, and Buchanan to McCluskey, February 11, 1915, folder 14-20t, box 190, General Correspondence, 1909–1925, Tulalip Agency, RG 75, NARA, Seattle; Joe L. Schell to Charles Buchanan, December 19, 1916, and Buchanan to Schell, December 20, 1916, file 18t, box 214, General Correspondence, 1916–1917, Tulalip Agency, RG 75, NARA, Seattle.

73. Russel Lawrence Barsh, "Banishing the Spirits: Indian Agents and the Pacific Northwest Winter Dance," *Journal of the West* 39, no. 3 (2000): 54–65, offers the explanation that motives for the emergence of the dance complex in public at this time included a struggle between different practitioners and their respective followers. Barsh also highlights the repressive efforts of Buchanan and other federal officials and tends to emphasize victimization rather than negotiation and agency. For other examinations of Spirit or Winter Dances among the Coast Salish, see Wayne Suttles, *Coast Salish Essays* (Seattle: University of Washington Press, 1987), 199–208; and Wayne Suttles, "Central Coast Salish," in *The Handbook of North American Indians, Vol. 7: Northwest Coast*, edited by Wayne Suttles (Washington, D.C.: Smithsonian Institution, 1990), 67.

74. Charles Buchanan to Lucien James, March 7, 1919; Buchanan to Schell, February 28, 1919; Buchanan to McCluskey, March 7, 1919, and April 10, 1919; McCluskey to Buchanan, February 11, 1919; Amelia Cush to Buchanan, January 17, 1919; and Buchanan to Cush, January 24, 1919, all in file 9c, box 92, General Correspondence, 1918–1919, Tulalip Agency, RG 75, NARA, Seattle.

75. Charles H. Burke to Lin. H. Hadley, March 28, 1928, and unsigned letter to the Commissioner of Indian Affairs, March 9, 1928, Decimal Files 072-073, box 269, Tulalip Agency, RG 75, NARA, Seattle.

76. Solomon Balch to Charles Buchanan, March 11, 1919, file 9c, box 92, General Correspondence, 1918–1919, Tulalip Agency, RG 75, NARA, Seattle.

77. McCluskey to Buchanan, February 11, 1919, ibid.

78. Ibid.

79. Ibid., March 24, 1919.

80. McCluskey to W. F. Dickens, February 4, 1921, file 2v, 4v, 5v, box 249, General Correspondence, 1909–1925, Tulalip Agency, RG 75, NARA, Seattle.

81. John Alexis to W. F. Fickens, January 25, 1921, ibid.

82. McCluskey to F. A. Gross, December 24, 1926, and Gross to McCluskey, December 21, 1926, Decimal Files 045-047, box 265, Tulalip Agency, RG 75, NARA, Seattle.

83. *Bellingham Herald*, January 23, 1931, 1 and 14.

84. *Bellingham Herald*, January 22, 1934, 2; January 23, 1935, 6; January 22, 1936, 6; January 22, 1938, 3; O. C. Upchurch to Charles Gable, July 9, 1936, Decimal File 072-073, box 269, Tulalip Agency, RG 75, NARA, Seattle.

85. *Bellingham Herald,* February 8, 1948, and October 10, 1955.

86. Ibid., January 21, 1978.

87. Ibid., January 21, 1981.

88. "'Cultural Genocide: Native Treaty Rights,'" videotape.

89. Buntman, *Robben Island,* especially 126–30, 236–51, and 264–71. Buntman builds on the now classic works of Scott, *Weapons of the Weak* and *Domination and the Arts of Resistance,* to offer a more nuanced and complex understanding of the ways resistance can be measured along a continuum and stresses the fact that resistance "aspires to power" (Buntman, *Robben Island,* 269). Resistance is part of building a political awareness of power and seeking control of it in opposition to oppression—an analysis that provides intriguing links between the antiapartheid struggles in South Africa and Native American struggles to use treaties as public transcripts to assert (or reassert) some degree of sovereignty.

90. Goldfarb, "Autonomy of Culture," 438–39; Silbey, "Everyday Life," 335–36; and Orville Lee, "Race after the Cultural Turn," in *Blackwell Companion to the Sociology of Culture,* 243–44.

6 Reserved for Whom?

DEFENDING AND DEFINING TREATY RIGHTS

ON THE COLUMBIA RIVER, 1880–1920

Andrew H. Fisher

O n May 15, 1905, the United States Supreme Court issued its landmark decision in *United States v. Winans*, a case concerning the treaty fishing rights of the Yakama Nation in south-central Washington State.[1] The ruling required fishwheel owners Audubon and Linnaeus Winans to stop impeding Indian access to traditional fishing stations at the Tumwater fishery along the Columbia River. Justice Joseph McKenna, writing for an eight-man majority, eloquently articulated the rationale: "The right to resort to the fishing places in controversy was a part of larger rights possessed by the Indians, upon the exercise of which there was not a shadow of impediment, and which were not much less necessary to the existence of the Indians than the atmosphere they breathed." An 1855 treaty had reserved that right, along with any others not specifically granted, which the Winans brothers could not legally restrict even on their own property. In reaching this conclusion, McKenna held further that treaties generally must be construed as the Indians understood them at the time of negotiation. Historians and legal scholars rightfully regard his opinion as a major victory for tribal sovereignty as well as treaty rights, but its legacy was more complicated and more problematic for the Native peoples of the Middle Columbia River.[2] From an ethnohistorical perspective there is cause to question whether the Court's construction of treaty fishing rights fully accorded with that of the Indians.[3]

The *Winans* decision, together with the related cases *United States v. Taylor* (1887) and *United States v. Seufert* (1919), helped redefine the nature of the very rights it protected. All three court actions were responses to challenges from non-Indian competitors who had obstructed Native access to traditional fishing sites on the Mid-Columbia River.[4] In each case the federal courts found illegal interference with treaty rights, but the litigation also made it clear that the government construed off-reservation fishing as a tribal entitlement belonging to the confederations established by treaty in 1855. Federal officials dealt primarily with reservation Indian leaders and treated fishing sites as tribal property. In doing so, they ignored indigenous traditions of village autonomy and family ownership of resource sites. Native trial testimony reveals that Indians did not immediately or universally accept the federal view. In legal terms, however, fishing rights and fishing sites became collective possessions rather than the privately held (though widely shared) assets of aboriginal custom. The fact that this transformation coincided with the allotment of reservation lands, an assimilationist policy designed to convert tribal property into individual private properties, is one of the many ironies that punctuate the history of federal Indian policy and law.

This case study of the *Taylor-Winans-Seufert* trilogy suggests that Indian treaties and their judicial interpretations became significant agents of tribal ethnogenesis and cultural change. As instruments of American colonialism, treaties and court decisions reshaped more than they reflected the complex realities of indigenous social and political life. They created powerful legal fictions that eventually compelled Native Americans to alter their diverse property regimes and legal cultures to suit the designs of the dominant society.[5] In the Columbia Basin this shift occurred slowly and with considerable debate among Indians. Some turned American law to their own advantage, using it to gain access to places they could not fish before, while others employed it as a club against competing groups. The decline of the salmon runs and the disappearance of traditional fisheries beneath reservoirs only deepened inter- and intratribal divisions as the twentieth century progressed. From the 1880s to the 1920s, however, the Indians' main antagonists were the fishwheel operators and cannery owners seeking to monopolize the riverfront. The non-Indians' attempts to nullify the treaties, or to categorically exclude entire tribes, forced the federal government to defend and simultaneously define the rights reserved in those agreements.

The so-called Stevens and Palmer treaties of 1855 laid the legal foundation for the reordering of indigenous property rights.[6] In order to gain title to Indian lands and remove Native inhabitants to reservations, the U.S. government had to identify the signatory "tribes," define their various territories, and select the proper "head chiefs" with whom to negotiate. This process, driven by political expediency rather than aboriginal reality, required the radical modification of Native institutions. On the Columbia Plateau winter villages formed the largest political units in a regional network of people who shared territory and cultural practices, engaged in economic exchange, and intermarried extensively. Family ties crisscrossed the area, bridging both geographic barriers and linguistic boundaries, and people moved in and out of different social groupings throughout the year. In this world of interconnected communities, individual Indians had multiple associations and multifaceted identities that greatly complicated attempts to categorize them.

Using pieces of the aboriginal pattern, American treaty commissioners partitioned the southern portion of the Columbia Plateau into territories to be ceded and grouped their residents into several purported confederations of tribes. Most of those living in villages north and west of the Columbia River became nominal members of the Yakama Nation, while those living south of it were ultimately folded into either the Confederated Tribes of Warm Springs or the Confederated Tribes of the Umatilla Indian Reservation. Some Indians actually settled on the reservations, but many stayed on the river or spent much of the year away from the agencies. On paper the treaty commissioners had arbitrarily broken up social networks, reassigned political loyalties, and restructured group rights in an effort to create a system they could better comprehend and control. However, as scholar Russel Lawrence Barsh has observed in this volume and historian Alexandra Harmon has shown in her work on Puget Sound, the multifarious nature of Native identity "did not collapse into reservation-based identities. On the contrary, residence continued to be a part of identity, along with geographically extensive networks of ancestry." The remaking of Native space along the Columbia River would take decades, but it had serious consequences for future generations of Indian fishers.[7]

Prior to the treaties, and for many decades after, kinship structured access to the fisheries where Indians had caught salmon for nearly ten thousand years before European contact. Although each village claimed its own fishing grounds, specific sites belonged to individuals and families. The rights to a particular cliff, rock, island, or scaffold descended through inheritance, and the owners had to grant permission for others to use it. Fishing rights thus created a major incentive to marry outside one's village, as a person could thereby acquire rights to several sites across a wide area. The language of the treaties reconfigured this system in subtle yet significant ways. Like the treaties on Puget Sound, which the treaty commissioners used as a model, the agreements in the Columbia Basin contained a nearly identical version of this familiar article: "The exclusive right of taking fish in all the streams, where running through or bordering said reservation, is further *secured to said confederated tribes and bands* of Indians, as also the right of taking fish at all usual and accustomed places, in common with the citizens of the Territory, and of erecting temporary buildings for curing them; together with the privileges of hunting, gathering roots and berries, and pasturing their horses and cattle upon open and unclaimed land."[8]

By vesting subsistence rights in the confederated tribes and bands, this clause purported to transform individual and familial rights into tribal possessions. At the same time the treaties permitted competition from American citizens, who eventually used their nation's land laws to reclassify the riverfront as private property. Within a century of the treaties' ratification, both Indians and non-Indians would be fishing in places they could not have fished before as kinship networks and salmon chiefs faced challenges from the state and tribal authorities empowered by Euro-American legal culture.

Conflict between aboriginal practice and settler policy first erupted in the 1880s. Following the arrival of the railroad and the fishwheel in the Columbia Basin, white homesteaders and packing companies began pushing aside Indian dipnetters and blasting channels for their water-powered harvesters. By 1900 five canneries and dozens of wheels lined the river between the Cascades and Celilo Falls.[9] Although many Native fishers eventually sold salmon to the packers, they deeply resented the usurpation of their treaty-reserved fishing grounds. As Yakama Indian agent James Wilbur explained in 1881: "The Indians have always regarded these fishing stands as their own property, as much as the house

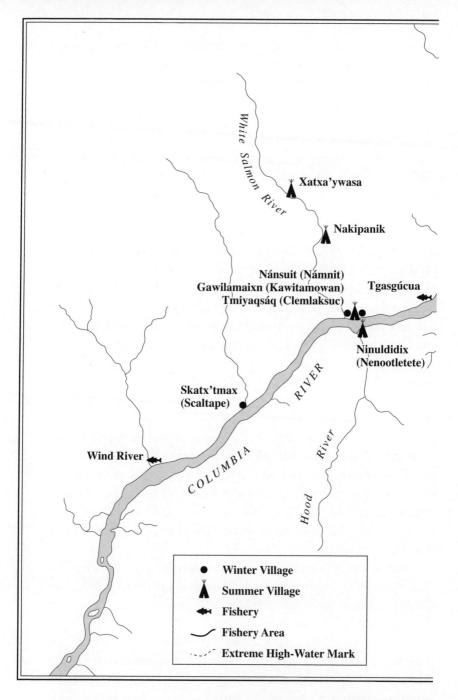

MAP 6.1 Columbia Gorge villages and fisheries. Inset: The Dalles area. Following Robert A. Habersham, comp., *J. K. Gill & Co's map of Washington Territory* (Portland, OR: J. K. Gill & Co., 1878).

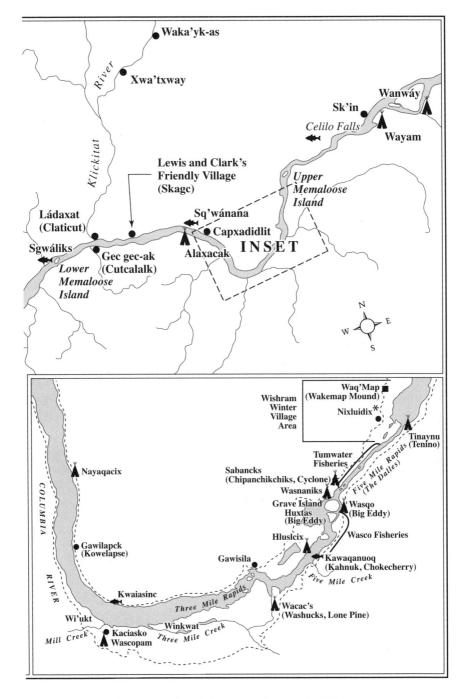

Waka'yk-as

Xwa'txway

Sk'in

Wanwáy

Celilo Falls

Wayam

Lewis and Clark's
Friendly Village
(Skagc)

Upper
Memaloose
Island

Ládaxat
(Claticut)

Sq'wánana

Capxadidlit

INSET

Sgwáliks

Gec gec-ak
(Cutcalalk)

Alaxacak

Lower
Memaloose
Island

N
W   E
S

Waq'Map
(Wakemap Mound)

Wishram
Winter
Village
Area

Nixluidix*

Tinaynu
(Tenino)

Nayaqacix

Sabancks
(Chipanchikchiks, Cyclone)

Tumwater
Fisheries

Five Mile Rapids
(The Dalles)

Wasnaniks

Grave Island
Huxtas
(Big Eddy)

Wasqo
(Big Eddy)

COLUMBIA

Gawilapck
(Kowelapse)

Gawisila

Huslcix

Wasco Fisheries

Kawaqanuoq
(Kahnuk, Chokecherry)

Five Mile Creek

Kwaiasinc

Three Mile Rapids

RIVER

Wi'ukt

Winkwat

Kaciasko
Wascopam

Three Mile Creek

Wacac's
(Washucks, Lone Pine)

Mill Creek

*Alternate names for Nixluidix: Echeloot, Spearfish, Spedis, Wishram or barn of any citizen; they never contemplated giving the whites the privilege of taking possession of them, but I believe when they signed the treaty supposed they were only giving the whites the privilege of taking fish at the fishery, from other stands."[10]

This culturally grounded and legally sound interpretation of the phrase "in common with the citizens of the Territory" held no water with white competitors, who read the treaty language to mean that they had equal standing at the tribal fisheries. They also assumed that Euro-American concepts of property ownership trumped whatever claims the Indians might have to their "usual and accustomed places." Accordingly, once citizens and companies had acquired land adjoining the fisheries, they often tried to block Native access to the river.

The trouble at Tumwater started with Frank Taylor, whose father William had cobbled together five contiguous homestead sections embracing the highly productive fishery across from The Dalles, Oregon. In 1881 he began leasing two prized fishing stands to a trio of white men intent on catching salmon for profit. They in turn prevented the Indian owners from using the rocks where their people had fished for generations. On several occasions, the Indians alleged, "the whites had taken away their dip-nets, and driven them from the fishing stands at the point of the revolver." Fearing starvation, the Indians beseeched the Yakama agency for assistance in reclaiming their ancestral inheritance. Agent Wilbur managed to negotiate a compromise, whereby the whites agreed to fish one of the stands on alternate days, but Taylor refused to concede that the Indians had a superior right. Since he had secured a fee patent from the federal government, "the fishery was his property, which he considered himself perfectly justified using to the best advantage, and had therefore leased." If the Indians wanted to fish there, he informed Wilbur, "he would dispose of his interest to the [Interior] Department for $3000.00, which he considered much below its real value." The Indian Office dismissed his offer out of hand, and the situation deteriorated rapidly.[11]

Taylor's provocative behavior finally compelled the federal government to take legal action. In 1884 he ran a barbed-wire fence across the Colwash Trail, the only path to the Tumwater fishery, arguing that it was necessary to stop the Indians from camping and pasturing horses on his land. When the Yakama agency dispatched some of its Indian police to keep the trail open, Taylor sued them for damages in county court. The Justice Department retaliated with a lawsuit on behalf of the Yakama Nation, *United States v. Frank Taylor*, which reached the Supreme Court of Washington Territory on appeal from the plaintiff. While recognizing Taylor's title to the land, the court held that "the Treaty privilege of the Indians to take fish was an easement upon it at the time the government conveyed the title and that such title did not extinguish the easement." In other words treaty Indians had the right to cross private property when passing to and from their traditional fishing sites. This opinion reversed the initial ruling of the district court and remanded the case for a new trial, resulting in an injunction against Taylor in October 1887. The tribes had won the first battle, but the war had only just begun.[12]

Neither the court order nor the transfer of title to Orson D. Taylor, an unrelated Baptist minister, ended white opposition to Native fishing at Tumwater. Indeed, the new owner turned out to be even less charitable and more devious than the previous one. Citing the fact that some Indian fishers lived off the reservation and claimed homesteads, which required them to forswear any tribal allegiances, Reverend Taylor contended that they had severed their tribal relations and forfeited their treaty rights. His argument followed a seductive but spurious line of reasoning. In fact, many Indians came to Tumwater from the reservations, drawn by the age-old lure of salmon and the enduring bonds of kinship. Even those who had obtained land on the public domain maintained de facto tribal relations through family ties and continued participation in the seasonal round. The Indian Office rejected Taylor's cynical manipulation of the law on the narrow grounds that the Indian Homestead Act permitted entrants to retain their shares of *tribal* property. However, the case showed that the notion of usual and accustomed fishing places belonging to tribes, not individuals and families, left some Indians vulnerable to attack. In the clashes yet to come, adversaries like Taylor would use the government's own categories against the people they supposedly defined.[13]

The concept of ceded tribal areas, central to the process of treaty making, proved irresistible to foes of Native fishing. Within nine months of the *Taylor* decision, the Oregon Railway and Navigation Company brought trespassing charges against Indians fishing at customary locations on the Washington side of the Cascade rapids. W. H. Holcomb, the company's general manager, insisted the charges were justified because the ceded territory described in the Yakama treaty "[did] not include the land where these Indians have been fishing, hence no agreements made in that Treaty could possibly be applied to this land." Furthermore, he argued, the railroad had purchased the property from a settler who perfected his claim under the Oregon Donation Land Act of 1850, nine years before Congress ratified the Yakama treaty. The *Taylor* case therefore had no bearing on the current dispute because the fishing easement had not been established when the land left the public domain. Holcomb was wrong on both counts. Besides accepting the false premise that the treaties had granted a privilege to the tribes, he assumed that Mid-Columbia Indians had once stayed within a fixed set of tribal boundaries. The Indian Office promptly pointed out these erroneous assumptions, which its own policies had fostered, but they remained potent legal weapons for adversaries committed to keeping Indians away from the river.[14]

Native fishers affiliated with the Warm Springs Reservation also lived in the shadow of the 1865 Huntington treaty, which supposedly surrendered the off-reservation hunting and fishing rights reserved ten years earlier. Although federal officials had never enforced that agreement because of its fraudulent character, white competitors claimed that the Indian parties to it had forfeited their fishing grounds on the Columbia. River dwellers and reservation residents alike faced a serious threat, since every Indian living south of the Columbia and west of the John Day River ostensibly belonged to the Warm Springs agency. In May of 1887 an OIA field inspector listened to anxious tribal leaders recount their understanding of the Huntington treaty. According to William Chinook, the elder statesman of the Kiksht-speaking Wascos, Oregon Superintendent of Indian Affairs J. W. Perit Huntington had said that the agreement merely required Indians to "get a paper or a pass when we wanted to go outside the Reservation." They had not knowingly surrendered their treaty rights, whatever the printed document said. "Huntington told lies when he said so," insisted Chinook. "We never sold any right to fish. I don't lie. My people would starve without their fish." The Warm Springs chief and former "renegade" Queahpahmah added a plea for the Sahaptin-speaking residents of the reservation: "I feel here in my heart that I and my people have been wronged by the white people, have been cheated by Huntington agent of our rights to fish, have been driven from [the] Columbia River like dogs, when we were promised protection. Tell this to the President, and ask him to help me, and the Warm Springs Indians at Simnasho."[15]

Help arrived the following summer in the form of two special agents, Thomas S. Lang and George W. Gordon, whose 1889 report furthered the transformation of the fisheries into tribal spaces. Lang, posted in The Dalles, spent the next five years trying to enforce the *Taylor* decision and resolve fresh disputes between Indians and whites. He faced stubborn resistance, however, and his own attitude made him a dubious advocate for tribal interests. While highly critical of Taylor and other "fishery whites," Lang accepted the legitimacy of the Huntington treaty and often appeared insensitive to Native concerns. The off-reservation Columbia River Indians especially annoyed him with their "very unreasonable" and "loud demands for immediate redress." When seeking potential witnesses to testify in court, Lang preferred to rely on the "best men" of the reservation rather than enlist "blowhards such as we have here."[16]

George Gordon shared his colleague's ambivalence about their assignment because it appeared to contradict the government's policy of forcing Indians to abandon their traditions and assimilate into American society. During the summer and fall of 1888, Gordon traveled the Columbia River from the Cascades to Wallula Gap seeking to buy land for Indians near the fisheries. Congress appropriated $3,000 for that purpose, but Gordon found few suitable tracts and fewer willing sellers. Except for a handful of marginal plots, which he proposed withdrawing from sale and settlement, virtually all the riparian property of value for fishing or camping had passed into private ownership. Gordon approached seven owners on the Oregon side of the river, including two Indian homesteaders, but he received only one attractive offer. While he advised taking it "upon the ground of abstract justice to the Indians of the Warm Springs Reservation," he agreed with their agent's opinion that off-reservation fishing "had been an injury to the Indians and an obstacle to their progress." At the end of his voluminous report Gordon suggested that the money go instead "to the development of their agricultural and stock raising interests, from which a more certain and permanent source of subsistence could be secured and a better state of morals and of society established among them." Considering his lukewarm support, it is hardly surprising that the government failed to acquire any property for Indian fishers.[17]

The Gordon Report further reinforced the idea that usual and accustomed fishing places belonged to recognized tribes. In the treaties the government had purported to transform personal and familial prerogatives into a collective entitlement governed by tribal affiliation. Hence, when Gordon visited the fisheries, he identified the various Indians he encountered with one or another of the neighboring agencies. Though not entirely arbitrary or inaccurate, his labels simplified the situation in a way that invited future conflict and endangered the rights of individual Indians. In his description of Celilo Falls, for example, Gordon associated the fishery with "the Indians of the Warm Springs reservation and the non-reservation Indians originally belonging to said reservation." This crude categorization not only ignored the presence of fishers affiliated with other bands at other agencies, it also implied that off-reservation Indians residing at the falls were bound by the Huntington treaty—an agreement their leaders had never signed. Opponents of tribal fishing had already made this claim and would do so again in the future. Even as Gordon fought against their exclusionary efforts, his report gave them potential ammunition.[18]

Many Indians already understood the significance of affiliation with a named treaty tribe, although they sometimes chose not to claim it. For those living within the ceded area of the Middle Oregon treaty, Huntington's handiwork offered an especially powerful incentive to avoid association with the Warm Springs agency. In an 1885 report on the problems at Celilo, agent Alonzo Gesner identified "six or eight hundred non-treaty Indians, who live along the Columbia River . . . and want to be let alone." While these people had many reasons for wanting to be left alone, including their general opposition to removal and assimilation, the fear of losing their fishing rights provided additional incentive to claim nontreaty status. Conversely, during Gordon's investigation of the trespassing dispute at the Cascades, the local Indians assured him that "they originally belonged . . . to the Yakima tribes or nation, though not now residing upon the Yakima reservation, and that they had been accustomed from time immemorial to take fish at these fisheries." Salmon remained a matter of survival for Mid-Columbia Indians, and federal policy tied access to tribal membership. The answers they gave to Gordon's questions could determine whether the government provided or withheld support in the struggle against white competitors.[19]

That struggle soon resumed at the Tumwater fishery. In the late 1880s brothers Audubon and Linnaeus Winans strung a fence across their homestead that impeded Native travel to the river. Echoing the Taylors, they insisted it was essential to protect their crops and pastures from Indian ponies, yet the brothers lost no time in building three fishwheels. Their barbed-wire barrier prevented Indians from reaching both the accustomed fishing stations and an important natural spring. As a river resident named White Salmon Charley recalled: "The children used to crawl outside of the fence for water and tear their clothes. That is the way the Winans are stopping the Indians from getting in." "I seen Winans Brothers," added Charley Ike, who lived in the nearby village of Wishram, "I said you have no right to blast rocks at salmon stations. They said the Indians had no right to claim any more a fishery. If the Indians want to make a fight, get them lawyers in Yakima and we will have all the Indians drove into the reservation, that is what they said last year to me." Federal officials called the brothers' bluff in 1897.[20]

The ensuing lawsuit, *United States v. Winans*, became a milestone in the history of American Indian law and the first of nine Northwest fishing rights cases to reach the U.S. Supreme Court. Hoping to overturn the *Taylor* precedent, defense attorneys Charles H. Carey and Franklin P. Mays raised several new arguments to bolster the Winans' property rights claim. First, they cited the Court's recent ruling in *Ward v. Race Horse*, which struck down Shoshone-Bannock treaty rights on the basis of the constitutional provision that new states join the Union on an equal footing with existing states. Because Washington's 1889 admission to statehood had supposedly abrogated treaties made during the territorial period, the Winans' lawyers contended, Indians held only the common right to fish enjoyed by all citizens of the state. The defense then advanced the rather contradictory assertion that their clients' use of state-licensed wheels gave them a right superior to that of Native dip-netters, "since wheel fishing is one of the civilized man's methods, as legitimate as the substitution of the modern combine harvester for the ancient sickle and flail." Even when erected at traditional grounds, fishwheels did not deprive Indians because their common right "[applied] to no certain and defined places." In other words, the Winans team alleged, Indians could always catch salmon somewhere else on the river.[21]

This final argument played on the notion that the fisheries originally belonged to recognized tribes with well-defined populations and boundaries. According to that logic, any member of the Yakama Nation or its fourteen constituent groups could take salmon at any usual and accustomed place within the tribes' ceded area. Fishing sites were thus interchangeable and open to all comers, regardless of their aboriginal ancestry and family history. In the courtroom, however, Native testimony exposed serious defects in this line of thinking. Take, for instance, an exchange between defense attorney Franklin Mays and Sam Tanawasha, a longtime resident of Wishram Village. When asked if he was a Yakama Indian, Tanawasha replied: "My mother is a Wisham [Wishram], I am right there at Wisham."[22] Mays then pressed him on the issue of fisheries, trying to elicit the desired response:

Q: Do you know about the fishery called Skin?
A: That is another tribe's fishing ground.
Q: Isn't there a good fishery there?
A: It is a fishing ground that belongs to another group of Indians.
Q: Couldn't you go there and fish?
A: No, I can't fish there, the Indians won't allow me, I couldn't go there.
Q: Are not the Indians that do fish there part of the Yakima Nation?
A: They used to go, some that have relatives there, go to Skin, at Wisham there is more salmon.[23]

Mays's cross-examination of other Indians produced similar results. Hoping to prove that people enrolled in the Yakama Nation could fish anywhere within their tribal territory, he instead demonstrated that indigenous conceptions of ownership still governed the fisheries almost forty years after the treaties became law.

Although Indian witnesses used the term "tribe," or at least had their words translated that way, their testimony showed that the concept still puzzled some people. They understood that the Yakama treaty protected their right to fish at all usual and accustomed places. They did not assume that it dictated universal access to those sites, however, as Wishram resident Martin Spedis later explained: "The various fishing stations were the private property of individual family groups and they were handed down from generation to generation . . . it had always been that way and the Indians always recognized their own rights to family stations."[24] People from Wishram and their relatives fished primarily at Tumwater, while residents of Skin and their relations generally caught salmon farther upstream at Celilo Falls. White Swan, named as one of the co-plaintiffs in the case, claimed fishing rights at Wishram because his wife came from that community, not because he served as head chief of the Yakama Nation. For many off-reservation Indians in particular, aboriginal attachments still mattered more than the tribal categories created by treaty. Hence, when Mays interrogated witnesses such as Joe Kolocken about their identity, it often produced confusion and consternation on both sides:

Q: You belong to the Yakima tribe or nation of Indians?
A: Yes, I used to go there.
Q: I am asking you if you belong to the Yakima tribe or nation of Indians.
A: I don't belong, I am not a Yakima.
Q: What are you?
A: Wisham.[25]

The sticking point was the difference between aboriginal identity and post-treaty tribal affiliation. Kolocken possessed legal rights under the Yakama treaty, by virtue of his membership in the signatory and constituent Wishram "tribe," and he sometimes visited the reservation where many of his people had settled. In his view, however, traveling to that place and associating with its residents did not make him a Yakama or give him the right to fish anywhere along the river.[26]

Native testimony also frustrated defense efforts to minimize the significance of salmon for tribal subsistence. Pointing to the idealized vision of land allotment, not its actual results, Mays suggested that Indians no longer needed fish because they had become farmers. This argument, aimed at the so-called progressives on the reservations, ran headlong into a wall of traditionalism. Bill Charley, a lifelong river dweller, raised some hay and potatoes on his allotment yet still depended on fishing for food and cash. "I don't know how the people live that went over [to Fort Simcoe], I have not been on the reservation," he told Mays, "but I used just as much salmon as I ever did." Speaking for reservation residents, White Swan declared: "I can't myself get along without the salmon, I don't know how to eat hog meat, I don't like it very well myself and that is the way it is with the other Indians, I suppose." As he understood it, the treaty assured them "you have your rights in the Columbia River to get this fish, the great father in Washington is not asking you for this river or this salmon, all the great father wants [is] the land for whites to settle by and by. But as long as the world stays here you will have all the salmon you want in this river all the time." A host of other witnesses said the same thing. Unable to prove its claims, and unwilling to accept the Native interpretation of the fishing clause, the defense team ultimately dismissed Indian testimony as "incompetent and inadmissible when it would tend to vary the plain stipulations of the treaty."[27]

The federal district judge agreed with the defense, but the Supreme Court overturned his decision on appeal and set forth two vital principles governing treaty interpretation. The first stated that treaties must be construed as the Indians understood them at the time and "as justice and reason demand," since the United States exerted superior power over the "unlettered" tribal representatives. The second, known as the reserved rights doctrine, held that treaties were "not a grant of rights to the Indians, but a grant of rights from them—a reservation of those not granted." Putting these principles into action, Justice McKenna declared that members of the Yakama Nation had retained their existing rights to cross the land, to fish at usual and accustomed places, and to erect temporary houses for curing their catch. Neither private property nor superior technology gave the Winans family an exclusive claim to the fishery, and they could not restrict the Indians in their use of it. Although Washington State might regulate their fishing, it too was bound to respect Indian treaties that preceded its admission to the Union.[28]

McKenna never explicitly addressed whether fishing rights resided in the tribe or with individuals because it did not bear directly on the issues at hand. In defining the scope of the treaties, he did recognize that they had reserved rights "to every individual Indian, as though named therein. They imposed a servitude upon every piece of land as though described therein." Throughout the opinion, however, he referred to the plaintiffs as "Yakima Indians" or "certain Indians of the Yakima Nation." While correct in the sense intended by U.S. treaty makers, such labels flattened persistent ethnic distinctions and implied that the Wishram fishery at Tumwater belonged to all "Yakima Indians," despite substantial testimony to the contrary. This construction of the treaties, conveyed to Indians by their agents and attorneys, laid the groundwork for tribal claims to the fisheries later in the century. Nevertheless, most Indians still adhered to the aboriginal conception of fishing sites. Writing in 1924, Yakama superintendent Evan W. Estep professed to be "doubtful about whether any one Indian can claim the exclusive right of fishing from a particular rock or island, yet I note that numbers of them claim this right as one which descended to them from someone else." The tension between these perspectives became glaringly obvious in the conflicts to come.[29]

The *Winans* decision, like the earlier *Taylor* case, failed to bring lasting peace on the river. Regulatory disputes with Washington State loomed in the near future, and the ruling changed nothing on the Oregon shore, where the Huntington treaty still threatened Indian fishing rights. Natives on that side of the river took salmon at the whim of the Seufert Brothers Company, which claimed most of the riparian property between The Dalles and Celilo Falls. By the time *Winans* went to trial, many local Indians had signed contracts to supply fish to the canneries. Seufert Brothers sold twine for nets, extended credit during the off-season, and allowed Indians employed by the company to take scrap lumber for fuel and scaffolding. The cannery's Chinese butchers also gave Indians discarded fish heads and tails, which they then dried and sold to visiting reservation residents. Owner Frank Seufert even allowed Indians to camp on his land as long as they did not damage his property or interfere with the wheels. His company had a history of aggressive land acquisition, however, and many Indians already resented him for blasting away traditional fishing sites near Tumwater. He antagonized them further by testifying for the Winans brothers and purchasing their land shortly before the case concluded. As his empire grew in the early twentieth century, he did not hesitate to challenge Indian fishing when it conflicted with his business interests.[30]

Seufert's principal confrontation with the treaties arose from the activities of an Indian named Sam Williams, an erstwhile company employee and the minister of the Indian Shaker Church at The Dalles. In 1907, Williams filed a homestead entry on behalf of his granddaughter for eighty acres adjoining Three Mile Rapids. Known to Native people as Wah-sucks, or Lone Pine, the area had once been a traditional fishing and camping ground for several villages on both sides of the river. Williams had obtained aboriginal rights to the fishery from its previous owner, Wasco Charley, but Seufert already claimed the surrounding land. By the time the General Land Office cancelled Williams's entry in 1915, he had begun operating a state-licensed fishing scow from a mooring on the contested point. Seufert tolerated Williams's presence and even helped him secure licenses as long as he sold his catch to the company.

In the summer of 1913, however, Williams switched to a buyer who offered better prices and hired several white men to work his scow. Their vessel competed with two of Seufert's Indian crews, which tried to stop Williams's scow from fishing that season. When his crew returned the following spring, Seufert took matters into his own hands—literally—and set their boat adrift. His employees repeated the offense four more times during the 1914 season, arguing that Williams had trespassed on company property. Williams sued for $2,000 in damages and requested an injunction to prevent the company from using the disputed river frontage. Anticipating a difficult battle, he called on the Yakama agency to help "protect my indian fishing right along river . . . [I] cannot fight millionaire corporation in courts without help of indian department." Another fish fight had begun.[31]

Throughout the ensuing trial, known as *United States ex. rel. Williams v. Seufert Brothers*, questions swirled around the identity of Sam Williams. Born to a Yakama father and a Cowlitz mother, he had spent part of his youth west of the Cascade Mountains. Although he had taken an allotment on the Yakama Reservation in 1897, he later sold part of it and moved to an Indian homestead along the Columbia River. Consequently, his rights as a member of the Yakama Nation seemed dubious to Seufert, who exploited popular notions of "blood" and "tribe" to argue that the treaty had no bearing on the case. In an angry letter to the U.S. district attorney, Seufert declared: "I cannot allow Indians of the Sam Williams stripe, who really do not belong here, but belong to western Washington Agency, to come here, gather up some white trash to stand behind them, so they can ask the Government to do their lawing for them. Williams belongs to the Quinault Reservation, and they have good fishing grounds there, and he should be made to go there."[32]

Echoing this sentiment, Seufert witness Charles Switzler informed a federal attorney that Williams "hasn't any more rights on that place then [sic] I have. I told him this Sam is a different person from all the Wasco's[,] he doesn't belong there and never was raised there. I said to the lawyer, '[E]ven I have a little Wasco blood in me and I don't bother about any fisherys [sic].'" In fact, Williams's right to fish at Lone Pine rested on his arrangements with the late Wasco Charley and his marriage to a Wasco woman named Susie, not on any personal claim to Wasco identity. Under the government's system of tribal classification, however, he remained vulnerable to charges that he had no place on the

Columbia River at all. Even the Justice Department harbored doubts and only agreed to proceed after the Indian Office assured that Williams had been allotted as "a straight Yakima Indian."[33]

Seufert's defense dropped the Cowlitz identity issue at trial, choosing instead to attack the rights of the Yakama Nation as a whole. Knowing that the company could not lawfully exclude treaty Indians in light of the *Winans* decision, his lawyers set out to prove that the confederated tribes possessed no fishing rights south of the Columbia River. The concept of ceded areas played straight into their hands. As the treaty commissioners had rendered it on paper, Yakama territory ended at the water's northern edge. The agency superintendent, Don M. Carr, privately admitted that to be his own understanding and also wondered whether the treaty applied to Indians fishing commercially with modern technology. Seufert's attorneys argued that even if Williams was an Indian and a member of the Yakama Nation, he could not possibly have a "usual and accustomed" fishing place on the Oregon shore. Those sites belonged to the tribes of the Warm Springs Reservation, which had supposedly given up their off-reservation rights in 1865. The logic was as clear and cold as the river itself. If the court accepted it, Seufert Brothers Company would become the principal owner and arbiter of fishing *privileges* on the Oregon side of the Columbia.[34]

At the initial hearing on May 24, 1915, district court judge Charles E. Wolverton leaned toward the defendant's point of view. The government avowed that "the Indians upon one side went to the other side, and vice versa, and that the fishing was a right in common," but he remained skeptical. In his opinion the Warm Springs Indians had surrendered their off-reservation rights in the Huntington treaty, leaving "the right as claimed by the Yakimas to be established upon their own customs, and upon their own practices, in fishing upon the south side." The testimony of several non-Indian witnesses and two elderly tribal leaders failed to satisfy Wolverton. He lifted a temporary injunction against Seufert Brothers but kept the case open, giving the government a chance to produce additional evidence and initiate further proceedings. If it chose to do so, he advised, "the plaintiff should enlarge the scope of his action, and include the Yakima Indians as a tribe, or their confederated tribes, so as to secure the community right belonging to those confederated tribes, if they have one."[35]

This final word of advice reflected Wolverton's judgment that fishing rights were indeed a tribal prerogative, which Williams had forfeited by accepting U.S. citizenship. Since he was no longer a member of an Indian community, one of a tribe or band, his lawsuit could not establish any rights on behalf of the Yakama Nation. Wolverton based this opinion on the fact that Williams had received a fee patent for his allotment and had taken an Indian homestead on the public domain, which required him to swear that he had severed "tribal relations" and adopted "the habits and pursuits of civilized life." On the surface Williams had met these stipulations. He resided off-reservation, held landed property, operated a fishing scow, wore Euro-American clothing, and presided over a nominally Christian church. For making such adjustments, the government had rewarded him with citizenship. Yet there is little reason to believe that Williams had truly severed tribal relations or ceased to think of himself as an Indian. Though more acculturated than many of his neighbors, he still spoke the Cowlitz language and lived among Indians in an off-reservation community. As a leader of the Indian Shaker Church, he ministered to Native people visiting the fisheries, healed their sick, and worked to protect their religious freedom against government persecution—all activities that entailed maintaining connections to his co-religionists on the reservations. Williams's life suggested no contradiction between "citizen" and "Indian," but the law framed them as exclusive categories.[36]

The Justice Department responded to Wolverton's advice by naming the Yakama Nation as a plaintiff and broadening the pool of evidence concerning traditional fishing practices. To counter Seufert's contention that Indians from the north never fished south of the Columbia, agency superintendents recruited an army of witnesses who had seen or done that very thing.[37] Tomar Handley, a venerable Wasco resident of the Warm Springs Reservation, testified to the historic mingling of diverse peoples at The Dalles:

Q: Did the Wasco Indians ever object to the Yakima Indians coming across to fish at Wah-sucks?
A: No.
Q: Well did the Yakimas ever object to the Wascos going over on their side?
A: No.
Q: Why did not one tribe, either the Yakimas or the Wascos, object to the other tribe fishing there?
A: Well, they were friendly, and they were related through marriage.[38]

The theme of kinship also permeated the statements of "Old Man" Pipeshire (Simtustus), an octogenarian Warm Springs Indian who traditionally fished at Celilo Falls:

Q: What were the relations of the tribes that met there, as to whether or not they would dispute or have trouble among themselves?
A: Never was any dispute, they married back and forth.
Q: What tribes were married back and forth?
A: The Indians married over to Wash-ham [sic] and the Yakima, and the Yakimas married over to the Wascos and Celilos.[39]

Again and again, Indians and non-Indians alike affirmed that the river was not a wall between separate and distinct tribes. "We knew no Oregon or Washington. We knew only that the shores were our fishing grounds," declared George Waters, who succeeded his brother White Swan as the head chief of the Yakama Nation. Even in 1915, said a resident of Skin called Doctor Sheawa, the Columbia remained "a table for [Indians on] both sides of the river. It laid right in between them, and they came and ate and were gone." Family relationships governed where people sat at this table, but many guests could choose from a number of different chairs.[40]

The weight of oral evidence presented at trial shifted Judge Wolverton's opinion in favor of the Indians. On May 1, 1916, he ruled that Lone Pine was indeed a traditional fishing site for the confederated tribes of the Yakama Nation and that Seufert Brothers "should be enjoined from exercising any pretended fishing right along or within this space." Citing the canons of treaty construction established in the *Winans* decision, Wolverton demolished the assumption that ceded areas limited tribal fishing grounds. "The Indian tribes did not themselves occupy definite territory with fixed and exact boundaries," he wrote, "and it is without doubt that the different tribes commingled more or less, and roamed about. . . . And so of their fishing—there was no monopoly by any one tribe of any specific and fixed territory." The ceded areas outlined in the treaties were merely a convenient device for extinguishing aboriginal title to the land. Drawn with that goal in mind, "they very naturally only followed in a general way the very general idea that the Indians had of their territorial delimitations." Native representatives agreed to these boundaries with the understanding that their people could continue to hunt, gather, and fish at their usual and accustomed places. Those rights had nothing to do with territorial boundaries, stated Wolverton, "since, to their mind, *all* such places were being reserved for their benefit anyway." Although the concept of tribal rights remained intact, the courts had seemingly laid to rest the illusion of tightly bounded and mutually exclusive tribal territories.[41]

Ironically, the Indian who had initiated the whole proceeding lost his own treaty rights as a result. Wolverton, expanding on his pronouncement at the hearing, declared that Sam Williams had become a citizen and could no longer demand government protection of his fishing rights. He had ostensibly lost his tribal status by accepting a fee patent, adopting "the habits of civilized life," and establishing his residence "separate and apart from any tribe." He possessed all the rights and privileges of an ordinary citizen but retained none under the Yakama treaty, which applied only to those still under the guardianship of the United States. Thus, even as Wolverton struck down artificial geographical boundaries between tribes, he reinforced the legal barrier between Indian identity and American citizenship.

Only a month later the U.S. Supreme Court's decision in *United States v. Nice* removed this barrier, and in 1924, Congress unilaterally conferred American citizenship on all Indians without stripping them of tribal membership. Even then, however, Seufert insisted that Williams was "not—so the court declared [—] an Indian." Seufert also continued to disobey the federal court order directing his company to vacate the contested river frontage. Judge Wolverton had cited him for contempt of court in 1920, but the Oregon Supreme Court subsequently upheld Seufert's property right in the separate damage suit that Williams initiated. Although Williams continued to fish at Lone Pine for several years, he did so as a regular citizen under contract with Seufert Brothers Company. Clearly frustrated by the arrangement and by the decline of his Shaker congregation, he moved downstream to Hood River in the late 1920s.[42]

While Seufert welcomed the court's dismissal of the "troublemaker" Williams, he had no intention of accepting the decision that members of the Yakama Nation possessed treaty rights at Lone Pine. "To my knowledge," he informed *The Oregonian*, "they have not fished there for thirty-five years, and to our witnesses' knowledge, about the same time. . . . None that fished for us were witnesses; those that did testify were drummed up from all parts, (except around the vicinity of our plant) old reservation Indians that never come to the river, and all this to create public sentiment." In Seufert's appeal to the U.S. Supreme Court, his lawyers challenged the tribal construction of the treaty on the grounds that it "imposes a servitude upon the Oregon soil." Since the Yakama treaty applied to Washington, they claimed, this servitude unfairly burdened property owners who had not anticipated it when they bought land in Oregon. The Supreme Court heard this argument in March 1919 but unanimously affirmed Wolverton's decree. The Indians' interpretation of the treaty was clear, declared Justice John Clarke, and their continued presence at the fisheries was so evident "that any person, not negligently or wilfuly [sic] blind to the condition of the property he was purchasing, must have known of them." After three decades of litigation, Mid-Columbia Indians had finally established their right of access to the river's precious salmon runs.[43]

In the process of defending the treaties, however, many Indians came to accept the government's legal restructuring of the fisheries. Indeed, some had already begun to act on the assumption that they could fish anywhere their tribe had recognized treaty rights. In 1915 an Indian homesteader named Emma Dave asked the Yakama agency to stop Olie Charley from fishing on her land along the Klickitat River. "He is a Tumwater Indian, and owns interest in fishwheels at Tumwater," she explained, but the poor spring runs had driven him to Klickitat Falls. "I have forbid him of coming on my premises but he says that he has a right to fish here because he is an Indian, and he is still fishing." Dave's complaint revealed the conflict brewing between the tribal right outlined in the treaties and the individual rights of aboriginal custom. Charley assumed that his membership in the Yakama Nation enabled him to fish at any of the aboriginal locations reserved by the treaty. Dave accorded him only the privileges of a visitor, and her family could not afford generosity because there was "not a very large run of salmon this year and we need them all for our own use." Because Charley no longer respected aboriginal practice, Dave could only hope that the government would enforce her rights as a landowner.[44]

Similar disputes erupted at Celilo Falls, where some Indians attempted to turn Seufert's arguments against fishers from the Yakama Reservation. In 1922, three years after the Supreme Court affirmed the *Seufert* decision, several witnesses accused the local headman Tommy Thompson and a Umatilla enrollee named Andrew Barnhart of trying to collect a $5 fee from members of the Yakama Nation before permitting them to catch salmon on the south side of the river. Two white men were also implicated in this alleged scheme, but Yakama Superintendent Don Carr focused his wrath on the Oregon Indians. Although the Indians' precise motives remain a matter of speculation, the cultural and historical context suggests something more than a desire for monetary gain. In recent years the Celilo fishery had grown increasingly crowded as irrigation dams on the Yakima and Umatilla rivers damaged the runs there and forced Indians away from their traditional locations. Many of the newcomers to Celilo had no customary place at the falls, and Chief Thompson rejected the claim that they had rights under the Yakama treaty. As he later testified in the 1930s, Yakamas already had "many favorable locations at which to fish on their side of the River . . . [where] Celilo and Oregon Indians are not permitted to fish."[45] The family table that Doctor Sheawa spoke of in 1915 was in danger of being overturned by an intertribal squabble that had started with rumors and false accusations made in court.

If Thompson and Barnhart did attempt to impose a fee on Yakama fishers, it may have represented an attempt to preserve Thompson's mediating role as the "salmon chief," who had traditionally regulated the fishery and adjudicated outsiders' requests to use particular sites. Such behavior clashed with the federal government's construction of the treaties, however, and the Yakama superintendent lashed out at Barnhart. "As a member of the Umatilla tribe I do not understand that you have any Treaty fishing rights on the Columbia River," he scolded, "and certainly you do not have any under the Yakima Treaty." The reprimand had little effect. In 1925 and again in 1927, Barnhart allegedly ordered Yakamas to leave Celilo because they had no rights in Oregon. The embarrassed Umatilla agent assured his colleague that "what [Barnhart knows] about the legal status of affairs on the Oregon side of the Columbia River would not fill a very large book." Thanks to the *Seufert* case, however, he knew enough to make trouble for other Indians.[46]

Disagreements within and between the tribes intensified over the next forty years, even as they struggled to fend off the common threat of state regulation. With salmon runs dwindling and other fisheries disappearing beneath reservoirs, many Indians migrated to the remaining sites between The Dalles and Celilo Falls. The Celilo Fish Committee (CFC), created in 1936 to settle the proliferating disputes, provided a forum for competing visions of the fishery. Local residents and people with ancestral fishing stations, such as Chief Thompson, viewed treaty rights as a legal umbrella beneath which traditional rules still applied. By contrast, newcomers and advocates of tribal control embraced the framework established in the treaties and reinforced through litigation.[47] As Barnhart explained to the CFC in 1942: "I was appointed a fish committeeman from my Umatilla Reservation to protect my tribal rights. I can remember the old people that fished here at Celilo—Wyam Indians. But the white man has come here and ruled your location as a tribal relation . . . this Committee will not determine one individual ownership to one location. But we must rule equal right."[48]

Two decades later the courts finally settled the question in the case of *Whitefoot v. United States*, which expressly defined treaty rights as tribal property.[49] Off-reservation activists such as David Sohappy still resisted the change, but the tribes embraced it as an opportunity to exercise their hard-won sovereignty. They began passing their own ordinances to regulate tribal fishing and eventually formed the Columbia River Inter-Tribal Fish Commission to oversee enforcement efforts. Perhaps the final blow to the "old ways" came in the early 1980s, when the Warm Springs and Yakama councils reluctantly backed federal efforts to evict the Sohappy family and other river residents from in-lieu fishing areas (built to replace those flooded by Bonneville Dam) on the grounds that the sites belonged to the tribes as a whole.[50]

Tensions among Indians, though more muted now, constitute but one legacy of the legal restructuring initiated in 1855. In 2005, as the Native nations that grew from the treaties staged their sesquicentennial commemorations, tribal leaders reminded the public that the United States did not give Indians territory, sovereignty, or identity; they already possessed all of those things. Rather, federal treaty commissioners and jurists took forms of social and political organization they did not fully understand and repackaged them as "tribes." Native people then had to sort out the meaning of this transformation, including its ramifications for such traditional activities as fishing. They have not always reached the same conclusion, and the debates within and between tribal communities provide a revealing window into Indian intellectual history.

Like contemporaneous discussions of tribal land tenure, which historian Alexandra Harmon has documented in her work on Indian Territory, intra- and intertribal disputes over treaty fishing rights constituted a "broad bilateral and intercultural discourse" about economic culture, political sovereignty, and group affiliation. Such debates are, Harmon notes, "a potent reminder that Indians have an intellectual history whose complex relationship to Euro-Americans' intellectual history deserves further research and thought." The *Taylor-Winans-Seufert* trilogy hastened the redefinition of Mid-Columbia Indian communities in the eyes of the law and eventually in the eyes of Indians themselves. To fully understand the dynamics of that process, scholars must engage in the sort of difficult, detailed genealogical research advocated by ethnohistorian Russel Barsh. Only then will they be able to determine precisely how the bonds of kinship that tied Indians to their fishing sites were strained and snapped by the lowering weight of federal policy and jurisprudence.[51]

NOTES

The author thanks the American Philosophical Society, the College of William and Mary, and the Center for Columbia River History for helping to fund his research.

1. In 1992 the Yakama Indian Nation reverted to the original spelling of its tribal name: "Yakima" is now spelled "Yakama." I have adopted this spelling to honor the tribe's decision and to distinguish the Indians from the river, county, and city of the same name. Quotations and citations containing the variant spelling have not been changed. Portions of this essay appeared previously in Andrew H. Fisher, "Tangled Nets: Treaty Rights and Tribal Identities at Celilo Falls," *Oregon Historical Quarterly* 105 (summer 2004): 179–211.

2. For the purposes of this essay, "Middle Columbia River" refers to the segment between the Cascades and Priest Rapids, and "Mid-Columbia Indians" to the various Kikst- and Sahaptin-speaking communities living along that stretch.

3. *United States v. Winans*, 198 U.S. 371 (1905).

4. For an overview of the Indian fishing controversy, see Fay G. Cohen, *Treaties on Trial: The Continuing Controversy over Northwest Indian Fishing Rights* (Seattle: University of Washington Press, 1986).

5. Russel Lawrence Barsh, "Ethnogenesis and Ethnonationalism from Competing Treaty Claims," paper presented at the Pacific Northwest Treaties in National and International Perspective Conference, University of Washington, Seattle, May 2005, copy in author's possession, 1–2; and Alexandra Harmon, *Indians in the Making: Ethnic Relations and Indian Identities around Puget Sound* (Berkeley: University of California Press, 1998), 72–85. On the role of law in American colonialism, see Sidney Harring, *Crow Dog's Case: American Indian Sovereignty, Tribal Law, and United States Law in the Nineteenth Century* (Cambridge: Cam-

bridge University Press, 1994); Charles F. Wilkinson, *American Indians, Time, and the Law: Native Societies in a Modern Constitutional Democracy* (New Haven, Conn.: Yale University Press, 1987); and Robert A. Williams, *The American Indian in Western Legal Thought: The Discourses of Conquest* (New York: Oxford University Press, 1990).

6. The Palmer treaties are named for Joel Palmer, Oregon superintendent of Indian affairs, who in 1855 concluded agreements with the peoples who became the Confederated Tribes of the Umatilla Indian Reservation and the Confederated Tribes of Warm Springs.

7. Robert Boyd, *The People of The Dalles: The Indians of Wascopam Mission* (Lincoln: University of Nebraska Press, 1996), 4–5; Helen H. Schuster, "Yakama and Neighboring Groups," in *Handbook of North American Indians*, vol. 12, edited by Deward E. Walker (Washington, D.C.: Smithsonian Institution, 1998), 327; Eugene S. Hunn, with James Selam and Family, *Nch'i-Wána, "The Big River": Mid-Columbia Indians and Their Land* (Seattle: University of Washington Press, 1990), 216–17; Barsh, "Ethnogenesis and Ethnonationalism from Competing Treaty Claims," this volume; and Harmon, *Indians in the Making*, 8.

8. Treaty with the Yakima, 1855, in *Indian Affairs: Laws and Treaties*, vol. 2, edited by Charles J. Kappler (Washington, D.C.: Government Printing Office, 1904), 699, emphasis added.

9. Joseph E. Taylor III, *Making Salmon: An Environmental History of the Northwest Fisheries Crisis* (Seattle: University of Washington Press, 1999), 62–64, 144. For detailed descriptions of fishwheels on the Columbia River, see Francis Seufert, *Wheels of Fortune*, edited by Thomas Vaughan (Portland: Oregon Historical Society, 1980); and Ivan J. Donaldson and Frederick K. Cramer, *Fishwheels of the Columbia* (Portland, Ore.: Binfords & Mort, 1971).

10. James Wilbur to Hiram Price, 21 May 1881, U.S. Bureau of Indian Affairs, Yakima Indian Agency Correspondence and Records (National Archives Microfilm Publication I6) (I6), Clifford C. Relander Collection, Yakima Valley Regional Library, Roll 2.

11. Ibid.; Joseph C. Dupris, Kathleen S. Hill, and William H. Rodgers Jr., *The Si'lailo Way: Indians, Salmon, and Law on the Columbia River* (Durham, N.C.: Carolina Academic Press, 2006), 61.

12. R. H. Milroy to John B. Allen, 22 June 1885, Vol. 3, 1882–1887, Press Copies of Letters Sent to Commissioner of Indian Affairs, 1882–1914 (Letters Sent, 1882–1914), Yakima Indian Agency (YIA), Records of the Bureau of Indian Affairs, Record Group (RG) 75, National Archives and Records Administration—Pacific Alaska Region (Seattle) (NARA-PAR); R. H. Milroy to John D. C. Atkins, 21 July 1885, Letters Sent, 1882–1914, YIA, RG 75, NARA-PAR; George W. Gordon, Report upon the Subject of the Fishing Privileges Etc. Guaranteed by Treaties to Indians in the Northwest, with Recommendations in Regard Thereto, 19 January 1889 (hereafter cited as Gordon Report), transcript, Les McConnell Collection (hereafter cited as McConnell), Portland Area Office (PAO), RG 75, NARA-PAR,

13–14, 41–43; *United States v. Taylor*, 3 Washington Territory 88 (1887); *United States v. Taylor*, 44 Federal Report 2 (1887).

13. Gordon Report, 16–17.

14. Ibid., 21–23, 25–26.

15. Report of Inspector Frank C. Armstrong, 14 May 1887, Records of Inspection of the Field Jurisdiction of the Office of Indian Affairs (National Archives Microfilm Publication M1070) (M1070), Records of the Bureau of Indian Affairs, Washington, D.C., Roll 58.

16. Thomas S. Lang to Thomas Priestley, 24 March 1890, I6, Roll 3.

17. Gordon Report, 1–4, 34–36; George W. Gordon to John H. Oberly, 12 January 1889, McConnell, PAO, RG 75, NARA-PAR.

18. Gordon Report, 88–89.

19. Alonzo Gesner to Nelson A. Miles, 15 May 1885, Vol. 4, 12 January 1885–25 July 1886, Letters Sent to Commissioner of Indian Affairs, 1869–1914 (Letters Sent, 1869–1914), Warm Springs Indian Agency (WSIA), RG 75, NARA-PAR, 161–62; and Gordon Report, 8–9.

20. Charley quote in Barbara Leibhardt, "Land Divided: Yakama Tribal Land Use in the Federal Allotment Era," in *Northwest Lands, Northwest Peoples: Readings in Environmental History*, edited by Dale D. Goble and Paul W. Hirt (Seattle: University of Washington Press, 1999), 213; Testimony in *United States of America, Thomas Simpson and White Swan, plaintiffs, vs. A. and L. Winans*, defendants, 1897 (typescript), MSS 4 (hereafter Winans Testimony), Oregon Historical Society, Portland (hereafter OHS), 55.

21. Cohen, *Treaties on Trial*, 55; and *United States v. Winans*, 382.

22. Winans Testimony, 60.

23. Ibid., 64.

24. Affidavit of Martin Spedis, in Edward G. Swindell Jr., *Report on Source, Nature, and Extent of the Fishing, Hunting, and Miscellaneous Related Rights of Certain Indian Tribes in Washington and Oregon Territory Together with Affidavits Showing the Location of a Number of Usual and Accustomed Fishing Grounds and Stations* (Los Angeles: Office of Indian Affairs, 1942), 175.

25. Winans Testimony, 68.

26. Ibid., 88, 18, 12–13; and *United States v. Winans*, 382.

27. Winans Testimony, 88, 18, 12–13; and *United States v. Winans*, 382.

28. *United States v. Winans*, 382; and Cohen, *Treaties on Trial*, 55–56.

29. *United States v. Winans*, 381; and Evan W. Estep to Cary W. Ramsey, 15 April 1924, Fishing Matters along the Columbia River (1924) (hereafter Fishing Matters), General Correspondence (GC), YIA, RG 75, NARA-PAR, 4.

30. Winans Testimony, 203; Francis Seufert, *Wheels of Fortune* (Portland: Oregon Historical Society Press, 1981), 45–46; F. A. Seufert to Clarence L. Reams, 15 June 1914, Box 2, Envelope 17, Seufert Brothers Company Papers, 1884–1954, MSS 1102 (hereafter Seufert Papers), OHS, 3; and I. H. Taffe to George W. Olney, 26 July 1909, Fishing Matters—Seufert vs. Olney (1912–15), GC, YIA, RG 75, NARA-PAR.

31. "Indian Chief, 103, Is Erect in Court," 15 May 1915, *The* (Portland) *Oregonian*, 12; Don M. Carr to L. A. Dorrington, 9 August 1915, Williams, Sam v. Seufert Bros. Co. (1913–18) (hereafter *Williams v. Seufert*), GC, YIA, RG 75, NARA-PAR; Seufert to Reams, 15 June 1914, Seufert Papers, OHS, 1–2; Don M. Carr to Commissioner of Indian Affairs, 18 May 1914, *Williams v. Seufert*, GC, YIA, RG 75, NARA-PAR; Dupris, Hill, and Rodgers Jr., *The Si'lailo Way*, 110–11; and Sam Williams to Don M. Carr, 31 July 1913, *Williams v. Seufert*, GC, YIA, RG 75, NARA-PAR.

32. F. A. Seufert to Clarence L. Reams, 15 June 1914, Box 2, Envelope 17, Seufert Brothers Company Papers, 1884–1954, MSS 1102 (Seufert Papers), Oregon Historical Society, Portland 4.

33. Charles Switzler to F. A. Seufert, 6 April 1915, Box 2, Envelope 18, Seufert Papers, OHS; Don M. Carr to Robert E. Rankin, 29 April 1915, *Williams v. Seufert*, GC, YIA, RG 75, NARA-PAR; and Dupris, Hill, and Rodgers, *The Si'lailo Way*, 105.

34. The Trial of U.S. versus Seufert Brothers (hereafter the Sam Williams Case), Celilo Indian Fishermen, 1947–1951, Tribal Records, 1897–1957, YIA, RG 75, NARA-PAR, 1–2; Don M. Carr to Clarence Reames, 25 May 1914, *Williams v. Seufert*, GC, YIA, RG 75, NARA-PAR.

35. Opinion of Court (typescript), 24 May 1915, Sam Williams Case, Box 2, Envelope 19, Seufert Papers, OHS, 1–7.

36. Ibid., 7; Dupris, Hill, and Rodgers, *The Si'lailo Way*, 105; Robert H. Ruby and John A. Brown, *John Slocum and the Indian Shaker Church* (Norman: University of Oklahoma Press, 1996), 169–70.

37. L. A. Dorrington to Gilbert L. Hall, 27 May 1915, Fishing Rights, Subject Files (SF), WSIA, RG 75, NARA-PAR; and L. A. Dorrington to A. M. Reynolds, 15 January 1916, Fishing Rights, SF, WSIA, RG 75, NARA-PAR.

38. Dorrington to Reynolds, 15 January 1916, 2.

39. Ibid., 2–3.

40. "Indian, 103, in Court," 12; *United States ex. rel. Williams v. Seufert Brothers Company*, 233 *Federal Reporter* (F.) 579 (1916); Trial transcript of *United States of America vs. Seufert Brothers Company*, John Wilson Special Collections, Multnomah County Library, Portland, Ore., vol. 2, 302.

41. Ibid., 583–84, emphasis added.

42. Ibid., 587–88; John R. Wunder, *"Retained by The People": A History of American Indians and the Bill of Rights* (New York: Oxford University Press, 1994), 49–50; Frank Seufert to Evan W. Estep, 14 August 1924, Fishing Matters, GC, YIA, RG 75, NARA-PAR; Don M. Carr to Commissioner of Indian Affairs, 15 May 1920, *Williams v. Seufert*, GC, YIA, RG 75, NARA-PAR; and Sam Williams to Evan W. Estep, 23 August 1924, *Williams v. Seufert*, GC, YIA, RG 75, NARA-PAR.

43. Frank A. Seufert to the Editor of *The Oregonian*, 12 May 1916, Box 2, Envelope 18, Seufert Papers, OHS, 3–4; Taylor, *Making Salmon*, 144–50; and *Seufert Brothers Company v. United States*, 249 U.S. 194 (1919), 198–99.

44. Emma Dave to Don M. Carr, 1 June 1915, Dave, Emma VHstd 3057, Allotment Case Files, ca. 1905–55, YIA, RG 75, NARA-PAR.

45. Tommy Thompson to Secretary of Interior, 27 August 1934, 115 Hunting and Fishing, Decimal Classified Correspondence, Umatilla Indian Agency, Record Group 75, NARA-PAR, 1-2.

46. Don M. Carr to Andrew Barnhart, 14 September 1922, Correspondence, Unallotted Indians, YIA, RG 75, NARA-PAR; Evan W. Estep to O. L. Babcock, 7 May 1927, 121—Indian Troubles, Visiting Among Indians (Indian Troubles), Decimal Subject Files (DSF), 1925–1967, YIA, RG 75, NARA-PAR; and J. B. Mortsolf to Evan W. Estep, 13 May 1927, Indian Troubles, DSF, YIA, RG 75, NARA-PAR.

47. Fisher, "Tangled Nets," 199–202.

48. Celilo Fish Committee Minutes, 2 September 1942, Meetings—1942, General Subject Correspondence, Records of C. G. Davis, Field Aide at The Dalles, 1939–50, PAO, RG 75, NARA-PAR, 5.

49. *Ambrose Whitefoot and Minnie Whitefoot v. United States*, 293 F.2d 658 (1961).

50. For a detailed history of the in-lieu fishing site controversy, see Roberta Ulrich, *Empty Nets: Indians, Dams, and the Columbia River* (Corvallis: Oregon State University Press, 1999).

51. Alexandra Harmon, "American Indians and Land Monopolies in the Gilded Age," *Journal of American History* 90, no. 1 (June 2003): 4–6; and Barsh, "Ethnogenesis and Ethnonationalism," 6–8.

7 Ethnogenesis and Ethnonationalism from Competing Treaty Claims

Russel Lawrence Barsh

Reinvented and imagined communities have been the focus of considerable study and theoretical debate in the quarter century since ethnonationalism replaced communism as a preoccupation of Western political leaders. Most case studies involve postcolonial environments in which indigenous and tribal societies find themselves marginalized and physically dispossessed within newly established states. This essay explores a rather different manifestation of ethnogenesis and ethnonationalism, involving a persistent colonial environment in which indigenous peoples reformulate their identities in a contest for legitimacy and state-controlled resources. Anthropologist Alcida Ramos has described a parallel competition among indigenous peoples in Brazil, where the prize is state demarcation of reserves.[1] In my case study, by comparison, the prize is the enjoyment of treaty rights: that is, rights recognized by the state 150 years ago. It is not about disputed land claims but rather about disputed inheritance or "successorship" among "tribes."

That "tribes" should dispute each other's rights at all is a significant development in the boundary waters of Washington State and British Columbia, a region frequently referred to as the Salish Sea because of its linguistic and cultural contiguity with Coast Salish–speaking peoples. The anthropologist Wayne Suttles has argued convincingly for a Coast

Salish "continuum" rather than a mosaic of socially and economically interrelated but politically distinct "tribes."[2] My experience since the 1970s as a lawyer for tribes, a traditional knowledge researcher, and a tribal program director is consistent with Suttles's characterization of the historical Coast Salish ethos as both competitively individualistic and strongly family based, with loyalties to family and class ordinarily trumping ties to such geographical groupings as houses or villages. As the historian Alexandra Harmon has shown, the underlying structure of Coast Salish society began to change in the late nineteenth century, with individuals thinking of themselves more broadly as "Indians" while also self-identifying more firmly with particular Indian reservations and tribes delineated by U.S. authorities.[3] One important component of this social transformation has been the association of harvesting rights, including fishing, with membership in "tribes" rather than membership in particular extended families.

I contend in this essay that the implementation of treaty fishing rights in western Washington since the 1970s has significantly increased the economic relevance of "tribal" boundaries and the salience of "tribal" affiliation in the public identities of Coast Salish peoples of western Washington State and their present-day communities. Treaty litigation culminated a process of replacing broad regional kinship networks with jealously exclusive, ostensibly homogeneous local polities—a process that began in the late nineteenth century with the establishment of Indian reservations and continued in the early twentieth century with the organization of federally approved tribal governments on those reservations. Coast Salish leaders and their lawyers asserted a "tribal" basis to fishing rights within the context of a federal legal system that already presumed the existence of discrete "tribes" and the collective nature of "tribal" resource rights. Collapsing the Coast Salish system of interconnected families and regional social classes into geographically discrete "tribes" was not foreseen or intended by Coast Salish treaty signers, however.

THE CONCEPT OF "TRIBE"

U.S. law assumes that "tribes" are collective owners of Indian property. Collective tribal ownership is a legal fiction, like the legal fictions that the Americas were legally vacant when Europeans first arrived, or that indigenous Americans lacked fixed settlements, institutions, or laws.

Unlike other legal fictions that legitimized Europeans' seizure of Indian territories, such as *terra nullius*,[4] the fiction of collective tribal ownership has not only survived but prospered in the so-called era of Indian self-determination, promoted by tribal governments. Emphasizing collective tribal ownership strengthens a central government bureaucracy at the expense of Indian families and indigenous customary laws.[5]

At the outset it is important to clarify the significance of the term "tribe" as it has typically been used in Euro-American law. A household, family, or lineage consists of a number of closely related individuals. They share common ancestors in each generation. A "tribe" is a larger group, comprised of many households, families, and lineages. They may assert some ancient shared ancestry and history, but they are linked more by shared institutions including language, systems of rank or leadership, and defense of a territory.[6] This is what the ancient Romans understood by "tribe" (*tribus*): a territorial polity with a hierarchy of power, smaller and less unified under law than a kingdom or state (*civitas*). In a tribe, ancestry and kinship compete with law as bases of solidarity and authority. In a state, law prevails over social solidarity, at least in principle.

It was convenient for European empires to categorize indigenous peoples as tribal and divide them into "tribes" with distinct, bounded territories. It is easier to exact a land cession from a few purported tribal chiefs than hundreds of families. What is more, a tribe was considered civilized enough to sell its land but not civilized enough to assert the right to keep its land for itself. A tribe was considered institutionalized enough to be given some form of internal self-government as part of an imperial scheme of indirect or proxy rule; but a tribe was supposedly too backward to function as an independent international actor without a protector or patron. Tribes were thus regarded as sufficiently mature to sign treaties with European powers but too childlike to be given access to the courts to enforce them.[7] Francis Jennings, Robert Williams, and John Borrows (among other scholars) have traced the Euro-American use of law to define indigenous peoples into division and submission.[8]

European imperial schemes profited from two complementary fictions: that tribal polities always entrusted their leaders with absolute authority over land and that all land was held and used in common, undivided in any way that could embarrass the generosity of the chiefs. (Anthropologist and national leader Jomo Kenyatta made this point forcefully when writing of his own people, the Kikuyu of East Africa.[9]) British Imperial courts accordingly ignored the existence of customary land tenure laws or substituted fictitious ones. In a 1919 appeal to the House of Lords in the case of *Southern Rhodesia*,[10] for example, the Law Lords maintained that the King of Pondoland was an absolute despot under Pondo law. Subsequent decisions in the British Commonwealth interpreted this as authority that tribal peoples generally *had no laws*—a pretense only recently abandoned in Australia and Canada.

In 1824 the U.S. Supreme Court took a somewhat different approach, ruling in *Johnson v. M'Intosh* that U.S. courts cannot inquire into the legitimacy of Indian signatures on a land cession: the validity and effect of a land cession is determined solely by U.S. law, and the disappointed customary owners or occupants of the land have recourse only to their own Indian leaders and institutions. The effect of this principle belies its pretended neutrality. Indigenous laws are irrelevant to land transactions with the colonial state and do not create rights directly enforceable in the state's courts. Hence, as far as U.S. judges are concerned, those indigenous laws are nonexistent. U.S. judicial deference to present-day tribal court systems has created an opportunity for Indians to reassert and enforce customary systems of land tenure, but as I have shown elsewhere in a survey of tribal court decisions, tribal courts themselves rarely invoke traditional or customary laws.[11] Rather, tribal courts generally act as if real estate was always inherently collective or tribal, to be disposed of as tribal leaders have seen fit.

International law (that is to say, the globalized European law of nations) has long maintained that private property rights persist through a transfer of sovereignty or regime change. Even if the new state or regime has constitutional authority to rearrange property rights, it must do so by express legislation.[12] Echoes of this principle appeared in early U.S. law concerning Indians—for example, in the rule that treaties and acts of Congress must be read strictly against any implied takings of property or limitations of "tribal sovereignty."[13] U.S. lawyers did not deem it necessary to learn about the norms and procedures of tribal legal systems, however, and U.S. courts have decided many intertribal disputes without referring at all to the customary laws of individual tribes or to customary principles widely observed by tribes in their dealings with one another. In general, each "tribe" was regarded as a discrete whole, and as a "tribal" matter property could only remain with the same tribe, or pass as a whole to another tribe. Individuals and families therefore had no enforceable interests in the tribal estate.

In 1914, drawing on thirty years of case law, the U.S. Supreme Court asserted as an ethnographic fact that all "lands and funds belonged to the tribes as a community, and not to the members severally or as tenants in common. The rights of each member to participate in the enjoyment of such property depended on tribal membership, and when that was ended by death or otherwise the right was at an end. It was neither alienable nor descendible."[14] This may seem a quaint old ruling, but it has been invoked more recently to deny claims by individual Indians that their tribal leaders sold their family property, including traditional shrines, without their consent.[15] U.S. courts persist in upholding communal ownership as being "in accord with normal Indian custom."[16] It has scarcely occurred to them that there are diverse indigenous cultures on this continent, with equally diverse systems of customary laws.

If Indian property is a tribal commons, what happens in the event that a tribe splits into two groups? It is remarkable how often this issue has come before U.S. courts. As a general rule, courts have sought evidence of collective tribal intent. Hence the Cherokees who refused to leave North Carolina for the Indian Territory as prescribed by treaty lost their share of the tribal estate;[17] whereas the Oneida families that moved from New York State to Ontario "by communal consent" retained their proportional share of Oneida property.[18] Similarly, the Delawares who became Cherokee citizens under the terms of an 1867 Cherokee-Delaware agreement obtained equal rights to the proceeds of Cherokee lands in Oklahoma.[19]

Tribes have sometimes been consolidated by a treaty or federal legislation.[20] In the absence of some overriding expression of federal intent, however, the courts have considered the customs and intentions of the Indians. In 1990, for example, two present-day federally recognized tribes unsuccessfully claimed the fishing rights of a third tribe that was no longer federally recognized. The membership rolls of both recognized tribes included descendants of the tribe whose recognition had been revoked. The Ninth Circuit Court of Appeals ruled there must also be evidence that all of the historical Indian tribes concerned intended "a consolidation or merger of the tribes, or cohesive bands thereof, sufficient to combine their tribal or political structures." For similar reasons a federal district court rejected the claims of the Swinomish Indian

Community to the fishing rights of the Samish Indian Tribe. A large number of Samish families had moved to the Swinomish Reservation and enrolled there in the nineteenth century, but there was no evidence that the Samish as a polity had decided to consolidate with the Swinomish.[21]

CUSTOMARY FISHERY LAW

Some indigenous societies in North America may have owned and managed land and fisheries collectively, but not in the Salish Sea. At the time of the treaties 150 years ago, Coast Salish social structure focused on the individual person, the household unit within a single cedar-plank house, and the extended family that linked households living in several plank house villages. In addition, a broader conception of place-of-origin exists in Coast Salish languages and may properly be interpreted as a type of ethnicity.[22] Families historically associated with the plank house village on Guemes Island still refer to themselves as *sapš* (Samish), for instance, and families that lived in houses on the lower Snohomish River still take pride in being *sdodobš* (Snohomish). But these are terms of historical affiliation, and like ethnicity they did not ordinarily confer rights to land or resources.

Status or "class" was more important than geographical or village origins. Status was individually earned, although the children of an influential family had opportunities and resources—including a regional network of kin and "friends"—to facilitate their rise. Like the European preindustrial middle class, Coast Salish society valued productivity, and families struggled to enhance their social standing and widen their connections with other high-class families through marriage and business partnerships. However, such material wealth as blankets, baskets, canoes, and preserved foods conferred no status merely by its possession. Status was a function of conspicuously distributing wealth at feasts in a way that created social debts—that is, calls on the labor, wealth, and support of others. As I have written elsewhere, Coast Salish "gentlemen" (*siiyém* in Northern Straits) were rich in people, rather than goods.[23]

Much status was earned through the sustainable stewardship and generous sharing of productive property. A wealthy individual could acquire a fishing site, keep it "clean" (*kwiát*), and invite his relatives and friends to fish there each summer. He could also hire a crew to fish the site for him and distribute the dried salmon at feasts. In either case the foundation of the owner's wealth was the continued productivity of the fishing site. If the fishery failed, its "owner" had nothing to give away at feasts. In this sense, individual "ownership" of productive living resources was intrinsic to the traditional Coast Salish status system, which in turn motivated the "owners" to take an active role in conserving biological productivity.

Rights to physical resources such as fishing sites, hunting grounds, and meadows for the cultivation or gathering of nutritious or medicinal plants tended to fall within the category of "inheritances" (čiləŋən in Northern Straits). Only worthy individuals could inherit, however; spirit power and demonstrations of the wise use of power and resources were also traditionally required. Thus when the custodian of a reef-net site passed over to the invisible world, stewardship of the site was not simply inherited by a close relative such as a sibling, child, or grandchild. A transfer would not be recognized unless it was made to someone who had demonstrated, by performances at the winter dances *and* by successful fishing, the support of powerful ancestors and guardians on the other side. The transfer was witnessed at a feast, moreover, where relatives of the former owner could denounce any impropriety. As a practical matter, this made it likely that fisheries remained in the hands of expert fishermen from influential families who had earned their status through productivity and generosity.

Of course, there have always been alternative sources of Coast Salish wealth, such as doctoring and the arts. Euro-American lawyers would call this intellectual property; in Coast Salish thinking it was spiritual property, conferred on worthy individuals by powerful ancestors and nonhuman beings in the invisible world. Although many of these gifts were traditionally associated with particular lineages and geographic areas, thus to some extent "inheritances," they must also be earned through individual effort. There was no sense of property being a "right" in the strict sense of Euro-American law. Birth into a high-class family or community could improve an individual's opportunity to seek some forms of property, but no one acquired property without personal merit and serious effort. Furthermore, a transfer of property was arranged by relatives of the former owner, and required approval by a public assembly, rather than by "chiefs" or by some elected or representative body. All property, then, was "private" at the individual and family levels, whether it consisted of land, goods, or knowledge.

A few years ago anthropologist Wayne Suttles and I visited Point Doughty on Orcas Island with Samish speaker and centenarian Lena Daniels and her grandson Randy. Lena remembered spending summers camping at this important reef-net site during the lifetime of her great-uncle Boston Tom, the traditional owner, who died in 1913. The summer sockeye season brought together her great-uncle's extended family: people from the old Eastsound and Rosario villages on Orcas as well as Samish from the Anacortes and Bay View areas, Lummi from the reservation near Bellingham, and Saanich and Cowichan households (like Lena's) from Vancouver Island. As Lena expressed it in Samish, Boston Tom had "many friends," which meant many to feed, as well as tacit authority to decide when to begin fishing. Point Doughty was "his place" (using the Northern Straits possessive prefix), but he did not turn anyone away or decide how many fish they could catch. Lena simply recalled his watching the salmon from a high spot every day. When he concluded that the "first run" of fish had passed the point, he announced that the season was open. In this simple way Boston Tom augmented his wealth by feeding his "friends" from many different corners of the Salish Sea, placing them in his debt at the feast hall. At the same time he conserved his wealth by ensuring adequate escapement each year.

Samish people as they are constituted today include direct descendants of owners of six reef-net sites on Lopez Island, one on south San Juan Island, and Boston Tom's site on Orcas Island. Other descendants of the same owners are enrolled today as S'Klallam, Lummi, Swinomish, and Upper Skagit and, on the other side of the international border, as Saanich and Cowichan. Individual members of many other present-day "tribes" have collateral or affinal links to the same site owners. Traditionally, any kinship ties could be sufficient to justify minimal seasonal access to a reef-net site, although the owner might be considerably more selective in choosing crew members for the most productive "sets" at the site—that is, allocating the largest shares of wealth. Closeness of kinship was always a consideration when choices had to be made; this is why it was important to listen to the family teachings, and why it is still said that people will be poor if they "don't know who they are" (that is, their kinship network).

When Boston Tom died, county officials usurped the family's traditional role and disposed of his property, including the reef-net site.[24] This was a taking of fish from all of Boston Tom's "friends," the value of each taking varying more or less in accordance with the strength of the kinship relationships and not a nominal "tribal" affiliation or place of residence. It is likely that rights to the fish would have changed little if the county had not intervened, no matter who was selected. The new owner would have been a successful reef-netter from the same broad network of families, widely recognized as a protégé of powerful spirit beings, perceived as generous and trusted to maintain the status quo. If a different sort of person was put forward, there would be accusations of impropriety in the feast hall, and the hosts would lose status and "pull down their names"—the Coast Salish equivalent of bankruptcy.

The factors traditionally considered in Coast Salish law with respect to claims to the ownership of "estates" such as fisheries, and claims to their use for the accumulation of wealth (as opposed to the casual use of resources while in transit—that is, for "lunch"), can be summarized simply. Claims to ownership were weighed against the claimant's lineage, personal merit, and power manifestly acquired from the invisible world, and they required recognition and validation at a public feast. Claims merely to the shared use of an estate could be asserted on the basis of any number of kinship relationships with the owner. Close lineal descent from the owner was the strongest argument; but in-laws, "friends" (business partners), and members of the same house group could ask for and receive the use of an estate with more or less expectation of recognition.

THE NEW DEAL AND TRIBALISM

The Coast Salish pursuit of "wealth in people" involved carefully arranged long-distance marriages, a kind of portfolio diversification that made nearly everyone living around the Salish Sea a relative to some degree, however small. Only the families of "slaves" tended to remain geographically or socially isolated. For a long time the establishment of Indian reservations did little to change Coast Salish social organization. People continued to travel and marry widely and to rely on far-ranging kinship ties for economic security. Reservations offered little in the way of farmland, and few Coast Salish pursued full-time farming. Most individuals who acquired "allotments" of reservation land earned their livelihoods elsewhere. For the most part the only Coast Salish who lost geographical mobility and developed localized reservation identities were government employees such as Indian policemen and clerks.

By 1900 most Puget Sound Indians were earning wages in logging camps, mills, and canneries, or working independently as seamstresses, knitters, and tradesmen.[25] The social, geographical, and economic mobility of Coast Salish people maintained the open fabric of traditional Salish Sea society. Men and women earned status through individual accomplishments, including earning power and the ability to mount lavish feasts. Status also continued to be a function of long-distance marriage ties. My census-based study of Puget Sound Indian residence and labor from 1880 through 1920 revealed a significant exchange of Indian population among reservations as well as between reservations and non-reservation towns. The multifarious nature of Coast Salish identity did not collapse completely into reservation-based identities. On the contrary, residence continued to be a part of identity along with geographically extensive networks of ancestry.

The Samish are one example. Federal officials never surveyed and set aside the March Point Reservation that the Samish believed had been promised to them by treaty in 1855. Eight influential Samish families remained on Guemes Island at their traditional feast hall (known as $x^{w}\acute{a}'imet$) and built a new plank house there in the 1880s.[26] Others stayed in the Bow-Edison area after settlers torched the Samish Island plank house. One large lineage took land on the Lummi Reservation and another on the Swinomish Reservation, where they are "tribal" members today. Another lineage moved to Cypress Island, off-reservation, where they comprised a majority of the island's "pioneer" population for two generations.[27] A Samish village of sorts was established by 1910 at the Fidalgo Island Packing Company's Ship Harbor cannery, where lived a number of individual households from the Guemes, Samish, and Swinomish aggregations of Samish people. Like their ancestors these people were all multiply hyphenated: for example, an individual might identify as *sapš* living at Swinomish with roots in the Guemes village—and with ancestral ties to Snohomish, Nooksack, Cowichan, and Musqueam.

Consolidation of "tribes" on reservations under the 1934 Indian Reorganization Act (IRA) promoted different ways of thinking about Indian identity. The act authorized "any Indian tribe, or tribes, residing on the same reservation" to organize local governments.[28] So few Indians were living on Puget Sound reservations by the 1930s that the Indian Office worried about the viability of reservation-based self-government; in some cases its field staff urged Indian families to relocate to reservations where they had historical ties.[29] The charters and constitutions adopted by reservation communities during the New Deal era emphasized residence at the expense of ancestry. Most striking of all, perhaps, was the decision of the "Indians residing on the Tulalip Reservation" to begin to refer to themselves as "Tulalip Indians." Tulalip residents had self-identified with more than thirty different ancestral groups in the 1920 census. Many of the membership rolls prepared by new tribal governments in the 1930s not only classified all resident Indians as one "tribe" but reset their Indian blood quantum to 100 percent. Thus, for instance, a Lummi Reservation resident of Nooksack, Sumas, Musqueam, Irish, and German ancestry could have been enrolled as full-blood Lummi.

To the extent that Coast Salish Indians of the New Deal era were protecting their families by staking their future on reservation-based identities in response to the promises of an "Indian New Deal" by the U.S. government, their motives cannot be faulted. However, the Indian Reorganization Act also began a process of transferring wealth such as reservation land and timber from regional kin networks to tribal governments elected by relatively small coresidential groups.

In the 1950s, ironically, the Indian Claims Commission treated compensation for lost land as an individual inheritance rather than "tribal" property. As a collectivity, for example, the "Tulalips" lacked standing to seek compensation from the United States, but most persons enrolled at Tulalip received individual shares of awards to one or more ancestral groups, such as Snohomish, Snoqualmie, and Kikiallos. Similarly, persons of Snohomish ancestry who did not live on a reservation, and were not enrolled in any IRA tribal government, shared equally in awards made to their ancestral group. Thus when the issue of Indian treaty fishing rights was litigated in federal district court in the 1970s, district judge George Boldt was confronted with two incompatible legal models of Indian rights: the IRA model, in which a relatively recent historical residential group, the "tribe," is exclusive owner on behalf of persons enrolled as tribal members; and the ICC model, in which individuals inherit rights from all of their ancestors, regardless of residence.[30]

THE BOLDT DECISION FRAMEWORK

In *United States v. Washington*, treaty rights were asserted by tribal governments, not by the traditional owners of marine resources. To be sure, tribal governments were acting on behalf of their members, who included traditional owners, but also included families that had not owned fishing sites.[31] The federal district court assumed that the fishery is a "tribal" (that is, collective) resource in which all tribal members are entitled to share equally regardless of their lineage or individual merit. The court's ruling therefore sanctioned the transfer of wealth from high-status families with inherited fishing sites to families with other forms of traditional wealth or no wealth at all, including families that had gained power in tribal electoral politics and thereby controlled boat loans, licenses, and harvest allocation under the court decision. It also greatly increased the number of families with enforceable rights to each historical fishing site, arguably weakening the link between harvesting fish and stewardship.

The federal government's expert witness, anthropologist Barbara Lane, provided the court with a fair overview of Coast Salish law relating to fisheries. She emphasized that case-area tribes were "very property-conscious."[32] She said in her deposition: "The individual groups had recognized places which were understood to be their places. They might invite other people in at various times and occasions to share resources in their area."[33] Stewardship of fishing areas had been "owned by groups," Lane explained, which were either "particular villages or, in the case of [trap sites on] smaller creeks, perhaps, individual families." However, the "title to them was said to reside in particular chiefs or leading individuals" and could be transferred at public ceremonies before witnesses.[34]

Lane continued: "At treaty times an individual had a right to fish at the place where he was born and raised and continued to live by virtue of being a member of that community at birth. If he changed residences during his lifetime, he would acquire rights to fish with the people in whose community he was now a resident member. He would not necessarily lose the rights to fish in the place that he originally came from, because even an individual who never changed residence had various levels of rights based on kinship and would normally have kin in several localities."[35] Hence an individual's community did not necessarily share in his or her distant fishing rights, since they were based on the individual's personal kinship ties. "You didn't go there unless you had a right to go either by residence or marriage or in-law relationships or descent," Lane testified.[36] Sharing fish during times of abundance with kin from other communities was governed by principles of generosity and reciprocity; but visitors were careful not to abuse this privilege.[37]

Guided by arguments advanced by tribes' lawyers, however, federal courts had already ruled that "each tribe bargained as an entity for rights which were to be enjoyed communally," including "the right to take fish at usual and accustomed grounds."[38] Citing precedent, Judge Boldt ultimately reasoned "the fact that certain Indians have been allowed to have sole use of a particular spot by the Tribe gives that individual no property right against the Tribe," since the fishery as a whole is a commons.[39]

The Lummi tribe submitted evidence of the individual ownership of reef-net sites to support its claim to an *exclusively Lummi* fishery in the San Juan Islands. The district and appellate courts dismissed the uncontested ethnographic evidence of individual reef-net ownership as "an aberration from the general communal pattern of Indian property ownership," and ruled that "as far as the United States is concerned, under the treaty the right to engage in reef net fishing belongs to the Lummi tribe" as a whole, and as such it is subject to the "same principle of equal division" as other treaty fishing rights.[40] Although the judges insisted that they were deferring to tribal law in the matter of regulating the individual exercise of fishing rights, they were in fact shaping a substantive rule of tribal property law ("equal division") that looks more like the English common law principle of wildlife allocation—that is, the "rule of capture"—inherited by most U.S. jurisdictions.[41]

Tribal governments had already used their New Deal powers to consolidate their ownership and control of reservation forests and grazing. *United States v. Washington* legitimized efforts by tribal governments to nationalize off-reservation fisheries that previously had individual or family owners. This kind of taking was an "internal affair" of the tribes and, in accordance with the principle of deference to tribal sovereignty, did not give rise to federal actions for abuse of power.[42]

In Australia and New Zealand, by comparison, traditional custodians (individuals) and landholding groups alone have standing to assert aboriginal rights and treaty rights. Australian courts have accepted Aboriginal arguments that land is not only a "resource" but sacred and therefore must be returned to the specific kinship group that has customary ties to the land and knows the stories, symbols, landmarks, and ceremonies associated with the land.[43] New Zealand courts follow the Waitangi Treaty Tribunal's reasoning that the treaty was made with traditional polities represented by chiefs chosen in accordance with customary laws.[44] Treaty rights accordingly belong to those historical polities, represented by leaders traditionally selected by their extended families or clans. Although Canada negotiates land claims with "bands" or "First Nations" constituted by federal ministers, the Canadian Supreme Court has ruled that traditional customary laws define the nature and exercise of "Aboriginal rights" such as fishing.[45] In the United States, then, where administrative powers were delegated to European-style "tribal" governments decades before the resolution of land and treaty claims, the administrative "tribe," which in large part was constituted externally, has become the holder of ancestral rights. In Australia and New Zealand, by comparison, where substantive claims *preceded* state recognition of institutions of indigenous self-government by more than a decade, rights to land and wildlife are still held and allocated by traditional custodians.

DEVELOPMENT OF A TREATY COMMONS

Judge Boldt's initial judgment in 1974 interpreted the phrase "usual and accustomed fishing grounds and stations," as it appears in the treaties with Puget Sound Indians, as every place that the members of a tribe "customarily fished from time to time, however distant from the then usual habitat of the tribe, and whether or not other tribes then also fished in the same waters."[46] Overlapping fishing areas were deemed to be typical of Coast Salish cultures; hence there was no requirement that a plaintiff tribe establish *exclusivity* of its historical use of an area before including it within claimed "usual and accustomed" fishing grounds.[47] "In determining usual and accustomed fishing places," furthermore, "the Court cannot follow stringent proof standards because to do so would likely preclude a finding of *any* such fishing areas."[48] It was unnecessary for a treaty tribe to prove by a preponderance of evidence that its ancestors customarily fished at each and every location that it claimed. Rather, a tribe's mere historical "presence in the area" could be sufficient to establish a prima facie case for fishing there as a matter of right.[49] Historical documents and scholarly studies were to be preferred over the testimony of living elders, however.[50]

Consistent with his view that the historical evidence was fragmentary at best, Judge Boldt invited tribes to enlarge their usual and accustomed areas incrementally in the future based on new evidence.[51] He also encouraged treaty tribes to resolve allocation disputes among themselves outside the courtroom.[52] However, several tribes attempted to expand their fisheries unilaterally by enlarging the geographic scope of their fishing regulations. "Such conduct evidences a disregard for the Court's rulings," Judge Boldt complained.[53] Intertribal disputes grew, particularly with respect to the boundaries of "primary" fishing areas, which the court agreed involved substantially different issues than the boundaries of tribes' usual and accustomed fishing areas.[54] In 1978, Tulalip alone was involved in four separate disputes with other tribes in the area encompassed by the litigation.[55]

At the outset the court was inclined to give treaty tribes the benefit of the doubt. Thus the Suquamish, for instance, with their treaty-era population concentrated on the Kitsap Peninsula in central Puget Sound, won herring fishing rights in coastal Skagit and Whatcom counties in the North Sound on the basis of a single recorded visit to the Hudson's Bay Company's Fort Langley post by a "small retinue" of Suquamish in 1827. Expert witness Barbara Lane testified: "It is my opinion that the Suquamish undoubtedly would have fished the marine waters along the way as they traveled [to Fort Langley]. It is likely that one of the reasons for travel was to harvest fish."[56] The Suquamish likewise won fishing rights in Hood Canal on the basis of five historical references to their fishing there, of which only three referred to specific locations or streams.[57] Similarly, the three Klallam tribes successfully asserted rights to the entire San Juan archipelago on the basis of a single reliable historical reference to the presence of some Klallams (among many others) fishing at Cattle Point.[58] Jamestown Klallam later claimed all of the North Sound on the basis of a single report that Klallams were with Skagits fishing Lummi Island in 1835 and "were met with" by early travelers in the San Juan Islands.[59]

Within the broader concept of "usual and accustomed" areas, however, the 1974 judgment distinguished between "permissive" fishing arising from individuals' historical kinship ties and "primary" fishing rights arising from communities' collective control of their territories.[60] While they expanded their "usual and accustomed" fishing areas in subproceedings before the court, tribes increasingly asserted "primary" rights to the most valuable fishing areas so that they could govern the allocation of quotas between their own members and other treaty tribes. The concept of "primary" rights was clarified in a lengthy dispute over rivers draining into the Strait of Juan de Fuca. Judge Boldt held that "east of the Hoko River was Clallam territory over which the Clallams exercised some control and that any Makah fishing on rivers within the Clallam territory was due to kinship, individual in nature and based upon inter-marriage, or a grant of permission."[61] The Skokomish tribe subse-quently won "primary" rights in Hood Canal.

Mixtures of peoples were settled on all Puget Sound Indian reserva-tions, "some more than others," but this did not enlarge individuals' fishing rights under traditional law.[62] Since present-day Indian tribes were claiming fisheries derivatively, from rights once enjoyed by indi-viduals or families, genealogical data should have been given great weight. However, tribes resisted releasing family history charts on grounds of privacy.[63] As a result, expert witnesses' broad assessments of relatedness between groups continued to be the basis of decision making resulting in broad generalizations by the court. In his First Supplemen-tal Treaty Status Order (issued on December 31, 1974), for example, Judge Boldt found that the Swinomish Indian Tribal Community and Tulalip Tribes of Washington are each "a political successor to certain tribes and bands and groups," without specifying which groups or their proportional representation on present-day tribal rolls.

The Swinomish government initially claimed fishing territory from Bellingham to Penn Cove, plus all of the San Juan Islands.[64] The evi-dence consisted of reports by anthropologists Sally Snyder and Wayne Suttles, consolidating what was known about "the Tribes forming the modern Swinomish community," which was to say the Swinomish, Lower Skagit, Kikiallus, and Samish. All fishing sites in the San Juan Islands were explicitly identified as historically Samish, but consistent with its broad conception of "usual and accustomed" fisheries, the court approved the overlapping Swinomish claim because at least some Swino-mish tribal members had Samish ancestry.[65] The Swinomish subse-quently challenged the Lummi Nation over the Cherry Point herring fishery, arguing that some Swinomish tribal members "can trace their ancestry to aboriginal tribes which fished herring in the areas which the Lummis now claim to be exclusive."[66]

The geography of these two disputes is significant: the islands have historically been the region's richest sockeye fishery, and Cherry Point its largest and most consistent herring fishery. Before the treaties influential

Lummi and Samish households "owned" these two fisheries. Individuals from Swinomish villages with strong kinship ties to those Lummi and Samish households would have had opportunities to fish with them. However, the court's approach gave all members of the Swinomish Tribal Community as it exists today an equal right to fish in areas historically owned by *siiyém* (leading men) who lived in the Lummi and Samish houses.

Similarly, the Tulalip Tribes initially claimed exclusive rights to the Snohomish, Stillaguamish, and Sauk-Suiattle river basins as successors to the aboriginal Snohomish-, Snoqualmie-, and Stillaguamish-area peoples.[67] The majority of Tulalip tribal members were of Snohomish ancestry, they argued, with many of Snoqualmie and Skykomish descent, and the Snoqualmie leader Patkanum had signed the treaty for the Snohomish, Snoqualmies, and Stillaguamish.[68] The Stillaguamish tribe objected "there could be no justice and certainly no order in the on-going fishery to grant to [one] tribe . . . the usual and accustomed places of any *single* individual tribal member."[69] In other words, they argued that since the largest part of the Tulalip membership was originally Snohomish, Tulalip could at best legitimately claim the traditional Snohomish fisheries. Furthermore, the majority of Snohomish "never went to the Tulalip reservation and are [still] organized off the reservation." Tulalip Reservation residents' decision to organize as a tribe under the Indian Reorganization Act could have no effect on the treaty rights of the aboriginal tribes, and Tulalip had thereby acquired no treaty fishing rights.[70] These objections had little effect in limiting the Tulalip "usual and accustomed area."

The Tulalip Tribes widened their claim in 1980 to include all of the marine waters between Port Angeles, Seattle, and the Canadian border, including the San Juan Islands, arguing that they had not presented their full case in 1975 because "unrecognized tribes were, at that time, making claims as successors to Tulalip treaty rights."[71] This referred to the Snohomish and Snoqualmie, who lost their initial bid for fishing rights in 1980 but continued to seek redress through administrative recognition of their Indian tribal status.[72] The Tulalip case for expanded fishing rights was circumstantial. The pleading stated: "Tulalip ancestors were not unlike those of other north and central Puget Sound tribes, in that they regularly and customarily fished throughout a wide marine area which was used jointly by the several tribes. They were not limited to their drainage system, nor were their fisheries activities restricted to the marine waters under their primary or 'territorial' control. [They] traveled widely and regularly [and] where the Indians regularly traveled, they regularly fished."[73]

Tulalip offered to establish by expert testimony "that the Tulalip predecessors traveled regularly and customarily throughout the San Juan Islands" and northern Puget Sound, where they "necessarily fished for subsistence" and sold some of their fish to settlers.[74] There were also historical reports of Snohomish traveling to Fort Langley to trade, and "no indication whatsoever of any other marine areas north to the Fraser which they did *not* use."[75] What is more, by claiming that the Snohomish had been "some of the most wide-ranging, widely-traveled and aggressive Indians on the Sound at treaty times,"[76] the Tulalip request implied that an extensive fishery could simply be assumed to have existed.

Evidence relating to the San Juan Islands consisted entirely of testimony by living Tulalip tribal members who were identified as Snohomish.[77] Consider the testimony of Harriet Shelton Dover, however, whose father identified as Snohomish and her mother and maternal grandmother as Samish. Dover stated that her father used to visit San Juan Island and Victoria, British Columbia, to attend "potlatches."[78] Her father and mother each had a different name for San Juan Island,[79] since they spoke different Coast Salish languages (Lushootseed and Northern Straits). Only her mother knew the Indian names for the other islands in the archipelago.[80] When asked directly which Indians fished in the archipelago, she replied: "My mother's Samish people did."[81] Over other case-area tribes' objections, the court accepted this as evidence of Tulalip fishing rights, without any direct evidence of Tulalip succession to Samish fishing rights.

At the same time the Tulalip directly challenged Lane and other ethnographers with respect to customary law, contending that at treaty time fishing "was characterized by the absence of strict territoriality" and all fishing grounds were held in common by all of the tribes.[82] The division of Coast Salish Indians into tribes was "artificial" and "arbitrary," masking the extensive alliances and kinship that once existed, resulting in many conflicts today.[83] "The confusion regarding the identity of the various tribal groups and their present somewhat arbitrary separation into (at times) mutually antagonistic legal units has resulted in a great deal of frustration and a number of ironic consequences," including a smaller "usual and accustomed" fishing area for the Tulalip![84] Arguably the most aggressive tribal party in the *United States v. Washington* proceedings, the Tulalip successfully changed the legal paradigm that had been originally adopted by the court (overlapping "tribal" fisheries) in order to gain the most extensive possible fishery for its fleet.

The Tulalip Tribes, moreover, asked for the right to fish chum in the South Puget Sound as a matter of "equity," since the chum in their own area had been depleted.[85] This invited the federal court to undertake the traditional role of redistributing local surpluses and minimizing local famines. The Northwest Indian Tribal Fisheries Commission endorsed the Tulalip proposal, and the court approved it. Federal lawyers went even further, arguing that one tribe "should not be required to curtail fishing on fish passing through its usual and accustomed places in order to assure fishing opportunity for another tribe on those same fish. Necessarily curtailments should be equitably shared by all."[86] This was consistent with traditional practices, they maintained. The court decision stated: "The Indians—whose survival and economy was so heavily dependent upon salmon—would go to where the salmon were if the runs at their usual places were severely curtailed for some reasons. This was especially true in marine waters where any concept of tribal ownership rights to fishing areas was far less pronounced than the case of freshwater river or stream areas."[87] This is a significant misstatement of the ethnographic record, however; redistribution had been based on the strength of kinship ties, not merely on need. Traditional incentives to conserve fish arose from *not* automatically reallocating fish to the needy. To compromise with the Tulalip Tribes, litigants contributed to making the treaty fishery a true commons.

In 1981 the Ninth Circuit Court of Appeals ruled that treaties had not affected tribes' relationships among or between themselves: they "reasonably understood themselves to be retaining no more and no less of a right vis-à-vis one another than they possessed prior to the treaty."[88] To address disputed "primary" fishing areas, the district court was to consider four factors: the proximity of the disputed fishing area to historical tribal settlements; the frequency and significance of different tribes' historical use of the disputed fishing areas; historical tribal perceptions of who controlled the disputed areas; and historical tribal behavior consistent with perceived control.[89] The goal was therefore to restore the status quo ante with respect to historical arrangements between communities. Instead, treaty tribes increasingly contracted out of their historical relationships. For example, the Tulalip subsequently signed agreements with five other tribes to recognize its claims to most of Puget Sound, and to share fish harvests "equitably" with the Tulalip.[90] The Lummi and Klallam tribes complained that the Tulalip fishing area thus recognized included Lummi and Klallam primary fishing grounds in the San Juan Islands and the Strait of Juan de Fuca without their consent.[91] An agreement was subsequently made to combine the three present-day Klallam tribes' usual and accustomed areas, on the grounds that the reassignment of families from a dozen villages into three federal recognized tribes was arbitrary.[92]

By the 1990s intertribal allocation was governed almost entirely by closed-door negotiations within the Northwest Indian Tribal Fisheries Commission. Allocation is no longer strongly tethered to customary law and history, but like the international allocation of fisheries, it is governed by the relative power of (relatively) sovereign states. The treaty fishery as a whole is like a commons, with the attendant management problems of multiparty coordination under conditions of mistrust and uncertainty.[93] How different might things be today, had the court in *United States v. Washington* incorporated the customary Coast Salish law of estates into its ruling? Disputes over individuals' right to fish in particular places would have been numerous, no doubt, and if not settled in the feast hall, would have been subject to the general civil jurisdiction of the Northwest Inter-Tribal Court system. Tribal governments would presumably have asserted inherent authority to regulate the exercise of individual fishing rights for the protection of fish populations, although their power to redistribute those rights would have been more limited. The administration of a customary law regime would have been contentious and complex, and it is possible that the individual owners of estates would have shared fishing rights about as widely as fishing rights are shared today under tribal government licenses. It is also possible that a customary law regime would have resulted in a concentration of fishing wealth in the hands of a small number of tribal members, becoming a kind of capital.[94]

ECONOMICS AND ETHNOGENESIS

In summary, present-day tribal governments have taken the position that *all* of their current members can fish wherever *any* of their members' indigenous ancestors could traditionally have fished. Because the most productive fishing grounds in the case area, such as the San Juan Islands, had supported the largest traditional networks of "friends" of the owners, nearly every treaty tribe was successful in claiming them.[95] The result is that all of the members of all the treaty tribes enjoy equal rights almost everywhere: a commons. However, the tribe with "primary" rights bears the responsibility of allocating annual catch quotas "equitably"—or as equitably as possible among parties with unequal wealth from such other sources as casinos. "Primary" rights thus confer on tribal governments the allocation function once held by the traditional owners of sites, but there is also an important difference. Formerly, in accordance with Coast Salish law, the owners of sites allocated fishing opportunities according to the strength of kinship ties. Under *United States v. Washington*, therefore, all enrolled members of tribes that have overlapping "usual and accustomed" fisheries must be treated the same.

From the perspective of ethnogenesis, moreover, the relationship between family and territory has been completely confounded. Enrolled members of recognized tribes have learned to regard their "usual and accustomed area" as a cultural fact, whether or not their families actually had customary rights there in the past. Thus, for example, Swinomish and Tulalip tribal members increasingly regard the San Juan Islands as their traditional territories, although only a small number of individuals on these tribes' rolls are actual descendants of people who had inherited rights or in-law privileges there a century ago. Likewise, Samish people have been told that they do *not* have a role in the culture or the stewardship of the islands because they do not yet have an adjudicated fishing area there. Court rulings and tribal side-agreements have been displacing family histories as a source of cultural knowledge and territorial identities.

Through the court-supervised process of litigating "tribal" treaty fishing grounds, tribe-based nationalism advanced at the expense of Coast Salish kinship. Polities arising from the federal reservation system and the Indian New Deal gained greater economic power through control of fish that previously had been resources belonging to individuals and their families. At the economically motivated urging of the tribes themselves, the federal courts in effect "modernized" Coast Salish social structure.

Social boundaries, particularly recently invented ones, are arguably only as strong as their relevance to everyday life and ordinary pocketbooks. In the 1970s fish remained an important source of food and income for Indian and non-Indian communities in western Washington. Treaty fishing rights had substantial cash value, intensifying intertribal competition for the most productive fishing sites. It is not surprising that some families initially switched their tribal affiliations to try to get access, through tribal fishing cards, to better fishing grounds; or that treaty tribes with large fleets invested hundreds of thousands of dollars to prevent landless, nonfederally recognized tribes from regaining their political status and treaty rights, although they were composed of people whose ancestors had signed the same treaties in 1854 through 1855. The economic salience of fish contributed significantly to reifying the idea of "tribe" as the primary ethnic group affiliation of Coast Salish peoples.

Much has changed since 1974, however. Many Puget Sound salmon and herring stocks have collapsed; some are even listed under the Endangered Species Act. Despite tribal, state, and federal efforts to restore stocks, competition from farmed Atlantic salmon continues to depress the wholesale price for wild Pacific salmon, making even the largest and most successful commercial operators think twice about keeping their Washington fishing licenses. At the same time much of Indians' employment has shifted from fishing fleets to casinos and retail business parks along the highway corridor connecting Portland, Seattle, and Vancouver. Constitutional developments in Canada have meanwhile recognized (but not yet implemented) the land and fishing rights of Coast Salish First Nations in British Columbia, and they are seeking greater political strength by advocating the renewal of a regional Coast Salish identity across "tribal" lines and across the international border.

As the treaty fishery loses its luster, and new opportunities arise from transboundary political and economic solidarity, it is conceivable that Coast Salish people will once again regard themselves as more alike than different. A continued decline in federal funding for tribal governments may contribute to such a shift if tribal technocrats respond to tight budgets by cooperating with other tribes and sharing programs. But this does not mean that some future, renewed Coast Salish identity will be the same as the Coast Salish "continuum" of the treaty-making era.

NOTES

1. Alcida Rita Ramos, *Indigenism: Ethnic Politics in Brazil* (Madison: University of Wisconsin, 1998). See, similarly, Natividad Gutiérrez, *Nationalist Myths*

and *Ethnic Identities: Indigenous Intellectuals and the Mexican State* (Lincoln: University of Nebraska Press, 1999); and Kay B. Warren, *Indigenous Movements and Their Critics: Pan-Maya Activism in Guatemala* (Princeton, N.J.: Princeton University Press, 1998).

2. Wayne Suttles, "Cultural Diversity within the Coast Salish Continuum," in *Ethnicity and Culture*, edited by Reginald Auger, Margaret F. Glass, Scott MacEachern, and Peter H. McCartney (Calgary: Alberta Archaeological Association and University of Calgary, 1987), 243–49; and Wayne Suttles, *Coast Salish Essays* (Seattle: University of Washington Press, 1987), especially 26–44.

3. Alexandra Harmon, *Indians in the Making: Ethnic Relations and Indian Identities around Puget Sound* (Berkeley: University of California Press, 1998), 155–58. "Coast Salish" is a term that originated with anthropologists to designate a family of languages spoken by the aboriginal inhabitants of a region on North America's Pacific coast encompassing much of present-day western Washington, Vancouver Island, and southwestern British Columbia. The largest precontact groupings recognized by Coast Salish peoples appear to have been linguistic; for example, between Ləšúcid ("Lushootseed") speakers of central and southern Puget Sound, and Lkə́ŋenəŋ ("Northern Straits") speakers of the northern Sound and its islands.

4. See the elegant review of *terra nullius* ("empty land") in Robert A. Williams Jr., *The American Indian in Western Legal Thought: Discourses of Conquest* (Oxford: Oxford University Press, 1990); and the more exhaustive technical analysis in James (Sakej) Youngblood Henderson, Marjorie L. Benson, and Isobel M. Findlay, *Aboriginal Tenure in the Constitution of Canada* (Scarborough, Ontario: Thomson Carswell, 2000).

5. Russel Barsh, "The Challenge of Indigenous Self-Determination," *University of Michigan Journal of Law Reform* 26, no. 2 (1993): 277–312; and Barsh, "The Nature and Spirit of North American Political Systems," *American Indian Quarterly* 10, no. 3 (1986): 181–98.

6. June Helm, ed., *Essays on the Problem of Tribe* (Seattle: American Ethnological Association and University of Washington Press, 1968).

7. See, for example, Charles Henry Alexandrowicz, *The European-African Confrontation: A Study in Treaty-Making* (Leiden, Netherlands: A. W. Sijthoff, 1973).

8. Francis Jennings, *The Invasion of America: Indians, Colonialism, and the Cant of Conquest* (Chapel Hill: University of North Carolina Press, 1975); Williams, *American Indian in Western Legal Thought*; and John Borrows, *Recovering Canada: The Resurgence of Indigenous Law* (Toronto: University of Toronto Press, 2002).

9. Jomo Kenyatta, *Facing Mount Kenya: The Tribal Life of the Gikuyu* (New York: Random House, 1965).

10. *In re Southern Rhodesia*, [1919] Appeal Cases (AC) 211 (UK).

11. Russel Barsh, "Putting the Tribe into Tribal Courts: Possible? Desirable?" *Kansas Journal of Law and Public Policy* 8, no.2 (1999): 74–96.

12. Russel Barsh, "Indigenous Rights and the *Lex Loci* in British Imperial Law,"

in *Advancing Aboriginal Claims: Visions-Strategies-Directions*, edited by Kerry Wilkins (Saskatoon, Saskatchewan: Purich Publishing, 2004), 91–125.

13. See, for example, *Menominee Tribe v. United States*, 391 U.S. 404, 413 (1968); *Washington v. Washington State Commercial Passenger Fishing Vessel Association*, 443 U.S. 658, 690 (1979).

14. *Sizemore v. Brady*, 235 U.S. 441 (1914).

15. For example, *United States v. Dann*, 865 F.2d 1528, 1533–36 (9th Cir. 1989).

16. *Whitefoot v. United States*, 293 F.2d 658, 693 (Court of Claims [Ct. Cl.] 1961); followed in *United States v. Washington*, 520 F. 2d 676, at 690–91 (9th Cir. 1975).

17. *Eastern Band of Cherokee Indians v. United States*, 117 U.S. 288, 308–9 (1886).

18. *New York Indians v. United States*, 40 Ct.Cl. 448, 460 (1905).

19. *Cherokee Nation v. Journeycake*, 155 U.S. 196 (1894).

20. For example, *Colville Confederated Tribes v. United States*, 4 Indian Claims Commission (ICC) 151, 193 (1956); *Yakima Tribe v. United States*, 5 ICC 196, 226–30 (1965); and *New York Indians v. United States*, 40 Ct.Cl. at 452.

21. *United States v. Suquamish Tribe*, 901 F.2d 772 (9th Cir. 1990); *Greene v. Lujan*, 943 *Federal Supplement* (F.Supp.) 1278 (Western District of Washington [W.D. Wash.] 1996). See, similarly, *Snoqualmie Tribe v. United States*, 9 ICC 25, 44 (1960).

22. Russel Barsh, "Coast Salish Property Law: An Alternative Paradigm for Environmental Relationships," *Hastings West-Northwest Journal of Environmental Law* 12, (2005): 1–29. Many present-day "tribal" names are also geographical in origin: early settlers named rivers for Native settlements and Native people for the nearest rivers. For example, settlers gave the name of the *S'duhúbš* house group near present-day Everett to the river that passed by there, "Snohomish." The S'duhúbš told settlers that the people of the headwaters were *S'dukʷalbixʷ* which is to say crazy, worthless, or nasty. This became "Snoqualmie" and was applied to one of the Snohomish River's tributaries and to the "tribe" that eventually formed of people with roots there.

23. Ibid.; also Suttles, *Coast Salish Essays*, 20.

24. County officials contacted the Indian Office (now the Bureau of Indian Affairs) before selling the property for burial expenses. Boston Tom's son was absent (overseas, according to family traditions), and the Indian Office had no interest in the property because it was not held in trust.

25. Russel Barsh, "Puget Sound Indian Demography, 1900–1920: Migration and Economic Development," *Ethnohistory* 43, no. 1 (1996): 65–97.

26. Wayne Suttles, "The Economic Life of the Coast Salish of Haro and Rosario Straits," Ph.D. dissertation, University of Washington, 1951, 43; reprinted in *American Indian Ethnohistory: Coast Salish Indians I* (New York: Garland Publishing Co., 1974), 41–570.

27. Shadrach Wooten homesteaded March Point with his Samish wife in the

1870s, then moved to Cypress in the 1880s, where they built the island's largest farm and raised a dozen children. Local historians regard the Wooten family as pioneers of Cypress; the family itself is enrolled as Samish tribal members. Karen Jones Lamb, *Native American Wives of San Juan Settlers* (Friday Harbor, Wash.: Bryn Tirion Publishing, 1994), 60–61. A similar duality of identities characterizes the Coffelts on Lopez Island and the Cayous of Orcas Island, among others.

28. Act of June 18, 1934, c. 576, section 16; 48 Statute 987 (1934); codified at 25 *U.S. Code* 476. Section 19 of the act, 48 Statutes at Large 988, 25 *U.S. Code* 479, extends the benefits of the legislation as a whole to "all persons of Indian descent who are members of any recognized Indian tribe now under Federal jurisdiction, and all persons who are descendants of such members who were, on June 1, 1934, residing within the present boundaries of any Indian reservation," as well as all persons "of one-half or more Indian blood."

29. Examples are found in Russel Barsh, "Political Recognition: An Assessment of American Practice," in *Who Are Canada's Aboriginal Peoples? Recognition, Definition, and Jurisdiction*, edited by Paul L.A.H. Chartrand (Saskatoon, Saskatchewan: Purich Publishing, 2002), 230–57.

30. Discussed also in Harmon, *Indians in the Making*, 199–205.

31. Only the Lummi Nation appears to have taken the issue of traditional law seriously, by emphasizing its individual members' ownership of particular reef net sites. See *United States v. Washington*, U.S. District Court, Western District of Washington at Seattle, Civil No. 9213, Complaint in Intervention of Lummi Indian Tribe, September 2, 1971, 2. Other tribal governments could have argued that they retained inherent power (as a matter of unextinguished tribal sovereignty) to mandate the perpetuation of traditional kinds of rights in fisheries, but they did not.

32. *United States v. Washington*, Deposition of Barbara Lane, December 5, 1979, 12.

33. Ibid., 14.

34. Ibid., 18–19, 23. Halibut grounds, sockeye reef net sites, and in-river fishing sites were treated more like "private property" than marine areas that were fished by hooked lines. *United States v. Washington*, Deposition upon Oral Examination of Dr. Barbara Lane, February 4, 1983, 15–16.

35. Ibid., 5–6.

36. Ibid., 7, 9; also *United States v. Washington*, Transcript of Trial, May 5, 1983, 74–75.

37. Ibid., Deposition upon Oral Examination of Dr. Barbara Lane, 8, at 74–75. She added: "Where people belonged and where they had rights to go was generally understood." Ibid., 20–21.

38. *United States v. Washington*, 520 F.2d 676, 688 (9th Cir. 1975) following *Mason v. Sams*, 5 F.2d 255, 258 (W.D.Wash. 1925): "The treaty was with the tribe; but the right of taking fish . . . was plainly a right common to the members of the tribe." In *Mason* a cannery had excluded reef net fishermen from sites on Point Roberts; the United States sued the cannery on behalf of the "Lummi Tribe" as a whole, although only a small number of individual Lummi tribal members tradi-

tionally owned reef net sites there. Daniel L. Boxberger, *To Fish in Common: The Ethnohistory of Lummi Indian Salmon Fishing* (1989; reprint, Seattle: University of Washington Press, 2000).

39. *Whitefoot v. U.S.*, 293 F.2d 658, 693 (1961); applied in *United States v. Washington*, 520 F. 2d at 690–91.

40. *United States v. Washington*, Complaint in Intervention of Lummi Indian Tribe; and *United States v. Washington*, 520 F. 2d at 690–91.

41. U.S. courts have long held that animals *ferae naturae* have no owner until they are lawfully captured, but also that Indian hunting and fishing involves rights of a more protected character. *Mitchel v. United States*, 34 U.S. (9 Pet.) 711, 746 (1835). See also the more recent Australian High Court case of *Yanner v. Eaton* [1999], HCA 53, finding that the right to hunt crocodiles existed as a form of property under Aboriginal laws and therefore can be protected under contemporary law.

42. *Settler v. Lameer*, 507 F.2d 231, 237 (9th Cir. 1974); and *Santa Clara Pueblo v. Martinez*, 436 U.S. 49 (1978).

43. Peter Sutton, *Native Title in Australia: An Ethnographic Perspective* (Cambridge: Cambridge University Press, 2003).

44. Kirsty Gover and Natalie Baird, "Identifying the Māori Treaty Partner," *University of Toronto Law Journal* 52, no. 1 (2002): 39–68. Determinations by the tribunal and related court actions can be found online at http://www.waitangi tribunal.govt.nz (accessed on October 18, 2005). For a general critical review, see Giselle Byrnes, *The Waitangi Tribunal and New Zealand History* (Oxford: Oxford University Press, 2004).

45. For example, *R. v. Van der Peet*, [1996] 2 Supreme Court of Canada (SCR) 507. See, generally, Kerry Wilkins, ed., *Advancing Aboriginal Claims: Visions-Strategies-Directions* (Saskatoon, Saskatchewan: Purich Publishing, 2004).

46. *United States v. Washington*, 384 F.Supp. 312, 322 (W.D. Wash. 1974).

47. This was an important departure from the Indian Claims Commission, which had required exclusivity of occupation and use, as a result of which no Indians were compensated for the taking of large parts of the United States. Russel Barsh, "Indian Land Claims Policy in the United States," *North Dakota Law Review* 58, no. 1 (1982): 1–82.

48. *United States v. Washington*, 384 F.Supp. at 322, emphasis added. The court decided to give little weight to recent judgments of the Indian Claims Commission demarcating traditional tribal territories because they had involved different kinds of claims—that is, compensation for the loss of land or underpayment for land ceded. *United States v. Washington*, 459 F.Supp. 1020, 1058-60 (W.D. Wash. 1975).

49. See, for example, *United States v. Washington*, Memorandum of Support Re: Port Gamble and Lower Elwha Usual and Accustomed Fishing Places, August 15, 1978, 4–5, and Supplemental Memorandum of Port Gamble Band of Klallam Indians, February 26, 1982, 4, both relating to "scattered references to Klallam *presence*" in the San Juan Islands (emphasis in the original). The court did not accept the argument of the Makah, however, that, as very aggressive people, they should enjoy a presumption that they did not ask anyone's permission to fish wherever

they pleased. See *United States v. Washington*, Reply Memorandum of Lower Elwha Tribe Regarding Usual and Accustomed Places of Lower Elwha Tribe, November 24, 1985, 1–2.

50. Ibid., Reply Memorandum of Lower Elwha Tribe, 3. But the court relied on living tribal members in the case of Tulalip, discussed below.

51. *United States v. Washington*, 384 F. Supp., at 419.

52. Ibid.

53. Order Re: Tulalip Tribes' Objection to Stillaguamish Fishing Regulations, March 10, 1976, 3.

54. See, for example, Memorandum and Order, February 24, 1983, 6–7, regarding the request of the Skokomish Tribe for a determination of their primary rights in Hood Canal. Treaty tribes' "usual and accustomed areas" had largely been settled during the early stages of litigation—that is, by 1974 and 1975.

55. Tribes' Status Report Re: Phase I Matters before the Court, August 8, 1978.

56. *United States v. Washington*, Barbara Lane, Identity, Treaty Status and Fisheries of the Suquamish Tribe of the Port Madison Reservation, December 15, 1974, 18; Order and Decree Re: Herring Fisheries, April 18, 1975, 2.

57. Supplemental Memorandum of Port Gamble Band, 12–13.

58. *United States v. Lower Elwha Tribe*; Post-Trial Brief Re: Usual and Accustomed Grounds of Port Gamble and Lower Elwha, May 7, 1979, 10–11; Magistrate's Report and Recommendation Re: Port Gamble and Lower Elwha Klallam Usual and Accustomed Fishing Area, September 24, 1981; Corrected Order Re: Request for Determination of Port Gamble and Lower Elwha Klallam Usual and Accustomed Fishing Places, October 28, 1981.

59. *United States v. Washington*, Memorandum in Support of Request for Determination: Jamestown Klallam Usual and Accustomed Fishing Areas, June 19, 198, 4.

60. *United States v. Washington*, 384 F.Supp. 351-53. The court also distinguished the right to fish casually while in transit, which it properly regarded as outside the scope of "usual and accustomed" fisheries.

61. Order Re: Makah Request for Reconsideration Re: Lower Elwha Usual and Accustomed Fishing Places, March 10, 1976, 4; affirmed, *United States v. Lower Elwha Tribe*, 642 F.2d 1141, 1144 (9th Cir. 1981).

62. Deposition upon Oral Examination of Dr. Barbara Lane, 76, at 114–15.

63. *United States v. Washington*, Motion for Leave to Depose Expert Re: Klallam Usual and Accustomed Fishing Grounds, April 3, 1979, 2; Objection to Makah, Lummi, and Tulalip Request for Production Re: Klallam Usual and Accustomed Fishing Grounds, March 28, 1979.

64. *United States v. Washington*, Petition of Swinomish Indian Tribal Community for a Determination of Usual and Accustomed Fish Areas, June 24, 1974.

65. *United States v. Washington*, Order and Decree Re: Herring Fisheries, April 18, 1975, 2.

66. *United States v. Washington*, Response of Swinomish Indian Tribal Community to Amended and Supplemental Request of Lummi Indian Tribe, Marsh 27, 1975, 1.

67. *United States v. Washington*, Complaint in Intervention of the Tulalip Tribes of Washington, August 20, 1974; Order Re: Tulalip Tribes of Washington's Usual and Accustomed Fishing Places, December 10, 1975.

68. *United States v. Washington*, Memorandum of the Tulalip Tribes of Washington on Usual and Accustomed Grounds and Stations, July 31, 1975, 3, 16.

69. *United States v. Washington*, Written Argument of Stillaguamish Re: Tulalip Determination of Usual and Accustomed Fishing Areas, August 4, 1975, 3.

70. Ibid., 7–8.

71. *United States v. Washington*, Request for Determination Re: Tulalip Tribes of Washington, September 5, 1980; Tulalip Pretrial Brief, April 13, 1983, 1. Note that the Tulalip Tribes characterized the Snohomish and Snoqualmie as claiming rights as successors to aboriginal Tulalips, and not the other way around.

72. The history and these tribes' loss of political status in the 1970s and efforts to regain their status can be found in Russel Barsh, "Political Recognition: An Assessment of American Practice," in *Who Are Canada's Aboriginal Peoples? Recognition, Definition, and Jurisdiction*, edited by Paul L.A.H. Chartrand (Saskatoon, Saskatchewan: Purich Publishing, 2002), 230–57.

73. Request for Determination Re: Tulalip Tribes, 2–3.

74. Ibid., 11.

75. *United States v. Washington*, Tulalip Submission in Support of Their Petition to Determine Usual and Accustomed Fishing Places, July 21, 1982, 14, emphasis added.

76. Ibid., 8–9.

77. *United States v. Washington*, Index and Citations to Be Used with Map Showing Presence of Tulalip Indians and Predecessor Groups in the Puget Sound Region, October 8, 1982.

78. *United States v. Washington*, Deposition upon Oral Examination of Harriette [*sic*] Dover, November 10, 1982, 31–32.

79. Ibid., 23.

80. Ibid., 24, 31, 35, 40, 47–48. Indeed, when she was asked repeatedly for the Indian name for Orcas Island, she finally gave "Changuanung," which is almost certainly the same as xʷčénkʷənəŋ, the Samish name for the reef net site on Watmough Bight on Lopez Island. Ibid., 48; Suttles, *Coast Salish of Rosario and Haro Strait*, 197.

81. *United States v. Washington*, Deposition upon Oral Examination of Harriette [*sic*] Dover, November 10, 1982, 38.

82. Ibid., 8.

83. Ibid., 9–10.

84. Ibid., 11.

85. *United States v. Washington*, Request for a Determination of an Equitable Adjustment of the Tulalip Tribes' Usual and Accustomed Fishing Places, October 16, 1975.

86. *United States v. Washington*, United States Memorandum Re: Tulalip

Motion for Equitable Adjustment of Usual and Accustomed Fishing Places, October 20, 1975, 1.

87. Ibid., 2.

88. *United States v. Lower Elwha Tribe*, 642 F.2d 1141, 1144 n. 8 (9th Cir. 1981).

89. Ibid., 1143, n4.

90. Stipulated Settlement Agreement of Swinomish Tribal Community and the Tulalip Tribes, June 13, 1983; Stipulation of Muckleshoot, Suquamish, and Tulalip Tribes Re: Tulalip Usual and Accustomed Fishing Places, June 13, 1983; Stipulated Agreement of Lower Elwha, Port Gamble, and Jamestown Bands of Klallam, Skokomish Tribe, and Tulalip Tribes, July 16, 1983; Stipulation of Nisqually, Puyallup, and Tulalip Tribes Re: Tulalip Usual and Accustomed Fishing Places, June 13, 1983.

91. *United States v. Washington*, Lummi Indian Tribe's Objections to the Settlements Involving the Tulalip, Muckleshoot, Suquamish, Swinomish, Puyallup, and Nisqually Tribes, June 30, 1982: "Put colloquially, the Tulalips, Muckleshoots, and Suquamish bought peace with Lummi fish." Ibid., 2. They also argued: "The Tulalip Tribes are not a tribe in the traditional sense of the word," but merely an aggregation of individual Indians. Objecting Tribes' Pretrial Memorandum, June 4, 1983, 10–11. However, other parties emphasized the fact that nonparties remained free to challenge any adverse impacts on their fisheries. Muckleshoot and Suquamish Tribes' Response to Lummi Indian Tribe's Objections, July 2, 1983.

92. *United States v. Washington*, Memorandum of Support of Proposed Magistrate's Report and Recommended Order, May 4, 1979, 5 (Port Gamble and Lower Elwha). After achieving federal recognition, Jamestown Klallam simply claimed the same areas as Lower Elwha and Port Gamble. Brief of Jamestown Klallam Tribe, December 29, 1983; Order Granting Summary Judgment on Jamestown Klallam Request for Determination of Usual and Accustomed Fishing Places, March 16, 1984.

93. Russel Barsh, "Backfire from Boldt: The Judicial Transformation of Coast Salish Proprietary Fisheries into a Commons," *Western Legal History* 4, no. 1 (1991): 85–102, and Barsh, "The Economics of a Traditional Coastal Indian Salmon Fishery," *Human Organization* 41, no. 2 (1982): 171–76.

94. Ironically, forty years after nineteenth-century "allotment" policy tried to make Plains Indians into capitalists, with some success stories, the Indian Service collectivized cattle herds and forced leading Indian ranchers into bankruptcy. Russel Barsh, "Plains Indian Agrarianism and Class Conflict," *Great Plains Quarterly* 7, no. 2 (1987): 83–90. Perhaps the greatest evil is vacillating national policy that continually redistributes Indians' wealth.

95. As of late 2006, seventeen treaty tribes fished in the San Juan Islands, and the Samish Indian Nation was in court poised to become the eighteenth tribal party.

8 The Stevens Treaties, Indian Claims Commission Docket 264, and the Ancient One known as Kennewick Man

Bruce Rigsby

The Ancient One, Kennewick Man, and Tiičáminsh Uytpamá Natítayt[1] are three among the names given to ninety-five-hundred-year-old human remains found in shallow waters of the Columbia River at Kennewick, Washington, in July 1996.[2] When regional Indian groups requested the remains so they could bury them promptly, a dispute ensued that attracted national and international media attention (including some right-wing culture warriors) and generated a popular literature as well as a considerable scholarly literature.[3] The controversy pitted a notable set of researchers, who wanted to study the skeleton, against some tribal governments and many Indian people in Washington, Oregon, and Idaho. It polarized American archaeologists, sociocultural anthropologists, and physical anthropologists; it reinforced old interpersonal antagonisms and intellectual differences, and created new ones.

In 2004 the U.S. Court of Appeals for the Ninth Circuit found for the eight plaintiff scientists who sought to study the remains and denied petitions for rehearing, so that further study could (and did) proceed. The bad feelings on both sides will be with us for years. That decision, known as *Bonnichsen v. United States of America et al.*, cannot have endeared archaeologists (especially) to people in Indian Country.[4] But beyond drawing attention to a cultural conflict between some scientists and

Indian traditionalists, the case should make us consider the likelihood that Indians reserved the right to curate graves and burial sites of people they considered their ancestors, even on lands they ceded in treaties with the United States. The discovery of a skull initiated the drama and conflict that put these issues in the public eye.[5] Within a few weeks after the find, the bones of an almost complete skeleton had been recovered and identified as those of an ancient man, soon dubbed "Kennewick Man" in the media. Indians of the nearby Confederated Tribes of the Umatilla Indian Reservation (CTUIR) responded by naming him "the Ancient One" in English. These Indians also have a name for themselves —for "(Indian) person" or "people"—in the Walla Walla Sahaptin language: *Natítayt*. I often use their term in place of "Indian(s)."

The CTUIR requested that the remains be turned over to them with no further study. They planned a quick reburial with proper ceremony. Other regional Natítayt groups joined in the request, but some wanted repatriation to themselves instead of the CTUIR. The Natítayt believe that the remains are those of an ancestral landowner. They asserted that therefore it was their religious duty to return their ancestor's bones to repose in the earth without the desecration entailed in DNA testing and other investigative procedures that scientists would employ.[6] Importantly, the CTUIR leaders drew attention to the fact that the bones were found on their traditional homeland, where they retained rights under an 1855 treaty that ceded other rights in the land to the United States. In a position paper Armand Minthorn of the CTUIR plainly stated the Natítayt argument about reserved rights and jurisdiction: "My tribe has ties to this individual because he was uncovered in our traditional homeland —a homeland where we still retain hunting, fishing, gathering, and other rights under our 1855 Treaty with the U.S. Government."[7]

In mid-September of 1996, the U.S. Army Corps of Engineers (COE) announced that they would return the remains to five Natítayt groups and let the groups decide among themselves how to deal with the Ancient One. A month later, however, eight scientists initiated an action to block repatriation and allow them to study the remains. When the CTUIR and later a tribal coalition requested possession of the Ancient One, they in fact asserted their reserved rights regarding burials. But in court they laid their claim under the Native American Graves Protection and Repatriation Act (NAGPRA), a 1990 act of Congress which provides that the owner of Native American human remains found on federal property shall be the Indian tribe whose land or area of aboriginal occupation encompasses that place.

The issue in the litigation became a question of whether and how NAGPRA applied and how certain terms (such as "indigenous" and "Native American") were to be read and given meaning. When trial judge John Jelderks and subsequently the appellate judges rejected the tribal coalition's request that the remains be repatriated, they were simply interpreting and applying NAGPRA. It was not for them to consider whether members of the coalition had reserved sovereign rights regarding burials. At the same time further legal action on the reserved rights question was effectively discouraged when the trial judge accepted that the site where the remains were found was not part of the aboriginal homeland of any CTUIR predecessor group. That finding is based on a superseded and now indefensible determination of the Indian Claims Commission (ICC).[8]

SOME ASPECTS OF THE *BONNICHSEN* LITIGATION

I focus here on two decisions—the opinion and order of Magistrate Judge John Jelderks issued on August 30, 2002, and the opinion of the U.S. Court of Appeals for the Ninth Circuit, written by Circuit Judge Ronald M. Gould and filed on February 4, 2004.[9] The plaintiffs/ appellants in the actions were eight scientists whom I would characterize variously as archaeologists, forensic anthropologists, and physical anthropologists. They were aggrieved not only by the COE's decision in 1996 but also by a decision of the Secretary of the Interior in September 2000 to repatriate the remains to a tribal coalition for reburial. They brought an action against the COE, the Department of the Interior (DOI), the National Park Service (NPS), and a small set of civil servants whose membership changed between the two actions. On appeal the coalition of five Natítayt groups joined the defendants-appellees as defendants-intervenors. The coalition consisted of the CTUIR, the Confederated Tribes and Bands of the Yakama Nation, the Nez Perce Tribe of Idaho, the Confederated Tribes of the Colville Reservation, and the Wanapum Band.[10]

The trial judge declined to remand the matter to the Secretary of the Interior with specific instructions. Among other things, Judge Jelderks found the remains were not "Native American" under NAGPRA because the evidence did not support the conclusion that they were "of, or relating to, a tribe, people, or culture that *is* indigenous to the United States." He noted: "The parties agree that the lineal descendants of the Kennewick Man, if any, cannot be ascertained, and the remains were not found on tribal land." He held that "the Secretary erred in assuming that the coalition was a proper claimant and in failing to separately analyze the relationship of the particular Tribal Claimants to the remains."[11] Finally, Jelderks concluded that the secretary also misinterpreted a key provision of NAGPRA when he determined that the Ancient One had turned up within the aboriginal territory of the petitioning tribes. That section of NAGPRA, now codified at 25 *U.S. Code* section 3002(a)(2)(C)(1), requires "a final judgment of the Indian Claims Commission" that the federal land where remains are found was "the aboriginal land of some Indian tribe." Jelderks said the secretary erroneously construed this language "to include cases in which no valid final judgment established aboriginal title, and misinterpreted . . . [it] by applying it to cases in which the ICC [Indian Claims Commission] had specifically found that the tribe *failed* to establish its aboriginal title."[12]

For all of the preceding reasons, the judge pronounced the secretary's decision "arbitrary and capricious," set it aside, and ordered the defendants not to transfer the Ancient One's remains to the tribal coalition. The three appellate judges affirmed, saying, among other things: "Because Kennewick Man's remains are so old and the information about his era is so limited, the record does not permit the Secretary to conclude reasonably that Kennewick Man shares special and significant genetic or cultural features with presently existing indigenous tribes, people, or cultures. We thus hold that Kennewick Man's remains are not Native American human remains within the meaning of NAGPRA and that NAGPRA does not apply to them."[13]

I have also read the expert reports and friend-of-the-court submissions, and I do not question the soundness of Judge Jelderks's black-letter legal reasoning about the meaning and intent of NAGPRA. It appears that the remains are not Native American as defined by NAGPRA.[14] I also accept his judgment that the evidence did not support a finding of "cultural affiliation" between the Ancient One and a contemporary Native American group. It is difficult to think of a case where remains that old might be linked to a contemporary ethnic group by the standards of proof required in court.[15] Furthermore, I understand the judge's legal reasoning that the tribal coalition did not have standing in the case.

However, the coalition was not just a fortuitous, unrelated set of neighboring groups. It represents the descendants of groups that participated in the treaty council at Walla Walla in 1855 and signed treaties proposed by Washington Territory governor Isaac Stevens (although some later rejected them). All the groups either had traditional territory that included the Kennewick Man discovery site or was close by. Ethnographically, we can describe the significant mid-nineteenth-century ancestors of the tribal coalition as people who were countrymen, fellow regional landowners, much intermarried, and who generally spoke or understood each other's languages.

The CTUIR includes the Cayuses, the Umatillas, and the Wallas Wallas. The Ancient One's remains were found on land that those tribes ceded in their treaty of June 9, 1855, and specifically on land that is recognized by the Natítayt throughout the region as belonging to Walla Walla people. A second coalition member, the Yakama Nation, made a treaty the same day at the Walla Walla council, and some of its signatories represented groups whose territories might have included the Kennewick Man site or come very close to it (these groups include the Palouses and the Wanapums). The Confederated Tribes of the Colville Reservation joined the coalition on behalf of Nez Perces, who are one of the confederation's constituent bands.[16] The Nez Perces too were major participants in the Walla Walla Council and signed their own treaty on June 11, 1855. The last coalition group—the Wánapam—are not a federally recognized tribe, although the earliest explorers observed and reported on them. Wanapum Band members are direct descendants of a local group headed by the prophet and holy man Šmúχala, who made his home near Priest Rapids after 1860. They are culturally conservative people who have resisted repeated efforts to move them to a reservation.[17]

These facts and Indian Claims Commission records persuaded John Leshy, a solicitor for the Department of the Interior, that the coalition's joint claim for the Ancient One's remains made sense: "Because, as noted above, *the ICC's findings of fact and opinions identify the recovery site of the Kennewick remains as the joint aboriginal land of numerous Indian groups, including at least two* [the CTUIR and the Yakamas] *of the claimant tribes,* I believe that these tribes collectively may successfully claim the Kennewick remains, if disposition is not appropriate under 25 U.S.C. 3002 (a)(1), (a)(2)(A) and (a)(2)(B)."[18] Leshy also observed that "multiple-use or non-exclusive use of an area did not preclude the ICC from" making a determination of joint ownership of a claimed area.[19] In fact, however, the ICC very rarely made joint-ownership determinations.[20]

In 1997, I wrote: "The requirement of exclusive use and occupancy prevented establishing Indian title over land where 'many tribes or bands were known to wander or occupy.' And it also required establishing that use and occupancy was sufficiently intensive that the tribe excluded 'white explorers, traders, miners, and settlers.'"[21] It is "conceivable that a similar shared aboriginal land holder [ICC] determination could have been made for the Mid-Columbia region at issue if the following tribes had brought a joint claim: Yakama, Umatilla, Nez Perce, and Colville," but the time for that is long past.[22]

THE ARGUMENT FROM RESERVED RIGHTS

When the Cayuse, Umatilla, and Walla Walla leaders signed their treaty in 1855, they explicitly ceded certain rights in lands and waters, but they reserved other rights.[23] The doctrine of "reserved rights" (or "implied rights") is a recognized part of established federal Indian law, along with canons of construction that require judges to give Indians' understandings the benefit of the doubt when construing treaties.[24] But the recognition of specific reserved rights has always been a matter of contention and litigation. The position I put in this essay is that the Natítayt treaty parties did not intend to cede, nor did they cede, their sovereign rights to deal with the remains of the dead then on their homelands and to access and look after the graves and burials there in traditional-customary ways.[25]

The argument for such Natítayt reserved rights, and thus for jurisdiction over the Ancient One's remains, is strong.[26] It rests on three legs —on the legal doctrine of reserved rights and precedents articulated by American courts, on past and continuing Natítayt understanding of the CTUIR treaty of 1855, and on the rights in land under traditional law and custom that the treaty-signing ancestors of the CTUIR possessed and exercised. I do not treat these three bases for the argument serially. The first is well known and beyond my competence as an anthropologist to do more than summarize, as done earlier in this essay. The second requires some knowledge of classical and postclassical Sahaptin culture and society, accessible through linguistic anthropological analysis and discussion of some key indigenous words, phrases, and concepts.[27] These provide background to the Natítayt understanding, past and present, of the treaty, which I discuss next, before considering evidence for the third basis of the argument—traditional-customary Natítayt rights in the lands they used and called home.

SOME SAHAPTIN WORDS, PHRASES, AND CONCEPTS

In the Walla Walla and other Northeast Sahaptin dialects, the word *Lč'ílč'ima* signifies the ancestors as a set, which includes the known and remembered dead as well as all the remaining dead since the beginning of time, when humans first occupied the earth. The word's counterpart in Umatilla, Yakama, and other dialects of Sahaptin is *Nč'ínč'ima*, and its Nez Perce equivalent is *Titlúume*. Good glosses are "the Ancestors, Old People." My observations on the Umatilla Reservation since 1997 are that speakers of the indigenous Sahaptin and Nez Perce languages regard the ancient man whose remains were found at Kennewick in 1996 as one of their Lč'ílč'ima, Nč'ínč'ima, or Titlúume. Those Natítayt who do not speak their heritage languages also regard the Ancient One as an ancestor.

These are terms of great respect. When I attended root feasts and other public events on the Umatilla and Yakama Reservations in the 1960s and 1970s, I heard people use them often in formal speeches to the audience or congregation as they invoked their Old People's experiences and admonishments. The Old People are exemplars and supporters of tradition and *natitaytwít*, *tananáwit*, or *tiináwit*—that is, "Indian-ness, Indian culture."[28] When I first read about Kennewick Man in early 1998, I also read the phrase "the Ancient One," the now customary Natítayt way of referring to the remains in English. I assumed that it was simply a translation into English of the important cultural concept of "the Ancestors, Old People," and I discussed the matter in my affidavit for the CTUIR later in the year.[29] I was concerned then with demonstrating that the Ancient One was not a New Age term, but one with its origin in indigenous tradition.

In early 2005, I learned that the CTUIR and other groups used the indigenous language phrase *Techaminsh Oytpamanatityt* when they requested the repatriation of the remains in February 1999. They gave the phrase no translation then. When the Yakamas filed to intervene in May 2000, their lawyer wrote: "The remains are called Techaminsh Oytpamanatityt ('from the land the first native') in the Yakama language." In technical linguistic orthography the phrase is properly three words— *Tiičáminš Uytpamá Natítayt*—and is well analyzed and glossed as "a human (or Indian) land-owner from the beginning of time." The first word, *Tiičáminš*, can be translated best as "landowner." It is a complex word built on the simple word or base *tiičám* ("earth, land, country") plus the derivational suffix *-inš*, which is the possessive-proprietive suffix. It gives the meaning "the one that has or possesses the thing signified by the base"—thus, "land-having" or "the one who owns (the) land."

I don't recall hearing or recording the word *Tiičáminš* during my fieldwork in the 1960s and 1970s. I encountered it first in September 2004, at a workshop review of the Sahaptin place-names atlas project.[30] It struck me as a perfectly well-formed comprehensible word, and because of my interest in traditional-customary systems of land tenure and use, I found it significant culturally and socially. Later, I learned that the anthropologist Melville Jacobs recorded a Northeast Sahaptin dialectal form we can reconstitute as *tiičámiš*, which he glossed as "landowner."[31] *Tiičámiš* is cognate with *Tiičáminš* "land-owner" in other Sahaptin dialects. This conventional form provides prima facie evidence for the existence and operation of a traditional-customary system of land tenure and use. Were I just starting fieldwork among Sahaptin-speaking people, the existence of this form would cue me to talk extensively and intensively with people about the traditional-customary ownership of land, now and in the past.

Uyt-pamá is also a complex word, and it is built on the simple word or base *(')úyt* ("beginning, start") plus the derivational abessive suffix *-pamá*, which we can translate here as "from, pertaining to." It is well translated as "from / since the beginning (of time)." As explained at the outset of this essay, *Natítayt* is the Walla Walla (Northeast) Sahaptin word that means "person, people." In an earlier period it implied or connoted simply "human being(s)," but since the early nineteenth century or so, its unmarked connotation is "Indian person, people." The remains of Tiičáminš Uytpamá Natítayt were found washed out at a place where the indigenous residents spoke the language from which these words come—that is, the remains were in country where Walla Walla people held the traditional aboriginal beneficial title.

The indigenous-language words for "law" are also relevant to the Natítayt interest in the Ancient One. The social philosopher Jeremy Bentham reminds us that where there is property, there is also law. Law and custom are signified by a single cognate term in Sahaptin and Nez Perce, *Tamánwit* and *Tamáalwit*, respectively, often translated as "the Law." In anthropological and general social science terminology, the term includes both law and custom, but its conventional reference is to traditional Indian law and custom.[32] God can also be called *Tamanwiłá* ("the Law-Giver, Ordainer") in Sahaptin. The same complex stem is also found in Nez Perce *tamánwi-* ("lead, plan, lay down the law, legislate") and *píitamalwit* ("treaty").[33]

The experts and friends of the court who opposed the tribal coalition assessed the myths and legends of traditional Sahaptin oral literature only for their historical veracity. They overlooked or ignored their chartering role in providing accounts of the events that were and are the root of Natítayt traditional-customary title to their homeland. But Natítayt communal title does not originate from acts of the sovereign, nor from sale and purchase, nor even inheritance; nor is it recorded on paper deeds. Instead, the oral literature tells us there was a time or period before there were human beings or people. The Spirit-Beings who lived on the land then are called *Walsákas*, *Walcáytsas*, and *Wat'ítaš* in Northeast, Columbia River, and Northwest Sahaptin, respectively. Principal among them was *Spilyáy* ("Coyote"), who fashioned many landforms and features and instituted the norms of human law and custom—that is, culture and society. Elements of the oral literature function as paper (or electronic) deeds do for owners and nonowners alike.

THE WALLA WALLA COUNCIL OF 1855

In May and June of 1855, Governor Isaac Stevens of Washington Territory and Oregon's superintendent of Indian affairs, Joel Palmer, held a treaty council with members of several indigenous groups at a site near present-day Walla Walla, Washington.[34] Of special interest to us are the Walla Walla people and their Cayuse and Umatilla kin and neighbors, but Nez Perces, Palouses, and Yakamas were also active players at the council. Over the century or so before 1855, their ancestors had undergone great social and economic transformation due to their acquisition first of horses, then later of cattle and other commodities acquired by trading and raiding trips into other regions, including the Spanish settlements in New Mexico, Arizona, and California, as well as from American emigrants transiting their homelands. From 1818 the policy and practice of the Hudson's Bay Company (HBC) (and later that of the missionaries) had encouraged political centralization and the development of explicit legal norms. The Natítayt had increasing material wealth; class distinctions were emergent between equestrian groups who went to the buffalo grounds on the Plains and those who "stayed home and ate cottontails"; and leaders had more power and scope to exercise that power.[35] The Natítayt leaders who negotiated with the American officials were also people of property and wealth who knew something of the wider world and had witnessed the dispossession and dislocation of Indian groups west of the Oregon Cascades and in upper California.

Stevens and Palmer discussed and negotiated three treaties with the Natítayt at the council, then wrote them down for signing. Their objective was to produce public documents that would, after ratification by the U.S. Congress, extinguish the Indian title to the land and thus enable the United States to provide secure titles to settlers. By U.S. law only the federal government was competent to extinguish the Indian title. Private companies (for example, the HBC) and individuals (for example, retired HBC men) might have gained possession of land by transactions with traditional owners, but they did not have titles recognized in American law.[36] The treaties were and remain the first and indispensable link on the chain of American titles to land in areas that the Natítayt ceded.

From what I understand of Natítayt law and custom in 1855,[37] I do not believe that the cession of lands was a proper act, but the Natítayt generally wanted to avoid war. Thus they tried to secure the best situation for themselves as peoples (and in some instances as individuals) by accommodating the American custom of providing for access to land and resources by formal treaty.[38] I believe the Natítayt did view the treaties as solemn covenants with the American government.[39] But I doubt that they realized the Americans thought the treaties consisted only of what was recorded in writing. The Natítayt would have regarded all that was said and agreed by talk at the council as binding on all parties.

People on both sides of the negotiations made efforts to communicate their intentions and desires as effectively as possible, but the factors preventing complete understanding were significant. Stevens and Palmer were concerned that the "chiefs, head-men and delegates" (whose agreement and signatures were essential to conclude the treaties) understand enough of the American proposal to discuss and negotiate points and issues, then reach accord and mark the documents.[40] Stevens and Palmer dealt with the Natítayt not only during the formal sessions but also in informal and even secret sessions. For their part the Natítayt were concerned about getting the best translations they could to understand fully what Stevens and Palmer proposed. Pyópyo Maqsmáqs, or Yellow Bird, the main Walla Walla chief, requested that there be more than one interpreter at the council.[41] Among the Natítayt leaders who spoke at the formal sessions, Pyópyo Maqsmáqs stands out for expressing concern about the need for good interpreting and the quality of particular interpreting.[42] The Natítayt also observed the commissioners not just to understand what they were saying, but to look into their hearts and assess their character and goodwill as well.[43]

English, Nez Perce, and Sahaptin were the languages used during the formal council proceedings.[44] Stevens and Palmer spoke in English, the Natítayt spokesmen (all males) spoke in Nez Perce or one or another Sahaptin dialect, and the interpreters (appointed and otherwise) translated into the addressees' language(s). When Stevens and Palmer spoke, the interpreters spoke their translations to two Natítayt "criers, heralds" (Nez Perce te'wyelene'wéet and Sahaptin sínwiłá), who relayed them loudly to the audience.[45] No doubt, many Natítayt understood both translations. The Natítayt also held meetings among themselves in the evenings, and the Nez Perce language was considered proper and fitting for such intergroup meetings. It had gained wide regional currency from the time of Lewis and Clark, and many Natítayt spoke Nez Perce as a second language, if not as their first.[46] It is possible that a few speakers on both sides also made some use of Chinook trade jargon, but the Natítayt did not regard the jargon highly, and indeed it lacked the referential and expressive power of the other languages.[47]

By 1855 power relations between the Americans and the Natítayt were so imbalanced and precedents were so powerful that Stevens and Palmer probably never considered framing the treaties in two languages, English and a Native tongue, as was done for the Treaty of Waitangi, concluded in New Zealand in 1840 and recorded in English and Maori versions. Instead, the treaties made at Walla Walla are written in a formal register of English. Their legal phrasing and terms had precise meanings and references for the Congress and the U.S. legal and political system. Had they been written otherwise, the treaties might not have been ratified by Congress, which included many lawyers. Some of the Natítayt were fluent speakers of English, perhaps even native speakers.[48] But I doubt that the treaties were completely clear and comprehensible to any native speaker of English—non-Indian or Indian—who lacked formal education, let alone training and experience in American law and politics. And some of the interpreters were illiterate; they made X marks instead of signing their names.

On June 9 the Walla Wallas, Cayuses, and Umatillas signed a treaty, and the Yakamas signed a separate one. Two days later the Nez Perces concluded their own treaty. On June 12, without waiting for Senate ratification, Stevens and Palmer prepared a public notice that the ceded lands, but not the reservations, were open to settlement, although the Natítayt retained possession of their "buildings and implements until removed to the reservations."[49] Newspapers soon published that announcement. War involving Yakamas and Palouses erupted some weeks later in late July, and hostilities continued into 1858, when Natítayt resisters were finally defeated and most began to remove to the reservations.

WHAT DID THE TREATY DO?

From the American perspective the treaty of 1855 accomplished four acts of importance:

1. It constituted a new nation—the Confederated Tribes of the Umatilla Indian Reservation (CTUIR)—as a party competent to treat with the United States and to cede land claimed or occupied by its constituent bands.[50]
2. It granted the United States some lands desired for its citizens.
3. It reserved some lands for the people of the new nation (who were not citizens of the United States).
4. It reserved certain rights, already held and exercised by the Natítayt under their own traditional law and custom, for the people of the new nation.

Stevens Treaties, Claims Commission and the Ancient One 255

Explicit reserved rights included the exclusive right to fish "in the streams running through and bordering said reservation" and "at all other usual and accustomed stations in common with citizens of the United States, and of erecting suitable buildings for curing the same; the privilege of hunting, gathering roots and berries and pasturing their stock on unclaimed lands in common with citizens." But the Natítayt were exercising other rights neither explicitly reserved nor explicitly relinquished in the treaty. We must understand, from the Natítayt perspective, that they did not leave the treaty council believing they had surrendered any unmentioned rights. And the treaty made no mention of burials, graves, or funerary customs. Since it did permit the Natítayt to be on lands other than the reservations, they had good reason for expecting that they could continue tending to the ancestors' resting places, wherever those were.[51]

WHO HAD PROPERTY RIGHTS AT THE KENNEWICK SITE IN 1855?

Now we consider the third base of the argument that the Natítayt reserved the right to deal in traditional ways with ancient human remains in the Kennewick area: the nature of customary Natítayt rights in that land. That entails reviewing evidence that connects the land in question to the people who occupied it in the classical period before the treaty. The evidence is convincing that Kennewick, Washington, is in territory that was occupied by Walla Walla people during the historic period and by their social, cultural, linguistic, and biological ancestors for some millennia previous.[52] The Walla Wallas are therefore the traditional owners of the land, and their leaders ceded it to the United States as part of the larger area ceded in the treaty of 1855.

On October 17, 1805, Captain William Clark visited a Natítayt fishing settlement near present-day Kennewick when he made a brief upriver reconnaissance from the camp of the Corps of Discovery near Kwʼsís at the mouth of the Snake River. Clark's account provides clear evidence that a Natítayt group was then in occupation of the general area where the Ancient One's remains surfaced 190-odd years later. He found men, women, and children living there and engaged in drying salmon. Among other things the people showed him the mouth of the Yakima River upstream.[53] According to the anthropologist Eugene Hunn (in an early

2005 e-mail with the author), there was an island, now flooded, across from the site where the Ancient One's remains were found, and its highest point might well have been sufficiently high to give Clark a view of the Yakima River's mouth.

In 1953, Pákayatut (also known as Johnny Buck), *wyánč'i* ("leader") of the Wánapam people at Priest Rapids, named the general Kennewick area on the right bank as *Ánwaš* ("Sun's Place")[54] Ánwaš is also the indigenous name of Clover Island, just downstream and now a marina. Pákayatut knew the area and the wider region well; his people (many of them descended from the nineteenth-century occupants of the area) still fished at Kennewick in 1950, although fish were scarce there by then.[55]

After departing their camp near K^w'sís on October 18, the Lewis and Clark party passed "eleven large mat lodges" at Walúula and proceeded a few miles down the Columbia to make their next camp on the north side of the river near a village of five lodges. Later that night they were visited by "the first Chief of all the tribes in this quarter," who set up camp nearby and came again early the next morning with three other chiefs, when they smoked, parleyed, and were given gifts. They called the main chief "Yelleppit" or "Yellept," described as "a handsome well proportioned man, about five feet eight inches high, and thirty-five years of age, with a bold and dignified countenance."[56] On their return upstream the next year, the Americans again met Yellept, who took them to his village on the northern side of the river, "about twelve miles below the mouth" of the Snake, and encouraged them to stop for a few days. The next evening a party of a hundred or so Chamnápam arrived and joined the Walúulapam for an evening of dancing with the explorers' party. Five years later the fur trader David Thompson met Yellept five miles below the junction of the Snake with the Columbia and subsequently described him as the "Chief of all the Shawpatin Tribes."[57]

Based on records of the Lewis and Clark expedition, other explorers' accounts, and information supplied by indigenous people, ethnographers have determined that there were three permanent Natítayt winter villages in the wider area where the Yakima, Snake, and Walla Walla rivers flow into the Columbia. From the south the village complex of Walúula or Walawála was on both sides of the Columbia at the Walla Walla mouth,[58] K^w'sís was on the point at the north side of the Snake mouth, and Čamná was on the north bank just inside the Yakima mouth. There were other named places (such as Ánwaš) in the area where people camped for shorter periods to fish and dry their fish and such. The people of the area spoke similar Sahaptin varieties. My coauthor Noel Rude and I have classified these dialects as belonging to the Northeast subgroup of the Northern groups of Sahaptin, but we can also call them Walla Walla Sahaptin.[59] Lewis and Clark identified the people at Kʷ'sís as the "Sokulk nation,"[60] their neighbors at Čamná as "Chimnahpum" and "Chimnapoos,"[61] and the "Wollawollah nation on both sides of the Columbia from the entrance of Lewis's [Snake] River, as low as the Muscleshell rapid."[62]

THE INDIAN CLAIMS COMMISSION DOCKETS 264, 264A, AND 264B CLAIMS

It has been little appreciated that the first court ruling in *Bonnichsen*, the so-called Kennewick Man case, rested in part on an earlier ICC finding that the area where the remains were found lacked aboriginal Indian owners. Scientific, legal, and public attention focused on whether there were demonstrable relationships of "lineal descent" or "cultural affiliation" between the remains and any contemporary Native American group. These issues arising under NAGPRA obscured important matters of tribal sovereign rights and jurisdiction. The earlier ICC proceeding was relevant because of a previously mentioned section of NAGPRA, which instructs the government to rely on a "final judgment" of the ICC when determining whether human remains were found on a tribe's "aboriginal land." In the CTUIR's case the relevant ICC proceeding began with a petition for compensation filed in August 1951.[63] Only Claim 1 for the ceded treaty area is directly relevant to the repatriation question, but two findings in Claim 4 provide evidence of the United States' general position that there was no Indian property in lands and waters.

The commissioners' final determination in June 1960 denied that the CTUIR's predecessor groups held "Indian title" based on "exclusive use and occupancy from time immemorial of any definable area in such ceded territory for each of the Indian tribes or bands who were parties to that treaty." If evidence had been shown to support the recognition of Indian title in some areas, the ICC determination continued, it was "in each instance . . . limited to the immediate vicinity of the respective village occupied by such Indians." Also rejected was an argument that the CTUIR's predecessor groups at least had "recognized title" to lands named in the treaty—recognized by American negotiators and the Congress that ratified the treaty.[64] In truth, the ICC thus denied that the Natítayt had owned the very land they ceded by treaty.

In December 1960 the CTUIR filed a Petitioner's Motion for Rehearing and Amendment of Findings. In September 1964 the ICC vacated (that is, annulled) its final determination and entered new findings of fact and opinion and an interlocutory order. Among them was a finding and opinion that the Cayuse, Umatilla, Walla Walla, the "Wayampam bands [from Celilo Falls and upstream a bit], the Nez Perce tribe, the Snake Indians, and other Indians jointly used the area where the remains were later found."[65] Consequently, there was no aboriginal or Indian title to be recognized. Nonetheless, the United States accepted a compromise proposal by the ICC to settle all CTUIR claims with an award for $2.5 million. The CTUIR appealed (Appeal Docket 1-65) the new findings in the Court of Claims on December 28, 1965. But shortly before that the CTUIR General Council met and voted to accept the final compromise offer. At hearings in Washington, D.C., on January 20, 1966, the ICC determined that the General Council meeting and vote of acceptance were proper and aboveboard. The final compromise settlement of February 11, 1966, consolidated Dockets 264, 264A, and 264B and awarded a "final judgement against defendant and in favor of petitioner in the net amount of $2,450,000." The agreement also included these passages:

> This stipulation and entry of *Final Judgment* shall finally dispose of all claims or demands which the Confederated Tribes of the Umatilla Indian Reservation have asserted or could have asserted against said defendant . . .

> *This stipulation, dismissal of the appeal and entry of the Final Judgment shall not be construed as an admission of either party as to any issue for purposes of precedent in any other case or otherwise.*[66]

It was the vacated 1960 final determination, among other matters, which led the trial judge in 2002 to reject the Natítayt argument that "a claim based on aboriginal occupation . . . was also a basis for" repatriating the Ancient One's remains to the tribal coalition defendants/intervenors. That rejection, though consistent with NAGPRA, especially section 3002(a)(2)(C), plainly disregards the second stipulation above "with regard to determining the ownership of Native American human remains and cultural items excavated or removed from Federal lands after November 16, 1990."[67]

The COE, DOI, and NPS defendants took the position that section 3(a)(2)(C) of NAGPRA does not apply because "the land where the remains were discovered [now managed by the Corps of Engineers] has not been judicially determined to be the exclusive aboriginal territory of any modern Indian tribe." They argued further: "*It is recognized by many, including the tribes, that the area around Kennewick was used heavily by many tribes and bands, so much so that the Commission found that no single tribe had a claim to exclusive use or occupancy.*"[68] I doubt many Natítayt hold the view that no specific classical group owned the area where the remains were found. That region was one of intensive occupation and use, but it was not without resident landowners. There are differences of opinion over who the classical owning group was: whether it was the Naχíyampam of Kʷ'sís and the Lower Snake, the Čhamnápam of the Lower Yakima, the Walla Walla or Walúulapam (whose classical estate was south of the Snake River junction on the Columbia), the Wánapam (whose southern boundary on the Columbia is unclear), or even the Palouses or Pelúuspem.[69] I have taken the position here that we can identify the Walla Wallas as its traditional owners at the time of the treaty in 1855 and the CTUIR as their successors at law, but the point is arguable.

THE INDIAN CLAIMS COMMISSION FINAL DETERMINATION IN HINDSIGHT

We anthropologists have made considerable advances in knowledge since the ICC hearings in the 1950s and 1960s. There is considerably more evidence available in the way of primary written sources and oral history (for example, the L. V. McWhorter, Verne Ray, and Click Relander Papers, Sam Black's 1829 report from Fort Nez Perces, and A. D. Pambrun's 1978 reprinted memoirs and his descendant's biographical sketch)[70] as well as scholarly research studies based on much new evidence.[71] We now understand classical Plateau social organization and land tenure better.[72] The same is true of comparative jurisprudence—specifically international law as it applies to the lands of indigenous peoples encapsulated in state-organized societies.[73]

More recent decisions in Australia and Canada (for example, the cases known as *Mabo No. 2* and *Delgamuukw*), also common law jurisdictions, provide new precedents and obiter on traditional aboriginal title to lands and waters and whether and how the common law (and statutory law) can recognize it. And finally, our general social theory understanding of the character of property[74] and of land tenure and use among hunter-gatherer-fishers[75] has increased and been refined in recent decades. The incidents of Natítayt title under traditional law and custom include much more than just usufructuary rights.[76] We social scientists can read and interpret the old and new evidence better these days, and we hope that our legal and judicial colleagues will give such improved analyses serious consideration when the opportunity arises, rather than accepting without question the findings of tribunals that heard testimony from an earlier generation of researchers.

The 1960 ICC final determination was based on a flawed theory and model of land tenure and use that privileged use and evidence for exclusion over normative law and custom. Put baldly, it held that the Indian occupation of the ceded lands did not give rise to Indian title because it was not based on exclusive possession from time immemorial. As the anthropologist Joe Jorgensen has noted: "The chief attorney of the Indian Claims Section [Ralph Barney] . . . took the position that Indians never really owned any land." The strategic and tactical positions taken by the United States' lawyers during the hearings reflected Barney's views consistently.[77] The vacated 1960 ICC final determination for Docket 264 can now be plainly seen as ethnographically unsound and legally not credible.

CONCLUSION

A recurring discourse in the popular media and among researchers was that the struggle for control of the Ancient One's remains was an instance of the battle between science and religion. There is no doubt that religious beliefs and practices widely shared among the Natítayt underlie their general opposition to studies of the remains and their intention to rebury them, but exclusive attention to those religious considerations ignores Natítayt concern about their treaties and treaty rights.

This oversight is understandable, since the CTUIR sought repatriation under the provisions of NAGPRA (which in turn is understandable, given the prominence of that legislation meant to right past wrongs and prevent new ones). When political leader Antone Minthorn said, "It is not science versus religion, . . . it is science versus the law," he identified NAGPRA as the law in question but neglected to mention the treaty and rights reserved under it.[78] The CTUIR's and the tribal coalition's reliance on NAGPRA had the unforeseen effect of foreclosing other possibilities. When the vacated ICC final determination came to light, the die was cast, precluding an action based on rights reserved by the treaties. No one had realized that they would have to contend with an ICC finding motivated at base by the United States' desire to minimize the costs of compensating Indians for and by an ideology of Indian assimilation.

When members of Congress approved the phrasing of NAGPRA's 25 *U.S. Code* section 3002(a)(2)(C)(1) to require "a final judgment of the Indian Claims Commission" that the federal land on which remains or object(s) were found was "the aboriginal land of some Indian tribe," they probably were unaware that historians have developed a negative assessment of the ICC's work. Nor, of course, were they aware of new anthropological and historical data proving traditional Natítayt ownership of the land where the Ancient One's remains were found. The 1964 ICC finding that the area was not held under aboriginal title or Indian title was based on incorrect interpretation of evidence that Indian people other than Walla Walla people were observed there engaged in such activities as camping, dwelling, fishing, drying fish, trading, conducting ceremonies, gambling, raiding, and performing servile labor.

The CTUIR and other members of the tribal coalition now need to establish more clearly just what land they ceded and what rights they reserved when their ancestors signed the treaties 150 years ago. The treaties are not just documents from the past, but they are living charters for the present and future. Despite the coercive, even deceitful circumstances of their origins, the treaties are authoritative guarantees for sovereign tribes and their own space in Indian Country. They offer opportunities for the future that we cannot always foresee, and as the historian Andrew Fisher has noted, they have also produced unexpected social changes.[79]

The task at hand includes reviewing the ICC claims documents and evidence as well as other documents and evidence that have come to light over the past forty years. Our new interpretation and assessment should be based on contemporary social theory and understandings. The old view that hunter-gatherers did not truly own their homelands or that they did not have, exercise, and recognize property rights and interests in them is no longer conventional wisdom in general social theory. When we look back at earlier records and oral histories of who was there and near about, we should be able to distinguish landowning groups and their members from people who were there as spouses, in-laws, and other relatives, trading partners, friends, travelers, war captives, or whatever. In this light I have taken the position that we can identify the traditional owners in 1855 of the site now on Columbia Park at Kennewick as Walla Walla people and that the CTUIR are their contemporary successors.

We cannot replay the ICC Docket 264 or its sequel in the Court of Claims. The enabling legislation ran its course long ago, and there is no way to appeal further and change its determinations. However, the Congress could achieve the same end in the future by amending the NAGPRA legislation to recognize that compromise final agreements with the ICC trump its vacated final determinations. Such amendment is unlikely unless there develops a wider public knowledge and acceptance that the CTUIR and/or the tribal coalition indeed should properly have jurisdiction because their predecessors occupied, were in possession of, and owned the lands and waters where the remains were found at the time they signed the treaty of 1855. That is linked to the proposition that the ICC final determination for Docket 264 was incorrect and that the current wording of 25 *U.S. Code* section 3002(a)(2)(C)(1) has worked an injustice on the CTUIR, successor to the Walla Walla signatories and traditional owners.

My argument is not simply a human rights and social justice one, but at base it is a jurisdictional argument, one of tribal sovereign right: that under the treaty of 1855 the CTUIR implicitly reserved the right to bury their dead in accord with their traditional law and custom and to look after and curate the many graves and burial sites on their ceded homelands, whether on reservation lands or not, and irrespective of their age and antiquity.[80] (It is useful to recall that if the remains had been found on current tribal land, whether reserved by treaty or acquired later, the CTUIR would have been able to require repatriation under NAGPRA —end of story!)

This argument does not require a finding or an assumption of direct biological descent from the Ancient One to present members of the CTUIR (although long-term continuity of the regional deme is likely, in my opinion). The argument is a legal one: that the present-day political successors of the sovereign indigenous parties to the treaties of 1855 did not cede, and therefore reserved, the right to care for or dispose of the remains of indigenous dead within their territories. This is a position the CTUIR took from the beginning. However—perhaps because their lawyers deemed NAGPRA the obvious and stronger basis for securing the Ancient One's remains—they did not pursue the argument in the litigation.

It is too late to reverse the situation of the Ancient One following the *Bonnichsen* decision, but the CTUIR, the other members of the tribal coalition, and their lawyers and researchers should consider ways to deal with such situations if and when they arise in the future. It is always useful to consider decisions in other common law jurisdictions, especially in Canada, which might offer alternative strategies and arguments. We also need to develop an ethnographically more adequate explanation of traditional-customary landownership and use to identify and secure better recognition of the rights reserved when ancestors of today's Indians ceded their lands by treaty; in other words, deeper knowledge of their past exercise of sovereignty and dominion in the region is needed. These should be put before the court of public opinion more effectively than has been done to date.

NOTES

I thank Bob Ackerman, Lillian Ackerman, Robert Boyd, Phil Cash Cash, Greg Cleveland, Steve Egesdal, Andy Fisher, Sasha Harmon, Gene Hunn, Joe Jorgensen, Jen Karson, Nancy Lurie, Tony Mattina, Thomas Morning Owl, Sam Pambrun, Ron Pond, Skip Ray, Bill Rodgers, John Ross, Noel Rude, Michael Silverstein, Rick Sprague, Darby Stapp, Deward Walker, Joe Watkins, Wilson Wewa Jr., John Wunder, David Yarrow, and Henry Zenk for their comments, suggestions, and help with references and other matters on drafts of this essay. I acknowledge the Board of Trustees of the Confederated Tribes of the Umatilla Indian Reservation for approval to do my research, and I also thank Tamástslikt Cultural Institute, its director, Bobbie Conner, and its staff for encouragement and support. The views expressed here are mine, except where attributed to others. *Naamí Lch'ilch'imaamíyaw Tí'aaχʷmaamíyaw* ("For all our Old People").

1. Sahaptin and Nez Perce language spellings are in linguistic orthography. See Bruce Rigsby and Noel Rude, "Sketch of Sahaptin, a Sahaptian Language," in *Languages*, vol. 17 of *Handbook of North American Indians*, edited by William C. Sturtevant (Washington, D.C.: Smithsonian Institution, 1996), 666–92; and Haruo Aoki, *Nez Perce Dictionary*, vol. 122, University of California Publications in Linguistics (Berkeley: University of California Press, 1994).

2. The remains reposed under dry land for millennia, but the construction of the McNary Dam downstream in 1953 filled Lake Wallula behind it, and a new terrace formed in its higher waters. It is thought that the wash from boat traffic and changing water levels caused the margin of the terrace to "calve" off (as icebergs do). The remains were washed from the surrounding earth as it disintegrated and were scattered just offshore over an area of three hundred square feet or more. The site is on the right bank of the Columbia, about midway between the mouths of the Yakima and Snake rivers, on the upstream end of Columbia Park inside Kennewick city limits.

3. For example, Ron Brunton, "Bones Connection Worth Fighting Over," [Brisbane] *Courier-Mail*, August 2, 1997; James C. Chatters, *Ancient Encounters: Kennewick Man and the First Americans* (New York: Simon & Schuster, 2001); Roger Downey, *Riddle of the Bones: Politics, Science, Race, and the Story of Kennewick Man* (New York: Springer-Verlag New York, 2000); Douglas Preston, "The Lost Man," *New Yorker*, June 15, 1997, 70–81; and David Hurst Thomas, *Skull Wars: Kennewick Man, Archaeology, and the Battle for Identity* (New York: Basic Books, 2000).

4. Many archaeologists regret the events and their damaging effects on relations with *Natítayt*. See Darby C. Stapp and Julie Longenecker, "'Working Together—the Times, They Are a-Changin': Can Archaeologists and Native Americans Change with the Times?" *Newsletter* [of the] *Society for American Archaeology* 18, no. 2 (2000): 18–20, 27; Darby Stapp and Julie Longenecker, "Learning from the Kennewick Man Controversy," *Anthropology News* (1999): 10–11; and Peter Jones and Darby Stapp, "An Anthropological Perspective on Magistrate Jelderks' Kennewick Man Decision," *High Plains Applied Anthropologist* 23, no. 1 (2003): 1–16.

5. Early media reports that Kennewick Man displayed "Caucasoid" features led to speculation that he might have been an ancient white man from Europe, which played well with parts of the public. If white people arrived in the Americas before the ancestors of contemporary Indian people, Indian claims to be the original owners of the land and to tribal sovereignty were thereby diminished.

6. For an excellent exposition of the notion of desecration, see Ronald L. Grimes, "Desecration: An Interreligious Controversy," in *The Future of the Past: Archaeologists, Native Americans, and Repatriation*, edited by Tamara L. Bray (New York: Garland, 2001), 91–105.

7. Armand Minthorn, "Human Remains Should Be Reburied," September 1996, available online at http://www.umatilla.nsn.us/kman1.html. Minthorn was then a member of the Board of Trustees of the CTUIR; he has since served as its chairman. For many years he has been the leader of the Wáašat, or Longhouse, religious community on the reservation, and his duties include leading the Sunday worship

services, funerals, and other ceremonies. His status among the Natítayt is like that of a minister, priest, rabbi, or imam in other communities.

8. Congress established the ICC in 1946 to resolve Indian claims and grievances once and for all, an aim consonant with the later termination policy "to get the government out of the Indian business." Nancy Oestreich Lurie, "The Indian Claims Commission Act," *Annals of the American Academy of Political and Social Science*, no. 311 (1957): 56–70; Charles Wilkinson and Eric R. Biggs, "The Evolution of the Termination Policy," *American Indian Law Review* 7 (1977): 139–84. On the ICC, see Nancy Oestreich Lurie, "The Indian Claims Commission," *Annals of the American Academy of Political and Social Science*, no. 436 (1978): 97–110; Harvey D. Rosenthal, "Indian Claims and the American Conscience: A Brief History of the Indian Claims Commission," in *Irredeemable America: The Indians' Estate and Land Claims*, edited by Imre Sutton (Albuquerque: University of New Mexico Press, 1985), 35–70; Charles Wilkinson and the American Indian Resources Institute (AIRI), *Indian Tribes as Sovereign Governments: A Sourcebook on Federal-Tribal History, Law, and Policy*, 2d ed. (Oakland, Calif.: American Indian Lawyer Training Program, Inc., 2004); and especially John R. Wunder, *"Retained by the People": A History of American Indians and the Bill of Rights* (New York: Oxford University Press, 1994), 89–93, 228–29, 257–58.

9. There are timelines and chronologies of events, copies of expert opinion evidence reports, and affidavits and such available at http://www.friendsofpast.org/kennewick-man, http://www.kennewick-man.com, and http://www.cr.nps.gov/aad/kennewick, which cover the longer and larger picture. See also Jones and Stapp, "An Anthropological Perspective"; Joe E. Watkins, "Beyond the Margin: American Indians, First Nations, and Archaeology in North America," *American Antiquity* 68, no. 2 (2003): 273–85; and Joe E. Watkins, "Becoming American or Becoming Indian? NAGPRA, Kennewick, and Cultural Affiliation," *Journal of Social Archaeology* 4, no. 1 (2004): 60–80.

10. The Society for American Archaeology and the National Congress of American Indians also were defendants-interveners.

11. Opinion and Order, *Bonnichsen and Others*, Civil No. 96-1481-JE, United States District Court for the District of Oregon, 2002, 33, 37 (emphasis added). Had the remains retained their ancient DNA, it is possible that molecular genetic analysis could link them to some contemporary person or people, but the absence of a demonstrable molecular genetic link does not rule out a chain with one or more genealogical links arising from adoption. All in all, the irrelevance of the NAGPRA requirement of lineal descent to the claim for the remains is not so much due to the difficulties of molecular genetic proof as to its disregard for general social theory— namely, that although based on a prototype of biological descent through successful matings, human kinship is a cultural not a biological phenomenon. Julie Finlayson, Bruce Rigsby, and Hilary Bek, eds., *Connections in Native Title: Genealogies, Kinship, and Groups* (Canberra: Centre for Aboriginal Economic Policy Research, Australian National University, 1999), 4–7. The requirement as stated is also blind

to whether "lineal descent" implicates or creates connection only to individuals or to whole groups, however defined.

12. 25 U.S. *Code* section 3002(a)(2)(C)(1) reads, "if the cultural affiliation of the objects cannot be reasonably ascertained and if the objects were discovered on Federal land that is recognized by a final judgment of the Indian Claims Commission or the United States Court of Claims as the aboriginal land of some Indian tribe— (1) in the Indian tribe that is recognized as aboriginally occupying the area in which the objects were discovered." Kosslak is incorrect to assert that Congress failed to specify what "aboriginal" meant in this statutory context. Renee M. Kosslak, "The Native American Graves Protection and Repatriation Act: The Death Knell for Scientific Study?" *American Indian Law Review* 24 (1999–2000): 147–48.

13. Opinion, *Bonnichsen and Others*, No. 02-35994, DC No. 96-1481-JE, United States Court of Appeals for the Ninth Circuit, 2004, 30.

14. There was a movement in Congress in 2005 to amend the NAGPRA legislation and change the wording of 25 U.S. *Code* section 3002(a)(2)(2), so that it would no longer be necessary to prove cultural affiliation to a contemporary Native American tribe, but the Bush administration opposed the change. See Les Blumenthal, "Debate over Kennewick Man's Remains Now with Lawmakers," *Tri-City Herald*, available online at http://www.kennewick-man.com/kman/news/story/6759384p-6646511c.html.

15. Wendy Crowther agrees these would be high, but Maura A. Flood disagrees. Crowther, "Native American Graves Protection and Repatriation Act: How Kennewick Man Uncovered the Problems in NAGPRA," *Journal of Land, Resources, and Environmental Law* 20 (2000): 286, 289; and Flood, " 'Kennewick Man' or 'Ancient One'? A Matter of Interpretation," *Montana Law Review* 63 (2002): 86. However, the case of ninety-five-hundred-year-old Cheddar Man fits with my view that regional human populations tend to display demic continuity even when there is immigration and conquest. Bryan Sykes, *The Seven Daughters of Eve* (London: Bantam Press, 2001), 169–84, 150. But the "umbilical cord" of ethnicity and culture that connects Cheddar Man to a high-school history teacher, two schoolchildren, and a butler, connected also by mitochondrial DNA, is a long and thin one indeed. Ernest Gellner, " 'Do Nations Have Navels?' " *Nations and Nationalism* 2, no. 3 (1996): 366–70; and Sykes, *Seven Daughters of Eve*, 181–84.

16. Many of the Colville Nez Perces are also Palouse descendents and identify sometimes as "Palouse-Nez Perce."

17. Click Relander, *Drummers and Dreamers: The Story of Smowhala the Prophet and His Nephew Puck Hyah Toot, the Last Prophet of the Nearly Extinct River People, the Last Wanapums* (Caldwell, Idaho: Caxton Printers, Ltd., 1956); and Julia G. Longenecker, Darby C. Stapp, and Angela M. Buck, "The Wanapum at Priests Rapids, Washington," manuscript, 21 pp.

18. John D. Leshy, "NAGPRA and the Disposition of the Kennewick Human Remains," letter to the Secretary of the Interior, 2000, emphasis added) available online at http://www.cr.nps.gov/archeology/kennewick/encl_4.htm.

19. John D. Leshy, "Attachment B, Review of the United States Indian Claims Commission's Decisions to Identify Cases Resolved through Compromise Settlements," letter to the Secretary of the Interior, 2000; available online at http://www. cr.nps.gov/archeology/kennewick/attach_b.htm. John W. Ragsdale Jr. remarked it significant that the provisions for repatriation could be based on "a sharing of aboriginal occupation in the area of discovery" but did not elaborate. Ragsdale, "Some Philosophical, Political, and Legal Implications of American Archeological and Anthropological Theory," *University of Missouri — Kansas City Law Review* 70 (2001–2): 50n239 and 52n242.

20. Ralph Erickson, "Aboriginal Land Rights in the United States and Canada," *North Dakota Law Review* 60 (1984): 114–15; Omer Stewart, "The Question of Bannock Territory," in *Languages and Cultures of Western North America: Essays in Honor of Sven S. Liljeblad,* edited by E. H. Swanson Jr. (Pocatello: Idaho State University Press, 1970), 201–31; and Omer Stewart, "The Shoshone Claims Cases," in *Irredeemable America,* 200; and Sutton, *Irredeemable America,* 136.

21. Bruce Rigsby, "Anthropologists, Indian Title, and the Indian Claims Commission: The California and Great Basin Cases," in *Fighting over Country: Anthropological Perspectives,* edited by Diane E. Smith and J. Finlayson (Canberra: Centre for Aboriginal Economic Policy Research, Australian National University, 1997), 29.

22. Leshy, "Attachment B."

23. See Charles F. Wilkinson and John M. Volkmann, "Judicial Review of Indian Treaty Abrogation: 'As Long as Water Flows, or Grass Grows upon the Earth'—How Long a Time Is That?" *California Law Review* 63 (1975): 603; and Wilkinson and AIRI, *Indian Tribes as Sovereign Governments,* 31–32.

24. Wilkinson and Volkmann, "Judicial Review of Indian Treaty Abrogation," 617–20, summarizes the conventional rules of interpretation: "ambiguous expressions must be resolved in favor of the Indian[s]," "treaties must be interpreted as the Indians themselves would have understood them," and "treaties must be liberally construed in favor of the Indians." Flood, "'Kennewick Man' or 'Ancient One'?" 73–74, applies these to NAGPRA and identifies the primary Natítayt interest as "the right to bury one's dead in accordance with cultural traditions and to expect their burial places to remain undisturbed."

25. For a similar argument, see Jack F. Trope and Walter R. Echo-Hawk, "The Native American Graves Protection and Repatriation Act: Background and Legislative History," in *The Future of the Past: Archaeologists, Native Americans, and Repatriation,* edited by Tamara L. Bray (New York: Garland, 2001), 17–18. Flood, "'Kennewick Man' or 'Ancient One'?" would seem to agree. Many such rights are also common law rights.

26. It is useful to recall a similar jurisdictional case. In 1991 the remains of another ancient man were found high up on the Schnalstal Glacier along the Hauslabjoch Pass, which crosses the ridge in the Ötzal Alps that separates Italy and Austria. He came to be known as "Ötzi, the Iceman," and he was "European" by genetic signature. Sykes, *Seven Daughters of Eve,* 5–8. The Austrians and the Italians both claimed him as their own and, after some survey work they agreed that

he had been found on Austrian territory. His remains were then placed at the Institute for Anatomy at the University of Innsbruck and studied by scientists. Radiocarbon dating showed him to date back some fifty-three hundred years to Neolithic times. A few years later, however, more ice melted, an old boundary marker appeared, and it became clear that Ötzi's remains had been found a few meters inside *Italian* territory. The two countries then agreed that Italy had jurisdiction, and in 1998 the remains were transferred to the South Tyrol Museum of Archaeology in Bolzano.

27. Sahaptin is an endangered language and has few fluent speakers as a result of language shift to English and consequent indigenous language loss. English is now the vernacular language of all Natítayt. Some scholars might object, then, that a discussion of Sahaptin language terms and concepts is thus irrelevant. That is a mistaken view that does not take into account the persistence and continuity of traditional cultural concepts, beliefs, standards and values, and customs among Natítayt, who no longer speak their heritage language. On the distinction between "classical" and "postclassical" social phenomena, see Peter Sutton, *Native Title in Australia: An Ethnographic Perspective* (Cambridge: Cambridge University Press, 2003), xvii. The former includes those "principles and practices . . . which may be considered to take substantially the same form as can be reconstructed for the early colonial contact period and the era immediately before it"; the latter includes those "that have developed distinctively since colonisation."

28. These are the Northeast / Walla Walla Sahaptin, Columbia River / Umatilla and Northwest / Yakama Sahaptin words. They are formed on the base that means "(Indian) person, people" plus a derivational suffix -wít or -áwit that forms abstract nouns.

29. Bruce Rigsby, "Expert Opinion Evidence Affidavit [in Support of the CTUIR's Request for the Repatriation of the Remains]," Brisbane, 1997.

30. In fact, the term occurs in an oral history text that I recorded from Chief Henry Thompson at *Wayám* / Celilo, Oregon, on March 11, 1964. Chief Thompson identified himself then as the *Tiičáminš*, "(traditional) landowner," there. I was reminded of this when I heard it on the recording again in late 2006.

31. Melville Jacobs, "A Sketch of Northern Sahaptin Grammar," *University of Washington Publications in Anthropology* 4, no. 2 (1931): 221. Jacobs identified the word as Walla Walla / Palouse, but during my 1960s fieldwork people told me that Cy Johnly, his main informant for Northeast Sahaptin, was a Naxíyampam man. Bruce Rigsby, "Linguistic Relations in the Southern Plateau," Ph.D. dissertation, University of Oregon, 1965, 40. See also Alexander Gunkel, "Culture in Conflict: A Study of Contrasted Interrelations and Reactions between Euroamericans and the Wallawalla Indians of Washington State," Ph.D. dissertation, Southern Illinois University at Carbondale, 1978, 11, 419.

32. Some readers might object that "traditional" always imports a past time, so that they speak of *traditional* as contrasted with *modern* culture and society. But if we understand that the process of tradition, the handing down of knowledge, belief, and the like, is a feature of all human societies, then we can speak of past and pres-

ent traditions, the products of what was handed down in the past and what is being handed down now. Bruce Rigsby, "Custom and Tradition: Innovation and Invention," *Macquarie Law Journal* 6 (2006): 113–38.

33. Aoki, *Nez Perce Dictionary*, 679, 1254.

34. See Theodore Stern, *Chiefs and Change: Indian Relations at Fort Nez Perces, 1818–1855*, vol. 2 (Corvallis: Oregon State University Press, 1996), 210, 242, 255, 275–77, on the council as an intergroup institution.

35. Rigsby, "Linguistic Relations in the Southern Plateau," 51.

36. Stern, *Chiefs and Change*, 230–31.

37. Ibid., 321–22.

38. They faced Hobson's choice. Wilkinson and Volkmann, "Judicial Review of Indian Treaty Abrogation," 609.

39. To judge by the morphology of the Sahaptin and Nez Perce terms for "treaty" (Sahaptin *pá'iniχ"at*, etc., and Nez Perce *píitamalwit* and *píweye'npt*, also "agreement"), they are not new words, and intergroup agreements were evidently not completely new phenomena. See Stern, *Chiefs and Change*, 293, on their prototypes. No doubt most of the parties considered the council to be a formal ceremonial event, although not all the Natítayt accepted the offer of the pipè from Stevens and Palmer. I thank historian Jim Miller for stimulating me to think the point through and check for evidence.

40. See Andrew H. Fisher, "People of the River: A History of the Columbia River Indians, 1885–1945," Ph.D. dissertation, Arizona State University, 2003, 58, 62.

41. Stern, *Chiefs and Change*, 298.

42. For some biographical details of the interpreters, see Edward J. Kowrach, ed., *Journal of Operations of Governor Isaac Ingalls Stevens of Washington Territory in 1855* (Fairfield, Wash.: Ye Galleon Press, 1978), 6; Stern, *Chiefs and Change*, 298, 302–3, 304; and Robert Boyd, *People of the Dalles: The Indians of Wascopam Mission* (Lincoln: University of Nebraska Press, 1996), 336–40.

43. Stern, *Chiefs and Change*, 302–3.

44. See Wilkinson and Volkmann, "Judicial Review of Indian Treaty Abrogation," 610–11, on the problems of language and translation (including "dishonest interpreters") often encountered at treaty councils and afterward.

45. (Colonel) Lawrence Kip, "The Indian Council at Walla Walla, May and June, 1855," *Sources of the History of Oregon* 1, no. 2 (1897): 14–15; Darrell Scott, ed., *A True Copy of the Record of the Official Proceedings at the Council in the Walla Walla Valley 1855 by Isaac Ingalls Stevens* (Fairfield, Wash.: Ye Galleon Press, 1985), 20, 114n16; and Stern, *Chiefs and Change*, 359n6.

46. Deward E. Walker Jr., "Mutual Cross-Utilization of Economic Resources in the Plateau: An Example from Aboriginal Nez Perce Fishing Practices," in *Washington State University Laboratory of Anthropology Report of Investigations No. 41*, edited by Roald H. Fryxell (Pullman, Wash.: Laboratory of Anthropology, Washington State University, 1967), 70, 18; Deward E. Walker Jr., "Nez Perce," in *Plateau*, vol. 12 of *Handbook of North American Indians* (Washington, D.C.: Smithsonian Institution, 1998), 425; and Theodore Stern, *Chiefs and Chief*

Traders: Indian Relations at Fort Nez Perces, 1818–1855, vol. 1 (Corvallis: Oregon State University Press, 1993), 36. Compared with Sahaptin, the Nez Perce language displays much less dialectal diversity, a fact in its favor remarked by early whites.

47. I found no mention of the use of Chinook jargon in the written accounts of the council. Apparently, the jargon became more widely used in the Southern Plateau during and after the Indian wars of the 1850s. A. J. Splawn, *Ka-Mi-Akin: Last Hero of the Yakimas*, 2d ed. (Yakima, Wash.: n.p., 1958).

48. Stern, *Chiefs and Change*, 178; and Kowrach, *Journal of Operations*, 8, 27.

49. This was a violation of the treaty terms. Wilkinson and Volkmann, "Judicial Review of Indian Treaty Abrogation," 611n49; Kowrach, *Journal of Operations*, 7; and Stern, *Chiefs and Change*. 318.

50. The Yakama treaty did the same, but the Nez Perce treaty recognized them implicitly as a single people or nation. In *Chiefs and Change*, 293, Stern observed that construction of the Cayuses, Walla Wallas, and Umatillas as "one nation acting for and in behalf of their respective bands and tribes, they being duly authorized thereto" was made with Congress in mind and "the Indians cannot have been aware" of it and its ramifications.

51. I know of no proposals at the treaty council or afterward to shift graves and cemeteries from the ceded area to the reservation, although the majority of burials since the treaty have been on the reservation. Instead, speakers at the 1855 council made reference to the bones of their ancestors interred on their homelands. There were and are local groups (for example, the Wayamłáma at Celilo, the Q'miłłáma at Rock Creek, and the Wánapam at Priest Rapids), families, and individuals who never shifted onto the reservations and continued (continue) to bury their dead in traditional-customary ways on their ceded homelands. See also Fisher, "People of the River." In the past, when the construction of dams threatened to inundate Natítayt graves, the remains were disinterred by archaeologists, measured, studied quickly and nondestructively with tribal approval, then reburied nearby above the projected waterlines. The remains were not generally, if at all, taken to cemeteries on the reservation. And recently, when remains are repatriated, they are generally buried not in cemeteries on the Umatilla Reservation, but near their original resting places.

52. Among non-Indians the group name Walla Walla gained a wider reference than just to the people of the Walúula village-complex by at least 1829, when trader Sam Black described the "Willa Walla" as living along the Columbia from the "Chutes" (the Deschutes River) to Priest Rapids. Black was then chief trader at Fort Nez Perces, later Fort Walla Walla. Dennis W. Baird, ed., *"Faithful to Their Tribe & Friends": Samuel Black's 1929 Fort Nez Perces Report*, Northwest Historical Manuscript Series (Moscow: University of Idaho Library, 2000), 17. See also Gunkel, "Culture in Conflict," 21–23, and Fisher, "People of the River," 51n51. Stern, *Chiefs and Change*, 329, wrote of the Walla Walla leader Pyópyo Maqsmáqs that while "his own people had dwindled through the years, he had taken under his aegis other closely related groups such as the Nahayampam [Naχíyampam] of the lower Snake and a large part of the Chamnapam."

53. Gary E. Moulton, ed., *The Definitive Journals of Lewis & Clark: Through the Rockies to the Cascades*, vol. 5 (Lincoln: University of Nebraska Press, 1988), 288.

54. Click Relander, "Categorical Answers to Comments upon Proposed Testimony from Johnny Buck in Connection with the Yakima Claim, EWV— Undated . . . Forwarded with Communication of September 18, 1953," 7, Relander Collection, Item 25-7, Yakima Valley Regional Library, Yakima, Washington.

55. Click Relander, "Interview: Puck-Hyah-Toot, 6/3/51, Interpreter, Son Frank Buck," 2, Relander Collection, Item 57-25, Yakima Valley Regional Library, Yakima, Washington.

56. Archibald Hanna and William H. Goetzmann, eds., *The Lewis and Clark Expedition by Meriwether Lewis*, 3 vols. (Philadelphia: J. B. Lippincott Company, 1961), 836, 427, 428; and Moulton, *Through the Rockies to the Cascades*, 298, 300n3, 303.

57. Gary E. Moulton, ed., *The Definitive Journals of Lewis & Clark: From the Pacific to the Rockies*, vol. 7 (Lincoln: University of Nebraska Press, 1991), 178–79; and Richard Glover, ed., *David Thompson's Narrative, 1784–1812* (Toronto: Champlain Society, 1962), 350. "Shawpatin" is doubtless an attempt to spell in English the pronunciation of Moses Columbia Salish *sháptənəxʷ*, their name for the Nez Perces. M. Dale Kinkade, *Dictionary of the Moses-Columbia Language (Nxa'amxcín)* (Nespelem, Wash.: Colville Confederated Tribes, 1981), 97. The word *sháptənəxʷ* is the prototype for the names Sahaptin, Shahaptian, and Sahaptian in English. For much of the nineteenth century the first two terms signified both the Nez Perces and the various Sahaptin groups (and their languages). From the 1960s linguists and anthropologists have used Sahaptin for the set of mutually intelligible dialects (i.e., the language-complex) that includes Umatilla, Walla Walla, Yakama, and others, while Sahaptian is the language family that includes the Nez Perce and Sahaptin languages, which are not mutually intelligible.

58. The first (Walúula) is its Northeast Sahaptin name; the second (Walawála) is its Columbia River and Northwest Sahaptin pronunciation. *Walawála* is a complex form built on the root √*wana-*, "flow (v), river, stream (n)." The consonant shift from -*n*- to -*l*- here is characteristic of Northeast Sahaptin. It and the reduplication signify the diminutive—that is, "a smaller river, stream"—perhaps the Walla Walla River. Less likely is that the reduplication signifies a distributive plural sense —that is, "smaller rivers, streams (distributed in space)." The Northeast Sahaptin dialects also have a phonological rule that reduces the sequence -*awa*- to -*uu*-. Thus *Walúula* developed from earlier *Walawála*, and it is now morphologically opaque to Sahaptin speakers.

59. Bruce Rigsby and Noel Rude, "Sketch of Sahaptin, a Sahaptian Language," in *Languages*, vol. 17, *Handbook of North American Indians* (Washington, D.C.: Smithsonian Institution, 1996), 666.

60. Hanna and Goetzmann, *Lewis and Clark Expedition by Meriwether Lewis*, 841–42; and Moulton, *Through the Rockies to the Cascades*, 284n8, 287, 296, 299.

61. The first (Chimnahpum) is the Sahaptin form of the name; the second (Chim-napoos) is its Nez Perce form. Hanna and Goetzmann, *Lewis and Clark Expedition by Meriwether Lewis*, 640.

62. The local group names Walúulapam ("Waluula people") and Čamnápam ("Chamna people") are built on the place-names Walúula and Čamná, but the people of Kʷʼsís were called the Naχíyampam, not the *Kʷʼsíspam. Naχíyam is the name of the lower Snake River from below Palouse to its confluence with the Columbia. I have never been able to identify the source of "Sokulk." Hanna and Goetzmann, *Lewis and Clark Expedition by Meriwether Lewis*, 841–42.

63. See Leshy, "Review of the United States Indian Claims Commission's Decisions to Identify Cases Resolved through Compromise Settlements," for a good recapitulation of events, findings, and such in the CTUIR Docket 264 claims. I have drawn on this item although I disagree with some of its assumptions and conclusions respecting the traditional ownership of land and waters. I do not know when it was first prepared and displayed. I wonder whether it might not have discouraged the CTUIR from pursuing the aboriginal possession argument for its right of repatriation much earlier. The interests of Natítayt do not always coincide completely with those of their Šuyápu allies and friends.

64. Findings of Fact, 8 Indian Claims Commission 513. When the United States recognizes the aboriginal title of a tribe by treaty or statute, we can speak of "recognized title," which is protected by the takings clause of the Fifth Amendment, unlike aboriginal title. John K. Flanagan, "The Invalidity of the Nez Perce Treaty of 1863 and the Taking of the Wallowa Valley," *American Indian Law Review* 24 (1999–2000): 75–98.

65. Leshy, "Outline for the Confederated Tribes of the Umatilla Indian Reservation's (Umatilla, Cayuse, and Walla Walla) Petition Brought before the ICC"; *Confederated Tribes of the Umatilla Reservation v. United States*, 14 Indian Claims Commission (1960), 14, 102–3. "Snake Indians" is the nineteenth-century term that includes the Bannock, Northern Paiute, and Shoshone peoples.

66. 16 Indian Claims Commission (1960), 484. Emphasis mine.

67. Leshy, "Review of the United States Indian Claims Commission's Decisions to Identify Cases Resolved through Compromise Settlements."

68. Francis P. McManamon, "The Initial Scientific Examination, Description, and Analysis of the Kennewick Man Human Remains, Report on the Non-Destructive Examination, Description, and Analysis of the Human Remains from Columbia Park, Kennewick, Washington," [October 1999], 2000, emphasis added; available online at http://www.cr.nps.gov/archeology/kennewick/mcmanamon.htm.

69. As Stern noted in *Chiefs and Change*, 387n6, scholars Clifford E. Trafzer and Richard D. Scheuerman wrote that three Palouse leaders, "Kahlotus, Slyotze, and Tilcoax," attended the initial meeting of the council but not its official sessions. Trafzer and Scheuerman, *Renegade Tribe: The Palouse Indians and the Invasion of the Inland Pacific Northwest* (Pullman: Washington State University, 1986), 49. Stern identified the first two as chiefs at Pelúus village (at the mouth of the Palouse

River), and the third we know to have been the chief at Kw'sɨs (at the Snake River mouth) during the 1855 council. The first man signed the Yakama Treaty as "Koo-lat-toose," and the third man, Tɨɬqawayks, also called "Old Man Wolf," signed the CTUIR Treaty as "Tilch-a-waix."

70. Baird, *"Faithful to Their Tribe & Friends"*; Andrew Dominique Pambrun, *Sixty Years on the Frontier in the Pacific Northwest*, edited by Glen C. Adams (Fairfield, Wash.: Ye Galleon Press, 1978); and Sam Pambrun, "Andrew Dominique Pambrun: A Biographical Sketch," report prepared for the Fort Walla Walla Museum of Living History, 2005, 1–33.

71. For example, Boyd, *People of the Dalles*; Andrew H. Fisher, "'This I Know from the Old People': Yakama Indian Treaty Rights as Oral Tradition," *Montana* 49, no. 6 (1999): 2–17; Andrew H. Fisher, "They Mean to Be Indian Always: The Origins of Columbia River Indian Identity, 1860–1885," *Western Historical Quarterly* 32, no. 4 (2001): 468–92; Andrew H. Fisher, "People of the River"; Andrew H. Fisher, "Tangled Nets: Treaty Rights and Tribal Identities at Celilo Falls," *Oregon Historical Quarterly* 105, no. 2 (2005): 178–211; Eugene S. Hunn, *Nch'i-Wána, "the Big River": Mid-Columbia Indians and Their Land* (Seattle: University of Washington Press, 1990); Helen H. Schuster, "Yakima Indian Traditionalism: A Study in Continuity and Change," Ph.D. dissertation, University of Washington, 1975; Helen H. Schuster, *The Yakimas: A Critical Bibliography*, edited by Francis Jennings and William R. Swagerty (Bloomington: Indiana University Press for the Newberry Library, 1982); Stern, *Chiefs and Chief Traders*, and *Chiefs and Change*; Walker, *Mutual Cross-Utilization*; Deward E. Walker, *Conflict and Schism in Nez Perce Acculturation: A Study of Religion and Politics* (Pullman: Washington State University Press, 1968); and especially the many chapters in Walker, "Nez Perce," in *Plateau*, vol. 17 of *Handbook of North American Indians*.

72. See especially Lillian A. Ackerman, "Nonunilinear Descent Groups in the Plateau Culture Area," *American Ethnologist* 21, no. 2 (1994): 286–309.

73. For example, see Kent McNeil, *Common Law Aboriginal Title* (Oxford: Clarendon Press, 1989); Kent McNeil, "The Meaning of Aboriginal Title," in *Aboriginal and Treaty Rights in Canada: Essays on Law, Equality, and Respect for Difference*, edited by Michael Asch (Vancouver: UBC Press, 1997), 135–54; and Kent McNeil, *Emerging Justice: Essays on Indigenous Rights in Canada and Australia* (Saskatoon: Native Law Centre, University of Saskatchewan, 2001).

74. For example, see James W. Harris, *Property and Justice* (Oxford: Clarendon Press, 1996); David Lametti, "Property and (Perhaps) Justice: A Review Article of James W. Harris, *Property and Justice*, and James E. Penner, *The Idea of Property in Law*," *McGill Law Journal* 43 (1998): 663–727; Stephen R. Munzer, *A Theory of Property* (Cambridge: Cambridge University Press, 1990); J. E. Penner, "The "Bundle of Rights" Picture of Property," *UCLA Law Review* 43 (1996): 711–820; J. E. Penner, *The Idea of Property in Law* (Oxford: Clarendon Press, 1997); Alain Pottage, "Instituting Property [a Review Article of Harris (1996) and Penner (1997)]," *Oxford Journal of Legal Studies* 18, no. 2 (1998): 331–44; Car-

ole M. Rose, *Property and Persuasion: Essays on the History, Theory, and Rhetoric of Ownership* (Boulder, Colo.: Westview Press, 1994); Carole M. Rose, "Evolution of Property Rights," in *The New Palgrave Dictionary of Economics and the Law*, edited by Peter Newman (London: Macmillan Reference Ltd, 1998), 93–98; and Jeremy Waldron, *The Right to Private Property* (Oxford: Clarendon Press, 1988).

75. See Bruce Rigsby, "A Survey of Property Theory and Tenure Types," in *Customary Marine Tenure in Australia*, edited by Nicolas Peterson and Bruce Rigsby (Sydney: University of Sydney, 1998), 22–46; Rigsby, "Aboriginal People, Spirituality, and the Traditional Ownership of Land," *International Journal of Social Economics* 26, no. 7/8/9 (1999): 963–73; Rigsby, "The Yorta Yorta Appeal Decision and Social Theory in Native Title Claims: Norms, Rights, and Interests," in *Aboriginal Title and Indigenous Peoples: Comparative Essays on Australia, New Zealand, and Western Canada*, edited by Louis Knafla and Haijo Westra (forthcoming); W. E. H. Stanner, "The Yirrkala Case: Some General Principles of Aboriginal Land-Holding," unpublished manuscript prepared for counsel in the *Milirrpum / Gove Land Rights Case*, Canberra, 1969; Peter Sutton, "The Robustness of Aboriginal Land Tenure Systems: Underlying and Proximate Customary Titles," *Oceania* 67 (1996): 7–29; Peter Sutton, *Native Title and the Descent of Rights* (Perth, Western Australia: National Native Title Tribunal, 1998); and Sutton, *Native Title in Australia*.

76. Some Americanist colleagues have commented that Indians only had usufructuary (not proprietary) rights to their lands during the classical period. The anthropologist Melville J. Herskovits first clearly stated the position. Herskovits, *Man and His Works: The Science of Cultural Anthropology* (New York: Alfred A. Knopf, 1948), 283, and *Economic Anthropology: A Study in Comparative Economics*, 2d ed. (New York: Alfred A. Knopf, 1952), 370. He missed the later insight that incidents of title generally include rights beyond those of use, such as rights to possess the object of property, to manage it, to its income, to alienate it, and to consume, waste, modify, or destroy it, to its security, and to transmit it. A. M. Honoré, "Ownership," in *Oxford Essays in Jurisprudence*, edited by A. G. Guest (Oxford: Oxford University Press, 1961), 104–47.

77. Joseph G. Jorgensen, "A Century of Political Economic Effects on American Indian Society, 1880–1980," *Journal of Ethnic Studies* 6, no. 3 (1978): 1–81. See Barney's letter of August 29, 1956, to Erminie Wheeler Voegelin for his views on Indian title, aboriginal occupation, "time immemorial," and so on. I thank historian Arthur (Skip) Ray for providing me with a copy. Note this phrasing in the defendants' objection to the 1960 ICC findings: "*Only after extended contact with the white man did these Indians obtain any concept of ownership of lands. No such concept was present with them in aboriginal times*" (emphasis added). Contrast this position with Australian High Court Justice Gerard Brennan's memorable phrasing in the case known as *Mabo No. 2*: "The ownership of land within a territory in the exclusive occupation of a people must be vested in that people: *land is*

susceptible of ownership, and there are no other owners" (*Mabo and Ors v. Qld* [No. 2] [1992] 175 CLR 1 F.C. 92/014 at 53, emphasis added).

78. Antone Minthorn, "Position Paper by Chairman Antone Minthorn: Kennewick Man Issue Damages Relationships," Confederated Tribes of the Umatilla Indian Reservation, 1998; available online at http://www.umatilla.nsn.us/kman 3.html. Antone Minthorn and Armand Minthorn belong to different families.

79. See Andrew H. Fisher's essay in this volume.

80. But not, of course, on ceded lands that are now held as freehold and so on.

PART IV

POWER RELATIONS IN CONTEMPORARY FORUMS

9 "History Wars" and Treaty Rights in Canada

A CANADIAN CASE STUDY

Arthur J. Ray

In recent years Canadian judges have presided over some lengthy trials of cases brought against the federal government for its failure to fulfill the obligations that arise from historic treaties. The longest and most expensive of these so far is that of the Samson Cree Nation of Hobbema, Alberta, which filed a claim in the Federal Court of Canada in 1989 (*Victor Buffalo v. Regina 2005*), alleging that the government had failed to meet its obligations to them as provided in Treaty 6 (of 1876). Their action asked for damages in the amount of $1.385 billion plus interest. Not counting closing arguments, the Samson litigation took 365 trial days, involved over twenty-five lawyers and sixty-five witnesses (including a former prime minister), generated fifteen thousand documents and over fifty thousand pages of transcripts, and cost the opposing parties more than $100 million collectively.[1] By all measures, to date, the Samson Cree case is the granddaddy of treaty claims in Canada. Indeed, its scope even surpassed the massive Gitxsan-Wet'suwet'en Aboriginal title claim in British Columbia (*Delgamuukw v. Regina*).[2] Such a case not only raises questions about the courts' accessibility to First Nations who cannot meet the massive costs of proving their claims in court, but it also raises questions about whether it is possible to "teach" judges the complex history on which they must base their decisions. I believe that this is an unrealistic expectation.

The complex *Victor Buffalo* lawsuit proceeded in two phases: Phase I concerned historical and treaty issues; Phase II addressed questions of money management. The opening historical segment took up almost half of the Court's time (174 days). It raised all of the core issues that arise in treaty rights cases concerning the use of diverse lines of ethnohistorical evidence and competing interpretive frameworks that are deployed to contextualize these historical, cross-cultural agreements. For instance, presiding Justice Max Teitelbaum listened to the testimony of thirty-five experts. These included Cree elders, who presented their evidence at the Hobbema Reserve, and other witnesses whose range of expertise represented the academic disciplines of archaeology, Canadian history, economic history, ethnohistory, historical geography, law, linguistics, and political science.

Collectively, the reports and testimony of this eclectic array of experts covered essentially all aspects of western Canada Native history, the fur trade, early colonial settlement, economic development, treaty making in western Canada, and federal-Indian relations after Treaty 6. This massive trial presents fundamental concerns about Aboriginal and treaty rights litigation, most notably, the decreasing accessibility of courts due to the mounting costs of legal battles (since few other First Nations have financial resources comparable to those of the oil-rich Samson Cree) and questions about whether it is possible to "teach" history in court when opposing sides are engaged in a hotly contested litigation. I address the latter issue in this essay, emphasizing the problems that arose in the *Victor Buffalo* trial and drawing on my experience as a historical expert in other Canadian cases.

"TEACHING" ETHNOHISTORY IN COURT

My first involvement as an expert witness in treaty rights litigation took place in 1985, when I was asked to take part in the case known as *Regina v. Horseman* (1990).[3] That case concerned First Nations' hunting rights in the Treaty 8 region, which lies north of the Alberta portion of Treaty 6. When the lawyer for the Cree defendant asked me to testify about the pretreaty economic history of the Treaty 8 area, I asked him, "What am I supposed to do as an expert?" He tersely replied, "You will be there to educate the court about Native history." Perhaps not wanting to alarm or confuse me, the lawyer did not add that the Court was a highly unusual student and the courtroom was unlike any university classroom. My involvement in subsequent cases from British Columbia to Ontario repeatedly forced me to confront these realities. They were particularly acute in the *Victor Buffalo* trial, where a battery of experts presented massive amounts of documentary and oral history evidence to the Court and provided contradictory interpretations of it. In this respect the case was very similar to the *Delgamuukw* trial.

The Court as Student

The "court" (a legal euphemism for a particular judge) usually poses substantial challenges for the expert witness/teacher. In my experience trial judges typically have little or no previous experience with Aboriginal rights litigation. The *Victor Buffalo* case was different in that respect, however. Justice Max Teitelbaum had extensive prior experience with such cases, including ones from western Canada.[4] More problematic for the ethnohistorical expert is the fact that trial judges commonly have little knowledge of the complex ethnohistory that is relevant to the case at hand. Likewise, they are unfamiliar with the nature and the methodologies of the disciplines that contribute to that history.

These problems were made starkly apparent to me in the *Victor Buffalo* and *Delgamuukw* cases. In the former, after I had testified extensively about the western Canada fur trade, Justice Teitelbaum revealed the limit of his previous education by asking me whether the Indians or the Hudson's Bay Company had built fur-trading posts in the Saskatchewan area.[5] In *Delgamuukw* the lawyers for the Aboriginal plaintiffs introduced me to the Court as a historical geographer. The problem they faced was that this specialty had not yet been recognized by Canadian courts, and opposing counsel did not think it was in their interests to have it recognized. As a result, counsel for the plaintiffs and lawyers for the Crown (representing the provincial and federal governments) engaged in a poorly informed, though sometimes entertaining, discussion about the nature of historical geography. Since I had not yet been recognized by the Court, I could not take part in this "seminar" discussion.

Once accepted by the Court, the expert faces formidable challenges as a teacher. In *Victor Buffalo*, as in *Delgamuukw*, experts were expected to bring the trial judge from a secondary-school level of historical knowledge to an advanced university graduate understanding—all this in an unreasonably short period of time. In the Samson Cree trial, for example, Justice Teitelbaum was given a crash course on Native history in western Canada from the time of initial contact (mid- to late-seventeenth century) to the present day in only fifty-eight days of conflicting testimony supported by reports and rebuttal and surrebuttal briefs.[6] It is not surprising that after trials of this magnitude, judges sometimes have difficulty absorbing the material and make basic factual errors. That happened in the *Delgamuukw* judgment.[7]

The trial judge's purpose poses another major challenge for the expert witness/teacher. The judge does not come to "class" out of curiosity, even if very interested in fur trade history, as may often be the case.[8] Rather, the court has to make findings of "facts" that are relevant to settling the dispute at hand. In the case of *Regina v. Marshall* (1999), Supreme Court Justice Binnie succinctly summarized the Court's approach to history when he wrote: "The law sees a finality of interpretation of historical events where finality, according to the professional historian, is not possible. The reality, of course, is that the courts are handed disputes that require for their resolution the finding of certain historical facts. The litigating parties cannot await the possibility of a stable academic consensus."[9] This perspective means that trial judges usually have little interest in the kinds of theoretical and methodological debates that excite the academic community, drive scholarly discourses, and lead to new interpretations with succeeding generations.[10] Rather, as Justice Binnie tersely put it, they search for, or make, findings of "facts" that address the current relevant case law. Therefore, to be effective teachers in the courtroom, experts must present facts in light of models that case law has generated rather than challenge the models, as scholars normally do in academic settings. This involves searching for data and theoretical frameworks that establish whether or not aspects of First Nations parties' ancestral practices meet the tests the courts have established to define surviving Aboriginal and treaty rights.

Another problem that expert witnesses/teachers face in developing a lesson plan for the court relates to the nature of the Aboriginal and treaty rights litigation process: it destabilizes "academic consensuses." In Canada a key reason for this is that before the Aboriginal title suit of the Nisga'a of British Columbia (*Calder v. Regina* [1973]),[11] the Canadian legal system and the academic scholarship concerning First Nations largely supported the dispossession and economic marginalization of Aboriginal people. Particularly important to the process were Lockean notions of property,[12] evolutionary models of cultural development,[13] and nation-building historical narratives that glamorized Canada's treatment of its Aboriginal people.[14] Ever since the *Calder* case, which launched the Aboriginal and treaty rights litigation era in Canada, First Nations have had to challenge this colonial legacy repeatedly by bringing new research findings to the court.

This means that the expert witnesses/teachers who appear for Aboriginal claimants and defendants frequently deliver revisionist lectures that contradict aspects of the established academic and popular understandings of Native history. Those who appear for the Crown, on the other hand, often reiterate older stories that are based on the extant and sometimes outdated scholarly literature.[15] The result is that the trial judge is forced to make difficult choices between revisionist perspectives, which often have not yet been subjected to peer review in the academy, and older outlooks, which often are based on literature that was subject to peer review in earlier times and therefore seemingly still bear the stamp of scholarly approval. Dated publications may be appealing to the court because they were not "tainted" by the claims process. As mentioned, however, these earlier works were often based on scholarly discourses that are prejudicial to current First Nations' interests. This problem arose in the case of *Victor Buffalo* as it had in *Delgamuukw*.[16]

Four Basic Issues

In the battle over revisionist and "standard" interpretations of Plains Cree history generally, and the Samson Cree specifically, four basic issues were hotly contested. The first issue concerned the historical locations of the ancestral Samson Cree. Historian Joan Holmes argued for the plaintiffs that the Western Plains Cree had lived in the region from the earliest times; archaeologist Alexander von Gernet countered for the defendant by arguing that published archaeological and historical research (including my work) suggested the ancestral Samson Cree did not move into the Hobbema area until the mid-nineteenth century.[17]

A second issue of sharp dispute concerned the question of whether the Cree understood and agreed to the written terms of Treaty 6. Witnesses for the Samson Cree, especially Cree linguist H. C. Wolfart, argued that the Cree would not have understood certain concepts, particularly the notion of surrendering the land, because of fundamental differences between English and old Cree (that is, before 1876).[18] For the Crown, political scientist Thomas Flanagan advanced the opposing proposition that the Cree fully understood the terms of the treaty because by 1876 they had established a long tradition of dealing with English-speaking fur traders. Also, he noted that interpreters were present. Accordingly, Flanagan contended there was no reason to suspect the Cree misunderstood the government's intentions.[19] In other words, he was advancing a traditional government proposition that the treaty was/is "plain on its face" to both parties. A substantial portion of trial testimony, including mine, addressed various aspects of this issue. The topics concerned questions about the competency of the interpreters, the extent to which the dialects of Plains and Swampy Cree and Plains Ojibwa interfered with translation efforts, and determining what the interpreters said to the Cree. The documentary records, on which scholars had largely relied prior to the case, say interpreters "explained" the treaty to the Cree. The problem is that those records do not provide detailed descriptions of the explanations.

A third question that arose, and one that is closely related to the interpretation issue, concerned the Samson Cree's own oral histories of Treaty 6. Through their oral history evidence, the Samson Cree advanced the proposition that their ancestors had agreed to share their lands, not surrender them, in exchange for promises that Canada would provide various social services, most notably education, health care, aid in times of famine and pestilence, and help in making the transition from a buffalo-hunting economy to a farming way of life. These ideas were put forward by the elders. One of the objects of my evidence and testimony was to consider whether documentary records would support Cree interpretations. This involved reviewing the history of the Cree's relations with the Hudson's Bay Company, which had been the Crown's representative in western Canada from 1670 to 1870. It also involved providing an economic context for the 1876 treaty and a discussion of Canadian treaty making in western Canada in the 1870s.

Given that Justice Teitelbaum had little prior familiarity with most of the historical characters and issues that were central to the trial, I opted to begin my "lecture" (as the first expert for the Samson Cree to follow the elders) with a brief PowerPoint slide presentation to "bring the history to life" in court by offering a visual summary of the main points of my written submission.[20] At the time this was an unusual technique for presenting evidence, and opposing counsel were reluctant to allow it. After receiving my assurance that I was not going to use the presentation as a Trojan horse to introduce new material other than that of a visual nature, they agreed to let me proceed with my slide presentation. I used it to emphasize the continuity that existed between the diplomatic and economic protocols that the Cree and their neighbors had established with the Crown through the Hudson's Bay Company and thought they had continued through treaties with Canada in the 1870s. The slide presentation afforded the best way to highlight the crucial symbolic dimensions of this Cree-Crown relationship by showing trade ceremonies from the eighteenth century and treaty proceedings of the nineteenth century. Central to both were gift-giving ceremonies, especially the clothing of Native leaders in British military uniforms, the smoking of the pipe, and speeches promising friendship, fair dealing, and mutual assistance in times of need.[21]

Subsequently, historian Winona Wheeler appeared for the plaintiffs to discuss the nature of oral history and the appropriate methodologies for its use inside and outside of the Cree community. She emphasized that once oral history sources are transcribed, they cannot be treated like any other documentary sources because, in the writing, they are transformed, become incomplete, and lose important contextual aspects.[22]

The Crown, however, mostly through the briefs and the testimony of Von Gernet, took a conventional stance. They argued that oral history must be treated like any other line of evidence and be subjected to testing against other sources.[23] Von Gernet posited that documentary sources contradict key points of the Samson Cree oral histories about Treaty 6. He had made this line of argument for the Crown in other cases, and generally the courts had received it favorably.[24] Only recently, in the case of *Regina v. Benoit* (2002), did a trial judge reject Von Gernet's testimony as biased against oral history evidence. That decision was overturned, however, by the federal courts of appeal.[25] Significantly, the intense battle in *Victor Buffalo* over the merits of oral history is part of an ongoing dispute in Canadian courts that began when the Supreme Court of Canada faulted the trial judge in *Delgamuukw* for not giving it sufficient weight.[26] Given the ongoing struggle in the courts about this line of evidence, it is not surprising that Justice Teitelbaum listened to the testimony about this subject, especially that of Wheeler, with great interest, although he gave no weight to her testimony.

The fourth subject of intense dispute concerned the question of whether the government acted in good faith in discharging the obligations assumed in Treaty 6. The Samson Cree and their experts, particularly economic historian Carl Beal, told Justice Teitelbaum that from the outset the Canadian government had often acted in ways that jeopardized this First Nation's interests.[27] Beal drew mostly on research he had undertaken for his doctoral dissertation in economic history[28] and the recent work of other historians, notably Sarah Carter.[29] Neither his dissertation nor Carter's work had focused on the Samson Cree, however, but they did address more generally questions concerning the Canadian government's approaches to the development of reserve agriculture in the Canadian Prairie West. In defense of the Crown, Flanagan advanced an older perspective, which holds that the government treated the Cree as well as could be expected given the economic and political circumstances that it faced during the late nineteenth and early twentieth centuries.[30]

Inevitably, these historical disputes raised basic questions about the nature of history and the methodologies that historians (broadly defined) use. Flanagan and von Gernet emphasized the merits of Western scientific methods and approaches to history that are rooted in the European Enlightenment. Many of the Samson Cree experts adopted a more postmodern and postcolonial perspective and argued for relativistic and polyvocal interpretations, which attempted to address the fact that the documentary records generated by colonizers and universalizing scholarly discourses of the past tend to silence the voices of the local colonized population. This has been an issue in other recent landmark trials, perhaps most notably in the case of *Regina v. Marshall* (1999).[31] Thus the briefs and testimony of opposing experts/teachers left Justice Teitelbaum with the problem of having to make decisions about the merits of revisionist and traditional interpretations of Western Cree history that are based on very different intellectual and philosophical positions concerning the best ways to study ethnohistory.

Expert Witness/Teacher

Having discussed the judge as a history student, I now consider briefly the expert witnesses/teachers who appear before the court. Expert witnesses/teachers typically have very disparate qualifications to address the particular and general historical issues of concern to the court. Like most university professors, some experts have established their Native history credentials through an active research and publishing agenda.[32] In effect, they are research-based teachers who bring to the court their in-depth knowledge of the history that is relevant to the litigation.[33] Typically these types of expert witnesses/teachers have earned doctoral degrees (the research degree of the academy), hold full-time university teaching/research positions, appear in court only occasionally, and do not depend on claims work for their income.

Because of the complex nature of ethnohistory, the domain of these witnesses' expertise often is limited to a few Aboriginal groups, or a small geographical area, or a narrow range of topics, methodologies, and lines of evidence. Perhaps the best examples would be experts whose research is based on archaeological, ethnographic (oral interviews), or linguistic fieldwork, because collecting these types of data is time-consuming, geographically focused, and often depends on the establishment of close working relationships with a First Nations group. The latter requirement means that academics who engage in this kind of research often are unwilling to appear on behalf of the Crown out of loyalty to their informants or because they fear their testimony for the Crown will jeopardize their future research prospects. This has been a problem in claims litigation since the earliest days of the United States Indian Claims Commission (USICC), which was created in 1946.[34] In my opinion it is becoming a critical problem in Canada today. The Crown finds it nearly impossible to retain experts who have close ties to Aboriginal communities. Barred from access to this line of evidence before trial, Crown counsel has little choice but to treat oral evidence in an adversarial way at trial.

In contrast to the preceding group of experts are those who do not hold full-time university appointments, are not publishing scholars, and make most of their livelihood from consulting work. The majority of these experts in Canada do not have doctoral degrees.[35] Often these full-time consultants lack in-depth familiarity with the history of the First Nation that is the subject of the litigation. Typically reports of these types of experts draw heavily on the secondary literature for theoretical and interpretive frameworks. Sometimes they support their interpretations with primary research. In other words they are generalists. Indeed, von Gernet claims that he is one of the few experts in Canada who is qualified to comment on archaeological, documentary, and oral history aspects of the ethnohistory of diverse areas and Aboriginal peoples of Canada, although his claim is not supported by a publishing record that demonstrates this expertise.[36]

In short, in most cases the trial judge receives history lessons from experts who have very uneven credentials. Some have in-depth knowledge of local histories based on long periods of study; others offer a broad perspective with little depth that often is based on a quick reading of the readily available primary and secondary sources. In the *Victor Buffalo* case all of these issues concerning the merits and problems of types of experts were aired, beginning with the exchange of experts' reports and rebuttal and surrebuttal briefs.[37] This raises questions about the ability of judges to assess ethnohistorical experts' credentials and evaluate their presentations in court. The process begins when the judge faces the decision of whether to accept an individual as an expert before evidence-in-chief can begin. The judge bases this decision on the presentation of the witness's vitae and any challenges from opposing counsel. Occasionally this process can be time-consuming, and that is especially likely if the field of expertise is unfamiliar to the court. What happened when I appeared in the *Delgamuukw* trial as a historical geographer is a good example. Prior to my being qualified, opposing counsel expressed their various understandings about what this field of expertise is and how perspectives drawn from it might, or might not, be useful to the Court.[38]

In the end Canadian courts rarely reject the qualifications of historical experts. (It has not happened in any of the cases in which I have been involved.)[39] Acceptance is essentially automatic when a historical expert already has been accepted by other courts in previous cases. Furthermore, it has also been my experience that the court at trial gives roughly equal weight to experts of various kinds—people the academic community would consider to hold sharply different qualifications. Usually, the court discounts the testimony of historical experts only when they display rather blatant biases in their interpretation. Finally, justices have shown little concern with experts who appear in court routinely but rarely, if ever, subject their court submissions to peer review in any of the usual forums provided by the relevant academic associations. In his briefs for the *Victor Buffalo* trial, for example, von Gernet cited positive citations of his testimony and briefs by courts in prior cases as proof of his authority and reliability.[40] In my opinion one of the reasons courts tend to weigh historical experts roughly equally is a common underlying notion that anyone can be a historian and that documents "are plain on their face."[41] Also, there is the notion that historians serve as clerks who simply bring to the court's attention documents that are deemed to be relevant.[42]

The Courtroom as Classroom

The most problematic aspect of the courtroom as classroom is its adversarial climate, which does not encourage opposing experts to search for common intellectual ground, advance explanations for their differences, or promote the acceptance of multiple interpretations and narratives of past events. Instead, a primary object of counsel at the trial is to rigorously "test" any evidence or interpretations that they deem to be prejudicial to their clients' interests and challenge the reputations of the experts retained by opposing counsel.[43] This practice serves to accentuate differences and often encourages experts to advance historical interpretations that push (and sometimes overrun) the boundaries indicated by currently accepted academic theoretical and methodological frameworks or warranted by new research. In the often heated courtroom battles, especially under cross-examination, experts can find it very difficult to avoid going beyond currently acceptable limits and thereby becoming mere advocates. Often the problem is exacerbated when litigation-oriented research uncovers new information that challenges current academic understandings of particular historical issues. In these instances the boundaries of reasonable expert opinion may not be clear. When I am confronted with such a situation, I ask myself whether I would be willing to present my research and conclusions to scholarly conferences and publish them in scholarly outlets (refereed journals and academic presses). Indeed, if experts are not simply being advocates and their claims work does lead to new understandings, I believe they have an obligation to take their findings out of the courtroom and present it to the academy. Too often this is not done.

Anthropologist Nancy Lurie, who is one of the veterans of Indian history "wars" before courts and commissions in the United States, has identified another key problem with the courtroom setting. She has noted that the ability of witnesses to educate the court is seriously hampered by the fact that they can only answer the questions put to them by the plaintiffs' or defendants' counsel or, less commonly, by the court.[44] The possibilities of real dialogue are further reduced by the fact that the evidence-in-chief and even cross-examination usually are tightly scripted. Lawyers do not like surprises in court.

Experts can address some of these constraints by helping counsel to develop the line of questioning they will face during the evidence-in-chief. My experience in this respect has varied greatly from one extreme, in which I wrote my own evidence-in-chief questions the night before I appeared, to the others, in which I had no input. In the case of *Victor Buffalo*, I spent a great deal of time working with the lawyers for the plaintiffs so that my evidence-in-chief was well structured and addressed key historical issues. Of course, experts have no control over the questions they will receive in cross-examination, but occasionally they can become heavily engaged in the preparation of questions for the cross-examination of opposing witnesses. In any event these are not very efficient or productive ways for experts to explore their differences or establish areas of agreement. Ethnohistorians addressed this problem in the earliest days of the USICC and recommended that pretrial (or prehearing) meetings of opposing experts be held for this purpose.[45] Rarely has this been done in an adversarial system.

A new problem has arisen in Canada recently. It is an increasingly common practice for the Crown to retain experts merely to have them prepare rebuttal briefs and give refutation testimony. There appear to be several reasons for this. It saves the Crown from having to commission expensive, case-specific research.[46] More important, in civil suits the plaintiffs have to carry the burden of proof, as the Samson Cree were required to do in *Victor Buffalo*. This means that the Crown merely has to raise what appear to be reasonable doubts about the evidence claimants bring forward. That is what happened in *Victor Buffalo*. The Crown's two experts, Flanagan and von Gernet, filed rebuttal and sur-rebuttal briefs. As noted previously, the archaeologist von Gernet challenged the work of Joan Holmes on general aspects of Plains Cree history and disputed Winona Wheeler on the use and reliability of oral evidence. The reality is that neither Holmes nor von Gernet has established expertise on Plains Cree history through normal academic channels of scholarly publishing or presentations at appropriate academic conferences, nor has Von Gernet done so with respect to oral history methods and interpretation.

CONCLUSION

The *Victor Buffalo* trial demonstrates many of the basic problems that have to be overcome when educating a court about the ethnohistory of a claimant group. A battery of opposing experts of very uneven qualifications presented the judge in that case with a massive amount of historical information and conflicting interpretations supporting or in opposition to the Samson Cree understanding of Treaty 6, which their elders presented. To weigh this material properly, when viewed from an academic perspective, the judge would have needed a level of ethnohistorical understanding that is equivalent to that of an advanced graduate student. He was expected to obtain this knowledge on the basis of barely two months of "class" time. Much of the "instruction" was not aimed at providing him with a nuanced understanding of the poly-vocal nature of that history; rather, it aimed to champion certain perspectives at the expense of others.

NOTES

1. "Samson Cree Lawsuit Wraps Up," available online at http://friendsof grassynarrows.com/item.php?205F (accessed 25 November 2006).

2. *Delgamuukw v. Regina*, Reasons for Judgment of the Honourable Chief Justice Allan McEachern, Supreme Court of British Columbia, No. 0843 Smithers Registry, 8 March 1991. This case took 365 days; it generated 9,200 documents and yielded a transcript in excess of 75,000 pages.

3. *Regina v. Horseman* [1990] 1 *Supreme Court Reports* (SCR) 901.

4. Justice Teitelbaum had been involved in the following cases: *Morin v. Canada* [2000] FCJ No. 1686 (Alberta); *Cimon v. Canada* [1999] FCJ No. 1736 (Ontario); *McLeod Lake Indian Band v. Chingee* [1998] FCJ No. 899 (British Columbia); *Yellowquill v. Canada* [1998] FCJ No. 1245 (Manitoba); *Tsawassen Indian Band v. Canada (Minister of Indian Affairs and Northern Development)* (1997), 129 Federal Courts Reports (FCR) 8 (B.C.); *Canadian Pacific Ltd. v. Matsqui Indian Band et al.* (1996), 111 FCR 161 (B.C.); *Wewayakum Indian Band v. Canada and Wewayakai Indian Band* (1995), 99 FCR 1 (B.C.); *Hunt v. Canada (Corrections Service)* [1993] FCJ No. 552 (Ontario, Aboriginal applicant); *Derrickson v. Canada* (1991), 49 FCR 295 (Ontario); *Obichon v. Heart Lake First Nation No. 176* (1988), 21 FCR 1 (Alberta); and *Blackfoot Band of Indians No. 146 v. Canada* (1986), 7 FCR 133 (Alberta).

5. Transcripts, 3 October 2000, lines 2806–7. The court asked: "Sir, these trading posts were set up by the Plains Cree?"

6. For comparative purposes it should be noted that my yearlong undergraduate introductory survey of Canadian Native history involves seventy-eight class hours, and most graduate students take a year or more of directed-readings courses to prepare for their doctoral preliminary examination in the Native history subject area.

7. For instance, in summary findings of fact, Fact #16, Chief Justice Allan McEachern mistakenly stated that "the fur trade in the territory began not earlier than the establishment of the first Hudson's Bay Company posts west of the Rockies . . . by Simon Fraser in 1805–06." In fact, Fraser worked for the archrival North West Company, which prevented the Hudson's Bay Company from expanding west of the Rocky Mountains until after 1821, when the two competing organizations merged. McEachern, Reasons for Judgment, viii.

8. In my first case (*Regina v. Horseman*), the lawyer for the Aboriginal defendant told me that judges at the lower court levels often fancy themselves local historians. The problem is that they are usually steeped in the local settler narratives and need to be reeducated.

9. *Regina. v. Marshall* [1999] 3 SCR 456: 35.

10. In the case of *Victor Buffalo v. Regina* lawyers for the plaintiffs did emphasize the methodologies of their experts, which is not the common practice. Although the trial judge stated he was interested in this discussion, he gave it little weight. This was evident in his reasons for judgment, where he remarked: "While at times it felt like the Court had been sent back to school, the historical information and interpretations presented were always interesting and, on many occasions, quite fascinating. It would have been all too easy to wander down the many well-trod avenues, lesser byways, and faint trails of our history." J. Teitelbaum, Reasons for Judgment, *Victor Buffalo v. Regina*, 2005 Federal Court (FC) 1622.

11. *Regina v. Calder* [1973] SCR 313.

12. This was the labor theory of property. It justified colonial regimes treating Aboriginal lands as vacant if they lacked visible signs of human alteration as exhibited at village sites, burial places, and so on. See Barbara Arneil, *John Locke and America: The Defence of English Colonialism* (Oxford: Clarendon Press, 1996).

13. These models emphasized subsistence and ceremonial use of the land, whereas most of the treaty rights cases I have been involved in address commercial hunting and fishing. Evolutionary perspectives concerning Canadian native culture history held sway until relatively recently. The best example would be Diamond Jenness, *Indians of Canada*. This work was first published in 1933 by the National Museum of Canada and went through seven editions. The last edition was 1977, which was published by the University of Toronto Press. The press reprinted the last edition several times. Until the 1990s Jenness's book was the only widely read general synthesis.

14. Usually these narratives portrayed Canada as a more humane colonizer than the United States. See Arthur Ray, J. R. Miller, and Frank Tough, *Bounty and*

Benevolence: A History of Saskatchewan Treaties (Montreal: McGill-Queens University Press, 2000); and Jill St. Germain, *Indian Treaty-Making Policy in the United States and Canada, 1867–1877* (Toronto: University of Toronto Press, 2001). Also, they tended to celebrate Canadian expansion and dismiss native resistance by casting the colonization process as a clash of civilization against barbarism. An example would be G. F. G. Stanley, *The Birth of Western Canada: A History of the Riel Rebellions* (1936 and 1962; reprint, Toronto: University of Toronto Press, 1992).

15. In these respects the Canadian circumstance is different from that of the early United States Indian Claims Commission cases, where government experts often advanced the new framework of cultural ecology, whereas experts for Indian tribes frequently championed the older cultural area perspective. Arthur Ray, "Kroeber and the California Claims: Myth and Reality," in *Central Sites, Peripheral Visions: Cultural and Institutional Crossings in the History of Anthropology History of Anthropology*, vol. 11, edited by Richard Handler (Madison: University of Wisconsin Press, 2006), 248–74.

16. In the *Delgamuukw* case, for example, the claimants' experts undertook new research on their history, which they presented to the court, whereas the defendants' experts countered mostly with anthropological research that had been published in the pre-1980s era, little of which focused specifically on the claimants' territories. See Ray, "From the United States Indian Claims Commission Cases to *Delgamuukw*."

17. Von Gernet, "Assessment of Certain Evidence Relating to Plains Cree Practices," 26 May 2000, and Von Gernet, "Aboriginal Oral Documents and Treaty 6," 21 March 2000, Federal Court of Canada Trial Division, Trial Division, T-2022-89 and T-1254-92.

18. It is generally accepted that the older, pretreaty Cree was very different from the Cree of the present day. Today very few Cree speak the older language. H. C. Wolfart, "Linguistic Aspects of Treaty 6," 24 February 2000, Federal Court of Canada Trial Division, Trial Division, T-2022-89 and T-1254-92.

19. Thomas Flanagan, "Analysis of the Plaintiffs' Expert Reports in the Case of Chief Victor Buffalo v. Her Majesty et al.," 21 July 1998, Federal Court of Canada Trial Division, Trial Division, T-2022-89 and T-1254-92; and Flanagan, "Surrebuttal to the Rebuttal Reports of Bob Beal, Carl Beal, Stan Cuthand, Arthur Ray, and John Tobia," 2 June 2000, Federal Court of Canada Trial Division, Trial Division, T-2022-89 and T-1254-92.

20. Arthur J. Ray, "The Economic Background to Treaty 6," Exhibit S-3, Federal Court of Canada, Calgary. Federal Court of Canada Trial Division, Trial Division, T-2022-89 and T-1254-92.

21. *Victor Buffalo v. Regina*, Transcripts, 3 October 2000, lines 2769, line 22—2784, line 25. I included paintings of the signing of the Hudson's Bay Company charter in 1670 to make points about the 1670 grant and the nature of the company: a painting of an eighteenth-century trading ceremony at York Factory to describe the nature of economic/diplomatic protocols; a picture of a fur trade "captain's coat" to draw parallels with treaty clothing allowances for chiefs; an etching

of the signing of Treaty 6 at Fort Carlton in 1876 to note the connection of Hudson's Bay Company with the process and the parallels in treaty and trade ceremonies; a picture of a blank treaty medal noting that medals had been used in the fur trade; a slide showing a trading ceremony and treaty negotiation side by side to emphasize continuity; a picture of Alexander Morris, who was the chief treaty negotiator for Canada in 1876; a picture of Alexander Christie, who was on the Treaty 6 negotiating team for Canada but had been HBC chief factor in Saskatchewan until 1869 to emphasize continuity to the Cree of those who spoke for the Queen; and last, an etching of the Hudson's Bay Company's post of Fort Pitt, which had been the other primary place of negotiation in 1876.

22. Winona Wheeler, "Indigenous Oral Tradition Histories: An Academic Predicament," Federal Court of Canada Trial Division, Trial Division, 2001 T-2002-89 and T-1245-92. For example, accounts given to outsiders and on the timetable of the court may be incomplete because some stories can only be told by certain individuals, at specific times of the year and in specific places.

23. Von Gernet, "Aboriginal Oral Documents" and "Comments on Winona Wheeler's Indigenous Oral Tradition Histories: An Academic Predicament," Report Prepared for the Defendants, 19 October 2001.

24. Ibid.

25. Federal Court of Appeal, *R. v. Benoit*, 2003.

26. Arthur J. Ray, "Native History on Trial: Confessions of an Expert Witness," *Canadian Historical Review* 84 (2): 259–62.

27. Carl Beal, "Report on Treaty Promises and Breaches, Treaty 6, Hobbema Reserve—1877–1930's," 6 June 1997, Federal Court of Canada Trial Division, Trial Division, T-2022-89 and T-1254-92.

28. Carl Beal, "Money, Markets, and Economic Development in Saskatchewan Indian Reserve Communities, 1870–1930s," Economic Department, University of Manitoba, September 1994.

29. Sarah Carter, *Lost Harvests: Prairie Indian Reserve Farmers and Government Policy* (Montreal: McGill-Queens University Press, 1990).

30. Flanagan, "Analysis of the Plaintiffs' Expert Reports."

31. For a good discussion of this issue in this case, see William Wicken, *Mi'kmaq Treaties on Trial: History, Land, and Donald Marshall Junior* (Toronto: University of Toronto Press, 2002).

32. An established publishing record can be a point of vulnerability in court for these experts, as opposing counsel may search it for any inconsistencies. For example, in the *Delgamuukw* and *Victor Buffalo* cases I was asked why some of my interpretations of the fur trade had changed since the time I published my first book in 1974.

33. Research-based or problem-based teaching is a common teaching model at research-oriented universities, where professors are expected to have active research careers.

34. I have discussed this in A. J. Ray, "Anthropology, History, and Aboriginal Rights: Politics and the Rise of Ethnohistory in North America in the 1950s," in

Pedagogies of the Global: Knowledge in the Human Interest, edited by Arif Dirlik (Boulder, Colo.: Paradigm Press, 2006), 89–112, as well as in Ray, "Kroeber and the California Claims," 269–74.

35. The teaching parallel here would be with those who teach in smaller liberal arts colleges and universities that emphasize teaching and do not expect professors to have active research and publishing agendas.

36. He explicitly stated: "I am among the few academic anthropologists in this country who have formal training and a publication record in all three major categories of evidence used to examine Aboriginal pasts: the archaeological record, written documents, and oral history and tradition." Von Gernet, "Assessment of Certain Evidence Relating to Plains Cree Practices," 2. At the time he wrote this in his court submission, his only referred academic publishing concerned the subjects of his doctoral research, which addressed aspects of the archaeology of the Iroquois. Regarding oral history, the "publications" he listed in his brief were a contract research report he prepared for the federal Department of Indian and Northern Affairs Canada, "Oral Narratives and Aboriginal Pasts: An Interdisciplinary Review of the Literature on Oral Traditions and Oral Histories," 1996, and a paper that he presented at a conference sponsored by the Fraser Institute, Vancouver, Canada, 1999. This presentation, entitled "What My Elders Taught Me: Oral Traditions as Evidence in Aboriginal Litigation," later was published by the Fraser Institute (a conservative think tank located in Vancouver, B.C.) in a collection of essays entitled Beyond the Nass Valley: National Implications of the Supreme Court's Delgamuuk Decision (Vancouver: Fraser Institute, 2002). In Von Gernet's biographical sketch promoting the book, he repeats the claim of expertise cited above. See http://www.fraserinstitute .ca/shared/author.asp?id=144 (accessed 25 November 2006).

37. Flanagan initiated this contest in his report when he noted that some of the plaintiffs' experts were not publishing scholars and/or held only master's degrees. This prompted counterattacks in rebuttal briefs filed by the Samson Cree's experts.

38. Delgamuukw v. Regina, Proceeding at Trial, vol. 202, 20 March 1989: 13328–329. Crown counsel (representing the provincial government) made the particular objection that "historical geography, or history is not a science at all, it's not a subject of expert opinion, it is not verifiable."

39. The exception has been in instances where the court determined that the expert was offering legal opinions.

40. See Von Gernet, "Assessment of Certain Evidence Relating to Plains Cree Practices," 2 and footnotes 1 and 3.

41. In Delgamuukw v. Regina, provincial Crown counsel advanced the latter proposition when I was being qualified as an expert. They argued that it was not necessary for me to explain the significance and meaning of Hudson's Bay Company documents because "in most cases the documents—the documents are plain on their face." "Proceedings at Trial": 13330. Frank Tough also discusses this issue. See Frank Tough, "Prof v. Prof in the Trial of the Benoit Treaty Eight Tax Case: Some Thoughts on Academics as Expert Witnesses," Native Studies Review 15, no. 1 (2004): 53–72.

42. In *Delgamuukw v. Regina*, for example, before I was qualified as an expert, the lawyers discussed at length whether they needed a historical geographer. In the end the judge decided it would be helpful to the court to have me direct them to the relevant Hudson's Bay Company records, given the vast size of that archive.

43. These problems have led noted historian Helen Hornbeck Tanner, who has extensive experience as an expert witness, to argue that the law is antithetical to history. See Tanner, "History vs. the Law: Processing Indians in the American Legal System," *University of Detroit Mercy Law Review* 76, no. 3 (1999): 693–708.

44. Arthur J. Ray interview with Nancy Lurie, Milwaukee Public Museum, October, 2001.

45. Sol Tax, "Minutes of a Meeting of AES and CSAS Meeting, Bloomington, Indiana, 5 May 1955," Bancroft Library, Kroeber Papers Series 4, Microfilm 158.

46. It should be noted, however, that even though the Justice Department may not commission research, other branches of the government, such as Indian Affairs, do so.

10 History, Democracy, and Treaty Negotiations in British Columbia

Ravi de Costa

What relationship do modern treaty-making processes, such as that under way in British Columbia in the twenty-first century, have with the histories of treaty making across the continent? This chapter explores the political context of current treaty making, comparing it with the era of imperialism, and argues that successful modern treaty processes need to acknowledge the democratic landscape on which they are taking place. The dense interactions and transformations inside and between indigenous and nonindigenous communities in settled colonies, such as those across the Pacific Northwest, require processes that allow for ongoing negotiation rather than "certainty" and "finality."

TREATIES AS DEMOCRATIC ACTS: INCLUSION & CONSENT

Two principles may be thought of as central to modern democratic societies: inclusion and consent. A democratic state requires popular legitimacy, which has historically meant the expansion of those able to participate and the need to seek all actors' consent, even if it is not forthcoming (though minorities' systematic refusal to give their consent damages the legitimacy of democratic orders). It is then a paradox that few states can point to their own birth as democratic acts on these terms. This is palpably true in the case of the colonies of European empires, which were founded on the tacit and often explicit assumption that indigenous peoples' inclusion and consent were not necessary. Modern treaty making strives for legitimation of this sort. But as I argue in this essay by drawing on a narrative of treaty making in British Columbia, the search for legitimacy situates the struggle for decolonization of colonial nation-states like Canada in a democratic context that both enables and requires new types of claims to be heard. The crisis of legitimacy faced by colonial nation-states can no longer be resolved by the simple, onetime transfer of consent from undifferentiated indigenous populations to the state.

Many theorists have criticized the liberal notion of consent, built on a thoughtful and informed, choosing individual. We can certainly consider the accumulated effects of colonization, with all its violence, disease, and genocidal intentions of policy, as creating a diminished capacity for indigenous consent. But we need to go much further, to accept that the social changes experienced by both indigenous and non-indigenous parties since colonization require a much more sophisticated and subtle approach to consent formation than that characterizing modern treaty processes so far. We need to embark on processes that are flexible enough to deal with the accumulated effects of colonization and the evolving ways that those effects are understood.

REPRESENTATIONS OF TREATIES

Scholars working for decolonization in Australia make frequent rhetorical recourse to the history of colonial treaty making in North America and New Zealand. This is sometimes portrayed as a centuries-long tradition of the recognition of indigenous peoples by European settlers and thus evidence of Australia's exceptionalism. Twentieth-century advocates of treaties in British Columbia have made similar remarks. Of course, close inspection of treaties with indigenous peoples reveals a history in which neglect by colonizers is at least as strong a theme as recognition. However, ample writing has demonstrated the moral power and precedent of the original treaties of the "peace and friendship" era and later ones, where two distinct and coherent peoples and traditions encountered each other and, through the wisdom of their respective leaderships, reached agreements giving the newcomers recognition and access to territory and resources.

As the scholar of legal history and philosophy Robert Williams has argued in his work *Linking Arms Together*, if historians include indigenous accounts of the encounter era in North America, a different picture of the frontier emerges in which cooperation and "rough equality" are central. Rather than devoid of agency in the face of the expansion of settler interests, indigenous peoples should be seen as "active, sophisticated facilitators on a multicultural frontier."[1] Rethinking treaties in this way allows us to see the moment that two discrete traditions and peoples were bound into mutual, enduring obligation. Indigenous diplomats honored the sacredness of treaties by insisting on such ceremonies as smoking the pipe before signing the documents. This, they understood, cleared the channels of communication and rendered the agreement sacred and permanent.[2] Treaties in the Indian tradition also meant the sharing of stories with a "jurisgenerative" or law-creating aspect. Treaties were the instantiation of a way of living and being together.

On this point Williams draws on political philosopher Richard Rorty's claim that solidarity relies on shared experiences (particularly shared hardships) more than the simple clearing away of misunderstanding and prejudice. Treaties between indigenous and settler groups that had faced each other in conflict exemplified this.[3] In such moments of encounter the performance of the leaders was of great significance for any future relationship, "made settled by the fact that the first or early performers' example is followed, their confidence confirmed, general expectation of further conformity strengthened and so a general custom launched."[4] In this sense treaties were living agreements that gave indigenous and settler peoples a framework for encountering each other and negotiating their interests as they arose. However, as indigenous peoples understood them, treaties as relationships also had a moral character, requiring that future encounters and negotiations would be conducted in keeping with the original agreement, respecting the autonomy of indigenous communities.

Memories of these aspects of treaty making persist, for example, in indigenous elders' understanding of the undertakings and spirit of Canada's Treaty 7, signed in 1877. In their view the treaty was an act of peace and coexistence, not the pretext for dispossession.[5] Recent work has recovered indigenous agency both in demanding and negotiating agreements; it has also exposed flaws in the colonial historiography of treaty making, in which triumphal narratives of extinguishment were abetted by complacent and complicit historians.[6]

In recent treaty-making endeavors, the rhetoric of Canadian governments both federal and provincial for building "new relationships" has drawn heavily on indigenous perceptions of the earlier treaties as sacred acts and performances.[7] But First Nations usually respond warily to government calls for new relations, suspecting that modern treaty making may work according to the same assumptions as those actually held by the original colonists: that treaties were conclusions to the matter of indigenous presence and did not provide a framework for the recognition of indigenous autonomy other than that which the state found convenient. Consequently, contemporary hopes that the moral force of the original treaties can be reproduced should be tempered by the fact that the parties to those treaties had differing views of what was actually taking place. Moreover, modern treaties must also acknowledge how much both parties have changed since the early period of colonization. The rest of the chapter demonstrates this by examining the British Columbia treaty process.

HISTORY OF TREATY MAKING IN BRITISH COLUMBIA

"Alone in the new world, with neither outside aid nor previous example to call upon, the Indians of British Columbia embarked on sustained political action within the new political system, demanding that it live up to its own official ideals."[8] For Europeans the will to treat has historically been a matter of necessity: treaty making has not been the consequence of Europeans' adherence to prior principles of inclusion and respect but a function of their need for assistance and stability during settlement processes. To understand how this is true of the present-day process, we need to examine how indigenous political representations, the nonindigenous authority, and the political landscape of British Columbia were all transformed, destabilizing the economy and eroding state legitimacy, so that treaty making was by the late 1980s inevitable. In the process, however, the original narrative of treaty making as performative encounter was superseded by the realities of modern pluralist politics.

A full account of Native mobilization would require a history of indigenous representations beginning in the second half of the nineteenth century. In this essay, however, I focus on the political mobilization and direct action of Natives in the province during the post–World War II period, when Native claims were able to connect more effectively with national and international currents of change. Indigenous subjectivities such as pan-Indianism and tribalism rose to significance during the course of the twentieth century and became the basis for cross-national or cross-clan political activity intended to present a united front to the absolutist settler state.[9] New political organizations started to reflect these shifts in political identity, with northern coastal Natives forming the Native Brotherhood of British Columbia in 1931 and interior Indians setting up the Confederacy of Indian Tribes of British Columbia in the mid-1940s.[10]

In 1951, as an international discourse of human rights gained momentum, the federal government of Canada lifted prohibitions on indigenous political activity in place under the Indian Act, the domestic legislation that oversaw indigenous life. Indigenous political activity expanded, rapidly so after a federal process of indigenous consultation on further reforms to the Indian Act was undertaken in 1968 and 1969. In 1969 the federal government tabled a new statement on Indian policy in the House of Commons, the so-called White Paper. Its ultra-assimilationist call for the abolition of Natives' special status immediately stimulated national opposition and the formation of a Native political organization that encompassed all of British Columbia, the Union of B.C. Indian Chiefs.[11] Political development meant Native leaders were dealing with broader constituencies, such as "non-status" indigenous peoples, and gaining greater access to federal funding for land claims activity.[12] New indigenous organizations sprang up: the Alliance of B.C. Indian Bands and the United Native Nations in 1974, the B.C. Coalition of Native Indians and the Tribal Forum in 1980, and finally the First Nations Congress in 1988. In their names no less than their policies, these organizations showed how rapidly Native political ideas were developing.[13]

These organizations cohered throughout this period in response to the lack of substantive government change on a range of issues and in particular the B.C. government's intransigence over land claims. In 1973 the land claim of the Nisga'a people of northern B.C. was adjudicated in the Supreme Court of Canada. In their finding, known as the *Calder* decision, the justices were split on the substantive matters, but their judgment raised the likelihood that aboriginal title continued to exist on

Crown lands where it had not been extinguished expressly. General land regulation or legislation that was not explicit could not extinguish aboriginal rights held "from time immemorial."[14] This led to fundamental shifts in federal policy and the beginnings of modern treaty making. Native people were suspicious about the motivations underlying what the federal government began to call a "comprehensive claims" process. However, within B.C. it was the continued refusal of the province to enter into any negotiations that became the focus of indigenous peoples' anger.

The political scientist Paul Tennant has suggested that 1973 was also the start of "the contemporary era of B.C. Indian political protest."[15] Although there had been earlier protests at Fort St. John and at Williams Lake, the timing seemed influenced by the American Indian Movement's standoff with the FBI at Wounded Knee in South Dakota. Direct action proliferated: in 1973 there was a blockade of Department of Indian Affairs (DIA) offices in Vancouver, and a traditional but allegedly illegal fish weir was built by the Cowichan people on Vancouver Island. In June 1974 there was a protest march on the legislature to pressure the New Democratic Party government to recognize Aboriginal title. That year as well, DIA offices across Canada were blockaded, the Nisga'a prevented a railway development on their territory, and armed Natives maintained a prolonged blockade of a highway near Cache Creek. The year 1975 saw an increase in confrontational actions, particularly the assertion of traditional resource rights.[16] That was a particular emphasis of interior groups under the leadership of Assembly of First Nations chief George Manuel. After a Lillooet "fish-in" in 1978, Manuel indicated that "sophisticated civil disobedience" would be an outcome of continued government intransigence; he also referred to an "army" of activists who would take up weapons in the struggle if necessary.[17]

In the early 1980s First Nations across the province began a second phase of direct action aimed in particular to disrupt the resource sector.[18] In 1984 first the Kaska-Dena people in the remote Northeast and then the Nuu-chah-nulth on Meares Island blocked logging access. In 1985 the Haida obstructed logging on Lyell Island. The following year, the Kwakiutl protested on Deare Island; the Nisga'a, Lillooet, and Nlaka'pamux all obstructed railway constructions, and Bella Bella paddlers arriving at Expo in Vancouver in 1986 encountered protests and speeches by the Native Brotherhood of British Columbia, angry at the appropriation of Native culture during the exhibition.[19] Also in 1986, Indians threatened not to participate in the census, which meant that British Columbia might lose up to $3,000 per person in federal transfer payments;[20] the Gitxsan Wet'suwet'en took offensive action, hurling marshmallows at fisheries officers; and the McLeod Lake band not only obstructed a logging road but actually started taking logs themselves.[21] Gitxsan Wet'suwet'en roadblocks and standoffs made it clear that the government's control was limited. David Mitchell, a member of the legislative assembly of B.C. and a vice president of the lumber company Westar, was quoted as saying the system has broken down completely. "It is no longer certain who controls the forests in north-west BC," he declared. Westar was eventually forced to reach a deal with tribal leaders.[22] The Nemaiah Chilcotin band forced Carrier Lumber, Ltd., to stop logging after unilaterally declaring their territory a wilderness preserve.[23]

In the 1970s protests had focused on the administrative concerns of bands—typically on reserves—and there was little media or court involvement. By the 1980s, however, the key difference was that the tribal basis of protests brought them to nonreserve lands and targeted resource companies that were perceived to be benefiting from the province's continuing refusal to negotiate. The media became more interested as protests offered the spectacle of traditionally garbed indigenous peoples confronting resource developers and the state. Native communities sought injunctions against developments in advance of preparing their land claims. Major churches became sympathetic as well as environmental groups. This was especially the case on the West Coast of Vancouver Island, where a broad coalition opposed to logging formed and included the local municipality.[24] It was, according one participant in the treaty process, "a very confrontational time in the province's history."[25] The province's dependence on natural resources made the confrontations and disruptions untenable, and the provincial Social Credit government rapidly reformed its policy from 1986.

Two points can be taken from this history. First, it demonstrates an inversion that has taken place between the nineteenth-century treaties and contemporary treaties. Now indigenous peoples must come into the colonists' world and demand recognition and inclusion in the dominant sociopolitical order. On the signing of the B.C. Treaty Commission agreement in 1993, George Watts of the Nuu-chah-nulth Tribal Council said, "I'm actually going to be part of this country in a little while."[26] Second, indigenous peoples' struggles for decolonization not only rely on the tools of the democratic order (such as formal political institutions and the public sphere of media and civil society), but also open the democratic realm as part of making claims. New ways of making their claims meant that indigenous peoples were envisaging a new shared moral order. Indigenous claim making not only strained and broke the bounds of "legality" but also forced the inclusion of new voices, such as those raised on behalf of nonstatus Indians or for tribal and other broader groups. The broader range of interests now working for decolonization in B.C. meant that the authorized parties to any treaty would have to reflect these newer ideas. Moreover, the forcefulness with which Natives had had to assert their rights would set in motion new kinds of state and social response.

THE PROCESS AND STATUS OF TREATY MAKING
IN BRITISH COLUMBIA

The political transformations of the 1960s and 1970s bore fruit in the 1980s. Indigenous claims severely disrupted the economic and social order of British Columbia, and by the late 1980s the province agreed to participate in a new comprehensive process of making treaties that would in many ways be distinct from the federal process under way since 1973. It was legislated in the early 1990s and began formally in 1993. The new process indicated how different a modern process needs to be from the early colonial "peace and friendship" treaties or the numbered treaties of the late nineteenth and early twentieth centuries. The difference was visible not simply in the new proceedings' technical nature but also in the range of ways that indigenous peoples could identify and represent themselves as part of the process and in the range of different nonindigenous interests that would be represented. Treaty making was also very much placed in the public eye, with effusive political rhetoric about how it would transform the collective identity of B.C. and correct the injustices of history.[27]

Six stages comprise treaty making as it was launched in 1993. Individual First Nations initiate negotiations by first submitting a formal statement of intent, comprising a rough indication of their traditional territories and a sense of who the relevant community is and how it is represented. Stage 2 requires both First Nations and the federal and provincial governments to demonstrate "readiness" for negotiations—that is, the capacity of each party to undertake negotiations and to demonstrate its "mandate." Stage 3 sees the parties develop their agenda for negotiations, known as a framework agreement. This includes details about the structure of the negotiations as well as a broad indication of the issues the parties wish to have discussed. Once a framework agreement is initialed at the table, it undergoes ratification processes set out at Stage 2. Stage 4 is the first substantive stage of negotiations: the parties work through the issues they have identified, the goal being to draft chapters of agreement on each topic, such as land and resources, fiscal relations, or wildlife management. The collection of these drafts is an agreement in principle (AIP) and requires ratification once again. The provincial government ratifies an AIP via cabinet approval.

Stage 5 attempts to turn drafts into a complete text that would become the final agreement. At this point a process of review is undertaken to ensure that nothing conflicts with the Constitution of Canada. This stage requires ratification by all three parties, a community referendum in the case of First Nations, as well as approval by both the British Columbia legislature and the parliament of Canada. On the "effective date" the final agreement becomes a treaty in the terms of section 35 of the Constitution Act (1982). Implementation, including transfer of resources and powers, comprises Stage 6 of the process. At this point the relevant indigenous community will no longer be administered under the Indian Act but under terms of its own making.

In mid-2008, in the sixteenth year of the process, only two First Nations have ratified Final Agreements. Tsawwassen and Maa-Nulth First Nations awaited passage of their Final Agreements through the Parliament of Canada.[28] Fifty-six other First Nations remained in negotiations at forty-six treaty "tables." Of these, thirty-four tables were making little or no progress.[29] As I have argued at length elsewhere, major impediments to agreements include the narrowness of what governments have been willing to discuss in terms of historical restitution, indigenous self-government, and the question of what treaties will do to aboriginal rights in a context of ongoing jurisprudence on those rights.[30]

We should not underestimate the difficulty for Native communities in consenting to treaties. For example, the Sechelt band rejected its AIP in July 2000; the Nuu-chah-nulth Tribal Council AIP was rejected in mid-2001 by Nuu-chah-nulth communities; the Snuneymuxw First Nation, who reached a draft AIP in April 2003, had still to gain community approval as of early 2007; and the Sliammon AIP failed its initial ratification vote in 2001 in the face of community disaffection, although it was eventually approved by a majority of 62 percent.[31] Such difficulties are likely to become more acute as communities are asked to ratify final agreements. Indigenous peoples realize that treaties increase the power of their own leaderships, and it has often been remarked that there are significant differences between those negotiating agreements and the community itself.[32] The community vote to ratify the Nisga'a Final Agreement (passed by only 61 percent of 2,376 eligible voters, with 23 percent against and 15 percent abstaining) included a ballot on a future Nisga'a constitution that had not yet been seen by the Nisga'a community.[33]

In some communities indigenous women have leveled criticism at the patriarchal membership of negotiation teams and at the inadequate attention paid to gender issues. In 1999 the commission that oversees treaty making convened a focus group on indigenous women's views about the treaty process. Women, the report concluded, played a highly subordinate role in treaty negotiations and felt isolated from them. The report found concern that a number of issues were not gaining a place in the treaty process discussions, including child welfare, domestic violence, and family health. Underlying these views was the concern that the process was dominated by the male Native elite.[34]

Conversely, lack of progress creates pressure within communities to prioritize more urgent social activities, such as education, or to pursue other political strategies. Some tables have effectively disbanded. Two First Nations—Ts'kw'aylaxw and Xaxli'p—have formally withdrawn.[35] The McLeod Lake band rejected the process of trilateral negotiations with B.C. and Canada, instead negotiating an "adhesion" with the federal government to Treaty 8 and securing a significant amount of land and resource rights through bilateral negotiations with Canada.[36] Furthermore, other First Nations in British Columbia, representing about one-third of the Native population, have never joined the process and continue to reject what they see as its basic assumption that the result will be extinguishment of aboriginal rights. They also object to the inclusion of the province in what they feel should be "nation-to-nation" negotiations with the federal government alone.

Indigenous people have criticized the definition of organizations that would represent First Nations.[37] One Secwepemc elder maintained that "it should be hereditary people who are signing these agreements. The tribal council is a civil servant who takes orders from the federal government."[38] In its 1998 Annual Report the Treaty Commission noted that there "may be as few as 10 or as many as 200 First Nations in B.C., depending on the definition used." Band councils, the bodies established by the Indian Act, are negotiating in most of the nearly fifty cases. Thirteen tables see indigenous interests represented by tribal councils (comprised of several bands), while three are based on traditional governance arrangements.[39] The enabling legislation described First Nations as any indigenous group, "however organized and established by aboriginal people within their traditional territory in British Columbia, that has been mandated by its constituents to enter into treaty negotiations on their behalf with Her Majesty."[40] The legislation made no reference to Aboriginal rights, which were rapidly evolving in the courts. In fact, major legal developments have shifted the ground on which modern treaty negotiations stand.

In 1999 the Treaty Commission prepared a confidential report for the principals, responding to the new environment created after the *Delgamuuk'w* judgment in 1997, which significantly expanded the conception of Aboriginal rights to allow indigenous peoples to enjoy their rights in a contemporary social and economic order. The report, *Strengthening First Nations for Treaty Purposes*, noted the potential that the changing jurisprudence of aboriginal title could "alter the very political foundations on which the treaty process rests."[41] Repeated admonitions of First Nations such as the Gitxsan for asserting their legal rights[42] seemed hypocritical when the commission concluded that "ultimately treaties are not only political documents but also legal ones . . . each party needs the assurance in treaty negotiations that the other parties have the legal capacity to deliver . . . , [raising] the spectre of negotiations being carried out with a First Nation that is not coterminous with the nation that holds title to a particular territory."[43] This reanimated divisions among Native people over their approach to the state and offered succor to more radical Native positions.

For example, Westbank First Nation went logging on their traditional territory in 1999, from the province's point of view, "illegally." Rather than pursuing criminal sanctions, however, the governments chose to negotiate "off the table," granting Westbank significant logging rights. One legal scholar suggested that the decision not to prosecute may indicate that the *Delgamuuk'w* decision shifted the balance of power significantly toward Natives, with an "onus of proof" of title now being on the provincial government.[44] The national indigenous organization, the Assembly of First Nations, developed a post-*Delgamuuk'w* strategy to "provide assistance and organizational capacity for First Nations considering asserting their title consistent with the *Delgamuuk'w* decision."[45] Indigenous organizations in British Columbia, representing those both in and outside the process, issued a joint "Consensus Statement" in early 2000, calling for the establishment of "a new policy of recognition, affirmation and implementation of aboriginal title."[46]

Even those First Nations who have been most attracted to the treaty process as it has unfolded, such as Lheidli T'enneh, have seen it as a matter of pragmatism at the very best. As their treaty analyst Rick Krehbiel put it: "Basically, there's only one process to work in. The Band was interested in getting itself built into the twentieth century in Canada, and there's really no other way to do it at this point. It's the only game in town."[47] Another analyst, Bernard Schulmann, noted that Ts'kw'aylaxw were motivated by economic isolation and dependence: "Ts'kw'aylaxw . . . entered the process in May 1994, and much of it has to do with the fact that they are sitting on 2000 hectares of rocks. Their land is utterly useless, they are in no position to pick up any other land through any other method, and they want to move from the past."[48] In the circumstances we should at least retain some skepticism about the extent to which absolute and final indigenous consent can be secured through the treaty process.

INCLUSION AND CONSENT: NONINDIGENOUS
PERSPECTIVES ON TREATIES

During the negotiations that led to the creation of the treaty process, indigenous peoples insisted on a "nation-to-nation" quality to treaty making, often speaking of a "one window" approach, where integrated and coherent indigenous communities deal directly and only with the (federal) government.[49] The metaphor of one window evokes the history of treaties made between the "elders" of each side, a single channel for recognition and exchange. Yet as we have seen, some now doubt the ability of such negotiations to take into account the range of indigenous groups that have interests in treaty making. The nonindigenous "party" to treaties is no less heterogeneous and certainly has had the means to demand the inclusion of multiple constituents.

The founding agreement of the treaty process made clear that "non-aboriginal interests are to be represented at the table by the provincial and federal governments." The governments, particularly the province, have been innovative in that respect. At the top of a pyramidal structure of consultation is the Treaty Negotiation Advisory Committee, a group of resource industry, labor, social, and environmental organizations that work with Canada and B.C. to identify the interests on which provincial negotiating mandates are based. Regional advisory committees are similar bodies of representatives from key economic and social sectors that support clusters of negotiations in particular regions and localities.[50] A special role was given to municipalities, because of their delegated authority for local government matters, through the creation of treaty advisory committees. In a memorandum of understanding with the body representing local governments in B.C., the province indicated that municipal representatives would be treated as "respected advisors of provincial negotiating teams" on transitional cooperation, public information, and British Columbia budget allocations.[51] Local government participants have been known to point out that they are nearly always the only elected members of negotiating teams.

Federal chief treaty negotiator Eric Denhoff publicly lamented the increasing complexity caused by the addition of local governments to provincial negotiation teams and the growing sophistication of "third party" demands like those of resource groups such as the Fisheries Survival Coalition.[52] Bruce Nelson was one such intervener, who sought to make room for the particular needs of ranchers in B.C.: "There is a new group trying to peer through that window. For them, not only are the images unclear, but they are becoming increasingly indiscernible. The group to which I refer is the other stakeholders, conveniently designated as third parties, people immersed in the land claims issue . . . we view the federal government as systematically abandoning the rights of rural, farming and ranching people in the government's efforts to achieve a politically correct solution to an extremely complex problem. . . . What has the government done to protect our minority rights?"[53] Voices like the British Columbia Citizens' Front stoked a new climate of litigation and conflict as when the Nisga'a Final Agreement faced provincial ratification in 1999.[54] The business community often portrayed itself as an innocent bystander in the internecine squabbles of vested interest groups. "We're the meat in the sandwich," said the president and CEO of the Mining Association of B.C., Gary Livingstone.[55] However, the distance from passivity to the maintenance of existing practices looked to be short indeed. In a publication setting out their perspective on treaties, the B.C. and Yukon Chamber of Mines asserted that "the industry just wants these contentious issues settled. Exploration needs access to the largest land base possible. . . . We need to work hard toward preventing . . . another set of regulatory hoops to jump through."[56]

Another resource group, the Council of Forest Industries, has consistently taken a tougher line, particularly after the *Delgamuuk'w* decision. It sees litigation as inevitable because the treaty process "has not provided any concrete deliverables."[57] It is "unreasonable, irrational and counter-productive," the group argues, "for native groups to claim the benefits of aboriginal title before such title is proved in court."[58] Most pointedly, treaties did not provide "enough certainty that land claims issues will be extinguished."[59] Jerry Lampert of the B.C. Business Council announced that "there have been major disappointments in achieving the certainty we are looking for."[60]

A provincial election in May 2001 appeared to absorb much of this tension, however. The British Columbia Liberals routed the governing New Democratic Party (NDP), taking seventy-seven out of seventy-nine of contested seats in the provincial legislature. Some part of this result, though by no means the whole, should be attributed to the delegitimation of the NDP and their strategy toward treaties. The combination of a resurgent Native opposition and the lack of actual progress in a costly public policy ensured that there were few votes the NDP could win on the treaty process and its promise of a "new relationship" in the province. Liberals spent considerable time positioning themselves as the guardians of democracy on treaty making. This came to a head during the legislative debates about the ratification of the Nisga'a Final Agreement in 1999. The intransigence of the opposition then led to the closure of the debate, providing fuel for the fire.

The problem with legislative scrutiny of treaty negotiations arises because of the recasting of power that takes place under treaty making: legislatures traditionally transmit their intentions to the populace, where they are digested by interest groups who lobby their responses and seek changes. Yet the legislation to enact treaties that have been agreed at treaty tables cannot be amended without undermining the entire process. This formal moment that decolonizes the democratic order thus appears to turn the parliaments into rubber stamps, where frustrated oppositions berate bored, even embarrassed governments.

A further rejoinder to treaty making has been that the principles on which it was based were rejected during a national referendum on constitutional reform—the Charlottetown Accord of 1992.[61] This did not prevent the opposition Liberals from including another referendum on provincial negotiating mandates as part of their Aboriginal policy platform. In 1999 the leader of the opposition, Gordon Campbell, asserted that, if elected, his party was committed to a policy of "bringing people into it." He said: "I am committed to giving all British Columbians a one-time province-wide referendum on the principles that will guide the province's negotiating mandate for future treaties. Make no mistake, the government under my leadership will not accept this Nisga'a treaty as a template for future treaty settlements. We will not endorse any treaty until there has been a genuine attempt to engage all British Columbians in a meaningful debate on the principles that they expect treaties to embrace."[62]

"All British Columbians" was unlikely to include many Native people, however. NDP premier Ujjal Dosanjh challenged Campbell to name one Native leader who supported his proposal, and Campbell could not.[63] Regardless, once the Liberals were elected in 2001, eight questions were put to the electorate, to provide clear instructions to members of the provincial negotiating teams.[64] The referendum was held under the British Columbia Referendum Act so that, if approved, the eight issues would become legally binding on the government under provincial law. All eight received overwhelming approval.[65] This was due in part to a concerted boycott by Native peoples and their supporters.

On one issue—the character of indigenous self-government to be agreed as part of treaty negotiations—we can see the potential effect of the referenda. Natives have been claiming recognition for autonomy and self-government since contact. In 1995 the federal government recognized self-government as an *inherent* right.[66] Canadian courts have repeatedly endorsed this position, perhaps most explicitly in a 2001 British Columbia Supreme Court ruling in *Campbell et al. v. Attorney-General of British Columbia / Attorney-General of Canada & Nisga'a Nation et al.* (an action brought by Gordon Campbell himself), which rejected the proposition that all power in Canada resides with the federal and provincial governments, stating that self-government was an Aboriginal right as protected by section 35 of the Constitution of Canada.[67] Nevertheless, the British Columbia government chose to ask residents of the province whether they agreed with the proposition that "Aboriginal self-government should have the characteristics of local government, with powers *delegated* from Canada and British Columbia."[68]

Eighty-seven percent approval of that question implies that provincial negotiators are now obliged under provincial law to discuss only delegated models of self-government at treaty tables. Although the exact effect remains unclear, few could argue that "delegated" and "inherent" mean the same thing. The position of the province that it will only consent to a "delegated" model is unlikely to survive a constitutional challenge, and indeed, recent agreements indicate that the "delegated" model is not being insisted upon.[69] However, the episode exposes the gulf between two notions of provincial political legitimacy: on the one hand, the wishes of the democratic majority and, on the other, the need to seek indigenous consent and inclusion. Although indigenous peoples succeeded in dragging a recalcitrant state into negotiations on decolonization through radical and more moderate forms of action that expanded the democratic realm, the new space they entered was porous to a range of nonindigenous actors who undermined the state's capacity (often with its approval) to act in the so-called one-window mode.

CONCLUSION

The memory of the earlier treaties as moments of recognition and esteem might still be a source of inspiration, but it can no longer be an example. In British Columbia discussions at treaty tables provide neither Native nor settler communities with models of exemplary behavior, other than perhaps the common-sense principle that it is good for people to talk to each other. In fact, the new treaty negotiations are highly technical blueprints for future systems of rule, the codification of exemplary behavior rather than its performance. It could be no other way. Compared with the early colonial examples cited by Robert Williams and discussed earlier in this essay, both "sides" are far less homogeneous than they were. The locus of authority in each case has been transformed such that when elders perform handshakes today there is as much skepticism as celebration. The hope that senior figures might enact a performance (or text) that is wholly representative, widely supported, and yet aspirational seems utopian amid the complexity of modern life.

Structures of legitimacy and authority are radically different than they were in previous centuries, and the traditional modes of authority of indigenous communities must now take into account the views of indigenous people living off-reserve as well as the concerns of women and Native youth, who all have their own desire to participate. Simultaneously, the colonial agent of empire has had to be reinvented for a pluralist democracy in which business interests, media representations, bureaucracy, civil society, and local government are all articulate and demanding. This is to say nothing, moreover, of the immensely complex relations that already exist between the two putative parties to a treaty, between indigenous peoples and others inside schools, workplaces, social settings, and families. We must assume these relations will continue to evolve, creating new representations of self and others, new challenges and problems.

Shorn of their rhetorical boilerplate and corporate dressage, modern treaties look nothing like the indigenous vision retold by Williams. Although I strongly agree with his conclusion that classical indigenous legal traditions have a great deal to offer contemporary conflicts, I wonder how such possibilities could ever find their way into current treaty practices, where those indigenous people most likely to want such agreements (elders and others dedicated to traditional commitments based on trust, shared stories, and the performance of exemplary behavior) are the most likely to be alienated from technical and legal negotiations. Some scholars are optimistic about the possibility that new frameworks of rights, such as the Canadian Charter of Rights, will enable new intercultural conversations and dialogue over core concepts like equality.[70] However, critics such as Taiaiake (Gerald) Alfred have attacked such processes (including the treaty process in B.C.) as simply another layer of colonization in the guise of indigenous recognition. Aboriginal rights and title, argues Alfred, are simply the colonial offerings available to those who "abandon their autonomy in order to enter the legal and political framework of the state."[71]

Does the treaty rationale reinforce rather than renounce fundamentally assimilationist foundations? Only indigenous peoples themselves can answer that question. My own view is that the British Columbia process is cast in anachronistic terms because of its commitment to "certainty" and finality.[72] We have not yet achieved a broad, meaningful social consensus about whether we should view the past as progress, misfortune, or genocide. Yet treaties seem to function for both the state and the nonindigenous public as ways to seal the past shut. For decolonizing states to insist that indigenous peoples reach consensus about the parameters of their futures in these circumstances seems quite unjust. That is a project that requires Native leaders, in the present moment, to set out the needs and desires of their communities comprehensively and conclusively for all time. It places great faith in the forbearance of everyone else not to use democratic institutions and values in ways that alter or undermine treaties.

Might we revitalize the performative character of treaty making? If so, how? Scholarly debates about theories of citizenship include concern about the integrating versus the differentiating implications of the recognition of difference. Critical advocates of treaty making urge both these goals simultaneously: a stronger and more trusting community based on a fundamental valuing of difference rather than mere tolerance of it. This would be difficult enough if the demarcations between indigenous and settler peoples were in every instance steady and clear, but in the "decolonizing democracies," they are not. For those committed to some notion of indigenous "authenticity," the transformation of indigenous peoples from the period of contact into the communities of today renders talk of rights or historical restitution unpalatable. The evidence from British Columbia suggests that it makes more sense to encourage a permanent culture of negotiation. Treaties are being conceived of as high-stakes moments that threaten existing, stable communities when the situation really calls for contingency and "uncertainty."

I conclude by reflecting on what this might mean for scholars. We can, for example, urge a better historical understanding on the assumption that wider knowledge of the ongoing illegitimacy of colonial nation-states will produce an alternative public discourse. I doubt that this will be easy or is even possible. Perhaps my own view on this is colored by the experience of Australia's reconciliation process—an attempt at democratic decolonization through a modest effort at public education, "sharing history," and "national healing"—where advocates grossly underestimated settler investments in the status quo.[73] In B.C. the referendum on the provincial government's treaty mandate as well as the building hostility to the recent agreements made on the Tsawwassen and Lheidli T'enneh tables suggest that even where there is wide support for reform, such a pedagogical strategy still faces real limits to convincing settler populations of shared alternative visions.[74] Scholars need to be far more candid than they have been about the prospects for *any* widely shared and meaningful visions in societies as complexly varied as contemporary liberal democracies.

Alternatively, we might learn from the historical evidence that social change requires new distributions of power and thereby urge indigenous peoples to take a more contrary stance, one that actually disrupts the assimilationist imperatives of treaty making—a return to the direct action and litigation that brought the governments to the table in the first place, or First Nations simply returning to traditional lifeways. This implies that nonindigenous people will also actively support and engage with that process, reinforcing the idea of illegitimacy through their own disobedience. The danger of provoking an entrenched opposition by doing this is unquestionably real. Moreover, we need to be careful that we do not repeat the oldest error once more, where nonindigenous peoples assume they know what indigenous peoples actually want and can formulate broad policies that will accommodate all claims to decolonization.

In light of the democratic imperatives of decolonization, I concur with the Canadian anthropologist Michael Asch who, drawing on Levi-Strauss, has argued that treaty making as consent-seeking should be "an uninterrupted process of reciprocal gifts, which effects the transition from hostility to alliance, from anxiety to confidence, and from fear to friendship."[75] We need to encourage the practice of perpetual negotiation and should do so in the knowledge that the "certainty" being sought in current treaty making can no more predict the future causes of hostility, anxiety, and fear than it can create new bases of alliance, confidence, and friendship.

1. Robert A. Williams, *Linking Arms Together: American Indian Treaty Visions of Law and Peace, 1600–1800* (New York: Oxford University Press, 1997), 29.

2. Ibid., 62–76.

3. Ibid., 92–97.

4. Ibid., 125.

5. Walter Hildebrandt, Dorothy First Rider, and Sarah Carter, *The True Spirit and Original Intent of Treaty 7* (Montreal: McGill-Queen's University Press, 1996), 67–82, 111–45. The so-called numbered treaties were made with indigenous peoples of the prairies beginning in 1871, as the newly independent Canadian government sought to consolidate its western expansion. See J. R. Miller, *Skyscrapers Hide the Heavens: A History of Indian-White Relations in Canada*, 3d ed. (Toronto: University of Toronto Press, 2000), 216–24.

6. Arthur J. Ray, J. R. Miller, and Frank Tough, *Bounty and Benevolence: A History of Saskatchewan Treaties* (Montreal: McGill-Queen's University Press, 2000).

7. For example: "We pledged to take action in a concerted way to forge a new relationship with the first nations people of this province, a relationship that was based on trust and mutual respect, a relationship that will enable first nations communities to move forward toward greater self-reliance and self-determination; and a relationship that will allow us all—aboriginal and non-aboriginal—to move beyond conflict and confrontation and work together to address our common concerns and goals. We pledged to build that relationship based upon a recognition of inherent rights and upon a foundation of just and honourable treaty settlements." See Andrew Petter (Minister for Aboriginal Affairs, British Columbia), *Official Report of Debates of the Legislative Assembly* (May 19, 1993), 6438.

8. Paul Tennant, *Aboriginal Peoples and Politics: The Indian Land Question in British Columbia, 1849–1989* (Vancouver: UBC Press, 1991), 83.

9. Hazel W. Hertzberg, *The Search for an American Indian Identity: Modern Pan-Indian Movements*, 1st ed. (Syracuse, N.Y.: Syracuse University Press, 1971); and Tennant, *Aboriginal Peoples and Politics*, 68.

10. George Manuel and Michael Posluns, *The Fourth World: An Indian Reality* (New York: Free Press, 1974), 97; and Paul Tennant, "Native Indian Political Organization in British Columbia, 1900–1969: A Response to Internal Colonialism," *BC Studies* 55 (1982): 28–30.

11. Harold Cardinal, *The Unjust Society: The Tragedy of Canada's Indians* (Edmonton, Alberta: M.G. Hurtig, 1969).

12. Tennant, *Aboriginal Peoples and Politics*, 176–80.

13. Ravi de Costa, "New Relationships, Old Certainties: Australia's Reconciliation and the Treaty-Process in British Columbia," Ph.D. dissertation, Swinburne University of Technology, 2002, 176–80; and Paul Tennant, "Native Indian Political Activity in British Columbia, 1969–1983," *BC Studies* 57 (1983): 112–36.

14. Douglas Sanders, "The Nishga Case," *BC Studies* 19 (1973): 16–18.

15. Tennant, *Aboriginal Peoples and Politics*, 174.

16. Ibid., 179–80.

17. Peter McFarlane, *Brotherhood to Nationhood: George Manuel and the Making of the Modern Indian Movement* (Toronto: Between the Lines, 1993), 249–50. See also Steven Point, "Understanding Native Activism," *BC Studies* 89 (1991): 129.

18. Nicholas Blomley, "'Shut the Province Down': First Nations Blockades in British Columbia, 1984–1995," *BC Studies* 111 (1996): 5–35.

19. Robert Weisnagel, "Paddlers Met by Angry Natives," *Vancouver Sun*, September 2, 1986, B3.

20. Larry Pynn, "Indian Snub of Census under Review Official Says," *Vancouver Sun*, September 4, 1986, A10.

21. Tennant, *Aboriginal Peoples and Politics*, 207.

22. Terry Glavin, "Westar Joins Northwest Timber Protest," *Vancouver Sun*, February 23, 1990, B3.

23. Scott Simpson, "Indian Court Case Prompts Firm to Halt Logging," *Vancouver Sun*, December 18, 1990, B2.

24. Tennant, *Aboriginal Peoples and Politics*, 208.

25. Interview with David Didluck, executive director of the Lower Mainland TAC, August 14, 2000. See also Blomley's maps of the density of blockades around the province and the complete list of direct actions, in Blomley, "'Shut the Province Down,'" 22–23, 31–35.

26. Scott Simpson, "Joe Mathias Possesses the Inner Strength of a True, Traditional Leader," *Vancouver Sun*, September 21, 1992, B1–2.

27. De Costa, "New Relationships, Old Certainties," 208–41.

28. It should be noted that the progress on the latter tables has been made by reaching agreements to give the First Nations access to resources and lands that are outside the main treaty text and therefore will not have constitutional protection. Miro Cernetig, "Delta First Nations Treaty Worth $120M: Tsawwassen Band Members Get Land, Lose Tax-Exempt Status," *Vancouver Sun*, December 7, 2006.

29. British Columbia Treaty Commission, *Annual Report 2007*, available online at http://www.bctreaty.net/files/pdf_documents/2007_annual_report.pdf.

30. Ravi de Costa, "Treaties in British Columbia: The Search for a New Relationship," *International Journal of Canadian Studies* 27 (2003): 173–96.

31. Jeff Thomas (Snuneymuxw Treaty Office), personal communication with the author, July 21, 2003.

32. Outside of British Columbia the recent decision to proceed with the diversion of the Rupert River in Quebec to enable further hydroelectric development has created divisions among affected Cree communities. Rheal Seguin, "Troubled Waters," *Globe and Mail*, December 19, 2006, A12.

33. Diane Rinehart, "Close Vote on Nisga'a Deal 'Disappointment,'" *Vancouver Sun*, November 12, 1998; "Nisga'a Head to Polls," *Vancouver Sun*, November 6, 1998; Peter Murrey, "The Nisga'a Treaty: Victory for Native Rights or Threats to Native Sovereignty," *On Indian Land* (spring 1999); and Neil Seeman, "Nisga'a Land Claim Challenges by Band Dissidents," *National Post*, March 23, 2000.

34. British Columbia Treaty Commission, Focus Group on Aboriginal Women and Treaty Making, *Focus Group Report*, March 9, 1999.

35. The Sto:lo Nation threatened to withdraw without substantial alteration in the government approach. See "Sto:lo Threatens to Withdraw from BC Treaty Process," Turtle Island Native Network, November 14, 2001, available online at http://www.turtleisland.org (accessed November 20, 2001).

36. British Columbia, "Overview of the Final McLeod Lake Adhesion to Treaty No. 8 and Settlement Agreement," 2000, available online at http://www.aaf.gov.bc .ca/news-releases/2000/mcleodover.stm (accessed January 14, 2001).

37. Janice Switlo, *B.C. Treaty Process — 'Trick or Treaty'? Giving Effect to the 'Spirit and Intent' of Treaties — Abandoning Treaty Rights*, February 1, 1996, unpublished report in Union of British Columbia Indian Chiefs (UBCIC) Vertical file: British Columbia Treaty process, 10.

38. Wolverine, quoted in "One Does Not Sell the Earth upon Which the People Walk: Against the Treaty Process," unsigned and undated pamphlet in UBCIC Vertical file: British Columbia Treaty process.

39. British Columbia Treaty Commission, "What Is a First Nation?" in *Annual Report* (Vancouver, B.C.: Treaty Commission, 1998).

40. British Columbia, *Treaty Commission Act* (1993), S.1(1).

41. British Columbia Treaty Commission, "Strengthening First Nations for Treaty Purposes," 6.

42. British Columbia Treaty Commission, "Treaty Commission Releases Report on Suspension of Gitxsan Negotiations," *Treaty Update* (April 1996), available online at http://www.bctreaty.net/files/pdf_documents/update_april-1996.pdf.

43. Ibid.

44. Kent McNeil, *The Onus of Proof of Aboriginal Title*, Delgamuukw / Gisday'wa National Process, 1999, 26, available online at http://www.delgamuuk w.org/research/onus.pdf (accessed November 12, 2001).

45. *The Delgamuuk'w / Gisday'wa National Process: Questions and Answers* 2000, 1, available online at http://www.delgamuukw.org/news/qa.pdf (accessed November 12, 2001).

46. First Nations Summit, Union of British Columbia Indian Chiefs and Interior Alliance, "Consensus Statement," January 29, 2000, reproduced in *Interior Alliance News* (July 2000): 10.

47. Interview with Rick Krehbiel, treaty analyst, Lheidli T'enneh First Nation, August 26, 2000.

48. Interview with Bernard Schulmann, treaty analyst, Pavilion Band, August 23, 2000.

49. De Costa, "New Relationships, Old Certainties," 205–6.

50. British Columbia Ministry of Aboriginal Affairs, *Advisory Committees*, 1996, available online at http://www.aaf.gov.bc.ca/aaf/treaty/process/comitees .htm#RACs (accessed November 12, 2000).

51. British Columbia Ministry of Aboriginal Affairs, "Union of British Columbia Municipalities Memorandum of Understanding," Victoria, B.C., 1993.

52. Eric Denhoff, chief treaty negotiator, Canada, in *Making Treaties in B.C.* (1998), directed by Richard Hersley, Motion Visual Productions, Vancouver, B.C.

53. Bruce Nelson, Pinantan-Pemberton Stock Association Land Claim Committee, Canada, *Proceedings of the Standing Senate Committee on Aboriginal Peoples*, March 21, 2000.

54. Dianne Rinehart, "Court Challenges of Nisga'a Treaty Faces Delays," *Vancouver Sun*, February 6, 1999.

55. Cited in Chris Wood, "History in the Making," *Maclean's*, July 27, 1998, 12–13.

56. British Columbia and Yukon Chamber of Mines, *An Informal Guide to Understanding First Nations and the Treaty-Making Process*, 1999, available online at http://www.bc-mining-house.com/aborig/Fn_guide.htm (accessed February 12, 2001).

57. COFI spokesperson Marlie Beets, quoted in Stewart Bell, "Fragile Détente on Land Claims Fades Away," *Vancouver Sun*, June 27, 1998.

58. Beets, quoted in Drew Hasselbank, "Aboriginal Title Fight," *Financial Post*, June 27, 1998, 16.

59. COFI press release, quoted in "Forest Industry Worried about Nisga'a Deal," *Canadian Press Newswire*, November 12, 1998.

60. Lampert, quoted in Justine Hunter, "Testy Exchange Reveals Tensions," *Vancouver Sun*, May 28, 1999.

61. Gordon Wilson, British Columbia Legislative Assembly, *Hansard*, May 19, 1993, available online at http://www.leg.bc.ca/hansard/35th2nd/ho519pm.htm.

62. Gordon Campbell speaking on December 18, 1999, quoted to Standing Senate Committee on Aboriginal Peoples: Evidence Hearings into Bill C51, Ottawa, February 23, 2000.

63. CBC Radio, Regional News, March 8, 2001.

64. British Columbia Ministry of Aboriginal Affairs, "Instructions to Negotiators," Victoria, B.C., 2002.

65. Elections British Columbia, *Referendum Final Results*, 2002, available online at http://www.elections.bc.ca/referendum/finalresults.pdf (accessed March 19, 2003).

66. Canada, Minister of Public Works and Government Services, "The Government of Canada's Approach to Implementation of the Inherent Right and the Negotiation of Aboriginal Self-Government," Ottawa, 1995.

67. *Campbell et al. v. Attorney-General of British Columbia/Attorney-General of Canada & Nisga'a Nation et al.*, [2000] British Columbia Supreme Court 1123.

68. Elections BC, Report of the Chief Electoral Officer on the Treaty Negotiations Referendum, emphasis added, p.2, available online at http://www.elections .bc.ca/referendum/refreportfinal.pdf.

69. See, for example, Lheidli T'enneh Agreement-in-Principle, July 2003, available online at http://www.bctreaty.net/nations/agreements/LheidliAiPJuly03.pdf (accessed March 19, 2003).

70. John Borrows, "Contemporary Traditional Equality: The Effect of the Charter on First Nations Politics," in *Charting the Consequences: The Impact of Char-*

ter Rights on Canadian Law and Politics, edited by David Schneiderman, Kate Sutherland, and University of Alberta Centre for Constitutional Studies (Toronto: University of Toronto Press, 1997), 169–99.

71. Gerald R. Alfred, *Peace, Power, Righteousness: An Indigenous Manifesto* (Don Mills, Ontario: Oxford University Press, 1999), 140.

72. De Costa, "New Relationships, Old Certainties," 279–89.

73. Ibid., 27–165.

74. Gary Mason, "Will Public Buy Treaties That Change B.C.'s Face?" *Globe and Mail*, December 9, 2006, A1.

75. Michael Asch, "Self-Determination and Treaty-Making: Consent and the Resolution of Political Relations between First Nations and Canada," paper presented at the Consortium on Democratic Constitutionalism: Consent as the Foundation for Political Community, University of Victoria, British Columbia, 1–3 October 2004.

11 Treaty Substitutes in the Modern Era

Robert T. Anderson

lthough the U.S. Congress prohibited treaties with Indians after
1871, there are significant parallels between treaty negotiations
prior to that ban and modern Indian tribes' negotiations with
the federal government regarding land and natural resource claims. The
power balance in both cases has been such that the Indian tribes have
had to concede that the United States can unilaterally determine most
issues about which it will negotiate. In no case has the government been
willing to put its ultimate sovereignty within U.S. borders at issue, and
certain rights that tribes may wish to obtain or reaffirm have been off
limits as a practical matter.

People familiar with Indian policy in the United States sometimes
assume that the doctrine of discovery—the claim that European nations
acquired title to American land they "discovered," leaving indigenous
inhabitants with a mere right of occupancy—is a relic of the past, along
with the corresponding colonial mind-set. On the one hand, since the
dawn of the current self-determination policy era in the mid-1960s, the
property rights of Indian tribes do seem to be held in higher legal and
moral regard than during earlier times. On the other hand, in recent
years when the Supreme Court and Congress have faced fresh issues
regarding aboriginal property rights, both bodies have returned to
approaches that have more in common with the proponents of manifest

321

destiny than the professed self-determination policy. Although current federal policy in support of tribal self-determination has undoubted benefits for the tribes, it is the federal government that defines the outer bounds of tribal sovereignty and dictates those outer bounds in much the same fashion as in the nineteenth century.

The early treaty period in the United States was marked by the use of diplomatic language reflecting tribal governmental status approaching that of nations under rules of international law.[1] At the same time there is little doubt that the U.S. government usually held the upper hand in the negotiations, and the tribes had little choice but to participate and achieve the best bargains they could. By the third decade of the 1800s the expansion of the non-Indian population, the growth in U.S. military prowess, and the retreat of the British as a competitor resulted in treaty terms that were increasingly one-sided. There were calls for the end of treaty making as early as the presidency of Andrew Jackson,[2] and federal policy generally reflected the notion that Indian lands would be acquired whether the tribes wanted to surrender their homelands or not. For example, Congress in 1850 authorized the president "to appoint one or more commissioners to negotiate treaties with the several Indian tribes in the Territory of Oregon, for the extinguishment of their claims to lands lying west of the Cascade Mountains; and if found expedient and practicable, for their removal east of said mountains."[3]

After Washington Territory was created from the northern portion of Oregon Territory in 1853, this mission fell in part to the new territory's governor, Isaac Stevens, whose biographer concluded that he "ran the treaty cessions as if he were a judge in a court of law. Though all had the opportunity to speak, to ask questions, and to demand explanations, and though there was room for minor modifications in the treaty drafts, the end result of the councils was inevitable."[4] The inevitable result was the cession of vast tribal territory to the United States in exchange for various payments, services, and the retention of smaller reservations. The tribes did obtain meaningful concessions from the United States in treaty negotiations, such as the right to fish at usual and accustomed stations, but the exchange of value was notoriously one-sided.[5]

Although formal treaty making in the United States ended in 1871, the U.S. government continued bilateral negotiations with Indian tribes over matters of mutual concern. But many of the "permanent" homelands promised in treaties prior to 1871 were substantially reduced in size when non-Indian settlers sought land previously guaranteed by treaty. The federal government accelerated its efforts to shrink the Indian land base through agreements that went to both houses of Congress for ratification.[6] Thus, although the United States in the Fort Laramie Treaty of 1868 promised to protect the Black Hills of the Dakota Territory for the Great Sioux Nation, the discovery of gold prompted a quick reversal and the taking of most of that land for non-Indian exploitation by an "agreement" that Indians signed under duress in 1876.[7] An early twentieth-century historian reviewed the situation: "As will be readily understood, the making of a treaty was a forced put, so far as the Indians were concerned. Defeated, disarmed, dismounted, they were at the mercy of a superior power and there was no alternative but to accept the conditions imposed upon them."[8] Indians frequently complained of fraud on the part of the United States in the negotiation or implementation of treaties,[9] but tribes with such complaints were left to appeal to an unresponsive Congress.[10] Through this process and supplementary federal legislation such as the General Allotment Act of 1887, the Indian land base was reduced from 156 million acres in 1881 to approximately 48 million acres in 1934.[11]

A major shift in federal policy occurred with the passage of the Indian Reorganization Act in 1934. That statute precluded the further allotment of communal reservation lands and provided permanent protection for allotments and tribal property from any form of involuntary loss.[12] It also marked a corresponding shift toward the support of tribal governmental institutions and their authority to exercise jurisdiction over members and territory.[13] The termination era of the 1950s was a brief interlude in which these pro-tribal policies were suspended and several tribes suffered disastrous consequences when their relationship with the federal government was severed.[14] But President Richard Nixon's announcement of the policy of self-determination marked a return to policies protective of the tribal land base and Indian sovereignty.[15] At a time of pro-tribal shifts in Congress and the executive branch, the courts also looked more favorably on tribal rights in some areas. Thus in 1980 the Supreme Court rejected the political question doctrine, which had allowed fraud by the United States in land dealings to escape judicial review. In a ruling challenging the federal government's expropriation of the Black Hills, the Court held that the United States must pay compensation when it takes recognized Indian title to land or water and that courts may not defer to congressional judgments of whether a "taking" has occurred.[16]

Those advances in federal policy have been qualified, however, by a number of other decisions restricting tribal jurisdiction over nonmembers in the criminal and civil contexts.[17] The Supreme Court's rejection of tribal regulatory power over non-Indians has been complemented by modern land claim settlements that restrict tribal powers to relatively small land areas and often subject tribes to some state authority. The settlements of modern Indian land claims, which are the closest contemporary analog to Indian treaties in the United States, have reflected continuing federal domination of negotiations. There remains essentially no chance for tribes to retain all aboriginal lands, and it is commonplace that land conveyed to non-Indians in violation of federal law will at best be only partially restored to tribal ownership. Thus, in the case of unextinguished aboriginal title to Alaska, the question was not whether the claims would be extinguished by Congress, but how much compensation would be awarded.[18] Likewise, in the case of the Maine Indian Land Settlement Act of 1980, invalid sales of Indian land to the state were certain to be ratified by Congress, with the amount of compensation the foremost question.[19] Settlements in Rhode Island, Connecticut, Massachusetts, and South Carolina share the pattern of extinguishing substantial tribal land claims in exchange for relatively small land areas.[20]

While some of the foregoing settlements have been criticized for tribal capitulation to state jurisdiction, more recent events indicate that the alternative of continued litigation in hope of substantial land recovery or large damage awards could have had worse consequences. For example, the land claims in upstate New York have not been settled despite nearly forty years of litigation, and once promising possible outcomes for the tribes in the courts now appear in doubt. In 1985 the Supreme Court ruled that Indian tribes whose lands had been sold in violation of federal law could sue for damages and recovery of the land.[21] However, in 2004 the Court held that land reacquired by the Oneida Indian Nation in its reservation claim area was subject to state taxation.[22] A federal appeals court quickly extended the Supreme Court's reasoning and rejected tribal claims for damages for non-Indian trespass on the ground that too much time had passed since the initial wrong.[23]

A brief examination of the Alaska land claims settlement and a recent

Indian water rights settlement reveals that, as in treaty times, indigenous groups are forced to negotiate in forums chosen by the colonizing nation and on terms that are implicitly or explicitly dictated. This is not to say that the outcomes were completely unjust. Rather, Native tribes end up with what the dominant society is willing to surrender instead of what the tribes might prefer. In that sense little has changed since the nineteenth century.

THE ALASKA NATIVE CLAIMS SETTLEMENT ACT: A SETTLEMENT IN THE TREATY TRADITION?

Although Alaska Natives were long neglected by the U.S. government, it is now well settled that they have the same legal status as Indian tribes in the lower forty-eight states.[24] The *Tee-Hit-Ton* case of 1955, in which the Supreme Court ruled that Alaska Native aboriginal title was not protected by the Constitution's prohibition on taking without the payment of just compensation, set a precedent applicable to tribes throughout the United States.[25] Despite that holding, the Alaska Statehood Act (passed in 1958) required the state to renounce any interest in lands claimed by Alaska Natives.[26] However, the act inconsistently granted the State of Alaska the right to select 102.5 million acres for its own use from "vacant, unappropriated, and unreserved" public lands. As the new state began to select lands, Native villages protested to the Secretary of the Interior, and on January 12, 1969, Secretary Stewart Udall imposed a freeze on further patenting or approval of applications for public lands in Alaska pending the settlement of Native claims.[27] Momentum for the extinguishment of aboriginal claims increased,[28] because oil development in northern Alaska could not occur so long as Native claims precluded the issuance of permits to construct the Trans-Alaska Pipeline, which was necessary to transport the oil.[29]

Although Natives would have some say in the terms of the settlement, they would not have a veto. As such, the situation differed little from the agreements dictated by the United States in the latter years of the treaty-making era and continuing through the late nineteenth and early twentieth centuries. Aboriginal claims would be settled, and the questions of how much land and money would be provided in compensation for the extinguishment would be decided by Congress, not Alaska Natives.[30] Furthermore, rather than taking the usual course of vesting existing tribal governments with the assets reserved after extinguishment of the aboriginal claims, Congress adopted an experimental model initially calculated to promote the speedy assimilation of Alaska Natives into corporate America.[31]

The Alaska Native Claims Settlement Act (ANCSA) of 1971 extinguished aboriginal title and also expressly extinguished "any aboriginal hunting and fishing rights that may exist."[32] In exchange, Alaska Natives alive on December 18, 1971, were permitted to enroll and be issued stock in one of thirteen regional corporations and in one of more than two hundred village corporations, according to their place of residence or origin.[33] Those corporations as a group were entitled to receive approximately 40 million acres of land and nearly a billion dollars.[34] In addition, Congress indicated its intent that there be some protection of Native hunting and fishing rights. While the Senate and the House could not agree on the means, the conference report expressed the conviction that "Native peoples' interest in and use of subsistence resources" could be safeguarded by the Interior secretary's "exercise of his existing withdrawal authority" to "protect Native subsistence needs and requirements; . . . The Conference Committee expects both the Secretary and the State to take any action necessary to protect the subsistence needs of the Natives."[35] Nothing other than this was done to provide generally for Native hunting and fishing rights, except to specify a subsistence preference for all rural residents of Alaska in 1980, after it became clear that the state and federal governments were doing little to provide for Native hunting and fishing rights.[36]

ANCSA did not even mention the governmental powers exercised by Native tribes in Alaska, so many assumed that those powers continued to exist, as would normally be the case under federal law. The inherent powers of self-governance over members and territory had been acknowledged in a number of ways,[37] and there is no evidence that Congress intended to extinguish them. The general rule is that when Congress determines to extinguish tribal property rights or governmental power, it must do so expressly.[38] Why was ANCSA silent on such a critical matter? The remote locations of Native villages and the relative lack of non-Native encroachment best explain the lack of concern for expressly securing rights of self-government. As a prominent Native leader involved in the negotiations explained:

Our focus was on land. Land was our future, our survival. In my region all we wanted was to get control of our space so we could live on it and hunt and fish on it and make our own way into the twentieth century at our own pace. Our focus was on land not structure. The vehicle for administering the land was not our focus. We weren't lawyers. We were battling the state tooth and tong. We were always afraid the President might create a pipeline corridor. We were afraid of failure, or not getting a settlement and not protecting the land for our future generations. As a minority group we knew we could only press the country so far. But none of us ever envisioned a loss of tribal structure. We never thought the tribal control would not continue.[39]

The matter is still not finally settled, but the United States Supreme Court dealt a major blow to the scope of tribal powers in Alaska when it ruled in *Alaska v. Native Village of Venetie* that land conveyed to Native corporations (approximately 40 million acres) pursuant to ANCSA was not "Indian country" and thus not territory subject to tribal jurisdiction under general principles of federal Indian law.[40] The Alaska Supreme Court subsequently ruled that Alaska tribes continue to have power over their members and others who consent to their jurisdiction notwithstanding the *Venetie* decision,[41] but that is small consolation following the loss of jurisdiction over a territory the size of Washington State.

Is ANCSA like a treaty? It is in the sense that a deal was presented to Alaska Natives by federal negotiators—a deal that could be tweaked around the edges and a deal whose provision for land and money distributions to Native people was negotiable to some extent. But there was no doubt that there would be a "settlement." Like treaties of the nineteenth century, the legislation agreed on accomplished the primary goal of removing indigenous claims to title to vast areas of land in order to facilitate non-Native settlement and resource extraction. In place of the backdrop of the military threat of the nineteenth century, there was the legal certainty (due to the *Tee-Hit-Ton* ruling) that aboriginal title could be eliminated unilaterally and without any compensation. And as in the treaty era, there were many who thought it right that the Natives be provided fair compensation, but the definition of "fair' would be largely dictated by the federal government with no realistic opportunity for Alaska Natives to insist otherwise.

The Nez Perce Tribe negotiated treaties and agreements with the United States throughout the second half of the nineteenth century, but one of the tribe's most important assets—water—was not dealt with in any formal and final way until the twenty-first century. After years of neglect the Nez Perce found themselves involved in a massive struggle over control of water needed by the tribe to protect their fishing rights. Encouraged and subsidized by the federal government, non-Indians had developed massive irrigation projects for out-of-stream water uses. The non-Indians fiercely resisted any change in the status quo. In the end the Nez Perce ended up with a substantial water right and other compensation, but they were forced to abandon their quest to substantially limit existing non-Indian out-of-stream uses. As in the nineteenth century, this was due in large part to the fact that U.S. law set out restrictive rules and a negotiation platform tilted in favor of non-Indian interests.

At the time of its initial treaty with the United States in 1855, the Nez Perce Tribe controlled an aboriginal territory of over 13 million acres in what is now Idaho, eastern Washington, and Oregon.[42] The 1855 treaty negotiated by Isaac Stevens established a "permanent" 7-million-acre reservation and promised that the tribe would retain the right to fish at all usual and accustomed stations outside of reservation boundaries.[43] Another treaty in 1863 reduced the original reservation to 700,000 acres.[44] By 2006 allotment of the reservation and measures to implement allotment had further diminished tribal and individual Indian land holdings to fewer than 100,000 acres. The 1863 treaty with the Nez Perce expressly guaranteed tribal rights to springs and fountains for tribal use and left the fishing provisions of the 1855 treaty intact.[45] Aside from the springs and fountains language, no further mention of water is found, although water would obviously be necessary to maintain tribal fisheries and sustain the Nez Perce. Nearly all Indian treaties fail to mention water explicitly, and yet the Supreme Court determined early on that when Indian reservations were set aside, they often included reservations of water.

The central case involving Indian reserved water rights is *Winters v. United States*.[46] In *Winters* the U.S. Supreme Court construed a congressionally ratified agreement between the Indians of the Fort Belknap

Reservation and the United States.[47] In the agreement the Gros Ventre and Assiniboine Bands of Indians surrendered most of their larger reservation and retained a much smaller reservation adjacent to the Milk River in Montana.[48] Non-Indians who had settled upstream of the reservation claimed paramount rights to use water from the Milk River based on the prior appropriation doctrine.[49] For the Indians to grow crops as contemplated by the agreement creating the reservation, they would need water being used by the non-Indians. The Supreme Court ruled that the federal government had the power to exempt waters from appropriation under state water law,[50] and that the United States and the Indians intended to reserve the waters of the Milk River to fulfill the purposes of the agreement between the Indians and the United States.[51] The Court stated that "ambiguities occurring will be resolved from the standpoint of the Indians. And the rule should certainly be applied to determine between two inferences, one of which would support the purpose of the agreement and the other impair or defeat it."[52]

Unfortunately for the tribes, the victory in the *Winters* case was not accompanied by federal action to protect tribal water rights. Instead, the federal government expended vast resources developing water projects for non-Indian use.[53] The National Water Commission in 1973 concluded that "in the history of the United States Government's treatment of Indian tribes, its failure to protect Indian water rights for use on the reservations it set aside for them is one of the sorrier chapters."[54] The commission also recognized the United States' trust responsibility to tribes with respect to water.[55] However, the hard fact is that non-Indian development resulted in much of the water in the West being put to out-of-stream uses pursuant to state law, such that the modern assertion of senior Indian rights has been fiercely resisted.

The *Winters* case is strong precedent for tribal reserved water rights, but those rights have been effectively weakened by the fact that Congress has permitted litigation over Indian water rights, unlike nearly all other disputes involving Indian rights, to be forced into state courts[56]— forums traditionally hostile to Indian tribes.[57] Tribes strenuously opposed the litigation of their rights in state courts, but the Supreme Court ruled that the McCarran Amendment—an act of Congress in 1952—provides for state court jurisdiction despite tribal objections, and it may occur without tribal participation.[58] In effect, Congress has derogated tribal rights by forcing tribes to litigate in forums hostile to tribal interests.[59] At the same time the federal executive branch is charged as a trustee with advancing Indian water rights as trustee.[60]

In 1987 the State of Idaho brought a lawsuit to determine the scope of all state water rights, along with federal and tribal reserved water rights, in the Snake River Basin, where Nez Perce aboriginal fishing areas and the Nez Perce Reservation are located.[61] Consistent with historical practice,[62] the U.S. Justice Department took a position firmly supportive of Nez Perce rights to water for in-stream flows to support fisheries on and off the reservation;[63] for on-reservation consumptive uses, including irrigation, domestic, commercial, and industrial uses; and for springs and fountains as guaranteed by the 1863 treaty. In 1998 the state district court hearing the case rejected the reserved right claims for in-stream flows[64] amid allegations that the trial judge had a conflict of interest.[65] The tribe's choice at this point was to appeal to the Idaho Supreme Court, which was known for its hostility to federal reserved rights, and/or to pursue settlement of its claims. The tribe and the United States pursued both avenues.[66]

The settlement they reached became federal law in 2004 with passage of the Snake River Water Rights Settlement Act.[67] The act's terms are certainly more favorable to the tribe than the result that would have been achieved in litigation. The tribe ended up with water to satisfy all the claims advanced by it and the United States,[68] but it made a major concession in subordinating all of its in-stream flow claims to existing non-Indian out-of-stream uses.[69] In exchange, the tribe received $22 million for water-delivery systems on the reservation, title to approximately 11,000 acres of land worth up to $7 million, and $60 million to restore fish and wildlife habitat.[70]

The Nez Perce faced a government (the State of Idaho) determined to use the jurisdiction Congress had provided in the McCarran Amendment as a device to define treaty-reserved water rights out of existence, or at least to limit any harmful effect those rights might have on existing state law water uses. By bringing the tribe and its trustee (the United States) into a state court in which a majority of judges were avowed opponents of federal water rights, the state secured an advantageous position from which it could negotiate to protect its interests. Despite the state's home-field advantage, however, the Nez Perce and the United States were able to use leverage afforded by the Endangered Species Act to obtain concessions on the water rights front. In short, since the federal government's regulatory power to protect salmon habitat under the Endangered Species Act threatened to disrupt water deliveries in much of Idaho, the state and powerful irrigation interests agreed to a settlement that accommodated the tribe's interests as well as non-Indian interests.[71] Although Congress in the 1950s had tilted the playing field against the tribe through the McCarran Amendment, the Justice Department and federal regulatory agencies (the departments of Interior and Commerce) were allied with the tribe and, at the tribe's urging, used their authority to advance a favorable settlement.

The funding and return of land certainly could not have been achieved outside of the settlement context. But as in the case of the Alaska land claims, successfully asserting senior reserved water rights to provide for treaty fisheries was not a realistic option.[72] The McCarran Amendment forced the tribe into a hostile forum for judicial determination of their water rights and foreclosed the tribe's preferred option—recognition of substantial senior reserved water rights. Given the Idaho Supreme Court's apparent bias against rights based on federal law, it would have been foolhardy to proceed to litigate without taking into account the reality of the Idaho courts' bias.[73] Although a review of an Idaho Supreme Court ruling on treaty right claims would have been available in the United States Supreme Court, that court has not been sympathetic to Indian claims in recent years.[74] In these inauspicious circumstances the Nez Perce Tribe managed to negotiate a surprisingly favorable settlement.

MODERN SETTLEMENT PROCESSES AND TREATIES

Tribal claims to unextinguished aboriginal title and reserved water rights are negotiated and litigated in an atmosphere that in many respects resembles the nineteenth-century treaty era. Many policy makers express the desire to deal fairly with the Indians, but as in treaty times it is the federal government that establishes the governing substantive rules and determines the forums for resolution.[75] Tribes generally do not have the option of forcing the government to respect complete tribal claims, although the courts now provide an avenue that was not generally available. But even in court the law is interpreted by judges who look sympathetically at non-Indian possessors of Indian land and water and tend to treat tribal claims with skepticism. Tribes are thus left to negotiate over what constitutes fair compensation for land and water in negotiated settlements. The settlements are presented to Congress for final approval —and possible unilateral modification. Given these significant legal and practical obstacles to achieving their important goals, tribes have done relatively well in both the treaty era of the nineteenth century and in modern negotiations over land, water, and sovereignty.

As shown earlier in this essay, Alaska Natives surrendered their aboriginal lands in a "settlement," but they really had no more choice in determining *whether* to surrender most of their aboriginal lands than the Indian tribes in Washington Territory who were presented with pre-drafted treaties by Governor Isaac Stevens. The fact was that the oil companies, non-Natives, and members of Congress who advanced statehood for Alaska proceeded on the assumption that Native title would be extinguished and the primary matter of debate would be the amount of compensation. It is the familiar tale of superior numbers and power accompanied by the sense of manifest destiny that drove the United States' westward expansion. Natives have achieved much with the proceeds of their settlement: the assets controlled by Native corporations ensure that they will remain among the most important economic forces in Alaska. Nevertheless, they had no real choice in the matter of whether to settle.

U.S. law and government practices have similarly forced tribes to make their claims to water in circumstances that give their adversaries the advantage. For years non-Indians dealt with Indian water rights and associated obstacles for development by simply ignoring the reserved rights doctrine and using water meant for Indians in massive reclamation projects. As awareness of the potential cloud on non-Indian water use grew, Congress (aided by the Supreme Court's generous interpretation of the McCarran Amendment) provided state courts with jurisdiction to determine the existence and scope of tribal water rights, to the decided disadvantage of tribes. Against these odds the Nez Perce turned an all-but-certain loss in state court into a settlement that provides great benefit to current and future tribal members and will allow substantial progress to be made in habitat restoration and thus advance treaty rights. Many other tribes have done the same in other water rights settlements. The tribes in nearly all modern settlements were compelled to accept less water than their legal entitlement under the *Winters* doctrine due to the fact that Congress authorized generally hostile state forums to adjudicate the tribal claims. However, the tribes have been very resourceful in obtaining other assets in exchange for the diminished quantities of water.

As in treaty times, tribes generally have no choice but to negotiate when summoned to the negotiation table over land claims and water rights. Furthermore, the federal government and states hold most of the political power and thus the negotiating edge. In a change from earlier times, however, the United States generally adheres to the notion that it must deal fairly with the tribes and acknowledges officially that the tribes are here to stay as sovereigns within the United States. Unlike treaty times, the federal courts have sometimes played a favorable role in shaping positive resolution of Indian land and water claims, and the federal government sometimes supports the tribes in litigation. Tribes are now assisted by their own lawyers (many of whom are Indians), and tribal leaders are skilled in the use of a wide variety of negotiation strategies. Tribes also have financial resources not previously available to influence public opinion and thus assure that Congress hears their views. But at the end of the day the tribes' subordinate position under U.S. law drastically diminishes their status at the negotiating table, just as they were disadvantaged in the treaty era.

NOTES

1. Felix S. Cohen, *Handbook of Federal Indian Law* (Washington, D.C.: Government Printing Office, 1942), 39. ("Until the last decade of the treaty-making period, terms familiar to modern international diplomacy were used in the Indian treaties" and "many provisions show the international status of the Indian tribes, through clauses relating to war, boundaries, passports, extradition, and foreign relations.") See also Robert A. Williams Jr., *Linking Arms Together: American Indian Treaty Visions of Law and Peace, 1600–1800* (New York: Oxford University Press, 1997).

2. See Nell Jessup Newton, Robert T. Anderson, Carole E. Goldberg, John P. LaVelle, Judith V. Royster, Joseph William Singer, Rennard Strickland, *Cohen's Handbook of Federal Indian Law* (Newark, N.J.: LexisNexis, 2005), 74–75.

3. Act of June 5, 1850, 9 Stat. 437.

4. Kent D. Richards, *Isaac I. Stevens, Young Man in a Hurry* (Provo, Utah: Brigham Young University Press, 1979), 206.

5. Charles F. Wilkinson, *Messages from Frank's Landing: A Story of Salmon, Treaties, and the Indian Way* (Seattle: University of Washington Press, 2000), 11, 14; and Francis Paul Prucha, *The Great Father: The United States Government and the American Indians*, abridged ed. (Norman: University of Oklahoma Press, 1986), 134.

6. Typical of such agreements is that recounted in *Winters v. United States,* 207 U.S. 564 (1908), which resulted in the creation of several smaller reservations for tribes that previously held the entire northern half of Montana. John Shurts, *Indian Reserved Water Rights: The Winters Doctrine in Its Social and Legal Context, 1880s–1930s* (Norman: University of Oklahoma Press 2000), 17–19. The Court in *Winters* established the rule that the establishment of an Indian reservation carries with it an implied reservation of water to fulfill the purposes of the reservation. The Court arrived at the rule in part by deploying interpretive rules that took into account the disparities in negotiating position. "By a rule of interpretation of agreements and treaties with the Indians, ambiguities occurring will be resolved from the standpoint of the Indians." Ibid., 576. See Newton et al., *Cohen's Handbook of Federal Indian Law,* 119–22.

7. The agreement was ratified by Congress in 1877. Act of February 28, 1877, 19 Stat. 254. See *United States v. Sioux Nation,* 448 U.S. 371, 377–78 (1980) (describing negotiations).

8. Doane Robinson, *A History of the Dakota or Sioux Indians* 442 (News Printing Co. Aberdeen, 1904).

9. See Francis Paul Prucha, *American Indian Treaties: The History of a Political Anomaly* (Berkeley: University of California Press, 1994), 173–74.

10. *Lone Wolf v. Hitchcock,* 187 U.S. 553 (1903); and Newton et al., *Cohen's Handbook of Federal Indian Law,* 413–14.

11. Newton et al., *Cohen's Handbook of Federal Indian Law,* 79.

12. Ibid., 1009–10.

13. Charles F. Wilkinson, *American Indians, Time, and the Law* (New Haven, Conn.: Yale University Press, 1987), 21.

14. Newton et al., *Cohen's Handbook of Federal Indian Law,* 95–96. As discussed below, proponents of this policy remained in Congress and had tremendous influence on the structure of the Alaska Native Claims Settlement Act.

15. Richard Nixon, Special Message to Congress, July 8, 1970, in *Public Papers of the President of the United States* (Washington, D.C.: Government Printing Office, 1970), 564. In a dramatic move, Nixon included language in his speech that also facilitated the return of sacred lands surrounding Blue Lake to the Taos Pueblo. Charles F. Wilkinson, *Blood Struggle: The Rise of Modern Indian Nations* (New York: W.W. Norton and Company, 2005), 214–16.

16. *United States v. Sioux Nation,* 448 U.S. 371 (1980).

17. *Oliphant v. Suquamish Tribe,* 435 U.S. 191 (1978); *Atkinson Trading Co. v. Shirley,* 532 U.S. 645 (2001). For a discussion of the Supreme Court's decisions in this area, see Newton et al., *Cohen's Handbook of Federal Indian Law,* 224–37.

18. See 43 *U.S. Code* 1601–23.

19. Wilkinson, *Blood Struggle,* 220–31. See 25 *U.S. Code* 1721–1735 (Maine Indian Claims Settlement).

20. See 25 *U.S. Code* 1701–1715 (Narragansett, Rhode Island); 25 *U.S. Code* 1751–1760 (Masantucket Pequots, Connecticut); 25 *U.S. Code* 1775–1775h

(Mohegan, Connecticut). 25 *U.S. Code* 1771–1771i (Gay Head, Massachusetts); and 25 *U.S. Code* 941–941n (Catawba, South Carolina).

21. *County of Oneida v. Oneida Indian Nation*, 470 U.S. 226 (1985).

22. *City of Sherrill v. Oneida Indian Nation*, 544 U.S. 197 (2005).

23. *Cayuga Indian Nation v. Pataki*, 413 F.3d 266 (2d Cir. 2005). See Sarah Krakoff, "City of Sherrill v. Oneida Indian Nation: A Regretful Postscript to the Taxation Chapter in Cohen's Handbook of Federal Indian Law," 41 *Tulsa Law Review* 5, 11 (2005).

24. Newton et al., *Cohen's Handbook of Federal Indian Law*, 336.

25. *Tee-Hit-Ton Indians v. United States*, 348 U.S. 272 (1955). Although the case arose in Alaska, the no-compensation rule was broadly stated and applies generally in the United States. For discussion and criticism of the decision, see Philip P. Frickey, "Domesticating Federal Indian Law," 81 *Minnesota Law Review* 31 (1996): 80–87.

26. Act of July 7, 1958, Public Law No. 85-508, section 4, 72 Stat. 339.

27. Public Land Order 4582, 34 *Federal Register* 1025 (1969). See *Alaska v. Udall*, 420 F.2d 938 (9th Cir. 1969).

28. See Melissa Berry, *The Alaska Pipeline: The Politics of Oil and Native Land Claims* (Bloomington: Indiana University Press, 1975), 123, 163–214; and Donald Craig Mitchell, *Take My Land Take My Life* (Fairbanks: University of Alaska Press, 2001).

29. See Robert D. Arnold, *Alaska Native Land Claims* (Anchorage: Alaska Native Foundation,1978), 137–47; and *Native Village of Allakaket v. Hickel*, No. 706–70 (D.D.C., April 1, 1971) (enjoining construction of trans-Alaska pipeline over Native-claimed lands).

30. Wilkinson, *Blood Struggle*, 234–35. For a review of the events leading to Alaska Statehood and the Native Claims Settlement Act, see Robert T. Anderson, "Alaska Native Rights, Statehood, and Unfinished Business," 43 *Tulsa Law Review* 17 (2007).

31. 43 *U.S. Code* 1606, 1607, and 1613. See, generally, Arnold, *Alaska Native Land Claims*; Douglas M. Branson, "Square Pegs in Round Holes: Alaska Native Claims Settlement Corporations under Corporate Law," 8 *UCLA–Alaska Law Review* 103 (1979); Arthur Lazarus and Richard West, "The Alaska Native Claims Settlement Act: A Flawed Victory," *Law and Contemporary Problems* 40 (1976): 132; and Monroe Price, "Region-Village Relations under the Alaska Native Claims Settlement Act," 5 *UCLA–Alaska Law Review* 58 (1975): 237.

32. 43 *U.S. Code* 1603(b).

33. 43 *U.S. Code* 1606-7.

34. Newton et al., *Cohen's Handbook of Federal Indian Law*, 340.

35. H. Conf. Rep. No. 92-746, at 37 (1971), reprinted in 1971 *U.S. Code Congressional & Administrative News*, 2247.

36. Newton et al., *Cohen's Handbook of Federal Indian Law*, 354–60.

37. See Aboriginal Fishing Rights in Alaska, Op. M-31634, 57 Interior Dec.

461, 474 (February 13, 1942); Custom Marriages, 54 Interior Dec. 39 (September 3, 1932); 25 *U.S. Code* 473a (application of the IRA to Alaska); *In re McCord*, 151 *Federal Supplement* (F. Supp.) 132 (D. Alaska Terr. 1957); and 18 *U.S. Code* 1162 (application of Public Law 280 to Alaska).

38. Newton et al., *Cohen's Handbook of Federal Indian Law*, 120 ("Tribal property rights and sovereignty are preserved unless Congress's intent to the contrary is clear and unambiguous.").

39. Wilkinson, *Blood Struggle*, 238–39 (quoting Willie Hensley). See also Imre Sutton, *Irredeemable America: The Indians' Estate and Land Claims* (Albuquerque: University of New Mexico Press, 1985), 306–16.

40. *Alaska v. Native Village of Venetie*, 522 U.S. 520 (1998). See Newton et al., *Cohen's Handbook of Federal Indian Law*, 362–63.

41. *John v. Baker*, 982 P.2d 738 (Alaska 1999).

42. *United States v. Webb*, 219 F.3d 1127, 1130 (9th Cir. 2000). See also William C. Sturtevant, ed., *Handbook of North American Indians*, vol. 12, *Plateau* (Washington, D.C.: Smithsonian Institution, 1998), 420–21.

43. Treaty with the Nez Perce, 12 Stat. 957, art. 3 (1855).

44. *United States v. Webb*, 219 F.3d 1127, 1130 (9th Cir. 2000).

45. Treaty with the Nez Perce, 14 Stat. 647, art. 8 (1863).

46. *Winters v. United States*, 207 U.S. 564 (1908).

47. Act of May 1, 1888, chap. 213, 25 Stat. 113 (1889).

48. Act of April 15, 1874, chap. 96, 18 Stat. 28.

49. All of the western states in the continental United States follow some form of the prior appropriation doctrine: "Under that doctrine, one acquires a right to water by diverting it from its natural source and applying it to some beneficial use. Continued beneficial use of the water is required in order to maintain the right. In periods of shortage, priority among confirmed rights is determined according to the date of initial diversion." *Colorado River Water Conservation District. v. United States*, 424 U.S. 800, 805 (1976) (footnote omitted). See, generally, Robert E. Beck, *Waters and Water Rights* (New York: LexisNexis, 2001, rep. ed.), section 12.02.

50. "The power of the government to reserve the waters and exempt them from appropriation under the state laws is not denied, and could not be." *Winters v. United States*, 207 U.S. at 577, citing *United States v. Rio Grande Dam & Irrigation Company*, 174 U.S. 702 (1899); *United States v. Winans*, 198 U.S. 371 (1905).

51. *Winters v. United States*, 207 U.S. at 576–77.

52. Ibid.

53. See Charles F. Wilkinson, *Crossing the Next Meridian: Land, Water, and the Future of the West* (Washington, D.C.: Island Press, 1992), 258–59.

54. National Water Commission, *Water Policies for the Future — Final Report to the President and the Congress of the United States* (Washington, D.C.: Government Printing Office, 1973), 475; and Daniel C. McCool, *Native Waters* (Tucson: University of Arizona Press, 2002), 36, stating that "the Bureau of Reclamation operates 348 reservoirs that provide water for ten million acres of farmland and 31 million people. . . . But the BIA has never finished an irrigation project."

55. National Water Commission, *Water Policies for the Future*, 477–79.

56. 43 *U.S. Code* 666.

57. Newton et al., *Cohen's Handbook of Federal Indian Law*, 1205–10.

58. *Arizona v. San Carlos Apache Tribe*, 463 U.S. 545 (1983).

59. Newton et al., *Cohen's Handbook of Federal Indian Law*, 1209–10. Some state courts, however, purport to be protective of tribal water rights. See Barbara A. Cosens, "The Measure of Indian Water Rights: The Arizona Homeland Standard, Gila River Adjudication," 42 *Natural Resources Journal* 835 (2002).

60. For a discussion of the federal government's institutional conflicts of interests, see Ann C. Juliano, "Conflicted Justice: The Department of Justice's Conflict of Interest in Representing Native American Tribes," 37 *Georgia Law Review* 1307 (2003).

61. See *In Re: Snake River Basin Water System (SRBA)*, 764 P.2d 78 (Idaho 1988).

62. See Robert T. Anderson, "Indian Water Rights and the Federal Trust Responsibility," 46 *Natural Resources Journal* 399 (2006): 434.

63. In its Brief to the Idaho Supreme Court on appeal, the Justice Department argued that "federal and state court decisions lead ineluctably to the conclusion that, at a minimum, water rights for fishery purposes were reserved on all streams located within the exterior boundaries of the 1855 [Nez Perce] Reservation and outside of that boundary, for all other streams where there is evidence of Nez Perce 'usual and accustomed' fishing places." *In Re: SRBA*, Case No. 39576, Subcase No. 10022, Brief of Appellant United States at 28 (November 22, 2003).

64. *In Re: SRBA*, Case No. 39576, Consolidated Subcase No. 03-10022 (Idaho Dist. Ct., November 10, 1999). For a critique of the court's analysis, see Michael C. Blumm et al., "Judicial Termination of Treaty Water Rights: The Snake River Case," *Idaho Law Review* 35 (2000): 449, 474–77.

65. Blumm, "Judicial Termination of Treaty Water Rights," 474–77.

66. They also asked the Idaho Supreme Court to set aside the trial court ruling on conflict of interest grounds but were unsuccessful. *United States v. Idaho*, 51 P.3d 1110 (Idaho 2002).

67. Public Law 108-447, 108 Stat. 2809, 3431.

68. K. Heidi Gudgel, Steven C. Moore, and Geoffrey Whiting, "The Nez Perce Tribe's Perspective on the Settlement of Its Water Right Claims in the Snake River Basin Adjudication," 42 *Idaho Law Review* 563 (2006): 589–93.

69. In addition, the instream flow rights are held by the State of Idaho in trust for all people in the state of Idaho. Idaho Code 42-1507, 2005 Idaho Sess. Laws, ch. 150, section 1. Presumably, however, the Nez Perce Tribe would be able to bring an action to enforce the flow regime if it were not being met.

70. Snake River Water Rights Act of 2004, Public Law No. 108-447, sections 8 and 9, 118 Stat. 2809, 3436–38; and Gudgel et al., "The Nez Perce Tribe's Perspective."

71. The components of the settlement dealing with the Endangered Species Act are detailed in the Mediator's Term Sheet and subsequent agreements. See Ann R.

Klee and Duane Mecham, "The Nez Perce Indian Water Right Settlement—Federal Perspective," 42 *Idaho Law Review* 595 (2006): 624–32.

72. This is not to say that the tribe would not have succeeded before an objective court. Indeed, the weight of authority supports their claim. See Blumm, "Judicial Termination of Treaty Water Rights."

73. The Idaho Supreme Court is an elected body, and when the court ruled 3-2 in favor of federal reserved rights for congressionally designated wilderness areas, members of the public mounted a concerted effort to prevent the reelection of Justice Cathy Silak. She was defeated, and Chief Justice Linda Trout then switched her vote to deny the federal reserved rights. See Michael C. Blumm, "Reversing the Winters Doctrine? Denying Reserved Water Rights for Idaho Wilderness and Its Implications," 73 *University of Colorado Law Review* 73 (2002): 173, 186–88 (detailing the political movement to oust Justice Silak based on her vote in the reserved water rights case).

74. See David H. Getches, "Conquering the Cultural Frontier: The New Subjectivism of the Supreme Court in Indian Law," 84 *California Law Review* (1996): 1573, 1640–41.

75. As Professor Getches has noted: "Perhaps Americans have set unreasonably high standards for themselves, but, whatever the reason, their attempts at 'justice' or 'generosity' have fallen short of expectations" (in Sutton, *Irredeemable America,* 303).

Contributors

ROBERT ANDERSON, a member of the Bois Forte Band of Chippewa, is an associate professor and the director of the Native American Law Center at the University of Washington Law School. He has served as counselor to the U.S. secretary of the Interior, associate U.S. solicitor of Indian affairs, and staff attorney of the Native American Rights Fund. He is coauthor and a member of the editorial board of *Cohen's Handbook of Federal Indian Law* (LexisNexis, 2005).

RUSSEL LAWRENCE BARSH has followed the politics of treaties since the 1970s, when he taught American Indian studies at the University of Washington and helped research and revive Mikmaq treaties in Atlantic Canada. For many years, in several capacities, he helped indigenous peoples assert land and treaty claims at the United Nations. He served as a treaty researcher for the Royal Commission on Aboriginal Peoples and as the first senior adviser to Canada's Office of the Treaty Commissioner before returning to his roots in science and the Pacific Northwest as director of KWIAHT, an ecology research laboratory in the San Juan Islands.

JOHN BORROWS is a professor and the Law Foundation Chair of Aboriginal Justice and Governance in the Faculty of Law at the University of

Victoria. He is Anishinabe, a member of the Chippewa of the Nawash Nation. He is the author of *Aboriginal Legal Issues: Cases, Materials, and Commentary* (Butterworths, 1998) and *Recovering Canada: The Resurgence of Indigenous Law* (University of Toronto Press, 2002).

RAVI DE COSTA is interested in comparative and global approaches to understanding the legacies of colonialism and indigenous politics. He completed undergraduate and doctoral degrees in Australia. His Ph.D. dissertation was a comparative study of treaty making in Canada and reconciliation in Australia. He is the author of *A Higher Authority: Indigenous Transnationalism and Australia* (UNSW Press, 2006). He is an assistant professor in the faculty of environmental studies at York University in Toronto.

ANDREW H. FISHER is an assistant professor of history at the College of William and Mary in Virginia. He is the author of several articles on Indians of the Columbia Plateau region. His essay in this volume is adapted from his book *Shadow Tribe: The Making of Columbia River Indian Identity* (University of Washington Press, forthcoming), which examines off-reservation communities and processes of tribal ethnogenesis in the Columbia Basin.

HAMAR FOSTER is a professor in the Faculty of Law at the University of Victoria, where he has taught courses in legal process, property law, criminal law, the law of evidence, legal history, and aboriginal law since 1978. He is coeditor (with John P. S. McLaren) of *Law for the Elephant, Law for the Beaver: Essays in the Legal History of the North American West* (Ninth Judicial Circuit Historical Society and Canadian Plains Research Centre, 1992) and *Essays in the History of Canadian Law, Vol. 6: British Columbia and the Yukon* (The Osgoode Society, 1995). He is also on the faculty of the Akitsiraq law program in Iqaluit, Nunavut.

CHRIS FRIDAY is a professor of history and the director of the Center for Pacific Northwest History at Western Washington University. He has published two books—*Organizing Asian American Labor* (Temple University Press, 1994) and *Leelooska: The Life of a Northwest Coast Artist* (University of Washington Press, 2003). He has also served as an expert historian and witness on behalf of a western Washington tribe, and has published essays on aspects of Asian American and Native American identities as well as issues of race and class in the American West.

ALAN GROVE is a legal historian who lives in Victoria, British Columbia. He is at work on a history of fishing on the Fraser River.

ALEXANDRA (SASHA) HARMON, a graduate of the Yale Law School, advised and represented Indian tribes in Washington State for approximately fifteen years. Wishing to explore questions that arose in her legal work, she subsequently earned a Ph.D. in history at the University of Washington. Since 1995, she has been on the University of Washington faculty in American Indian Studies. She is the author of *Indians in the Making: Ethnic Relations and Indian Identities around Puget Sound* (University of California Press, 1998).

DOUGLAS C. HARRIS is an associate professor in the Faculty of Law at the University of British Columbia, where he teaches and writes in the areas of property law, fisheries law, Aboriginal peoples and the law, and legal history. He is the author of *Fish, Law, and Colonialism: The Legal Capture of Salmon in British Columbia* (University of Toronto Press, 2001) and *Landing Aboriginal Fisheries: Indian Reserves and Fishing Rights in British Columbia, 1849–1925* (UBC Press, forthcoming).

KENT MCNEIL is a distinguished research professor at Osgoode Hall Law School, York University, and a Canada Council Killam Fellow. He is the former research director of the University of Saskatchewan Native Law Centre. He is the author of *Common Law Aboriginal Title* (Oxford University Press, 1989) and *Emerging Justice? Essays on Indigenous Rights in Canada and Australia* (University of Saskatchewan Native Law Centre, 2001).

PAIGE RAIBMON is an associate professor of history at the University of British Columbia. She is the author of *Authentic Indians: Episodes of Encounter from the Late-Nineteenth-Century Northwest Coast* (Duke University Press, 2005) as well as several articles on indigenous peoples and colonialism, indigenous migrations and labor, and public representations of Indians.

ARTHUR J. RAY is a professor emeritus of history at the University of British Columbia, a faculty associate of the Faculty of Law at the University of British Columbia, a fellow in the Royal Society of Canada, and a Senior Canada Council Killam Fellow. He is the author of seven books, including *I Have Lived Here since the World Began: An Illustrated History of Canada's Native People* (1994; reprint, Key Porter Books, 2004); with J. R. Miller and Frank Tough, *Bounty and Benevolence: A History of Saskatchewan Treaties* (McGill-Queen's University Press, 2000); *Indians in the Fur Trade* (1974; reprint, University of Toronto Press, 1998); and more than sixty articles on Native history, the fur trade, and the use of ethnohistorical evidence in aboriginal and treaty-rights cases, including the landmark *Regina v. Powley* (2002), *Delgamuukw v. Regina* (1997), and *Regina v. Horseman* (1990).

BRUCE RIGSBY is emeritus professor of anthropology at the University of Queensland, where he taught from 1975 to 2000. He has done anthropological and linguistic research with the Sahaptin-speaking people of eastern Oregon and Washington since 1963. He coedited (with Nicolas Peterson) and contributed to *Customary Tenure in Australia* (Oceania Monograph 48, 1998) and *Donald Thomson: The Man and Scholar* (Academy of the Social Sciences in Australia, 2005). He received a Centenary Medal in 2003 "for distinguished achievements through anthropology and native title in Australia."

Index

Carey, Charles H., 197
Carlson, Keith, 22
Carr, Don M., 203, 208
Carrier Lumber, Ltd., 303
Carter, Sarah, 286
Cascadia, 60, 102, 107, 109
Catholic Church, 166, 174
Cayuse people, 248, 249, 252, 255, 259, 271
Celestie, Josie, 171
Celilo Falls, 189, 196, 198, 201, 205, 207–8, 259
Celilo Fish Committee (CFC), 208–9
censuses, 224, 303
Charley, Bill, 199
Charley, Olie, 207
Charley, Wasco, 201–2
Charley, White Salmon, 197
Charlottetown Accord (1992), 311
Charter of Rights, Canadian, 147, 313
Cheddar Man, 267n15
Cherokee people, 219
Chinese immigrants, 64, 107, 112, 201; and conflicts with Indians, 69–70
Chinook, William, 194
Chinook jargon, 6, 27n2, 171, 254, 271n47
Chowitsut: personal wealth of, 161, 180n21; and Treaty of Point Elliott, 19, 160–61, 163; and South Saanich treaty, 162–63, 181n27; successors to, 166
Christie, Alexander, 294n21
Church Missionary Society, 107, 125n116
chum. See salmon
Clark, J. W., 62
Clark, William, 256–57
Clarke, John, 207
Clubshelton, Chief, 171
coal, 95, 105, 112, 117n24
Coast Salish people: development of treaty commons, 228–34; and

Douglas treaties, 90, 128, 130; economics and ethnogenesis of, 234–36; and fishing rights, 134, 216, 220–23, 226–27, 234–26; language of, 215, 220, 232, 237n3; redefining of tribes among, 215–16, 223–25, 232, 238n22; society of, 216, 220–25, 228, 235–36. See also Cowichan; Musqueam; Lummi
Cohen, Fay, 146
colonialism: ending of, 298, 304; genealogies of, 56–61, 68–75; Indian role in, 77–78
Columbia River Intertribal Fish Commission, 209
Columbia watershed, 44, 187
"comprehensive claims" process, 302
Confederacy of Indian Tribes of British Columbia, 301
Confederated Tribes of the Colville Reservation, 246, 248–49
Confederated Tribes of the Umatilla Reservation, 188, 245, 255, 259, 264. See also Umatilla
Congress, U.S.: Alaska Native Claims Settlement Act, 324–27; McCarran Amendment, 329–32; property rights, 321–22; and treaties, 164–65, 321
Connolly, William, 123n90
conservation, 129, 131, 134–35, 145–46
Constitution Act (Canada, 1982), 125–26n116, 305
contiguity doctrine, 45
Convention of 1818, 37, 43, 47
Cook, James, 43
Corp of Engineers, U.S. Army, 245–46, 260
Council of Forest Industries, 310
court cases: *Alaska v. Native Village of Venetie* (1998), 327; *Bonnichsen v. United States et al.* (2004), 244–49; *Calder v. Attorney-General of*

court cases (*continued*)
British Columbia (1973), 35, 89,
107, 113, 282–83, 301; *Campbell v.
British Columbia* (2000), 36, 312;
Delgamuukw v. Regina (1991), 279,
281–83, 285, 288, 295n41, 307–8,
310; *Duwamish et al. v. United
States* (1927), 171, 173, 176; *Ex
Parte Crow Dog* (1883), 108, 113,
123n91; *Geary v. Barecroft* (1667),
51n30, 52n36; *Hunt v. Canada*
(2004), 145; *Johnson v. M'Intosh*
(1824), 40, 218; *Kie v. United States*
(1886), 108–9, 127n127; *McKay v.
Campbell* (1871), 122n80; *Regina
v. Benoit* (2002), 285; *Regina v.
Ellsworth* (1992), 145; *Regina v.
Gladstone* (1996), 135–37; *Regina
v. Horseman* (1990), 280, 292n8;
Regina v. Hunt (1995), 145; *Regina
v. Jack* (1979), 133–35; *Regina v.
Marshall* (1999), 136, 146–47, 282,
286; *Regina v. Morris* (2006),
152n51; *Regina v. Sparrow* (1990),
134–36, 147; *Regina v. St. Catherine's Milling and Lumber Company*
(1885), 126n116; *Regina v. Vander
Peet* (1996), 135–37; *Saanichton
Marina Ltd. v. Tsawout Indian
Band* (1989), 144; *Snuueymuxw
First Nation v. British Columbia*
(2004), 145; *In re Southern Rhodesia* (1919), 218; *Tee-Hit-Ton Indians v. United States* (1955), 325,
327; *United States v. Nice* (1916),
206; *United States v. Seufert* (1919),
187, 200–207, 210; *United States v.
Seveloff* (1872), 102–3, 108–10;
United States v. Taylor (1887), 187,
192–95, 210; *United States v. Tom*
(1854), 100–103, 105–11, 113,
120n62, 124n100; *United States v.
Washington* (see *Boldt* decision);
United States v. Winans (1905),

186–87, 197–201, 205, 210; *Victor
Buffalo v. Regina*, 279–86, 292n10,
293–94n21; *Ward v. Race Horse*,
197; *Washington v. Washington
State Commercial Passenger Fishing
Vessel Association* (Passenger Fishing Vessel, 1979), 129, 132, 133,
136, 146; *Whitefoot v. United States*
(1961), 209; *Winters v. United
States* (1908), 328–29, 332, 334n6;
Worcester v. Georgia (1832), 39,
52n31, 123n91
Cowichan people, 64, 90, 118nn34–
35, 133, 222, 224, 302; and
"treaty," 91, 94–98, 105–6, 110,
116n17, 118n32, 118n39, 123n93,
150n22
Cowlitz people, 202–4
Crease, Henry Pering Pellew, 107, 112
Cree people, 123n90, 283–85, 290,
293n18, 293–94n21, 317n32. *See
also* Samson Cree
Crockett, David, 166–68
Cushing, Caleb, 101, 106, 121n68

dancing, 174–77, 184n73, 221, 257
Daniels, Lena, 222
Dart, Anson, 99
Dave, Emma, 207
Davie, Theodore, 125n116
Davis, Jennie, 170
Deady, Matthew P., 102, 107–13,
122n80, 123–244nn96–97,
124n100, 125n105, 126n127
decolonization, 19, 298, 304, 312, 315
de Costa, Ravi, 19–20, 22, 25
Delaware people, 28n10, 219
Delgamuukw v. Regina (1991), 279,
281–83, 285, 288, 295n41, 307–8,
310
Denhoff, Eric, 309
dependency, 159, 168, 172–73
Dickson, Brian, 133–35
Didian, Joe, Sr., 64

Fort Langley, 162, 229, 232
Fort Laramie Treaty (1868), 323
forty-ninth parallel, 11, 37, 44, 46, 47, 98, 104, 106, 128
Foster, Hamar, 16, 60, 139
Foucault, Michel, 58–59, 76
France: and claims of sovereignty, 39, 42; and Indian sovereignty, 36, 54n53; and Louisiana Territory, 37
Fraser, Simon, 292n7
Freeman, Victoria, 60, 78
Friday, Chris, 18–20, 22, 26
fruit, 63, 69

Garrett, A. C., 96
gathering rights, 70, 245
Geary v. Barecroft (1667), 51n30, 52n36
gender issues, 73, 306
genealogies: of colonialism, 56–57, 68–75; figurative and literal, 59; Foucault's definition, 58; of land alienation, 58, 61–68; microhistory and, 59; of scholarship, 60, 75–78
General Allotment Act (1887), 323
Gesner, Alonzo, 196
Getches, David H., 338n75
Gitxsan Wet'suwet'en people, 279, 303, 307
Gold River, 64, 67
gold rushes, 94, 110, 323
Goldstream River, 145
Gordon, George W., 195–96
Gordon Report, 196
Gould, Ronald M., 246
Grant, Ulysses S., 108, 124n101, 182n37
Gray, John Hamilton, 112
Gray, Robert, 43–44, 56–57, 79
Great Britain. *See* Britain
Grey, George, 116n18
Groberman, Harvey, 145
Gros Ventre Band, 329
Grove, Alan, 16, 30n23, 60, 139
Gurand, Lucy, 160

Haida people, 64, 161, 302
halibut, 129, 239n34
Hall, Emmett, 113
Handley, Tomar, 204
Harmon, Alexandra: and Indian identity, 179n7, 183n60, 188, 216; and treaty councils' ceremonial value, 159–60; and tribal land tenure, 209–10
Harris, Cole, 58, 67, 84–85n74, 93, 105, 139
Harris, Douglas, 16–17, 30n23
Heiltsuk people, 135–36
herring, 129, 135–36, 229, 230, 236
Hillaire, Darrell, 157
historical geography, 281, 288
history scholarship: academic consensus on, 282; academics' weaknesses in, 76–78; by First Nation researchers, 76; genealogies of, 60, 75–78; interpretation in court of, 282–83; source material for, 75–76
HMS *Hecate*, 95
Hobbema reserve. See *Victor Buffalo v. Regina* (2005)
Holcomb, W. H., 193
Holmes, Joan, 283, 290
Homalco community, 64
house openings, 180n21
Hoxie, Frederick, 20
Hudson's Bay Company, 43–44, 253, 284–85, 293n21; American settlers and, 103–4; and fishing, 141, 142, 147; and beginning of fur trade, 292n7; role in treaty making, 90–91, 137
human rights, 301
Hunn, Eugene, 256–57
hunting rights: Douglas's position on, 93; and treaties, 70, 139–41, 152n51
Huntington, J. W. Perit, 194
Huntington treaty (1865), 194–96, 201, 203
Hunt v. Canada (2004), 145

Iceman. *See* Ötzi, the Iceman
identity, Indian, 179n7, 183n60, 188, 216
Ike, Charley, 197
inclusion, 297–98
Indian agents, 64, 65, 69, 200
Indian Claims Commission (ICC), 225, 240n47–48, 246–49, 258–63, 267n12, 268n19, 273n63, 287, 293n15
Indian country, 98–100, 102, 108, 110–11, 120n64, 327
Indian Homestead Acts, 193
Indian Mutiny (1857), 97
Indian Reorganization Act (1934), 224–25, 231, 323
Indians: conferring of U.S. citizenship on, 206; cooperation among, 172–73; as farmers, 166–67, 172; history of dispossession of, 19; off-reservation, 196, 307, 313; role in colonialism of, 77–78; status of, 72–73, 84n63; as term for indigenous people, 14; traditional dancing of, 174–76, 184n73. *See also* Aboriginals; Indian treaties; Native Americans
Indian-settler relations, 63–64, 299; Chinese-Indian conflicts, 64, 69–70; genealogical approach to, 57–61
Indian Shaker Church, 201, 204, 206
Indians of the Tulalip Agency, 168, 173
Indian Trade and Intercourse Acts (1790, 1834), 98–99, 100, 108–9, 125n105
Indian treaties: as attempts to stem conflicts, 19; as badge of sovereignty, 20; British Columbia Treaty Commission Agreement (1993), 303–4; with the British Crown, 10–11; and character of Native-newcomer relations, 13; Congressional delay in ratification of, 164–65; Congressional prohibition of, 321; Cowichan

Treaty, 94–98, 105; cross-border linkage in study of, 11–16; focus of, 168–69; Fort Laramie Treaty (1868), 323; history of, 157–58; hunting and fishing rights, 139–40; Huntington treaty (1865), 194–96, 201; indigenous people's role in evolution of, 12–13, 20; Makah Treaty (1855), 149n4; Medicine Creek Treaty (1854), 148n4, 158, 164; Nanaimo Treaty (1854), 90, 94–95, 97, 105; Nisga'a Treaty(2000), 35–36, 89, 310–11; Olympia Treaty (1855), 149n4; oral knowledge of, 169–71; payments rendered in blankets, 90–91; Point No Point Treaty (1855), 149n4, 158, 165; purpose of, 165–68; and remembrance, 173–77; representations of, 298–300; and resistance, 168, 173, 176–78; South Saanich treaty (1852), 162–63, 181n27; status in international law of, 14; strategies for, 159; Supreme Court rulings on, 10–11; and treaty countil, 159–65; Treaty 6, 280, 283–84; Treaty 7 (1877), 299; Treaty 8 (1899), 35, 62, 137, 280, 306; as understood by Indians, 20–24. *See also* Treaty of Point Elliott (1855); treaty making
intellectual property, 221
Interior, U.S. Department of, 246, 260
intermarriage, 19–20, 60, 72–74
International Court of Justice, 54n56
international law, 44–45, 218; Eurocentric nature of, 45; indigenous people and, 260, 322; status of Indian treaties in, 14; territorial sovereignty and, 38–43, 47; used to justify colonialism, 21

Jacobs, Melville, 251, 269n31
Jefferson, Juanita, 157
Jefferson, Thomas, 37

Jeffries, Alfred, 63–64
Jelderks, John, 246–47
Jennings, Francis, 217
Johnnie, Charlie, 64
Johnson v. M'Intosh (1824), 40, 218
Jones, Jimmy, 170
Jorgensen, Joe, 261

Kahlotus, 273n69
Kanim, Hetley, 164–65
Kanim, William, 169
Kaska-Dena people, 302
Kautz, Augustus, 160
Kelsomaht people, 64
Kennedy, Arthur, 123n93
Kennewick Man: Court of Appeals
  decision on, 244; dispute as science
  vs. law, 262–64; dispute as science
  vs. religion, 261; finding of, 244–45,
  265n2; and Indian Claims Commis-
  sion dockets, 258–61, 273n63; lin-
  eal descent issue of, 247, 258,
  266n11; litigation on, 245–50;
  property rights (1855) at site of,
  256–58; Sahaptin terms related to
  Indian positions on, 250–52
Kenyatta, Jomo, 217–18
Kie v. United States (1886), 108–9,
  126–27n127
Kikiallus people, 70–71, 73, 230
Kikuyu people, 218
kinship ties, 222–24, 226, 229, 231,
  233, 235
Kolocken, Joe, 199
Kosslak, Renee M., 267n12
Krehbiel, Rick, 308
Kwakiutl people, 145–46, 161, 302.
  See also Kwak'waka'wakw people
Kwak'waka'wakw people, 128. *See
  also* Kwakiutl people
Kwina, Henry, 169

labor theory of property, 292n12
La Forest, Gérard, 134

Lambert, Douglas, 136–37, 148
Lamer, Antonio, 55n58, 135–36
Lampert, Jerry, 310
land alienation genealogies, 61–68
Land Ordinance of 1861 (Canada), 63
land title: in Canada, 261; in common
  law, 97, 261; extinguishing of, 90,
  97–98, 110, 326, 332; and immi-
  grants, 62; and settlers, 99
Lane, Barbara, 160, 226, 229, 232
Lane, Robert Brockstedt, 160
Lane, Vernon, 157–58, 177
Lang, Thomas S., 195
law of nations. *See* international law
Lawrence, T. J., 52n36
Leschi, 102, 121n74
Leshy, John, 248–49
Levi-Strauss, Claude, 315
Lewis and Clark expedition, 43–45,
  55n60, 254, 256–58
Lheidli T'enneh people, 308, 315
L'Heureux-Dubé, Claire, 135–37
Lillooet people, 302
Linking Arms Together (Williams),
  299
Livingstone, Gary, 310
Locke, John, 81n21, 283
logging, 64, 71, 169, 224, 302–3, 308
Louisiana Territory, 36–37
Lower Skagit people, 169–70, 230
Lummi people: and treaties, 18–19,
  157–58, 160–63, 166, 169; as farm-
  ers, 166–67, 172; and fishing, 172,
  222, 227, 230–31, 234, 239n31,
  243n91; Treaty Day celebration of,
  174, 176; Tribal Business Council,
  183n60; and "working bees," 172–
  73
Lurie, Nancy, 289–90
Lushootseed language, 232, 237n3

Maa-Nulth people, 305
Macdonald, John A., 107–8, 111
Mackenzie, Alexander, 43

Maine Indian Land Settlement Act (1980), 324
Makah people, 230, 240n49
Makah Treaty (1855), 149n4
Mallet, Edmond, 168
Manuel, George, 302
Maori people, 90, 116n18, 255
Maori Wars, 97
March Point Reservation, 224
marriage, 19, 107; diplomatic, 162; among pioneers, 72; and status, 202, 204, 220, 224, 226
Marshall, John, 39–41, 51–52n31, 129
Martin, August, 169–70
Martin, Joe, 79
Marx, Karl, 73, 78
Maynard, Dr., 6–7
Mays, Franklin P., 197–98
McCarran Amendment (1952), 329–32
McCluskey, William, 175
McEachern, Allan, 292n7
McFadden, Obadiah B., 102, 120nn62–64, 124n100
McKay, Jim, 176
McKay, Thomas, 103, 122n80
McKay v. Campbell (1871), 122n80
McKenna, Joseph, 186, 200
McKenna-McBride Royal Commission, 62
McLachlin, Beverley, 135–37
McLaren, John, 107, 112
McLeod Lake Band, 303, 306
McLoughlin, John, 103–4, 122n87
McNeil, Kent, 21, 35
McWhorter, L. V., 260
Merivale, Herman, 152n58
Metlakatla, 89, 107, 111, 113
Mexico, 42
microhistory, 59, 177
Mi'kmaq people, 136
Miller, J. R. (Jim), 13, 270n39
mining, 169

Mining Association of British Columbia, 310
Minthorn, Antone, 27, 262
Minthorn, Armand, 245, 265–66n7
missionaries, 44, 75, 176, 253
Mitchell, David, 303
Morris, Alexander, 293–94n21
Mowachat/Muchalaht people, 64, 67
Mukilteo, 3, 8, 28n1
Murphy, Justice, 145
Musgrave, Anthony, 96, 107
Musgrave, Zoe, 106–7
Musqueam people, 119, 134, 224, 225

National Park Service (NPS), 246, 260
National Water Commission, 329
Natítayt, 251, 253, 265–66n7, 260–62. See also Walla Walla Sahaptin language
Native American Graves Protection and Repatriation Act (NAGPRA) (1990), 245–47, 258–64, 266n11
Native Americans, 14, 20, 187. See also Aboriginals; Indians
Native Brotherhood of British Columbia, 301, 303
Native space, 58, 60, 67, 69, 188
natural law, 41, 52n36
Navajo Reservation, 11
Nelson, Barnard, 64
Nelson, Bruce, 309
Nemaiah Chilcotin band, 303
Newcastle, Duke of, 91, 94, 116nn16–18, 122n86
New Zealand, 113; and bilingual treaty-making, 254–55; and Maori, 90, 116n18, 140; and native title, 97, 102; and treaty rights, 227–28
Nez Perce language, 254, 270n39, 271n46, 272n57
Nez Perce people, 25, 103–4, 252, 328–31, 337n63
Nimrod, James, 169

Puyallup people, 102, 148–49n4, 160, 164
Puyallup River, 160
Pyópyo Maqsmáqs (Yellow Bird), 254, 271n52

Queahpahmah, 194
Quinault people, 131

Raibmon, Paige, 19, 26, 30n23, 181n30
Ramos, Alcida, 215
Ray, Arthur, 22, 24–26
Ray, Verne, 260
Regina v. Benoit (2002), 285
Regina v. Ellsworth (1992), 145
Regina v. Gladstone (1996), 135–37
Regina v. Horseman (1990), 280, 292n8
Regina v. Hunt (1995), 145
Regina v. Jack (1979), 133–35
Regina v. Marshall (1999), 136, 146–47, 282, 286
Regina v. Morris (2006), 152n51
Regina v. Sparrow (1990), 134–36, 147
Regina v. St. Catherine's Milling and Lumber Company (1885), 126n116
Regina v. Vander Peet (1996), 135–37
regional advisory committees, 309
Relander, Click, 260
reservations, 7, 27, 166, 174, 193, 204, 216, 256, 322; administration of, 165, 168; moving to, 71, 99, 102, 188, 255, 271n51; and resources, 169, 199, 230, 328, 329, 334; society on, 176, 223, 224, 250. *See also* reserves
reserved rights doctrine, 17, 147, 200, 245–46, 249–50, 256, 330, 332, 338n73
reserves, 73, 127, 143, 152, 165, 215, boundaries/size of, 59, 66–67, 68, 96; and Douglas, 93, 96, 123n93,

144; Indian goals for development of, 166–68; local governments on, 224–25; as "making Native space," 58, 60; and preemptions, 65, 109; tribal authority over non-Indians on, 324; and water rights, 67, 69. *See also* reservations
resistance, 74, 77, 158–59, 168, 173–78, 185n89, 195, 292–93n14
Richards, Kent D., 179n7
Rigsby, Bruce, 21–22, 25, 30n26
Roberts, Charlie, 63
Roeder, Henry, 161–62
Rorty, Richard, 299
Roth, Lottie Roeder, 161
Royal Proclamation of 1763, 10, 11, 97–98, 102, 105, 109, 123n92, 125n109
Rude, Noel, 258
rule of capture, 227, 240n41
Russia, 36–37, 42–43, 109

Saanich Peninsula, 137
Saanich people, 119n42, 144, 162, 222. *See also* South Saanich Treaty
Saanichton Marina Ltd. v. Tsawout Indian Band (1989), 144
Sahaptian language family, 272n57
Sahaptin languages, 194, 210n2, 245, 250–52, 254, 258, 265n1, 269nn27–28, 269n31, 270n39, 270–71n46, 272nn57–58, 273n61
Salish Sea, 215, 220, 222, 223, 224
Sallequun people, 94
salmon, 172, 193; and Boldt decision, 129, 131, 134; dried, 221, 256; fishery, 136; habitat of, 67, 83n45, 331; Indian reliance upon, 233; Indian rights to, 136, 143, 145, 162, 187, 189, 192, 196–201, 207–8, 222; stocks of, 236
Salt Spring Island, 65, 71, 73–74, 77, 83n53
Sam, John, 171

steelhead. *See* salmon

Steh-shad, 174

Stevens, Isaac I., 10–11, 16, 23, 152n54; Chowitsut's meeting with, 163; dividing the Oregon Territory, 128; Indian concepts of property rights, 21; Indian fishing rights, 141; intent in treaty making by, 159, 179n7; Leschi trial, 102; Nez Perce water rights, 328; as power in treaty making, 8–9, 322; and Treaty of Point Elliott, 3, 6; treaty ratifications by Congress, 164; and Walla Walla treaty council, 248, 252–55, 270n39

Stillaguamish people, 231

Sto:lo people, 22, 318n35

Supreme Court, Alaska, 327

Supreme Court, British Columbia, 36, 145, 312

Supreme Court, Canada, 89; defining holders of treaty rights, 228; fishing rights, 133–37, 147, 228; history's value, 282, 285; hunting rights, 152n51; Nisga'a claims, 35, 301; sovereignty of Indian nations, 36

Supreme Court, Idaho, 330–31, 337n63, 338n73

Supreme Court, New Zealand, 97, 102

Supreme Court, Oregon, 100–101, 120n62, 206

Supreme Court, U.S.: "Indian country" defined by, 108, 327; moderate livelihood limit on treaty rights, 129, 132, 151n43; *Nice* case, 206; *Passenger Fishing Vessel* case, 136; political question doctrine, 323–24; property rights, 321–22; *Seufert* case, 206; tribal authority over non-Indians, 324; validity of Indian treaties, 10–11; water rights, 328–29; *Winans* case, 186, 197, 200

Supreme Court, Washington, 131, 193

Suquamish people, 170, 229

Suttles, Wayne, 215–16, 222, 230

Swinomish people, 174, 176, 219–20, 222, 224, 230–31, 235

Switzler, Charles, 202

S'ya-whom, 162

Tanawasha, Sam, 198

Tanner, Helen Hornbeck, 296n43

Taylor, Frank, 192–93. See also *United States v. Frank Taylor*

Taylor, John, 169, 171

Taylor, Orson D., 193

Taylor, William, 192

Tee-Hit-Ton Indians v. United States (1955), 325, 327

Teitelbaum, Max, 280–82, 284–86, 291n4, 292n10

Tennant, Paul, 92–93, 105, 302

termination era, 323

terra nullius, 54n56, 217

territorial rights. *See* sovereignty

Thelen, David, 12

Thompson, David, 257

Thompson, Henry, 269n30

Thompson, Tommy, 207–9

Thompson, William, 64

Thoms, Michael, 153n62

Thomson, Duane, 68

Thurston, Samuel R., 98, 113, 120n59

Tiiĉaminsh Uytpamá Natítayt. *See* Kennewick Man

Tilcoax, 273n69

timber, 64–65, 67, 71, 161, 165, 172, 225

Tla-o-qui-at people, 56–57, 79

Tlingit people, 121n77, 161

Tolmie, William Fraser, 112, 118n32, 121n74, 122n85

Tom, an Indian, 100–101. See also *United States v. Tom*

Tom, Domonic, 64

traditional laws and customs, 269–70n32, 313, 315; decision making, 182n42; laws, 218, 228, 230, 239n31, 249–50, 255, 269n27, 207,

Northwest, 36. *See also* Congress, U.S.; Supreme Court, U.S.

United States ex. rel. Williams v. Seufert (1919), 187, 200–207, 210

United States v. Frank Taylor (1887), 187, 192–95, 210

United States v. Nice (1916), 206

United States v. Seveloff (1872), 102–3, 108–10

United States v. Tom (1854), 100–103, 105–11, 113, 120n62, 124n100

United States v. Washington. See *Boldt* decision

United States v. Winans (1905), 186–87, 197–201, 205, 210

Upper Skagit people, 170, 222

Vancouver, George, 43

Verney, Edmund Hope, 95

Victor Buffalo v. Regina (2005): expert witnesses/teachers in, 280–83, 286–89, 292n10, 293–94n21; and government good faith, 286; as longest Canadian treaty case, 279; oral history of Treaty 6, 284–86; phases of, 280

Von Gernet, Alexander, 283, 285–86, 288–91, 295n36

Waitangi Treaty Tribunal, 227

Wakashan people, 90

Walla Walla council (1855), 248, 252–55

Walla Walla people, 26, 248–50, 252, 256, 259–60, 262–63, 271n52

Walla Walla Sahaptin language, 245, 250–51, 258, 269n28, 269n31, 272n57. *See also* Natítayt

Wánapam people, 248, 257, 260, 271n51

Wanapum people, 246, 248

Ward v. Race Horse, 197

Warm Springs tribes, 188, 194–96, 203–5, 209, 211n6

Wascos, 194, 204, 205

Washines, Arlen, 26

Washington, Joe, 176

Washington, Louis, 175

Washington Territory: significance of, 10–11; and Stevens treaties, 4–5, 9, 26; defining tribes in, 23

Washington Treaty (1846), 37, 44–47, 98–99

Washington v. Washington State Commercial Passenger Fishing Vessel Association (Passenger Fishing Vessel, 1979), 129, 132, 133, 136, 146

water rights, 67, 69, 325, 328–33, 336n49, 337n63

Waters, George, 205

Watts, George, 304

Westar (lumber company), 303

Westbank people, 308

Whatcom County Human Rights Task Force, 157

Wheeler, Winona, 285–86, 290, 294n22

Whidbey Island, 70–71

White, Elijah, 103

White, Richard, 71

Whitefoot v. United States (1961), 209

White Paper, 301

White Swan, 198–99, 205

Wickaninnish, Chief, 56

Wilbur, James, 189, 192

Willamette Valley, 44

William, Tyee, 174

Williams, George H., 100–101, 108, 120n63, 124n101

Williams, Robert, 217, 299, 313

Williams, Sam, 201–4, 206

Winans, Audubon, 186, 197. See also *United States v. Winans*

Winans, Linnaeus, 186, 197. See also *United States v. Winans*

Winters v. United States (1908), 328–29, 332, 334n6

Wishram people, 197–200

Witgen, Michael J., 29n13

Wolfart, H. C., 283
Wolverton, Charles E., 203–6
women, 3, 6, 100, 165; indigenous, 72–75, 84n68, 306, 313; mixed-heritage, 60, 72, 75; and salmon, 256; and status, 224
Wooten, Shadrach, 238–39n27
Worcester v. Georgia (*1832*), 39, 52n31, 123n91
"working bees," 172–73
Wounded Knee, 302
Wunder, John, 12

Xaxli'p people, 306

Yakama people, 26, 208, 249, 271; and Bonnichsen litigation, 246, 248–49; Confederated Tribes and Bands of the Yakama Nation, 246, 248, 273–74n69; and fishing, 131, 186, 188, 189, 192, 194, 197–200, 202, 205, 209; and language, 250, 251, 269n28, 272n57; and name reversion from Yakima, 210n1; and Walla Walla Council, 252; and war of *1855–1858*, 255. See also *United States ex. rel. Williams v. Seufert Brothers*; *United States v. Frank Taylor*; *United States v. Winans*
Yakama treaty, 271n50
"Yelleppit" or "Yellept," 257
Yellow Bird (Pyópyo Maqsmáqs), 254, 271n52